ARCHAEOLOGY AND MODERNITY

Archaeologists have long recognised that they study past worlds which may be quite unlike our own. But how are we to cope with the difference of the past if our own circumstances are unique within human history? What if archaeology itself depends on ways of thinking that are specific to the modern Western world?

This is the first book-length study to explore the relationship between archaeology and modern thought, and to demonstrate that, while we may believe our approaches to be based on value-free techniques and thinking, archaeology is still dominated by philosophical ideas that developed in the seventeenth to nineteenth centuries. Julian Thomas discusses the modern emphasis on method rather than ethics or meaning, our understanding of change in history and nature, the role of the nation-state in forming our views of the past, and contemporary notions of human individuality, the mind, and materiality.

He also addresses the modern preoccupation with depth, which enables archaeology to be used as a metaphor across other disciplines. *Archaeology and Modernity* concludes by calling for a reformed, 'counter-modern' archaeology, which refuses to separate material evidence from political, moral, rhetorical and aesthetic concerns, as well as meaning.

Julian Thomas is Professor of Archaeology at the University of Manchester. He writes and teaches on the neolithic of Britain and Europe, and the philosophy of archaeology. His publications include *Time, Culture and Identity* (Routledge 1996) and *Understanding the Neolithic* (Routledge 1999).

ARCHAEOLOGY AND MODERNITY

Julian Thomas

LONDON AND NEW YORK

First published 2004
Reprinted 2006
by Routledge
2 Park Square, Milton Park, Abingdon, Oxon OX14 4RN

Simultaneously published in the USA and Canada

270 Madison Ave, New York, NY 10016

Routledge is an imprint of the Taylor & Francis Group

© 2004 Julian Thomas

Typeset in 11/12pt Garamond 3
by Graphicraft Limited, Hong Kong
Printed and bound in Great Britain by The Cromwell Press,
Trowbridge, Wiltshire

All rights reserved. No part of this book may be reprinted or reproduced or utilised in any form or by any electronic, mechanical, or other means, now known or hereafter invented, including photocopying and recording, or in any information storage or retrieval system, without permission in writing from the publishers.

British Library Cataloguing in Publication Data
A catalogue record for this book is available from the British Library

Library of Congress Cataloging in Publication Data
Thomas, Julian.
Archaeology and modernity / Julian Thomas.
p. cm.
Includes bibliographical references (p.   ) and index.
1. Archaeology.   2. Archaeology—Philosophy.   I. Title.
CC72.T48 2004
930.1′01—dc22
                          2003018161

ISBN 0-415-27156-8 (hbk)
ISBN 0-415-27157-6 (pbk)

IN MEMORY OF MY BROTHER,
GAVIN RICHARD THOMAS,
1963–2000

CONTENTS

List of figures	viii
Preface	x
Acknowledgements	xii
1 The emergence of modernity and the constitution of archaeology	1
2 Archaeology and the tensions of modernity	35
3 The tyranny of method	55
4 History and nature	78
5 Nation-states	96
6 Humanism and 'the individual'	119
7 Depths and surfaces	149
8 Mind, perception and knowledge	171
9 Materialities	202
10 Towards a counter-modern archaeology: Difference, ethics, dialogue, finitude	223
Bibliography	249
Index	268

FIGURES

1.1	The Aristotelian cosmos	9
1.2	The Ptolemaic universe	10
1.3	The cabinet of Ferrante Imperator	14
1.4	The cabinet of Olaus Worm	14
1.5	Aldrovandi's illustration of 'Pesce Istrice'	25
1.6	Aldrovandi's illustration of Mandragora	25
1.7	Title page of Jonston's *De Insectis*	26
2.1	Stone tools from the Somme gravels	45
2.2	Comparison of the Magdalenian skull with that of a recent Eskimo	52
3.1	Descartes' representation of the human sensory apparatus	58
3.2	Pottery design change at Snaketown, Arizona	68
3.3	The Carter Ranch site	71
4.1	Georges Cuvier	88
4.2	The Divine Cow of Queen Hapshepsut	92
5.1	Title page of Hobbes's *Leviathan*	102
5.2	Neolithic settlement at the Knap of Howar, Orkney	114
5.3	Skara Brae, Orkney	114
5.4	Map of hypothetical tribal areas in neolithic Orkney	115
6.1	The Bronze Age warrior: equipment from northern Italy	142
6.2	Memorial messages following the death of Diana, Princess of Wales	145
6.3	The 'Ice Man' in the Alps	146
7.1	Ditch section from the Wor Barrow long mound, Dorset	159
7.2	Sigmund Freud with his collection of antiquities	162
7.3	Freud's 'topographic' model of the psyche	167
8.1	Descartes' illustration of the brain	172

FIGURES

8.2	Descartes' image of visual information being conveyed to the mind	178
8.3	Spear-thrower from Mas d'Azil	193
8.4	The 'Sorceror' at the cave of Trois Frères	197
9.1	Image of a mammoth at the cave of Bernifal, France	220
9.2	Garnwnda chambered tomb, south-west Wales	221

PREFACE

Over the past few decades the role of contemporary preconceptions in forming our image of the past has become a growing concern for archaeologists. Very often it has been a familiarity with anthropology that has alerted us to the likelihood that our own everyday practices are not shared by all human beings, and cannot be assumed to have prevailed in the past. As a result, it has been possible to interpret prehistoric and protohistoric societies in counterintuitive ways, which emphasise gift exchange, ritual, the collective appropriation of resources, the meaningful character of landscape or the symbolic role of material things. However, it has often been pointed out that there is a danger of imposing the ethnographic present on the past, particularly as many of the communities that we study through archaeology have no close analogues amongst living groups. An alternative, or complementary strategy is to attempt to identify those aspects of our own existence that are diagnostic of a particular contingent condition, which we might identify as 'modernity'. This, at least, would provide us with an indication of what we should *not* expect to find in the past. Where this has been attempted it has often been on a piecemeal basis, and I have personally been as guilty as anyone of referring rather glibly to the influence of Enlightenment ideas or ethnocentric modernism on archaeological practice.

This book is an attempt to be a little more systematic about the identification of modern ways of thinking and acting, with the aim of facilitating a more productive engagement with the past. As such, it follows up some of the issues that were addressed in *Time, Culture and Identity* (Thomas 1996), while being more explicit about the connections between the Western philosophical tradition and the formation and subsequent development of the archaeological discipline. Such an approach leads one very quickly to a significant irony. It is arguable that the modern world is qualitatively different from any other epoch of human history: its defining features are quite singular. Consequentially, the worst possible location from which to attempt to understand past societies is in the modern West. Our contemporary habits, ways of life, commonplace ideas and daily experiences conspire to make it all but impossible to comprehend lives that were ordered in entirely different ways. But at the same time it may be that our desire to investigate those past lives through the medium of material culture is itself distinctively modern. If we were not modern, it might not occur to us to do archaeology at all. It is this double-bind that inspires the principal aim of this book: to identify those aspects of modern thinking which have contributed to the formation of archaeology, and to consider whether archaeology's attachment to modernity can be transcended. At the very least, it is hoped that this project will help to identify those conditions from within which we presently conduct our archaeology, inherited as they are from quite specific traditions of thought.

The volume is structured in such a way as to lay out the general issue of the interconnectedness of archaeology and the modern experience in a broadly chronological fashion over the first two chapters, and then to address a series of more specific themes. These are epistemology, historical and natural change, the role of the nation-state, humanism, depth, mind, and materiality. Finally, the conclusion makes some suggestions regarding the overcoming of modern thought in archaeology. It will be noticed that the arguments in the various chapters cross over and interconnect at various points. This demands a certain amount of recapitulation and overlap, but my decision has been to accept this, and to make each chapter as far as possible complete in itself. This enables each to be read to some degree as a separate essay.

ACKNOWLEDGEMENTS

I would like to thank all of my colleagues in Manchester who helped in the production of this book in various ways. Thomas Dowson, Chris Fowler, Siân Jones, Stephanie Koerner and Colin Richards have all read parts of the text, and provided invaluable comment and encouragement. Ina Berg, Suzy Butters, Stuart Campbell, Eleanor Casella, Mark Crinson, Tim Insoll and Lynne Vickers have all given support of one kind or another. Thanks to Bob Eaglestone, John Pickstone and Peter Ucko for discussions and references over the past few years, and to Richard Bradley and Alasdair Whittle for help that made the book possible. I gratefully acknowledge the support of the Arts and Humanities Research Board and the University of Manchester for providing two semesters of research leave in 2002–3, which gave me the opportunity to write most of the text. Thanks, finally, to Sue, Morag and Rowan, who have done so much to make life better while this book has been coming together.

Every effort has been made to obtain permission for the use of copyright items. If any proper acknowledgement has not been made, we invite copyright holders to inform us of the oversight.

1

THE EMERGENCE OF MODERNITY AND THE CONSTITUTION OF ARCHAEOLOGY

> Archaeology . . . a discipline devoted to silent monuments, inert traces, objects without context, and things left by the past.
> Michel Foucault, *The Archaeology of Knowledge*

Introduction: why modernity?

Archaeology investigates the past through the medium of material things. Yet it is increasingly clear that we do not simply reconstruct the way that things were. Instead, we establish a relationship between the past and the present. This relationship can be conceived as a kind of conversation, to which we bring a variety of expectations and prejudices, and from which we receive challenges and surprises (Gadamer 1975: 236). The past never fully reveals itself to us, but through our continued engagement we learn more, both about past worlds and about ourselves. The self-recognition that emerges from this process involves an increasing awareness of our own assumptions and prejudices: the conceptual 'baggage' that we tend to impose on the past. Considered in this way, the perceived distance between the past and the present is not so much a barrier to understanding as a productive space (ibid.: 264). Yet the dialogue between the two cultural and historical contexts is one that requires our active participation in giving the past a significance, and in appreciating our own position in the present (Warnke 1987: 68; Johnsen and Olsen 1992: 426).

It is arguable that while archaeology has made considerable advances in the methodological and theoretical skills required in order to address the past, we often lack an appreciation of the conditions under which we ourselves operate in the present. Indeed, in many disciplines that seek to draw up a contrast between the modern West and some other society the conception of our own context is superficial, based principally on personal experience (Pickstone 2000: 34). This in turn means that our understanding of the past continues to be hamstrung by what Gadamer calls 'the tyranny of hidden prejudices' (1975: 239). This book is intended to facilitate some recognition of the circumstances in which the discipline of archaeology finds itself at the start of the twenty-first century, and of the reasons why we address the past in the ways that we do. The central argument that I will be seeking to make is that modernity represents the condition of the possibility of archaeology. By that I mean that archaeology as we presently practise it is intimately connected with the modern experience, and indeed amounts to a distillation of a modern sensibility (see Olsen 2001: 43).

In everyday language, something that is 'modern' is generally contemporary, up to date, or progressive. It is worth saying at the outset that the sense in which I will be using the word is a philosophical one, which refers to a phase of history that succeeded the medieval era in the West. According to some commentators this period may be coming to a close (or may even have ended). Over the years, a number of historians of archaeology have suggested, whether implicitly or explicitly, that the growth of the discipline coincided with this epoch. For instance, Crawford (1932) argued that the Industrial Revolution promoted archaeological discovery through the excavation of canals, railway cuttings and coal mines, and created a leisured middle class who had the opportunity and the motivation to study the past. Piggott (1976) drew attention to the incremental process by which improvements in transport opened up the landscape to antiquarian travellers. Schnapp (1996) emphasised the growth of learning that facilitated the appreciation of artefact typology and stratigraphy. Trigger (1989) foregrounded both changing social relations and developing conceptions of history. While agreeing with the importance of all of these factors, I will seek to subsume them within what I consider to be a more fundamental process: the emergence of modernity.

Modernity may represent a chronological division of human experience, but more importantly it is distinguished by the growth of a particular philosophical outlook, and by particular ways in which human beings have operated socially. A range of obvious characteristics are particular to the modern era: capitalism, the emergence of nation-states, industrialisation, improvements in communications and transport, mercantilism, the control of violence by the state, surveillance, constant political struggle, an increasingly urban way of life, and an experience of agitation, turbulence and continuous change (Giddens 1991: 15; Berman 1982: 18; Olsen 2001: 42). Equally important has been the decline of tradition and (in the West at least) of religious conviction. Moreover, the erosion of established sources of social stability has been widely recognised within modern communities, with the effect that the modern condition is also characterised by general unease and dissatisfaction. Modern societies are unusual in recognising their own material and social conditions as being unlike those of the past, and this has fuelled a continuous critique of modernity from within (Kolakowski 1990: 12). The recognition that 'things could be otherwise' promotes a sense of continuous crisis, yet without any clear prospect of resolution. All of these conditions have been related to increasing social fragmentation, individualism, and efforts on the part of states to impose secular codes of moral behaviour (Gray 1995: 152). Order is recognised as a problem in the modern world. This begins to explain the peculiarly important role that philosophical thought has played in modernity. Throughout this book I will be discussing what may seem at times to be somewhat abstract philosophical themes, but in the modern world such ideas have continually 'trickled down' into everyday discourse, reconfigured themselves as 'common sense', or informed the policies and legislation of national governments. This is all the more so because, as Zygmunt Bauman argues, modern philosophy is often *legislative* in character, attempting to lay down a moral order, identify the good, or tame and organise a seemingly chaotic world (1992: 119). In the modern world, abstract thought is often considered to precede action: indeed, the two are held to be separate events. For this reason, modern life is overwhelmingly *designed and planned*. The construction of buildings and artefacts, the planning of towns, and the organisation of societies is composed in theory before being put into practice. This is one of the reasons why utopian thinking is so distinctive of modernity (ibid.: xv).

Utopias are by definition located in the future, and it is a unique aspect of modernity that it conceives of itself as a project, leading to some future state. Yet this project is forever unfinished (Smart 1992: 183). The modern condition strives for some form of closure that cannot be achieved. Both modern philosophy and modern state politics operate on the premise that perfection can be achieved, provided that a new foundation for thought and action can be secured. This imperative lies behind the *foundational philosophy* of the likes of Descartes, Locke and Kant, as identified by Richard Rorty (1979).

Frederic Jameson warns us against the dangers of periodisation: to talk of 'modernity' or 'post-modernity' risks setting up an image of cultural homogeneity within a chronological phase (Jameson 1984: 56). With this in mind, we might think of modernity less as a block of time with hard edges, and more as a *process*, in which certain practices and relationships emerged to cultural dominance over time. We might talk of a modern era that began with the Italian Renaissance, but the ruling ideas of modernity have roots that descend back as far as the Greeks and Romans. What made the modern period modern is that a particular cluster of understandings which had been in a rarefied circulation for many centuries achieved a position of hegemony, and began to operate as the principles around which people structured their lives. Here we find a first point of connection with archaeology, for while there are isolated instances of what we might choose to call 'archaeological thinking' identifiable in the depths of antiquity, the emergence of a definable archaeological tradition is contingent upon that of modernity.

Modernity was (or is) neither spatially nor temporally homogeneous. Forms of organisation and understanding which matured (but were not necessarily generated) in Western Europe have gradually spread over much of the world, but in doing so they have been transformed. Similarly, the process of modernity was one that involved changes of focus and emphasis. Renaissance humanism was eclipsed by the religious conflicts of the later sixteenth century. The New Philosophy of the seventeenth century provided the impetus for the universalising intellectual project of the Enlightenment. This in turn gave way to a more historicised understanding of humanity in the nineteenth century. Such an attempt to break the modern age down into a series of phases is undoubtedly far too neat. However, the point that I wish to make is that the many twists and turns of the way in which modern people understood their own place in the world provided the context within which archaeology emerged. Moreover, this history provides the legacy that still burdens archaeology. Our ways of thinking about the past and about material things remain distinctively modern.

The roots of modernity

Histories of archaeology lay some stress on early examples of the uncovering of ancient ruins. Perhaps the earliest of these was the excavation of the temple of Larsa in Iraq by Nabonidus in the sixth century BC (Daniel 1950: 16; Schnapp 1996: 17). Attention is also sometimes drawn to the opening of ancient tombs by the classical Greeks (Schnapp 1996: 26), and to the excavations conducted by Bishops Earldred and Eadmar in St Albans in the eleventh century, partly in search of building stone (Piggott 1976: 5). Yet while these cases demonstrate an awareness of the remains of the past surviving into the present, there is no sense in which these remains were being used as evidence in the construction of a systematic knowledge of a past society, or of the diversity of humankind. So, arguably, while these early excavators were *addressing the archaeological*, they were not practising archaeology. Such a practice could only come into being once a particular series of understandings of humanity, time, and materiality had developed. A critical step in this direction was taken with the emergence of the belief that human beings are creatures of infinite value, possessing immortal souls, and inhabiting a world that is perishable. Such a view is to be connected with Christianity, and might be contrasted with the ancient Greek conception of humans as mortals, who are placed in an eternal world (Gray 1995: 158). This could be seen as the beginning of a process whereby humanity gradually came to supplant God as the subject of history.

Such a transient world would come to its end with the Last Judgement, and during the Middle Ages the belief that the Last Days were at hand was widespread. There was little recognition of the depth of human history, and consequentially any diversity amongst people was understood in spatial rather than temporal terms. Thus, as Hooper-Greenhill points out, Roman tombs discovered in Europe were rationalised as those of Saracens, while the remains of ancient cities were described as the work of giants (1992: 32). Medieval Europe did possess a linear conception of history, but it was one that was based around the decline from grace, followed by redemption. As a number of authors have suggested, this narrative resonates with the classical notion of humanity's decline from a Golden Age (Trigger 1989: 34; Schnapp 1996: 68). This implied that human abilities and skills were likely to have devolved over time, denying the possibility of the accretional growth of learning, or the progressive elaboration of technology. Yet while Hesiod's account of the ages of gold, silver and bronze presented an image of historical decline, it also contained a periodisation, which was explicitly linked to technological change (Daniel 1950: 14). Arguably, then, a linear view of time was already implicit in European culture by the time that the classical authors were revisited by the Renaissance. The change was to be one of emphasis, away from predestination and towards human achievement (Burckhardt [1860] 1995: 226).

Renaissance humanism reintroduced human agency into history, as manifest in Leon Battista Alberti's claim that 'men can do all things if they will' (ibid.: 107), and Giovanni Pico della Mirandola's *Speech on the Dignity of Man*: 'To thee alone is given a growth and a development depending on thine own free will. Thou bearest in thee the germs of a universal life' (ibid.: 264). Renaissance scholars affirmed that human beings could change their own conditions of existence through action, and looked back to both Aristotle and Plato as models of intellectual achievement (Appleby *et al.* 1996b: 25). These influences were to mature into quite different intellectual traditions. While Aristotle had been revered by medieval scholasticism, it was his emphasis on human diversity and difference, and on the contextuality of historical events and ethical judgements that interested the humanists. Renaissance humanism was distinguished by its toleration of the plurality of humankind, its attentiveness to alterity, and its acceptance of ambiguity in morality and metaphysics. Indeed, Mirandola's conclusion that 'man is free as air to be whatever he likes' suggests that a protean human pluralism was viewed as a source of emancipation (Bauman 1991: 22). The concern with Plato, by contrast, was wholly new, having been facilitated by the re-emergence of Plato's works in Greek from Constantinople after 1400, and their translation by Marsilio Ficino. Plato's emphasis on a mathematical conception on the world was to inspire Renaissance natural philosophy, and ultimately prepared the way for the new science of Copernicus, Galileo and Kepler (Goodman 1991: 28).

That the Copernican model of the universe would lead to a collision with Christian orthodoxy was perhaps to be expected, but equally significant was the growing conflict between faith and reason. Both the scholastics and the humanists had placed great emphasis on the role of reason, but the latter had tied it to free will, rather than presenting it simply as a principle to guide disputation. This meant that reason was to become increasingly active in social conduct and political strategy. The model of free rational action was defended on the grounds that God allows human beings free will in order to give them moral responsibility (Carroll 1993: 49). However, this implies that humans are in a position to work out for themselves the correct course of action at any given time, as opposed to simply putting their faith in the creator. This dilemma was instrumental in bringing about the Reformation, which some have seen as a kind of 'counter-Renaissance'. The dispute between Erasmus and Luther of 1524–5 turned on the contrast between the person as a free agent and as a bearer of total guilt (ibid.: 67). Yet both humanism and Protestantism subscribed to a conception of the person that was increasingly individualised. As we will see, believing oneself to be an 'individual', whether by taking responsibility for one's own salvation or acting in one's own interest, is a distinctively modern attitude.

It was the Renaissance rediscovery of the classical world, of course, that prompted the growth of antiquarianism. Here we have both an orientation on the past, and a specific interest in the remains of the past as being of value in their own right. From the late fourteenth century onwards, collections of Greek and Roman artefacts began to be amassed, while architectural devices and sculptural forms drawn from antiquity began to come back into fashion. This development was closely related to humanism (Schnapp 1996: 132), and while ruins and artefacts were not used as evidence in the full sense, they were recognised as an indication of past human achievements. Initially, this was taken as a confirmation of a decline of the world since ancient times. In the terms of the Renaissance cosmology, the earth was understood as a living organism, and the relative lack of accomplishment in contemporary human crafts was considered to be a symptom of its sickness (Hooper-Greenhill 1992: 33). Nonetheless, the gradual growth of an awareness that architecture, the arts, dress, legal structures and modes of conduct had changed since classical times was to have a positive effect. The Renaissance differed from the medieval period in recognising past people as qualitatively different from those of the present, and being of interest by virtue of that difference. Integral to this outlook was the awareness that different political, ethical and religious systems had existed in the past. The past therefore achieved a relationship of exteriority to the present, and could be appealed to by way of precedent or example (McVicar 1984: 55). Trigger (1989: 35) argues that for the humanists, taking an interest in classical antiquities was sometimes a coded way of expressing a preference for the republican politics of the past, in opposition to the despotisms and monarchies of early modern Europe. In practice, the ancient world provided a range of political blueprints that might be alluded to, ranging from the authoritarianism of Augustan Rome to the Athenian democracy (Day 1996: 74). What was new about the Renaissance was the understanding that society could be changed by act of will, and that a range of alternative possibilities had existed in the past, which might be preferred to the currently prevailing conditions.

Renaissance humanism was predominantly sceptical, pluralist and tolerant of diverse points of view. The Reformation can be seen in part as a reaction to one aspect of what the Renaissance embodied: wilfulness, the arrogation of God's authority to humankind, the hubris of reason. Yet after the Council of Trent of 1545–63 Protestantism itself became a heterodoxy that was not to be tolerated by the Catholic nations. Catholicism reasserted the authority of the Pope, the unquestionable validity of tradition, the centrality of a unified body of dogma and the monopoly of the Church over the interpretation of the scriptures (Goodman 1991: 97). As Stephen Toulmin has argued, the later sixteenth and earlier seventeenth centuries were a period in which the philosophical and religious diversity that had been fostered by the Renaissance hardened into polarised positions, which then formed the basis for political struggles (Toulmin 1990: 12). France suffered a series of religious wars between Protestants and Catholics, central Europe was ravaged by the Thirty Years War, and the English civil wars played out a series of antagonisms that were not merely religious but involved governance, freedom, property and representation (Hill 1967: 129). Having entertained the possibility of alternatives to the absolute monarchy, political elites found themselves beginning to be challenged by popular demands for reform, as in the case of the Putney debates in England (Thompson 1963: 24–5).

By the seventeenth century, then, there was a growing imperative to repudiate diversity, ambiguity, plurality and scepticism, and to replace them with certitude and firmly grounded truth (Bauman 1992: xiii). Philosophy was to find this certainty in a restatement of its concern with reason and logic, and with an enhanced emphasis on the Platonic preoccupation with mathematics. Most of all, there was a growing concern with epistemology, which arose from the desire to overcome the authority of the ancient texts while not allowing knowledge to become chaotic and undisciplined. For Bacon, this was to be achieved by collective scholarly activity, but Descartes argued that rigour was only to be found in an individual adherence to a method that would guarantee a truthful outcome to inquiry (Shapin 1996: 130). However, given the severity of the conflicts that had engulfed Europe from the time of the Reformation onwards, the demand for order and certainty was no longer a purely academic matter. If religion was to be a source of discord rather than a foundation for the right of rulers to rule, legitimation and legality would have to be found elsewhere by the modern states. From the sixteenth and seventeenth centuries onwards, the growth of learning was increasingly bound up with that of the state, not simply in terms of patronage and support but also in the way in which political authority was constructed and maintained. My suggestion is that the flourishing of antiquarianism in this period was no coincidence. Antiquarianism at once fed off the growing importance of intellectual activity, and helped to provide a temporal grounding for the European nation-states. The importance of constructing a historical origin for peoples, ruling lineages, customs and places was all the greater at a time when the precise character of political power and the national community was both fragile and unresolved. This may have been all the more so in the case of Protestant England, where the monarchy, the legal system and the Church needed to reconstruct their legitimacy following the break from Rome in the 1530s (McVicar 1984: 56).

The new science

The early modern 'scientific revolution' was founded upon Copernicus's and Kepler's models of a solar system in which the earth rotates around the sun, and Galileo's innovative use of the telescope. Each demonstrated that scientific activity could add to what was known about creation from the existing Greek, Ptolemaic and Arabic sources. However, it would be a mistake to subscribe to the belief that modern science had simply restarted the onward march of knowledge in Europe, which had been halted by the collapse of the Graeco-Roman world. Galileo's work, for instance, was a challenge to the accepted order of the cosmos. If telescopes could reveal 'new' stars that were not visible to the naked eye, the universe might be infinite in extent rather than the bounded structure presented by Aristotle and Ptolemy (Shapin 1996: 18). The new sciences that would gain their coherence in the seventeenth century did not just add new observations and theories to what had been known before. Instead, the seventeenth century saw a fundamental change in the way in which knowledge was organised. Michel Foucault (1970: 57) has argued that in the Renaissance all of creation was conceived of as a single fabric, in which individual phenomena were networked to one another by resemblance, analogy and sympathy. Unravelling the order of the universe was thus an interpretive task, in which the manifold connections between different forms of knowledge were followed and catalogued. The world was conceived as a book to be read, in which things and language were imbricated with one another (Pickstone 2000: 39). Words led one to things, and things led one back to words, in a ceaseless process of identifying the creator's design. Importantly, this meant that meaning was intrinsic to the world. People inhabited a universe of meaning, and of moral value (Figure 1.1). For in the Ptolemaic model of the cosmos (Figure 1.2) the earth and the heavens were arranged in a series of concentric spheres. Different elements gravitated towards their fitting place in the overall scheme of things, and those that were higher were of greater worth. Thus human beings fitted into the order somewhere between angels and plants (Hooper-Greenhill 1992: 35). Consequentially, the notion of a heliocentric universe was actually a challenge to the established moral order.

In the Renaissance cosmology, no firm distinctions were maintained between science, magic, erudition and ephemera, since any piece of information could add to the understanding of the whole (ibid.: 32). This whole was a bounded entity of possible knowledge, in which access to the macrocosm

THE EMERGENCE OF MODERNITY

Un missionnaire du moyen âge raconte qu'il avait trouvé le point
où le ciel et la Terre se touchent...

Figure 1.1 The Aristotelian cosmos. The sphere of the heavens is separate from that of the sub-lunar world, and operates in a different fashion. Here an astronomer seeks to penetrate the void (after Camille Flammarion, *L'Atmosphere: Météorologie Populaire*, Paris, 1888. Courtesy University of Oklahoma History of Science Collections)

could reasonably be achieved by way of the microcosm. Related to this holism was the teleology of Aristotelianism, which had held that all existing things tended over time towards the realisation of their ideal forms, which did not yet exist in a worldly manifestation (Collingwood 1945: 93). Movement towards this *telos* was therefore the final cause of all changes that took place within the world, and in this sense all matter was essentially active (and indeed, in some views, animate). By contrast, the 'efficient causes' of the action of physical bodies upon one another were held to be abnormal and relatively inconsequential (Smith 2002: 35). This meant that mechanical explanations for worldly happenings were considered to be less significant than the teleological process by which things were tending towards their fruition. Furthermore, the efficient causes that were believed to operate

THE EMERGENCE OF MODERNITY

Figure 1.2 The Ptolemaic universe. The various spheres are ordered in a way that reflects their respective moral worth (public domain image from www.whisperingstone.com/.../reference_graphics-page4.htm)

included some that would come to be rejected by the natural philosophers of the seventeenth century. For instance, it was believed that action at a distance could be brought about by attraction, repulsion and sympathy (Shapin 1996: 42).

At roughly the same time as Western political thought began to stress the need for order and structure, science itself changed its focus from the interpretation of resemblances and associations to classification and ordering. Instead of attempting to establish the system of connections that held creation together, science began to construct the means to typify, discriminate, measure, segregate and tabulate phenomena. As Foucault puts it, the 'figure' of knowledge in the seventeenth and eighteenth centuries is the table: a universal mathematical ordering of things (Foucault 1970: 75; Sheridan

1980: 51). At the same time, the causal action of discrete entities upon each other began to supplant theories of tendency, maturation and the perfection of form. Matter became the passive object of forces rather than active.

It is important to remember that seventeenth-century science was conducted within a Christian world-view. Galileo and Kepler were never atheistic, but believed that by using a coherent conceptual structure and precise measurement it would be possible to identify God's handiwork in nature (Cassirer 1951: 42). The challenge that this perspective offered to the Church was that it implied that the intentions of the creator could be approached through material things, rather than exclusively through scripture. Effectively, science was proposing an alternative to the Church's exclusive position as interpreter of God. The danger of this position was fully appreciated by Francis Bacon. In his *Novum Organum* ([1620] 1878) Bacon argued that the creation of new knowledge would only serve to magnify the glory of God. But he had already been careful to distinguish in his *Advancement of Learning* ([1605] 1920: 5) between the first cause (the will of God) and second causes (the physical mechanisms through which this will was made manifest) (Appleby *et al.* 1996a: 3). This transformation of the distinction between final and efficient causes enabled Bacon to claim that his science did not deal directly in the interpretation of God's plan, which was properly the domain of religion. Instead, science should describe creation at one remove from the creator. Even when Descartes was to set up a philosophical system which effectively excluded miraculous happenings from the world, he was to do so from within the framework of Christian belief, so that he and others were able to continue to combine religious faith with a belief in science (Kolakowski 1990: 8).

The distinction between first and second causes helped to set the tone of Bacon's empiricism. This so-called 'experimental philosophy' was to become one of the more important currents in modern thought. Both empiricism and Cartesian rationalism shared the desire to find a new foundation for knowledge, and as we will see this is a recurring theme throughout modernity. For Bacon, such a foundation is to be found in the sensory experience of material things. Bacon presents the world as being composed of bounded entities that interact in discrete events which proceed according to fixed laws. The aim of experimental science should be the identification of these laws through experience (Jones 1961: 58). Bacon's inductive method was intended to work from the specific results of experiments to broader generalisations, which would eventually yield a universal natural history. While advising his readers not to be over-hasty in expecting concrete results from science, Bacon believed that the ultimate outcome of his natural history would be the human mastery of nature, which had been lost in Adam and Eve's fall from grace (Shapin 1996: 139).

This natural history was to be a body of knowledge pieced together from observations and experiments, supplanting the unsound information that people had hitherto had to work with, forming a basis for inductive reasoning. As such, it would represent a store-house of experiences gathered over time. It was to be experimental in the sense that it was to involve forms of natural-historic description in which forces and conditions were invoked that might not be observed in the everyday run of things. Pickstone (2000: 138) suggests that this is to be distinguished from post-nineteenth-century experimental science, which has involved the systematic creation and control of novelty in the service of innovation. There was no sense in which Bacon's science was intended to create new products, compounds, or artefacts. Bacon's approach to science was highly sceptical, for he believed that the mind was easily misled by a variety of 'idols' (popular misconceptions, traditions, imperfect education), and needed to be continually directed by the evidence of the senses. The more that science relied on logic alone, the more likely it was to indulge in flights of fancy. Rather than allowing such errors to arise, theorisation should be held off until sensory experience of natural things had been acquired. However, Bacon distrusted the senses almost as much as the mind, considering them to be dull and imperfect. It was for this reason that experiments needed to be very carefully put together, so as to maximise the yield of the limited powers of perception (Jones 1961: 50). Significantly, in identifying the danger that the understanding should become a 'false mirror' of the outside world, Bacon subscribes to the same division between the mental and the material, or mind and body, as was to inform Descartes' work in quite a different way.

From an archaeological point of view there are two aspects of Bacon's influence on Western thought that are supremely important. The first concerns the growing conflict between 'ancients' and 'moderns', or between a continued adherence to the written word of classical knowledge and the new learning (Smart 1992: 12). Throughout the Renaissance the rediscovery of the classical past and the residual concern that the present might be inferior to the past had meant that the rediscovered texts had maintained considerable authority (Pickstone 2000: 43). Bacon was deeply antipathetic towards a reverence for the ancient authors, and was much taken with the notion that human understanding grows by increment. This belief in the gradual expansion of knowledge embodies a conception of progress, which was to inform an entirely new historical narrative. That the human condition is progressively improved by the growth of learning was to be a keystone of the Enlightenment, and in turn facilitated the consideration of both social and biological evolution. The second, related point is that Bacon recognised that new knowledge could be created. While this point is now virtually taken for granted, at the time that he was writing there was a strong belief that too much learning weakened the mind (Appleby *et al.* 1996a: 4). Bacon had to justify learning, and struggle against the 'evil' belief that all truth had already been discovered. Bacon's stress on experiment was in part a means of asserting that the sum of possible knowledge was not to be found in books, and that the experience of material things could lead to understandings that were entirely novel. There could be no archaeology without this recognition that one can learn new things by attending to the material world.

The growth of empiricism reflected a more general conviction that material things represented a legitimate source of understanding. For some while, antiquarians had been prone to point out that, unlike texts, artefacts could not lie. They thus formed a more secure form of evidence (Schnapp 1996: 181). Now it began to be more widely recognised that objects were entities from which new knowledge could be drawn. This made interesting samples and specimens the effective equivalents of books, rather than simply illustrative examples of particular phenomena: they could be studied. This was to have considerable implications for the well-established cultural practice of collecting. In the medieval world, objects such as relics of the saints had been collected together in churches and monasteries. These had been displayed, yet that display was not seen as an end in itself so much as a means of glorifying God. Conversely, kings and princes had long gathered treasure together in their vaults, but this had been a largely private activity (Prior 2002: 12). In the Renaissance, these two practices of treasure-gathering and display were brought together in the much more ostentatious palaces of the mercantile princelings of Italy. The fifteenth-century courts generated a culture of competition and rivalry, in which the display of wealth and splendour was a means of maintaining the precarious social status that had been built on commercial enterprise rather than dynastic inheritance (Hooper-Greenhill 1992: 47). The glorification of the patron (rather than God) was achieved through the deployment of taste and novelty as well as raw wealth, creating a spectacle which substantiated the claim of the prince to be a person of significance. It was in the context of this culture of ostentation and connoisseurship that the new innovation of the cabinet of curiosities was to emerge. Typically, such a 'cabinet' might have been either a piece of furniture or a room set aside for the collection and display of remarkable items ranging from geological specimens, plants, antiquities and stuffed animals to paintings (Figure 1.3). Related to these were gardens, in which exotic species that were increasingly being encountered on voyages of discovery were planted, and rarer zoological gardens.

While much of the value of these collections doubtless lay in diversion, amusement, and above all their role as a means of social competition, conventional histories of archaeology have sometimes underestimated their scholarly significance. Cabinets are often presented as random and pointless accumulations of oddities, and their unsystematic character is generally identified in the lack of distinction made between cultural and natural phenomena (Figure 1.4). Fossils and prehistoric stone tools might have been displayed alongside one another, for instance. It might be more accurate to recognise the cabinet as a transitional cultural form which attempts to represent the entire world as a unified image, but through the framework of the Renaissance

Figure 1.3 The cabinet of Ferrante Imperator (from Imperator's *Historia Naturale*, 1672)

Figure 1.4 The cabinet of Olaus Worm (from his *Musei Wormiani Historia*, 1655)

world-view rather than the tabular and typological lens of the seventeenth and eighteenth centuries (Hooper-Greenhill 1992: 82). Rather than attempting to arrange objects into arrays of like things, the cabinets of early modern Europe were structured as a microcosm of creation, ordered by sympathy, allegory and correspondence. As Hooper-Greenhill argues (ibid.: 84), this organisation of material things in enclosed space drew on both the arts of memory and occult principles. While later museums would establish a classificatory order amongst entities that could then be observed from a position of exteriority, the cabinet materialised a cosmology in such a way that a person might enter into it, and gain influence over it. Pre-modern magical practices were understood to achieve their aims through the congruity of words, things, and ideas, rather than through the distanced manipulation of things characteristic of modern science (Horkheimer and Adorno 1973: 11). Over time, the role of the cabinet as a memory theatre and focus of sympathetic magic may have declined, but this does not reduce the sense in which they continued to be structured according to a set of principles which was not ancestral to the modern museum but alien to it.

Where the cabinet does indeed represent a precursor to the museum is in the way that the collection of objects had come to be recognised as the equivalent to a library. Indeed, many of the early cabinets actually contained books, in keeping with the Renaissance view of words as integral to the world of things. By the middle of the seventeenth century, gardens and cabinets had become subject to recreational visiting, as a casual means of acquiring new information (Jardine 1999: 253). This tendency was initially most marked in botany, and indeed the Tradescant collection (which would eventually form the nucleus of the Ashmolean Museum) was begun as a botanical collection. Well into the seventeenth century, private collections continued to be composed of items that we today would separate as biological, geological and archaeological. This clearly demonstrates the sustained influence of the scheme of knowledge structured around resemblance and association: everything was still potentially connected to everything else, and classificatory order was yet to have its impact on the private collector. However, by 1675 the Ashmolean Museum had been founded in Oxford, with the expressed intention of making the collection available for study by the university students (Trigger 1989: 47). As sources of potential new knowledge, collections of material things began to be assembled by the universities in the same way as they had amassed libraries, and before they ever came to build scientific laboratories (Pickstone 2000: 73). Furthermore, in 1663 King Frederik III had set up his *Kunstkammer* in Copenhagen, establishing the notion of the national collection. From this time onward, as the nations of Europe began to acquire overseas dependencies, collections of plants, animals, minerals and artefacts from other continents began to develop in capital cities as an unmistakable element of the apparatus of colonialism. To labour the point: objects had become things from which knowledge could be extracted, and had become the business of the state. Removed from their original location, and recontextualised in the museum, objects could be studied comparatively, and could serve as a means of instructing future bureaucrats and administrators. This is a uniquely modern configuration.

Rationalism and mechanism

> I am much occupied with the investigation of the physical causes. My aim in this is to show that the machine of the universe is not similar to a divine animated being, but similar to a clock.
> Johannes Kepler (quoted in Shapin 1996: 33)

Baconian empiricism was one of the two great pillars of seventeenth-century science and philosophy, which sometimes stood apart from one another, and were sometimes combined in various ways. The other was the rationalism of René Descartes. Both were foundationalist, in attempting to find a new and fundamental ground for knowledge and action, but the means in which they went about this were radically different. While Bacon demanded a closer attentiveness to physical things, harnessed and strengthened by the discipline of experiment, Descartes was more thoroughly sceptical. Doubting everything, Descartes came to focus on pure, abstract reason as a means of overcoming the potential chaos threatened by competing cosmologies (Toulmin 1990: 71). Descartes followed Plato in presenting mathematics and geometry as the most fundamental forms of knowledge, and considered a range of abstract ideas to be innate in the human soul, having been placed there by God. The apex of Descartes' argument is the knowing subject: the only thing that I can be certain of is that I am aware. The metaphysical sanction for the mind's awareness of innate concepts that it can use to understand the world is then found in religious faith: God is not a deceiver, thus our mental apparatus must be accurate. The most important of the innate capacities of the mind is the ability to reason, and from this it follows that reason is to be trusted more than the information about the world that the senses provide us with. For this reason, Descartes was thoroughly opposed to the Renaissance view of the world as structured through resemblance. We cannot trust the outward appearance of things, so resemblances can be deceptive. Similarly, language may be an imperfect tool for describing things, or may be untrue (Foucault 1970: 43).

In place of similarity and connection, Descartes sought to differentiate and order things by measurement and comparison. In the *Discourse on Method* he suggested that problems could be resolved by dividing them into their constitutive elements, which should then be ordered from simple to complex (Descartes [1637] 1912). Here, rather than beginning with experiment and observation, reason is the principle that organises worldly things

(Foucault 1970: 53). One can begin with the study of pure geometry, and move from there to the particularities of matter. What Descartes was hoping to achieve by this means was the identification of the fundamental principles of nature. These in turn could be expected to be concerned with geometry and motion, since all worldly bodies essentially consisted of a substance with a geometrical extension (Cassirer 1951: 50). So like Bacon, Descartes wanted to create a total system of knowledge; the difference was that he wanted to work outward from a set of grounding principles, rather than building upwards from observations. In contrast with Bacon's 'experimental philosophy', Cartesian rationalism came to be known as the 'mechanical philosophy' because it relied on the notion that the universe was like a great machine, operating according to a series of relatively simple laws (Coley 1991a: 179). It had been noted by Kepler and others that clocks and automata could give the outward impression of being animate entities, but that an acquaintance with their inner motions demonstrated that they were entirely mechanical. Descartes argued that the same was true of nature: the notion that the world and its creatures might possess some form of intentionality was based on an illusion. Machines, having been engineered to fulfil a particular task, were entirely intelligible (Shapin 1996: 36). Accordingly, Robert Hooke held that increasingly powerful microscopes would eventually undermine all theories of influence and sympathy between material bodies by revealing the 'small machines of nature' (ibid.: 50). This conviction that the world was entirely comprehensible, but that some aspects of its workings were beyond the capability of the unaided senses to apprehend, contributed to the popularity of the so-called 'corpuscular theory'. This held that all matter was composed of tiny atoms in continual motion. Accordingly, all problems of matter were problems of mechanics. Any complex circumstance could be reduced by a 'calculus' to a set of ordered principles.

The structure of Descartes' argument in the *Discourse on Method* was to have decisive implications for modern Western culture. We have seen that for Descartes the absolute certainty of innate first principles can be attributed to the truthfulness of God. But it was equally important to him in overcoming his own scepticism to place human consciousness at the centre of his analysis. This single move had the effect of at once defining conscious reason as the essence of humanity, and constructing a pre-eminent position for epistemology as prior to any other kind of knowing (Carroll 1993: 119; Heidegger 1993a: 297). At the same time it rendered humanity as a kind of fixed point in the cosmos: that which was knowable became that which was known by a human subject (Derrida 1978: 278). Rather than being one kind of phenomenon created by God alongside other phenomena, humans were now in the privileged position of being the interpreters of reality. As we have mentioned already, the emergence of Christianity began a process by which the world slowly changed from being an aspect of eternal divinity to a facility at the disposal of humankind. Christianity had imagined a God who operated as an agency, a creator and first cause, and this might be identified with the origins of instrumental reason (Zimmerman 1990: 171). With Descartes, the position of God was further marginalised, for the certainty of the existence of material things was now to be vested in human consciousness. All things could be assayed and measured, and humanity was to be the measure (and creator) of all things (Gray 1995: 153).

Just as Descartes mistrusted the appearances of things, so he rejected the attempt to uncover the multiple connections and contexts in which things are embedded. In place of such a relational hermeneutics, he advocated the imposition of an order on the world (Foucault 1970: 74). Human reason is able to stretch a grid over creation and divide it up in a comprehensible way because, being God-given, it is infallible. Provided that we attend to the voice of reason we cannot commit any error. Error arises from hastiness, and the imperfect application of reason, or from submitting to the demands of authority, which compromises reason (Gadamer 1975: 246). Yet because reason was a capacity of the mind, and was applied freely by human subjects who had autonomy of will, while the material world was a mechanism that obeyed invariant laws, Descartes was obliged to separate mind from body and subject from object. The relationship between the observing subject and the observed object became critical to human understanding, and it was this that led to the privilege afforded to epistemology. Indeed, it is as soon as one imagines that a problematic relationship exists between a subject and an object that one has brought epistemology into being (Critchley 1999: 56). Moreover, splitting the mind from the body, and hypothesising that mental activity takes place in a realm that is separate from the material world, has the additional effect of constituting *perception* as a problem. How information is gathered from the world and internalised becomes an issue.

In their different ways, Baconian empiricism and Cartesian rationalism attempted to refound human knowledge by clearing away the impediments that had been scattered about by unsound thinking. Both attempted to cleanse and purify the operations of thought, and both advocated the construction of holistic systems of knowledge. While the divisions between the two were profound, they shared a desire to introduce universally acknowledged criteria to govern what was and what was not to stand as truth. Effectively, they together embody an imperative to banish ambiguity and multiplicity, and to impose a single authoritative system of knowledge on the world.

The New Philosophy

During the seventeenth century the works of Bacon, Descartes, Locke and Hobbes, amongst others, began to define a distinctively modern conception of society and nature. One of the most characteristic elements of this new thinking was the claim that knowledge could be framed in ways that were context-free, and were consequentially universal in their applicability. While these arguments were prominently articulated in relation to physics, they were applied equally to political and ethical issues. As Toulmin argues, seventeenth-century philosophy replaced a consideration of the context and language of arguments with an insistence on abstract logic, and a concern with the particular, local and timely with an emphasis on permanent, universal generalisations (1990: 21). Descartes' influence was greatest in promoting the kinds of rational certainty that could be promised by mathematics, while Bacon's concern with empirical verification eclipsed an interest in the rhetorical structure of arguments. As we will see, the ultimate effect of the transfer of these imperatives into the ethical sphere was to be the creation of an abstract moral philosophy (ibid.: 76). These approaches advocated the construction of a system that would integrate all possible forms of knowledge, and this further encouraged the belief that the same kinds of regularities that were being identified in physical processes might also be found in the human world (Cassirer 1951: 6). Yet until the later seventeenth century this notion of a total system of knowledge was largely presented as an achievement to be aspired to in the longer term.

To begin with, then, the new philosophies had their impact at the level of procedure: they suggested ways in which headway could be made towards the establishment of a coherent new science. In this respect, Descartes' methodological arguments were of critical importance. Descartes had suggested that reason should proceed by dissolving a complex reality into its component parts, and then reassembling these parts in order to understand the totality (ibid.: 14). Consciousness therefore achieves command over things by reconstructing the process of creation. Arguably, this implies that humanity is conceived as following in the path of the creator, rethinking the thoughts of God. Furthermore, this process of dissolution and reconstruction is one that involves agency: again, humanity was usurping the position of the creator, and Being was becoming predicated upon acting. Finally, the idea that the world can be made comprehensible by reducing it to fragments is an utterly modern conception (Bauman 1991: 12). Rather than attempting to understand things in the context of a broader set of relations, they are abstracted and presented as being in the first instance free-standing entities. Any totality is to be understood as being composed of a collection of objects that logically precede the whole. Descartes himself believed that any substance could be divided an infinite number of times, and that there are consequentially no fundamental particles, but his methodology nonetheless lies behind a broader tradition of 'atomism' in science and social theory. This manifests itself both in systems theory, which dissolves complex phenomena into multiple 'sub-systems', and in liberal social thought, which privileges the rights of the individual over community, tradition and obligation (Taylor 1985: 187). We might choose to connect this specific conceptual isolation of entities to the more general processes of alienation that characterise modernity, through which economic and social relationships are dissolved, and people and things are made to appear to exist in a state of reciprocal independence. Associated with this development was the removal of meaning from the world. If in Renaissance thought phenomena had been networked to each other by their symbolic significance, associations, mythological connotations and etymology, meaning was now increasingly identified as the content or product of the human mind, as we shall see below.

In Britain, rationalism and empiricism provided the intellectual milieu in which the Royal Society was formed, following the restoration of the monarchy, after the civil wars. That Charles II was favourable towards science was highly fortunate for the founders of the Society, for experimental science had been promoted by Puritan elements during the period of the Commonwealth. Empiricism was believed to show industriousness, in contrast with the slothful ways of the scholastics. The Royal Society followed this precedent, with a programme that was vigorous, optimistic, and at times grandiose. Robert Hooke, for instance, set the tone by arguing that there was nothing in nature that lay beyond analysis (Coley 1991b: 211). Similarly, Robert Boyle proposed in 1666 that a complete natural history of Britain should be undertaken by the Society. Interestingly, one of the elements of this project that he advocated was a questionnaire survey on the antiquities of the regions of the nation (Piggott 1985: 21).

This is an indication of the extent to which antiquarianism was embedded in the scientific revolution, the New Philosophy, and the Royal Society in particular. Many of the more prominent antiquaries of the period, like Robert Plot and Edward Lhwyd (the first two curators of the Ashmolean Museum) presented their own studies as a facet of natural history (Schnapp 1996: 198). More importantly, the seventeenth-century antiquarians were often part of the same social networks as the philosophers and experimentalists. John Aubrey, for instance, was a friend of Hobbes and was very familiar with the works of Bacon and Descartes (ibid.: 190). It is barely conceivable that Aubrey's recognition that artefacts could be classified, and that their character changed through time, was not informed by what he had learned through these professional connections. Moreover, when the Society of Antiquaries was established in 1717 with William Stukeley as its secretary (Piggott 1985: 15), its structure was explicitly based upon the Royal Society and the other learned societies that had recently been founded. All of these were sustained by Bacon's advice that science must be a collective activity involving the accumulation of observations and experiments.

Newton and the ordering of nature

The reconciliation of rationalism and empiricism, and the construction of something approaching a coherent structure of scientific knowledge, was first achieved by Isaac Newton. His *Principia Mathematica* of 1687 can be seen as the culmination of the scientific revolution of the seventeenth century, presenting a unified theory of gravitation that had profound consequences for the way in which matter was to be understood (Newton [1687] 1995). Like Boyle and Hooke, Newton was part of the experimental tradition that had been founded by Bacon, yet he shared with Descartes a belief that nature obeyed a series of laws which could be expressed in mathematical form. He simply held that those laws should be directly accessible by empirical means. Like Hooke, he believed that all things could be known by science, yet he acknowledged that some natural laws were more general in their applicability than others. Newton's work also followed on from that of Descartes and Bacon in that it elaborated the mind/body dichotomy. He argued that human experience involved the re-presentation of the outer world in an 'Inner Theatre' or *sensorium communae*. The nervous systems and sensory apparatus had the function of bringing information about the world to this inner space, and taking back the mind's commands to the executive faculties (Toulmin 1990: 108). On this basis, Newton contrived to argue both that there was a real order in nature, and that it could be fully comprehended by the systematic gathering of sensory evidence (Cassirer 1951: 8). Like Descartes, Newton imagined the structure of the universe to be something like a complex mechanism. On the other hand, he also believed that this mechanism was effectively regulated by God, who, having created the cosmos, actively intervened in its preservation (Coley 1991b: 223). Most significantly, Newton followed Copernicus and Galileo in arguing that there was a single universe which obeyed a uniform set of laws (Pickstone 2000: 87). This was effectively a refutation of the Aristotelian cosmology, in which the physics of the heavens were distinct from those of the earth (Shapin 1996: 17). Aristotelianism had held that the elements which resided below the moon were affected by change and decay, and moved in a rectilinear fashion. The celestial bodies, by contrast, were perfect, eternal, and underwent no change. The burden of Newton's argument was that principles that had been demonstrated by experiment on earth could be expected to apply elsewhere in the universe.

Newton's ideas are significant, not simply because they transformed the ways in which physics, astronomy and mathematics were to operate but also because any fundamental change in the conception of nature had immediate consequences for the understanding of human society. For Newton, scientific knowledge is knowledge of God's creation. Science is the means by which reason apprehends the work of God. Newton presents nature as something like a clockwork machine, the cogs and wheels of which have been assembled by God. This places God in an external relationship to the orrery, still a creator, but one who stands back from His creation. In contrast, the Renaissance had seen God as present within nature. Giordano Bruno, for instance, had argued that God was the internal principle of motion in nature, so that nature itself was continually coming into being, rather than a made thing that was 'finished' (Cassirer 1951: 40). Clearly, this was a variation on the Aristotelian theme of the continuous movement of things towards their *telos*. Bruno presents the world as a whole as being animate, through the immanent presence of the deity, just as Aristotle had seen worldly entities as having something like a 'soul'. The implication of the Newtonian view is that material things do not and cannot move themselves; they are only ever subject to external agency, whether human or divine.

Newton's vision promoted a more thoroughly instrumentalist conception of the universe. Not only was God a creator, the world was a product. The more that the material world came to be seen as a created substance that obeyed physical laws, and the more that reason became the prerogative of a mind that operated under quite different conditions, the more it became possible to separate humanity from the rest of creation. Bruno Latour has argued that the hallmark of modernity is a kind of conceptual 'purification' in which the knowledge of physical things is held apart from that of politics and social power (Latour 1993: 3). The laws of nature could be distinguished from the conventions of society, and yet once the two had been separated, similarities could be identified between them (ibid.: 130). Most importantly, reason was capable of elucidating both natural and social order. However, while nature had been created by God, and the investigations of the scientist should lead one to marvel at His handiwork, society was made by people. Thus the work of reason in understanding human relations might be expected to result in the improvement of the conditions under which people lived. That is to say, reason could produce progress and civilisation in the human world, as well as mastery over the natural world.

However, to begin with, the potentially radical implications of Newton's work were not fully worked through. The emphasis on order, structure and stability proved congenial in a political climate where cohesion and certainty were to be desired (Toulmin 1990: 109). It is highly significant that the idea of a scientific analysis of society emerged at the very point when modernity was gaining its coherence (Smart 1992: 7). However, those commentators who initiated this form of study were not necessarily seeking new, utopian social forms. Hobbes, for instance, was much influenced by Descartes' mechanical conception of nature, and argued that the state is like a machine or a body composed of organs (Goodman 1991: 22). Just as nature is made up of stable systems that obey causal laws, so humans can use reason to create stability in society. In this process, the overcoming of wilfulness and emotion may involve submitting to established authority. For Hobbes, the state is made up of the wills of many individual persons, who together constitute a collective will (Cassirer 1951: 19). This picture of innumerable separate entities coming to form a greater whole is clearly related to the corpuscular conception of matter. Both Hobbes and Locke suggested that human beings exist in the first instance in a state of nature, and are transformed by a civilising process (Taylor 1985: 190). The implication is that the state of nature has both a conceptual and a historical priority, so that as well as humans being socialised in the course of their lives, there was presumably a time when all people existed in a 'natural' condition. Locke places these arguments into the context of education, arguing that a new-born child is a 'blank slate' of which anything can be made by learning. Hobbes, however, argued that human nature was essentially evil and violent. It was the task of reason to replace this condition with order. In *Leviathan*, Hobbes ([1651] 1996) argued that it was necessary for the monarch to impose a total authority on the populus in order to overcome the negative aspects of humanity.

In the work of Hobbes and Locke there is an emerging tension between the individual and society. The individual human being has now come to be associated with reason and will, and exists prior to the social. Yet the social can be understood as an entity in itself, operating in something like a law-like fashion. The polarisation of the individual will and the social will had the effect of enhancing the growing dichotomy between the person and the community, while the community itself came to be seen as the product of the acts of individual persons. These tendencies would mature into the 'social physics' of Smith and Ricardo, in which it came to be recognised that there may be unintended consequences of human actions (Appleby *et al.* 1996a: 7). Thus while society is created by individuals, the collective whole may operate in ways that are not willed by individuals. Although the notion of social order goes back at least as far as Plato, Hobbes in particular was to emphasise the role of consciousness in reflecting on that order. Moreover, the understanding that social order was a human achievement lay behind the development of statecraft and what we would now call 'social engineering'.

We have argued that Newton's era, the end of the seventeenth century, was one that found or created order in nature and society. One of the consequences of this was that the practice of classification took on a much greater importance. Natural history was now dominated by the description of objects, and their positioning within taxonomic schemes (Foucault 1970: 137). While the Renaissance had relied upon similarities of appearance, it was now held that God's ordering of the world was sufficiently complex as to be hidden. On the surface, nature appeared to be chaotic and confused, but on a deeper level there would be some form of organisation. Taxonomic classification was the means by which the order of nature might be made apparent. What is particularly significant about this way of thinking is that it shows the first hint of the importance of the distinction between surface appearance and hidden depths, which must be uncovered by human effort. This is another distinctively modern conception, and one that would become much more significant at the start of the nineteenth century with the emergence of the notion of hidden structures.

As we have seen, classification places all things within a grid or table. They are thus rendered as equivalents, or signs within a classificatory system. While this approach was first applied to living things, it soon provided the format for the ordering of files, archives and libraries (Foucault 1970: 132). Given the close connections that we have already noted between natural history and antiquarianism, it is not surprising that these methods were also applied to artefacts. Indeed, Edward Lhwyd was to move towards the typological ordering of antiquities on the basis of work that he had already undertaken on fossils (Piggott 1976: 20). Schnapp (1996: 266) refers to the way in which Aubrey, Caylus and Winckelmann were able to recognise that typology might provide a means of seriating and dating artefacts. However, it is important to recognise that their achievements were built upon a fundamental change in the way in which the material world was understood. We have seen that within the early cabinets of curiosities and museums little distinction was made between geological or botanical specimens and objects of human manufacture. The temptation is to suggest that this is a measure of the relative ignorance of the collectors concerned. Yet it is instructive at this point to note the contrast that Foucault draws between two natural historians, Ulisse Aldrovandi (1522–1605) and John Jonston (1603–75). Aldrovandi's works are concerned with animals, both real and mythical, and represent an exhaustive chronicling of all of the information that could be assembled concerning particular creatures (Figures 1.5, 1.6). This included descriptive material, travellers' tales, myths and legends. Jonston's writings, however, are concerned with more exclusively classificatory information: anatomical details, means of locomotion, diet, means of reproduction, and so on (Figure 1.7). Within half a century, there had been a complete change in natural history, from relational chronicle to descriptive ordering (Foucault 1970: 129). Rather than seek the connections between creatures, the imperative was now to segment and classify them.

Significantly, one of the collections to which histories of archaeology sometimes refer was that of Aldrovandi himself, which contained both stone axes and flint arrowheads of prehistoric date (Piggott 1976: 103). These objects were not separated from the biological and geological specimens. However, Aldrovandi himself was active in the continuing debate over the possible human origins of such artefacts, and presented different arguments at different times (Daniel 1980: 35; Trigger 1989: 53). So Aldrovandi was not ignorant of the character of the objects that he possessed. Rather, we could suggest that with the change in the organisation of human knowledge that took place during the seventeenth century came a further change in the significance of collections. For Aldrovandi, the collection might already be a store of potential knowledge, but the form that it took was that of a microcosm of the physical world, in which all relationships were potentially significant. Just as a book or a library should gather together all the knowledge that might be worth knowing, so any interesting specimen might throw light onto any other. Aldrovandi's collection was ordered by correspondences and relational sequences, including alternations of like and unlike things, and sought to bring art and nature together (Hooper-Greenhill 1992: 124). In

Figure 1.5 Ulisse Aldrovandi's illustration of 'Pesce Istrice', from his *Tavole di animali* IV

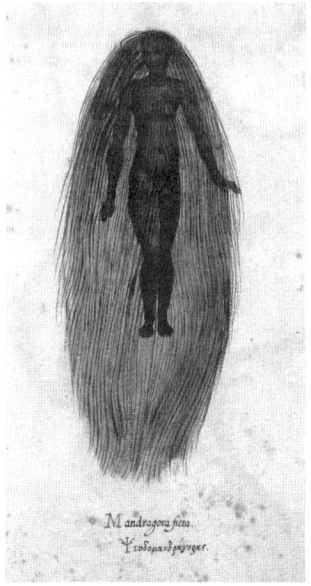

Figure 1.6 Ulisse Aldrovandi's illustration of Mandragora (Mandrake root), from his *Tavole di piante* IX

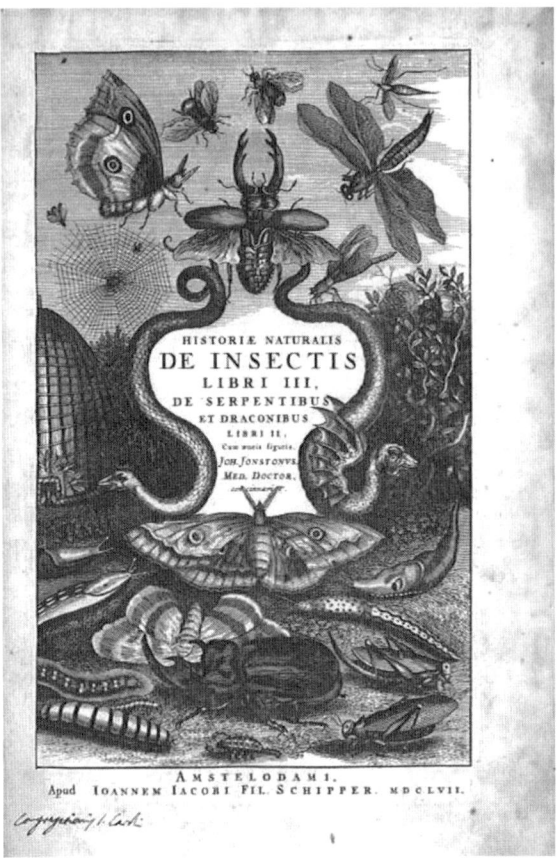

Figure 1.7 Title page of John Jonston's *De Insectis* (1655–7) (Biblioteca Panizzi)

some cases, items were grouped thematically rather than according to physical similarity. While Aldrovandi's cabinet may not have represented the kind of occult machinery that some of the early Renaissance collections amounted to, it was nonetheless integrated by ties of meaning rather than taxonomic structures.

By the later seventeenth century, though, information existed to be classified and organised. Collections and museums provided the raw material for systems of classification, which are fundamentally exclusionary. Taxonomical ordering defines which aspects of a phenomenon are not significant, as much as which are. In the wake of Newton, the separation between the human and non-human worlds, culture and nature, was absolute, and this now provided the principal basis for ordering collections of material things. If the cabinets of curiosities had been the materialisation of a cosmology structured around meaning and significance, the subsequent development of museums demonstrates the attempt to make the classificatory table manifest. Description was now prioritised over meaning, and museum collections were gathered in such a way as to assure representative coverage of species, genera, and types (Pickstone 2000: 61). Rather than mystical influence, the museum collection now enabled the observer to gain mastery over the things of the world from a position of exteriority, looking down on the array of specimens and appreciating their classificatory order (Hooper-Greenhill 1992: 45). The museum now became the world-picture, facilitating the understanding of a world that was expanding rapidly through commerce and colonialism.

This desire to apprehend the world in its entirety was matched by new strategies of graphical representation. The 'realistic' images of architecture and landscape that were made possible by linear perspective have been linked by a number of authors to the development of the object/subject dichotomy, and the separation between people and things fostered by capitalist economic relations (Berger 1972: 16; Cosgrove 1984). We can identify a connection between this kind of art and the naturalistic depiction of objects in science, including the convention of drawing things to scale (Pickstone 2000: 63). Implicitly, this mode of representation relies on the notion that material things have an unproblematic character which is fully available to the sensory apparatus, and that by rendering them accurately as they appear to one viewing subject, their fundamental character can be conveyed to another. Both perspective art and scientific drawing are evidence of the eviction of meaning from the world. The project of realism in representation relies on the understanding that the depicted thing is what it is: a meeting of matter and light. Meaning is always secondary to the way that the thing objectively is, and the way that it is conveyed to us by our senses. As Andrew Jones has pointed out, the kind of standardised scientific graphic depiction that emerged in the seventeenth century is one of the fundamental disciplinary practices of archaeology (Jones 2001: 337). Any excavation report contains large numbers of scale drawings of objects, while the 'corpus' publication depicts all known examples of a given class of artefacts, according to a standardised set of conventions. All of these objects are therefore 'seen' from a single point of view, and this has the effect of *constituting* artefactual categories. Arguably, then, the way in which archaeologists define the kinds of things that they find is a consequence of the early modern project of presenting the world in such a way as to be viewed by a transcendental subject.

The Enlightenment

By the end of the seventeenth century, the new science had established the project of a search for order in nature, and the implication that a similar order might be created in the affairs of humans had been widely accepted.

The Enlightenment of the eighteenth century was to take the emphasis on reason and analysis and propose that they should form the basis for all human knowledge (Cassirer 1951: 6). Newton's combination of rationalism and empiricism proved persuasive, so that authors like Diderot ([1754] 1999) advocated a move away from abstract mathematical science towards a more descriptive approach. Increasingly, the intention was now to generalise the analytical framework that he had proposed to all areas of human enterprise. John Locke had argued in his *Essay Concerning Human Understanding* ([1690] 1998) that human beings acquire information from their experience of the world, and that their knowledge is therefore not innate. Consequentially, through education and access to information, they can improve their own conditions. The Enlightenment built on this argument to propose that greater knowledge of the world leads to greater self-understanding, and this in turn will generate social progress (Cassirer 1951: 37). According to Montesquieu, all human beings naturally possess an insatiable thirst for knowledge. Providing that all obstacles are removed, human beings will progress from one idea to the next, and will eventually arrive at a perfect and enlightened understanding. This confidence in the growth of knowledge was reflected in Diderot and D'Alembert's *Encyclopaedia*, which was arguably the most distinctive product of the Enlightenment. The *Encyclopaedia* was a new kind of book, which was written in the understanding that it could not represent an eternal order of knowledge, and would be overtaken by the escalating accumulation of facts (Rosenberg 2001: 51). It was presented as a tool to enable the reader to increase their own understanding, with an alphabetical dictionary order to facilitate browsing.

Although it is unwise to suggest that the Enlightenment was characterised by a single, uniform point of view, it is fair to say that most Enlightenment thinkers equated legitimate knowledge with experimental science. The success of the scientific revolution appeared to be self-evident, and therefore the growth of understanding in other areas depended upon the adoption of a method as similar as possible to that of physical science. It has been argued that the Enlightenment represents the defining project of modernity: consequentially the privileged position that was afforded to science in the Western world during the eighteenth century has been maintained ever since (Gray 1995: 145). Moreover, the Enlightenment laid absolute stress on the autonomous operation of reason, unfettered by tradition or authority. Reason was considered to be homogeneous and universal, the same at all times and all places, so that one thinking being was much the same as another regardless of their temporal or spatial location (Cassirer 1951: 6). What this amounted to was a denial of human finitude, the very attribute which many authorities would argue renders us human, as mortal beings (Falzon 1998: 11). In emphasising the universality of reason, the Enlightenment suggested that it is possible for humans to transcend their historical and cultural conditions. This was to have the very positive effect of inspiring emancipatory political movements, but it also tended to promote an arrogant disregard for cultural diversity. Moreover, it presented the differences between human beings (culture, gender, ethnicity, class) as superficial rather than constitutive, with the result that the difficulties that afflicted those who did not approximate to the idealised 'Everyman' were underestimated.

Equally seriously, the Enlightenment proposed a moral and political order supported by rationality and atomistic logic. Human beings were understood as being in the first instance autonomous individuals, whose fundamental characteristics could provide the basis for an ethical code. The relationships between individuals, the state, and nature were increasingly seen as a matter of logical calculation. The logical and rational foundation of human conduct would be easier to achieve if pre-existing obstacles were swept away, so Locke's notion of the 'clean slate' began to be applied at the level of the society as well as the person. If a fresh start were made in social relations, a rational and ordered community might be created (Toulmin 1990: 175). This was the thinking that ultimately inspired the French Revolution. Autonomous reason might be expected to create a better society, because all humans shared the same rational faculties, and because if those faculties were allowed to operate unimpeded they would recognise that it was in their own interest to co-operate with others. However, it was acknowledged that in the present imperfect circumstances many people were irrational, because they were operating under the deluding influences of prejudice and superstition. Therefore, laws had to be constructed in such a way as to force people to act as if they were being rational (Bauman 1993: 27–8). The Enlightenment is thus responsible for the idea that 'rational' ways of life can be imposed on communities for their own good.

Because they compromise the work of reason, the Enlightenment presented tradition, prejudice and superstition as being in all cases undesirable. As Gadamer puts it, the Enlightenment's most fundamental prejudice is that against prejudice itself (1975: 240). If a universal, rational civilisation created *de novo* was capable of bringing about the perfection of humankind, then any society based upon traditional values or religious faith was by definition inferior (Gray 1995: 123). It has been this argument that has enabled the modern West to disrupt and undermine countless non-Western societies. At the risk of a gross oversimplification, such 'traditional societies' are often oriented on the past, and maintain their order through the continuity of custom and belief (Giddens 1991: 29). Tradition provides people with an orientation in the world, and limits risk and uncertainty. 'Westernisation' has often had the effect of stripping out traditional practices and authority, replacing them with a 'rational' order that amounts to no more than unfettered capitalism and perpetual insecurity. However, the Enlightenment's emphasis on the social consequences of the exercise of reason also meant that it was more openly critical of existing political institutions than

Locke or Hobbes had been. Authority, as much as tradition, was seen as an impediment to reason, and Voltaire once remarked that men would never be free until the last priest had been strangled with the entrails of the last prince (Appleby *et al.* 1996a: 8).

While Bacon, Descartes and Newton had all held that science was engaged in revealing the work of God, the philosophers of the Enlightenment were more hostile to religion. The aim of science was to divest nature of its secrets, and this could be achieved by human reason alone, without the intercession of a divine being. Moreover, theology was placed alongside superstition as an irrational influence that was dangerous when it became involved in the moral order (Cassirer 1951: 47). We have seen that over a period of two millennia since the emergence of Christianity the way in which the relationship between humans and the deity had been conceived had gradually changed. From being at the centre of all things, God had slowly been marginalised by a developing humanism which now presented humanity as the creator of a cultural world (Carroll 1993: 117). Instead of the discoverers of God's creation, the Enlightenment cast humans as the masters of their own fortunes. During the eighteenth century, the deists had effectively taken the first steps towards an atheistic cosmology by claiming that God had created the world before leaving humankind to their own devices. This went well beyond the Newtonian image of a God who periodically tinkered with the clockwork of the universe. Christianity had instituted a temporal narrative that led from the fall of man to judgement and salvation. Now a series of similarly linear narratives were developed, which still focused on the fate of humankind but which made people the agents of their own transformation rather than subjects of divine grace.

While some aspects of Christianity had emphasised the freedom that God had given humans, to choose to sin or to be saved, freedom was much more central to the Enlightenment project. As Rousseau argued, only humans are free to choose their own perfection: a choice that is not open to animals (Day 1996: 68). Freedom was thus connected with reason as a human prerogative, and the more that reason supplanted tradition and prejudice, the more humans became free individuals. The progressive freeing of the individual is consequentially at the centre of the metanarratives created by the Enlightenment (Carroll 1993: 121). The individual becomes 'unencumbered' by overcoming a series of restrictions: traditional social forms, the limitations of nature, the shackles of belief (MacIntyre 1981: 32). Just as Christianity had presented a narrative that reached fulfilment with the Last Judgement, so Enlightenment narratives stressed closure in the perfection of individuals or the resolution of conflicts. Because the Enlightenment promoted the idea of a universal, rational civilisation, it was possible to argue that there would be a single answer to all social problems. Different points of view could be brought into dialogue, and logically resolved. The implication of this is that both for the individual and for society, history must have an end. There must be a point of culmination at which communities have achieved their potential. Moreover, because reason was both universal and homogeneous, and because all humans were in principle capable of perfection, the notion of the psychic unity of humankind was influential in the Enlightenment (Appleby *et al.* 1996b: 27). This encouraged the belief that human history was a universal history.

The metanarratives of the Enlightenment mark the development of a modern conception of historical time. The medieval world had largely seen the universe as changeless, save for the creation and the judgement. Aristotelianism had presented the entire world as being in motion, but the movement towards the *telos* had relatively little to do with human intercession. By the eighteenth century, there was a growing sense that human beings were bringing about progress, transforming their own conditions of existence by their own actions. The implication of this was not only that the future would be unfamiliar, but that the past would have been unlike the present. While the Renaissance looked back to the past for its learning and its social ideals, in the eighteenth century the past came to be of interest because it contained the origins of developments that are not yet complete. Ironically, this resulted in the revisiting of ideas that had been discussed in the classical era, although they were utterly transformed in the process. Epicurus and Lucretius, for instance, had advanced the concept of evolution, proposing that it was responsible for the gradual diversification of phenomena (Harris 1968: 26–7), while Varro had proposed a series of stages of historical development, leading humans from savagery through pastoralism to tillage (Schnapp 1996: 68). Enlightenment historical philosophy harnessed these ideas to a vision of the progressive perfection of human existence through the application of reason and the construction of order. Generally, this process was understood as having begun with a 'state of nature', in which the absence of culture coincided with disorder. While Rousseau was to argue for the nobility of savage peoples, for the most part Enlightenment thinkers saw the distant past as a time in which reason had been weakly developed, and thus a period inferior to the present. Here again, the belief that universal criteria can be defined to cover morals and values had the effect that quite crude value judgements could be made, both in respect of the past and in relation to non-Western people who were judged to be less 'developed'.

In one important sense the metanarratives of the Enlightenment were quite distinct from any account of human development that had existed in the ancient world. Both Plato and Aristotle had, in different ways, adhered to the belief that each creature or phenomenon that existed in the material world aspired to achieve a state as far as possible akin to its ideal form. The structure of the universe was attributable to the relationships between the forms or ideas, and the teleological vision of history saw the direction of temporal change as being determined by the movement towards the perfection of worldly phenomena. Change therefore took the form of the maturation of a pattern that was already implicitly in existence, and these ideas remained influential during the revival of learning in the Renaissance. All things had their own 'natural motion', which took them towards perfection, and towards their appropriate place in the moral and cosmological order (Shapin 1996: 29). By contrast, from at least the seventeenth century onwards, the Western tradition rejected any notion of ideal forms, whether existing in some other sphere or immanent in worldly things themselves. Rather than being parts of a cosmological order, worldly entities were increasingly understood as singular, and linked by mechanistic relations. Consequentially, the Enlightenment view was not that history was advancing towards a predetermined *telos*, but that progress would lead to a perfection of the human condition that had not yet existed in any form. The outcome might be inevitable, but was only to be attained through the realisation of human potential in the application of reason. The perfect ordering of society and nature was not intrinsic in the universe, but would be a human achievement. By implication, this view radicalised the sense in which historical change was directional and non-reversible.

The Enlightenment's universal histories were based upon a series of philosophical premises, and tended more to the rationalist than the empiricist pole. As a result they relied more on the coherence of their arguments than on any use of what we would now define as archaeological evidence. Nicholas Mahudel's description of ages in which tools of stone, bronze and iron were in use, presented in 1734, is an example (Trigger 1989: 60). The force of the hypothesis lies in the conception of technological evolution and its relationship to the development of reason, rather than any observations on prehistoric artefacts. Similarly, Robert Jacques Turgot's *Plan for Two Discourses on Universal History* of 1750 drew on Locke's works on education and the debate on psychic unity to propose that human beings would have advanced through successive stages of hunting, pastoralism and farming (Harris 1968: 28). So although these works deal with the distant past, they are best considered alongside books like Condorcet's *Outline of the Intellectual Progress of Mankind* ([1795] 1822) as part of a general intellectual framework that provided the context in which ideas of the temporal development of material culture developed. They were generally more concerned with explaining the contemporary state of society and economy than with understanding the past for its own sake. Pluciennik (2001: 742) has recently contrasted those eighteenth-century conjectural histories that were based around stadial schemes for the development of subsistence economy with those that focused on technological change. While the latter were to be of critical importance to archaeology, the former were more significant in political economy and anthropology. It would not be until the 1920s that the two would be brought together in the notion of 'periods' of time characterised by distinctive combinations of food procurement and material culture (ibid.: 748).

We have noted already that many of the early antiquarians were directly acquainted with the philosophers and scientists of their time, so that their approaches to material things were directly informed by current ideas. Another example of this pattern is provided by William Stukeley, who had known Halley and Newton in his years as a physician in London (Piggott 1985: 42). Influenced by Newton's work on planetary gravitation, and by the idea that God had vested a coherent pattern in nature, Stukeley wrote an essay on the notion of the 'music of the spheres' in 1720. His argument was that the orbits of the planets had been created according to a set of mathematical relationships that might be expressed as musical harmonics (Ucko *et al.* 1991: 97). Although this seems a bizarre idea, the theory reflects Newton's belief that the creator is directly involved in the regulation of nature. Later, when Stukeley was to argue that the builders of Avebury and Stonehenge were members of a monotheistic society comparable with that of ancient Egypt (ibid.: 74), it is arguable that he was again in tune with current debates. Stukeley argued that monotheism was a universal stage in human development, more sophisticated than pantheism. His suggestion was that monotheistic societies in different parts of the world could be used to illuminate each other, an argument that is reminiscent of more recent evolutionary approaches in archaeology (e.g. Renfrew 1973a; Earle 1991). While Stukeley's later work is often criticised as being inferior to his descriptive fieldwork, being influenced by religious ideas, it is also possible that by the 1740s he was reflecting contemporary notions of universal progress. As a person of some religious conviction, Stukeley would not have been a wholehearted supporter of the Enlightenment. But the view of the past that he adopted was one that was only possible within a modern framework of thought.

Similar arguments can be made in relation to Christian J. Thomsen, and his role in applying the 'three-age system' to material culture. Thomsen developed his classificatory scheme as a means of organising the collection of prehistoric and protohistoric artefacts of the Royal Commission of Danish Ancient Monuments in Copenhagen (Schnapp and Kristiansen 1999: 32). Yet we should remember that before taking on this task in 1816 Thomsen had studied in Paris, and had already classified collections of coins and medals. While numismatic research would have helped him to recognise the ways in which the form of artefacts changes through time, it is equally probable that exposure to the academic environment of Napoleonic France would have brought Thomsen into contact with the historical philosophies of the Enlightenment. What Thomsen was able to do was to take the speculative history of technology that Mahudel and others had proposed and use it as a basis for ordering an assemblage of artefacts into a chronological succession. But this itself depends on the understanding that time forms a logical order in which different subsistence practices, social types, and kinds of artefacts give way to each other in a sequential fashion. Yet Scandinavia, and Denmark in particular, was in any case sympathetic to the ideas of the Enlightenment, and to the French Revolution. It is therefore unsurprising that archaeological innovations that rely on order, sequence, classification and typology were often first established in northern Europe. Thomsen and his student Worsaae both placed great stress on the importance of the classification of artefacts, and saw function, substance, decoration and association as multiple dimensions according to which things could be categorised (Daniel 1950: 46). In short, the grid of modern ordering practices had been laid onto the chaos of prehistoric material culture in the attempt to purge its ambiguity. Admittedly, Thomsen and Worsaae applied the three-age system in an idiosyncratic manner, for they did not suggest that the stone, bronze and iron eras were universal stages in human development. Instead, they argued that this was the sequence in which more complex technologies had been introduced into Scandinavia from central Europe by migrating communities. However, Nilsson was to propose something more in keeping with a universal narrative of social evolution: particular artefacts were to be associated with successive stages of human development, from savage and herdsman to agriculture and civilisation (ibid.: 49).

2

ARCHAEOLOGY AND THE TENSIONS OF MODERNITY

Reason and morality

Between the sixteenth and eighteenth centuries, fundamental changes overtook the ways in which people in Western Europe understood the world. While these changing patterns of thought were most clearly articulated by philosophers, scientists, and writers, the decline of tradition and faith and the rise of reason was much more widespread in these societies (Toulmin 1990: 12). Indeed, this period was characterised by a variety of attempts to transform a social structure based upon the ruler's proximity to God into one founded on a rational moral and legal code. For this reason, the efforts that were made to define the relationship between reason and morality in the later eighteenth century are of the greatest possible interest. The idea of a moral order has been fundamental to modernity. The moral order is the ideal to which modernity appeals, the point at which sequences of historical development are presumed to eventually arrive. The imperative to create an orderly nation-state, founded on a rational legal code that could discipline the base natural drives of the population, was bound up with the same forces that produced the discipline of archaeology. This kind of social arrangement could be assumed to be the destination of all humanity, because the moral sense is universal, rather than culturally relative.

This argument was most forcefully expressed by Immanuel Kant. According to Kant, certain aspects of our mental faculties are a priori, or given, rather than developed out of experience. Indeed, Kant argues that if we are to make sense of our experiences, we need to make use of certain principles that are already present in our consciousness (Walker 1998: 26). Without a priori principles, no knowledge or experience is possible: for example, humans have an a priori grasp of time and space that precedes the experience of any positive thing *in* time and space. The human understanding provides us with a range of concepts and categories that enable us to organise our 'sensory intuitions' of the world. Reason, then, allows us to link our individual acts of understanding together in a logical way (Burnham 2000: 12). What this means is that the human subject, armed with its cognitive

35

faculties and a priori concepts, achieves its conception of the world by ordering it (Falzon 1998: 22). Indeed, any knowledge of the world that we can achieve is acquired through categories and concepts, rather than though unmediated experience (Simons 1995: 14). For Kant, the evidence of our senses is only a set of appearances, and it is impossible to have direct access to things in themselves, as they really are. This places categorisation in an even more central place than Locke had afforded it, and while Kant entertained the possibility of the existence of God he clearly implied that the order that we discover in nature is a human order. Reason is itself an a priori mental faculty, and the moral law is known to reason, rather than to experience.

Kant argues that it is inherently rational to act morally. We do not learn to act morally: it is a categorical imperative. Reason commands us to act morally. Any rational being who is aware of the moral law cannot fail to recognise it as an instruction to act (Walker 1998: 24). Because reason is a distinctive faculty of human intelligence, the moral law is not natural. Natural things obey the natural laws of physics, but the moral law operates in a space that is exempt from this kind of causal relation (Burnham 2000: 23). The moral law can only be followed where there is freedom, in the sense of the choice to do otherwise. Thus human beings are the only creatures that can act morally, precisely because they have autonomy of action (Carroll 1993: 129). So again, while Kant does not deny the existence of God, he finds no place for religious injunctions or the observance of tradition in morality. Kant's argument suggests that the moral law is unitary: there is one correct way to behave in any particular circumstance, and the more that one acts in a rational fashion the more likely one is to obey the moral law. One implication that can be drawn from this is that those who are in a better position to exercise reason than others are in a better position to dictate the laws of society (Bauman 1991: 22). Here again, we can recognise the connection between philosophy and legislation.

Perhaps because the modern world is aware of historical change, and does not imagine that things will always be precisely as they are now, modern societies are concerned with their own contingency. Dynasties collapse, empires rise and fall, and the maintenance of order and continuity comes to be recognised as a problem. Effort needs to be exerted in reproducing the existing set of social relationships. Once this problem began to be reflected upon, the role of philosophy was transformed. In articulating the relationship between the moral law and the laws of nature, Kant was providing an abstract conception of justice and governance that could be put into practice by state legislators. Kant's arguments are concerned with the moral duty of treating other human beings as ends in themselves, rather than means, and showing an 'active sympathy for their fate' (Kant [1797] 1998: 457). Yet the implication was that if the moral law was obeyed, the social order would be maintained. By identifying the moral law with the willed action of individuals, Kant had located a transcendental ground for the contingent institutions of the modern state, which nonetheless gave the human subject a foundational role in civil society.

In their different ways, both Kant and the French Enlightenment *philosophes* minimised the belief that the world contained any inherent meaning, preferring instead the view that meaning entered the world through the ordering activities of human beings. The role of the human individual was to give meaning to a world that already existed as a blank slate. Into a meaningless and chaotic world, human beings bring structure and design (Bauman 1992: xi). The natural world is composed of so much meaningless stuff, which awaits being formed and rendered meaningful by humans but which does at least obey the laws of nature. The human world, however, does not yet obey the moral law. It is wayward and unruly. As a result, there is an abiding sense of failure in the modern West: the universal civilisation has not yet arrived, and human beings are not yet as law-governed as the things of nature (ibid.: 187). Therefore, the lives of humans need to be administered, designed, moulded and engineered by the state.

The discovery of finitude, and the problem of Man

While Hobbes and Locke had held that human societies should be expected to obey laws equivalent to the laws of nature, we have seen that the end of the eighteenth century brought a growing concern with historicity. Hobbes had argued that the state represented a means of rising above the 'state of nature', but now there was an increasing belief that the process of achieving a rational society would be a protracted one. Seventeenth-century thinkers had imagined that human societies were composed of fixed structures, which would achieve their fruition or culmination as history progressed. By the end of the eighteenth century, notions of development or evolution were taken more seriously as historical narratives began to involve changes through a series of distinct stages (Sheridan 1980: 49). The important innovation here is that instead of merely amounting to static objects 'in' time, societies were now increasingly understood as dynamic entities. This much is implicit in Thomsen's use of the three-age system, where classification, which had hitherto involved the organisation of entities on a synchronous grid, came to be connected with *sequence*. So objects as well as people are not simply contained in time, they operate in different ways as time progresses.

This shift of intellectual preoccupations from a static classificatory order of nature to a developmental sequence of social forms, which eventually came to be applied to natural things as well, may be one of the most decisive consequences of the Enlightenment. It has been argued that high modernity has been dominated by time (Jameson 1984: 64), in that constant change, restlessness and a belief in progress have been endemic in the modern West. Claude Lévi-Strauss (1977: 29–30) once drew a distinction between 'hot' and 'cold' societies, those which were and were not disposed to historical transformation. Since the beginnings of agriculture, he argued, some societies have been subject to accelerating change and progressive internal differentiation. Yet what is remarkable is that over the past 200 years people in the Western world have become accustomed to the idea that material and technological progress is routine, and to be expected (Vattimo 1988: 4). Modern Western people acknowledge that they live in a world that is different from that of their grandparents, and presume that their grandchildren will live in a different world again.

That not merely social relationships, but the whole fabric of creation was in a state of constant flux was an idea that first took hold in geology. James Hutton, in his *Theory of the Earth* ([1788] 1795), was to argue that the study of rocks and their formation addressed quite different problems from those dealt with by Newtonian mechanics, for it was concerned with constantly changing conditions (Toulmin 1990: 124). That such processes could be understood at all depended upon the implicit use of what would later be defined as the principle of uniformitarianism, which holds that some aspects of physical processes in the past were the same in principle as those that can be observed in the present. Hutton argued that if processes of heating, pressure and weathering can be recognised affecting rocks in the present, it is reasonable to assume that the formation of those rocks can be attributed to the influence of those same agencies operating over very long periods of time. Of course, the depths of time involved would have been far longer than the biblical timescale then in orthodox use, so that Hutton's ideas were an implicit challenge to the accepted account of the creation. A little later, William Smith was to add the insight that rocks had been laid down in an orderly sequence, in his *Strata Identified by Organised Fossils* (1816). Thus the relative age of rock formations could be identified according to their juxtaposition. As with Thomsen, Smith was making the link between time and sequence: distinctive events were to be located in a non-reversible series. Interestingly, the idea that the earth was composed of a series of layers of material had been discussed as early as the beginning of the seventeenth century by Verelius, and Oolof Rudbeck had drawn a stratigraphic section of a megalithic tomb in 1697 (Schnapp 1996: 200). What these antiquarian approaches to stratification had lacked was the recognition of dynamic processes at work in the formation of strata.

The outcome of these developments was that while nature and culture had been split apart into different domains, one ruled by the natural law and the other an arena in which free will might operate, both were now conceived as subject to directional change. According to Foucault's analysis, this was the point at which *Man* began to emerge as a problem to be addressed by the sciences (Sheridan 1980: 79). By the start of the nineteenth century, Man had become at once the subject who acquired knowledge, an organism with a distinctive physiology, and a historical subject. Foucault argues that at this point those academic disciplines that were concerned with humanity were transforming themselves in order to accommodate the relationship between historical process and human finitude. Cuvier had revolutionised natural history, changing it into biology by emphasising the functioning of organisms rather than the classification of species. Ricardo had transformed the study of wealth into economics by focusing on the functioning of markets. And the history of language was developing into philology, concerned with the conditions of speaking (Foucault 1970: 312). All of this meant that the sciences were absorbing themselves with the historical continuities that provided the conditions of the possibility of human functioning. Human beings were finite, mortal beings, but there was now a conceptual entity that transcended the person, created at the intersection of the organism, artefacts and words. Man was the issue that lay behind labour, language and life (ibid.: 318). This was all the more of a problem because Man had taken on the role of the subject for whom knowledge is possible, the creator of culture and the transformer of nature. Understanding Man was now a priority, since it amounted to understanding how a knowable world had come into being.

The formation of the notion of Man can be seen as the culmination of the modern project. Its consequences for archaeology cannot be overstated. When archaeologists talk of 'the origins of Man', or 'the history of Mankind', they mean Man in the sense referred to by Foucault. That is to say, the particular concatenation of biological and cultural conditions that provides the ground for a certain kind of existence. Archaeology is a product of this discursive formation. It charges itself with uncovering the deepest roots of this kind of being. It concerns itself with the origins of 'anatomically modern Man', of consciousness, language, signification and economic relations. Yet Man is a product of modernity, and a concept that could not have been thought before the start of the nineteenth century.

This brings to mind the argument made by Martin Heidegger in his essay 'The Age of the World Picture' (Heidegger 1977). Here Heidegger suggests that in the period since the Middle Ages human beings have come to look on the world less and less as a divine creation that they inhabit and more and more as an object that they stand outside of and are free to manipulate. The world becomes a picture, in that it is subject to re-presentation, an object of scrutiny. The important change is that the ground of a thing's existence had changed from its being made by God to its being observed by humanity. From Descartes onward, it is human subjectivity that is the guarantee of existence, rather than faith in God. This means that human beings are now the beings upon whom existence is grounded. Humanity has become the subject, and the world has become the object. Finally, as the analytical gaze of humanity turns inward, people become objects as well as subjects. This is the point at which Foucault would say that the figure of Man has appeared on the horizon. Man is at once the ground of knowing, and the greatest mystery to be uncovered.

Modernity and its discontents

The Enlightenment sought to re-establish human knowledge by doing away with metaphysics. All that would matter would be the unfettered exercise of reason upon the natural world. However, it is possible to argue that modernity has simply seen one metaphysical structure replaced by another. We have seen that in the modern age science has been recognised as the supreme form of knowledge. Yet science is itself established upon a metaphysical basis. For instance, science often maintains that only statements that can be empirically tested can stand as true. Yet this statement itself cannot be tested: it is metaphysical (Lawson 1985: 19). In the same way, science generally bases its observations on the world on the premise that material things are simply present at hand in an unproblematic way. Things do not conceal themselves from us, and the question of how it is that we notice things, how they become recognisable or intelligible to us, is not an issue. This is because much of modern science inhabits a Cartesian world in which material things are defined in terms of their spatial extension and their spatio-temporal motion. No place or direction of motion is any better or worse, or more or less significant, than any other. Locations are just points on a grid. Therefore events can be registered by measurement and calculation (Heidegger 1977: 119), and events are only significant if they *can* be measured. All of this makes up what Heidegger calls the 'ground-plan' of modernity, a set of assumptions that is already known but which never has to be stated before observation takes place.

Throughout the first two chapters of this book I have been arguing that in the modern world philosophy and science have become far more than the ethereal discourses of specialist practitioners. Aspects of their arguments and the kind of rationality that they have promoted have gradually come to replace religious faith or customary practice as the 'common sense', everyday way of thinking that large numbers of people have applied to their lives. That science is always metaphysically based, and always has to assume more than it can empirically prove, suggests that modernity itself rests upon a metaphysical foundation. This in part explains why the modern West has had to rely so heavily on metanarratives, which give the impression that the unrelenting change of the modern era is focused and directional. Science and reason always leave unanswered questions, and consequentially have to find other supports for their legitimacy. As Lyotard argues, it is characteristic of the modern sciences to assert their legitimacy with reference to their place in some overarching process: the emancipation of Man, the freeing of the human spirit, the creation of wealth, the discovery of the universe (1984: xxiii). Yet the social role of these metanarratives is quite different from the place that narrative occupies in many non-modern or non-Western societies. The stories and myths that circulate in traditional or customary societies are integral to, and embody, social relations. As Lyotard puts it, they transmit the relationships that make up the social bond, the relations between the storyteller, the person about whom the story is told, and the audience (ibid.: 21). Myth and legend are at once a kind of performance that brings a community together, and also an explanation for why the community is as it is. Such a community has no need for a past, other than perhaps a mythic past. Tradition, custom and narrative form a seamless whole that integrates, reproduces and provides an exegesis for society, rendering any further clarification superfluous.

Science, however, is a form of knowledge that asserts its independence from social relations, its objectivity. It cannot be legitimated by the social relations in which it is embedded, because it claims to stand outside of society, context-free. Any explanation of society now needs to take on an objective character. Modern societies need to understand how they have come to be as they are, but they cannot do this through myth. They need a rational explanation, involving causes and effects, and fixed in linear time. They need a past that has been researched, and which can aspire to the criteria of validity that have been established by science. History and archaeology exist in the modern world because modern societies demand an origin in order to render them legitimate, and because modern science requires a context to distract attention from its groundlessness. An objective past that can be demonstrated to have really happened is now part of the strategy of legitimation (ibid.: 28). The past serves as the fixed point of origin for metanarratives that extend into the future. The inquiry into the past serves to substantiate that the path that we project into the future is credible.

So in the modern world, history as well as nature has become an object of scrutiny and analysis. A considerably more worrying aspect of modern metaphysics arises from the way in which it reduces the world to matter and motion. We have seen that modern science separates significance from meaningfulness by defining legitimate facts as those that can be measured and quantified. This means that the world can be understood as a collection of matter, linked by a network of predictable causal relationships (Vattimo 1988: 40; Zimmerman 1990: 124). This perspective can be seen as the ultimate outcome of the lengthy process in which being has come to be associated with the production and transformation of matter. As Heidegger would put it, the 'ground-plan' of modernity can only be put into operation if we have first carried out an 'un-worlding'. Our world is comprehensible to us because it represents a context of intelligibility. That is to say, we inhabit a world that is revealed to us in its meaningfulness. The modern West often presents meaning as an extraneous quality that is added 'on top of' a world of geometrical extension and spatio-temporal motion, as if as an afterthought. The world is first of all composed of matter, to which human beings 'give' meaning. As we have seen, this casts humans as meaning-giving intelligences. It is more helpful to understand the world as being meaningful 'all the way down'. Meaning and significance are not different things: we recognise something as significant because of what it means to us. We do not add meanings to objects, we identify them as meaningful in the first instance. What this means is that in order to see something as a 'mere' thing, a lump of matter or a geometrical form, we must strip away its meaning, and reduce it to the form in which it can be registered by science.

What has happened in modernity is that this process of 'un-worlding' has become generalised. Putting this another way, the world has been subject to a 'disenchantment', in which it has been rendered a docile object, rather than representing a subject in its own right (Bauman 1992: x). The world has been subordinated to human will, and made to exist merely at the service of humans. Heidegger describes this process as 'enframing', in which the world comes to present itself to us as a mere stock of resources, a 'standing reserve' (Heidegger 1977: 20). Enframing is a mode of revelation in which we look at the world through the lens of science and technology, and challenge it, in the attempt to gain mastery over it. It can be contrasted with *poisis*, in which the world is revealed in its meaningfulness, as an integrally connected context of life. While the ancient Greeks may have begun the movement towards this 'productionist metaphysics', by connecting being with having been made, they also recognised *techne* as a kind of making or forming that allows a substance to reveal itself as it is (Zimmerman 1990: 230). Christianity, by contrast, presented the world as a whole as something that had been forged by the creator. Eventually, the world is not merely a product, but the raw material for the handiwork of humans. For modern science, nature exists to be ordered, manipulated and subdued.

Contradictions of modernity

While I have argued that our modern world has been built upon a set of philosophical understandings that have achieved a kind of hegemony, it would be a mistake to imagine that these ideas have been universally accepted. For as long as modernity has been in existence, critical arguments have been developed against it, and these will be considered in greater detail throughout this book. One of the problems in identifying a 'post-modern' position is that these critical perspectives have been around for a long time, and might more properly be described as 'counter-modern'. Just as we have argued that it is a unique aspect of modernity that it is conceived as a project, so we could suggest that it is a further characteristic of the modern age to generate criticisms of itself. In other words, modernity is self-aware, and consequentially self-critical. In most cases, counter-modern positions were clearly initiated within the developing traditions of modern thought. Romanticism is a case in point. Romanticism was based upon Rousseau's repudiation of reason, yet its other characteristics were definitively modern. The Romantics replaced reason with myth and passion, but placed a radical stress on individuality, autonomy and freedom. It was the modern individual self that was celebrated by Romanticism, a self with an inner world boiling over with emotions, straining against the restrictions of tradition. The overcoming of tradition provided a historical narrative for Romanticism which paralleled that of the Enlightenment, and it simply reversed the relationship between reason and emotion without transcending the opposition between the two (Gadamer 1975: 243).

If Romanticism can be seen as part of the unfolding of modernity, it certainly played a crucial role in the formation of archaeology. In northern Europe, a nostalgic attachment to castles, abbeys and megalithic monuments and an interest in the sublime qualities of landscape resulted in a shift of interest away from classical antiquities in the course of the eighteenth century. Moreover, Rousseau's emphasis on the nobility of 'savage' peoples began to render the prehistoric peoples of Europe of interest in their own right (Daniel 1950: 22). These changing priorities can be recognised in the case of the English antiquarian Sir Richard Colt Hoare. Hoare, like many other wealthy young men of his time, travelled on the Continent, intending to take the 'grand tour' (Piggott 1976: 124). However, his efforts were frustrated by the French Revolution and the outbreak of the revolutionary wars. As a substitute for Italy, Hoare chose to travel in Wales, and developed an interest in Celtic and medieval antiquities (Symmons and Simpson 1975: 7). Furthermore, his imagination was fired by the Gothick, and while he was at pains to stress the objective and empirical character of his researches into the ancient monuments of Wiltshire (e.g. Hoare [1812] 1975: 7), he often reflected on the gruesome character of the skeletal remains that he and William Cunnington had hired workmen to unearth.

Yet archaeology does not simply reflect the complex patterns of modern thought. In some cases the study of the past has provided the arena within which conflicting ideas have been worked through. For instance, we have seen that throughout the modern period the extent to which God was held to be directly responsible for the creation of the world and its contents has gradually declined. Hutton and Smith had demonstrated that no direct divine intervention needed to be invoked to explain the formation of geological strata, and that these strata contained distinctive sets of fossil remains. It followed from this that the organisms contained within these layers had changed over time. Now, Lamarck's suggestion that organic evolution over a period of many thousands of years had transformed fish into human beings was greeted with incredulity when it was proposed in his *Hydrogeology* of 1802 (Harris 1968: 110). Yet the idea that living species changed over time was already accepted within the framework of the 'great chain of being'. What this suggested was that the entire living world formed a single structure, which was advancing forward in concert. All individual species were gradually developing, but their mutual relationships with each other remained constant, and all remained infinitely distant from God, even if it was towards Him that they advanced. No species will ever overtake another, for each link in the chain is moving forward at the same speed. As Foucault puts it, before Cuvier it was as if all the living species made up a classificatory table, which was constantly in motion, or alternatively that new squares on the table were continually being revealed (Foucault 1970: 151–2). Thus the aspect of biological evolution that could not be accepted was that of the progressive development of hierarchy, since this would disrupt the classificatory system. Cuvier's innovation was to consider species as organisms that functioned in distinctive ways, rather than entities defined by distinctive attributes. His use of comparative anatomy flowed from this outlook, and it was this that enabled him to recognise the exotic character of the extinct mammals represented in geological deposits.

That these species became progressively less familiar in deeper strata demanded an explanation, and both Cuvier and William Buckland responded with the doctrine of 'catastrophism'. This held that God had first created the world, and had then at different times created new sets of animals, which had been exterminated by a series of deluges, each equivalent to Noah's flood (Trigger 1989: 90). The geological strata concerned were therefore defined as 'diluvium', the products of a succession of floods. What is revealing here is the changing conception of the creator's involvement with the world. Quite beyond Newton's view of God's continuous intervention in the world, Buckland imagined a succession of new suites of animal species, each wiped out by catastrophe. Cuvier hypothesised that the deluges might have been regional in extent, allowing animals to migrate into areas that had been depopulated, while Charles Lyell was to suggest that each species was fitted by God to a particular environment, and condemned to extinction by environmental change (Harris 1968: 112). This is a God who is not simply a creator but a designer, or even a scientific experimenter. While these debates have generally been discussed in terms of the attempt to maintain a role for God, and to sustain a Christian tradition in science, the changing character of the causality involved may be equally significant. Nature was now understood as something that was designed and administered in an intricate way. God was not 'in nature' in a mystical way, but 'tried out' successive sets of creatures while manipulating the variables of the environment in which they were deployed.

Diluvialism, the belief in a series of deluges, relied on the notion that the most recent of the floods had been the one that was reported in the Bible. This being the case, human remains should not be expected to be found in the deposits laid down by the earlier catastrophes. The eventual discovery of human bones or stone tools alongside the remains of extinct species by Boucher de Perthes at Abbeville in the Somme Valley should thus have been decisive (Trigger 1989: 91–3). While Perthes was to make the curious argument that he had uncovered the remains of antediluvian human species, his discoveries were largely discounted until after Pengelly's excavations at Brixham Cave, twenty years later, in the 1850s. It was following this that

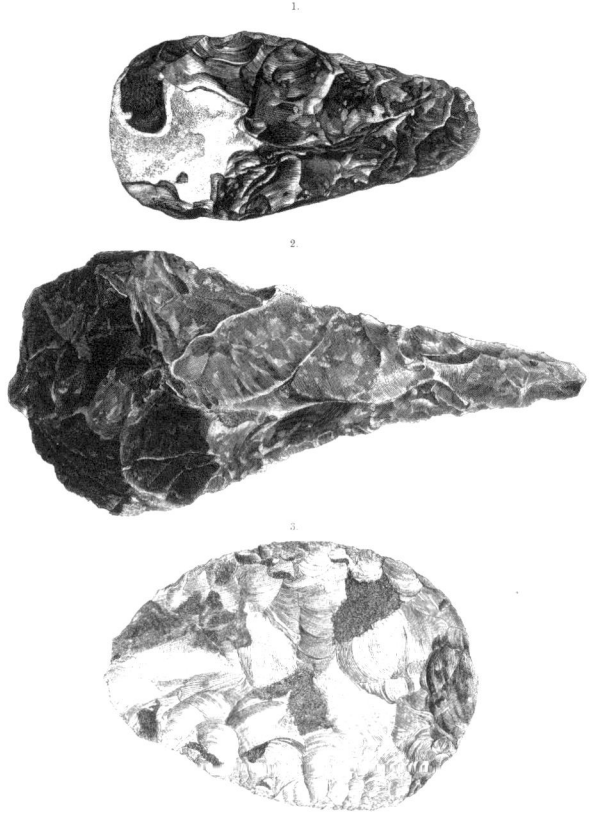

Figure 2.1 Sir John Evans's illustration of palaeolithic stone tools from the Somme gravels (from *Archaeologia* 38, 1860)

Joseph Prestwich visited the Somme under the auspices of the Geological Society to verify Perthes' finds, taking John Evans with him to study the stone tools (Evans 1860: 283) (see Figure 2.1). As Trigger (1989: 94) notes, this visit coincided precisely with Darwin's publication of *Origin of Species* (1859). What had happened is that a new and powerful metanarrative had become established: that of the evolution of humankind. Without this, the Abbeville evidence could not be thought through in the ways that we now find self-evident. While the great Enlightenment narratives of historical development could explain changes in the material conditions under which human beings existed, the narrative of human evolution could not be formed in the absence of the concept of Man. That is to say, the existence of any given human being at any point in time had to come to be seen as made possible by biological, cognitive and technological circumstances, all to a greater or lesser extent linked through the figure of Man. The gradual excision of God from these arguments is significant, but it may be less a consequence of the victory of scientific reason over religion, and more a reflection of the new position of centrality assumed by Man.

The crisis of modernity

Archaeology dramatises and elaborates the conflicts and contradictions of modernity, because it embodies so many of the key aspects of modern thought. And it must be said that modernity has been filled with contradictions; even that they have provided it with much of its dynamic character. Modern thought has attempted to free itself of ambivalence by placing things into clear categories. Yet as Latour points out, the attempt to separate human from non-human and culture from nature always fails, for modern technologies and social systems depend on creating integrated hybrids of people and things (Latour 1993). Modernity seeks order and stability, but ends up creating a social world that is unstable, restless and unresolved (Bauman 1991: 9). Modern philosophy promotes reason as a means of achieving freedom, justice and toleration, but the modern West has more often been exclusive and intolerant of difference. The universality that the Enlightenment proclaimed for its values has often excluded women, people of colour, Jews, and homosexuals. Modern science has stressed the need for knowledge to be based upon firm foundations, but these foundations have turned out to be metaphysical. Modern politics has attempted to resolve conflicts by bringing opposing views into dialogue, but very often this has simply confirmed that they are incommensurate. This is because the prejudices, traditions and beliefs around which they cohere have not withered away in the face of reason. The progress which has unquestionably been achieved in technology, communications, healthcare and standards of living has always been bought at a price: increased social divisions, the 'dumbing down' of culture, the impoverishment of the Third World, environmental degradation (see arguments in Horkheimer and Adorno 1973). Progress has not been an inclusive or a comprehensive process. Finally, Renaissance humanism and Protestantism both began as high-minded attempts to reconsider the basis of human existence. But the outcome of their interaction has been the development of the bourgeois world-view, and liberal individualism (Carroll 1993: 102). What has survived is free will and instrumental reason.

Because the modern age has understood itself to be progressing in a particular direction it has periodically been beset with concerns over its failure to achieve its goals. I have argued that from the end of the eighteenth century onwards the West has increasingly recognised the significance of qualitative historical change. This has meant that the progress of reason would involve not simply the fulfilment of the potential of existing structures but a series of transformations. Furthermore, it was slowly acknowledged that nature as well as society transforms itself through time (Toulmin 1990: 145). This is the broader significance of the replacement of the notion of the great chain of being by theories of organic evolution. Yet the growing emphasis on humans as finite beings located within historical processes placed a greater investment in modern metanarratives. If people were less assured of achieving the kingdom of heaven they might at least have faith that their actions would contribute to the fulfilment of the national destiny, the attainment of the New Jerusalem, the perfection of human knowledge, or the freedom of the human spirit.

A major challenge to modern orthodoxy was presented by the First World War. While science and reason were widely understood to be influences that would lead humanity to well-being and emancipation, the conflict of 1914 to 1918 appeared to demonstrate the opposite. Science and technology had been complicit in a slaughter on a scale that had previously been unimaginable. The Great War had notoriously been a war run on railway timetables, in which the mobilisation of huge armies had been facilitated by sophisticated systems of transport and deployment that were literally impossible to stop once they had been initiated. Technology seemed to have escaped human control. Vast quantities of high explosive were rained down on the battlefields, creating landscapes in which human existence was virtually impossible (Saunders 2001: 38). New weapons like mustard gas, tanks, aircraft, airships and submarines compounded the destruction, and yet for much of the time the strategies in which they were employed achieved little. Only minor gains of ground were made in offensives that cost colossal numbers of lives. The tactical skills of the general staff on both sides appeared to have been unequal to the destructive capacity of the ordnance at their disposal. The war was widely considered to have been not only costly but futile.

The recognition that technoscience had played such an instrumental role in the war was responsible for several of the more influential intellectual developments in the period from the 1920s onwards. If there was to be any hope of a future society based upon reason, science would have to be refounded, or purified. The different ways in which it was suggested that this might be achieved were highly diverse, however. The logical positivism of the Vienna Circle, for instance, represented something like a return to the strict empiricism and rationalism of the seventeenth century. Science should be based exclusively on observation and logic. Any indulgence in speculation and metaphysics had to be rooted out, because it was in straying away from what could be directly learned through experiment that scientists compromised their objectivity (Bryant 1985: 111). Any statement that went beyond what could be proved by experience was not only dangerous but meaningless. By contrast, the critical theory of the Frankfurt School attempted to identify the social, economic and cultural factors, many of them unrecognised or unacknowledged, that surrounded the production of knowledge (Jay 1973: 46). The Frankfurt School sought to elaborate the Marxian theory of ideology, in which societies are seen as saturated by the ideas of the dominant class, by introducing Kant's conception of critique. By interrogating contemporary culture, the critical theorists hoped to understand how ideology functioned to constitute the consciousness of those who created academic knowledge. Where they differed amongst themselves was on the question of whether ideology could be purged from scientific knowledge, yielding a kind of objectivity, or whether human knowledge was inherently ideological.

Different again was Edmund Husserl's transcendental phenomenology. Rather than simply advocating a knowledge based on empirical experience, Husserl argued that there had hitherto been little understanding of what happens when consciousness apprehends worldly things. Science could only be reconstituted when the nature of experience had been problematised. Husserl proposed to achieve this through the process of *phenomenological reduction*, through which experience could be boiled down to its most fundamental constituents, the primordial units of perception (Moran 2000: 146). These were understood as universal, transcendental, and installed in consciousness. It is worth noting that all of these attempts to rebuild science, with the partial exception of critical theory, were repeating the original injunctions of Bacon and Locke: to clear away false knowledge and lay a new foundation that would be absolutely secure. Effectively, they were arguing that modernity had faltered because *it had not been modern enough*. And indeed, the period immediately after the First World War saw a proliferation of hyper-modern intellectual movements of one sort or another, like the Futurists and the Vorticists. Arguably, then, the general reaction to the way in which science and reason had been compromised by the carnage of the Great War was to restate the cardinal values of modernity, and emphasise certainty and clarity (Toulmin 1990: 154). In some cases this involved reducing the modern project to its barest fundamentals, or distilling some aspect of modernity, such as the metanarrative of national destiny and technological progress. In this sense, the challenge to modern thought in the aftermath of the First World War can be seen as responsible for the rise of Italian Fascism and Spanish militarism, if not actually for Nazism.

The First World War challenged the idea of reason because of its sheer stupidity. The notion that a complicated tangle of diplomatic issues should result in a stubborn war of attrition in which millions would die, at the start of the twentieth century, seemed to negate any belief that human wisdom was growing incrementally through the ages. This negation could only be overcome by asserting that the triumph of reason had not yet been achieved. Far more damaging to the modern picture of history and the Enlightenment project that it nurtured was the Second World War, and in particular the Jewish Holocaust and the other Nazi mass killings of Romany people, the disabled, homosexuals, Jehovah's Witnesses, communists, socialists and Soviet prisoners of war that took place from 1933 onwards. For the Holocaust required that a modern nation-state should mobilise its people, and the technological and organisational resources of railways, gas chambers, crematoria and police forces, in the systematic project of annihilating part of its own population. As Zygmunt Bauman has cogently argued, various attempts have been made to represent the Holocaust as something exotic and unconnected with modernity (Bauman 1989: 85). The Holocaust has been portrayed as a specifically Jewish matter, or an outburst of the barbarism that had been repressed by modernity, or a consequence of the restricted nature of modernisation in Germany, which had only been unified as a nation since the 1870s.

Bauman makes the counter-argument: that the Holocaust was entirely characteristic of modernity, and is only thinkable in the context of a modern world. In the modern Western nation-states, the cultivation of order had promoted notions of social engineering in which the 'health' of the national community was often associated with homogeneity. The rational planning of societies might involve public health projects, state housing and public education, but it was very often the same class of professional administrators and welfare workers of the earlier twentieth century who entertained notions of eugenics (Bauman 1991: 32). Intervention into selection and heredity could be understood as a means of hastening human perfection. Moreover, the belief that science was objective and value-free had the effect of severing the practice of 'racial science' from any consideration of its ethical content. As a result, the notion of racial hygiene was already well established in European science long before the Nazis came to power (ibid.: 41). With instrumental rationality freed from moral constraints, slave labour in munitions factories and patented apparatuses of mass killing became logical extensions of the modern programme of finding total solutions to perceived problems of ambivalence and heterogeneity.

The burden of Bauman's argument is that modernity is genocidal. Modern reason seeks uniformity and clarity, and the resolution of problems. In combination with runaway technology and political systems based on national identity, this produces a lethal mix. The twentieth century saw repeated instances of mass killing in mass societies: Armenia, the Belgian Congo, the Russian pogroms, Manchuria, the Soviet Gulag, the Cultural Revolution, Vietnam and Cambodia, Chile, Rwanda, Indonesia, the former Yugoslavia. Premeditated and administered mass murders on this kind of scale did not take place in the pre-modern world: they were not instances of a 'reappearance' of barbarism. Bauman therefore concludes that the Holocaust was simply typical of the modern age. Indeed, as a number of authorities have pointed out, Hitler may actually have been responsible for fewer deaths than either Stalin or Mao Tse Tung. However, in another sense the cultural significance of the Holocaust may be unique. Germany was one of the nations within which the Enlightenment was formed. Indeed, it was Kant who most thoroughly explored what human enlightenment might entail. Yet rather than progressing inexorably towards a state of perfect knowledge, universal toleration and freedom from prejudice, the Germans elected a demagogue, constructed a state based on fear and hatred, and set about murdering millions of Europeans in cold blood, using the most sophisticated technology available to them. In the light of these developments it is simply no longer possible to place any faith in the Enlightenment project of universal emancipation through reason.

Therefore, it is highly illuminating that Jean-François Lyotard defines *postmodernity* as an 'incredulity towards metanarratives' (1984: xxiv). Theodor Adorno once famously wrote that after Auschwitz it would be a criminal act to write poetry. It is just as pertinent to say that after Auschwitz it is impossible to show any confidence in universal schemes of historical progress. In this sense, it may be accurate to suggest that we now live in a postmodern age, and that the Holocaust was one of the decisive factors that brought modernity to an end (Eaglestone 2001: 7). More cautiously, we might say that it is unclear whether the world that we inhabit is postmodern, late modern or high modern, and that this will only become clear with time. Yet undoubtedly, Lyotard is correct to suggest that something fundamental has changed in Western society over the past fifty years, and that on the whole people do not now consider themselves to be contributing to the forward march towards some future utopia. Or as Gianni Vattimo puts it, recent years have seen the collapse of the idea that history represents a single unified process of events (Vattimo 1988: 9). But it is difficult to suggest any particular point at which a radical break with the past took place (Jameson 1984: 53), and perhaps more accurate to suggest that over the course of the latter half of the twentieth century a variety of the central aspects of modernity started to show signs of decline.

Over this period, technology has continued to become more elaborate, and yet science has become the subject of greater scepticism. As a result, science has tended to concentrate its efforts on devising new technologies that work, as opposed to revealing ultimate truths (Lyotard 1984: 47). At the same time, the nation-state, the characteristic political formation of modernity, has increasingly come under attack. In Western Europe, the established nations have faced calls for the devolution of power from regional movements in areas like the Basque country, the Pays d'Oc, Catalonia, Brittany, Scotland, Wales and various parts of Italy. In Eastern Europe a series of new nationalisms have developed, and in North America and Australasia there have been calls for self-determination on the part of indigenous peoples. At the same time, the ability of nation-states to control their budgets, capital reserves and internal markets has been compromised by the globalisation of financial markets and the instantaneous electronic transfer of capital.

The process of globalisation has had other effects beyond the speeding up of capital flows and the erosion of the state. Just at the same point when modernity has been revealed as a questionable project, it has expanded across virtually the whole of the globe (Gray 1995: 166). A significant element in the modern West's construction was the rendering of non-westerners as 'others'. As we have argued, the 'universality' of modern Man was achieved at the expense of a series of exclusions. Such a distinction between the West and the rest of the world is now difficult to sustain. Modern technology and instrumental reason have come to be incorporated into a wide variety of societies, but with very diverse results. In the Islamic world the resilience of religious belief does not seem to be in question, and there is considerable resistance towards what are understood as the profane indulgences of the West. Similarly, Japanese modernisation has not been precisely the same thing as Westernisation (ibid.: 169). In many parts of the world the modern scientific innovations appear to have been adopted without necessarily requiring the introduction of liberal democratic political arrangements. China would seem to be a case in point in this respect. It may be a mistake to imagine that modernity is an integrated totality that has been formed in the historical experience of Europe and North America, and can be transferred intact to other geographical areas. If modernity is a project, it is one that is radically incomplete. Indeed, it could never be completed, since its various utopias could never be achieved. As Latour (1993) argues, we have never *been* modern because we are still struggling to achieve the state of *being modern*. As modernity has become established in other places, new groups of people have begun to create new forms of modernity (Miller 1994). Increasingly, then, modernity has become something plural, as fragments of the Western framework have been assimilated and recontextualised by different communities.

Of course, while this process has been most accentuated in the period since decolonisation, it has roots that go back as far as the mercantile ventures of the Renaissance. The events of exploration and colonisation brought Western communities into contact with a much greater range of human diversity than had been familiar in the medieval era. Here again, archaeology has been absolutely central to the modern experience. The various attempts to make sense of the encounter with non-Western peoples were to have a formative effect on archaeology. In the Renaissance, exploration gave further impetus to the humanist concern with human difference and plasticity. When indigenous North American communities were discovered to be able to manufacture tools from flaked stone, this fuelled Robert Plot's suggestion in his *History of Staffordshire* (1686) that certain objects in antiquarian collections might also be tools made by humans, rather than 'thunderstones' or 'elf-shot'. This helped to establish the idea that European people in the distant past might have had a less sophisticated technology, and by implication the notion of material progress. But at the same time, it also promoted a renewed conflation of temporal and spatial difference, whereby non-Western peoples came to be seen as the equivalents of 'primitive' prehistoric Europeans, at an earlier stage in a universal ladder of development. This would eventually have its crudest manifestation in W.J. Sollas's *Ancient*

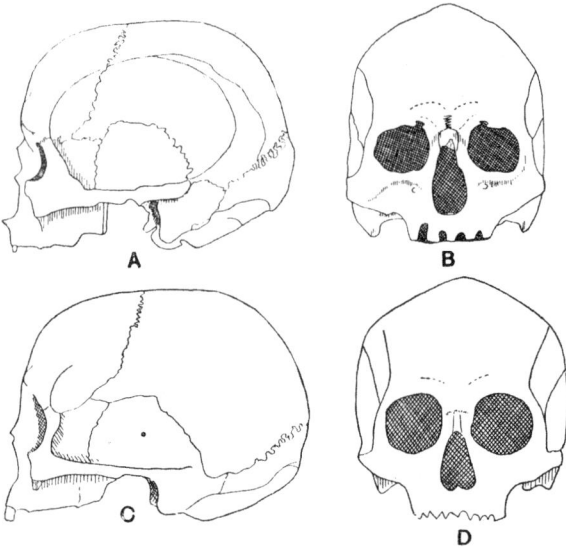

Figure 2.2 W.J. Sollas's comparison of the Magdalenian skull from Chancelade (A, B) with that of a recent Eskimo (C, D) (from *Ancient Hunters and their Modern Representatives I*, 1911, Macmillan and Co. Reproduced with permission of Palgrave Macmillan)

Hunters and their Modern Representatives (1911), in which the Tasmanians, Australian Aborigines, Bushmen and Eskimo were presented as survivors of various prehistoric groups who had once occupied Europe (see Figure 2.2). Each had been ejected into the furthest extremities of the globe by the incursions of new and more sophisticated communities. In these ways, archaeology has drawn on the recognition of human diversity, and has sought to explain it in ways that have substantiated the modern imperative to organise difference, and in the process to control it. If universality and homogeneity could not be achieved immediately, difference could be fixed in a narrative that led towards the utopia of its dissolution.

Conclusion

In this first section of the book I have attempted to identify some of the significant currents of modernity, while at the same time demonstrating the ways in which archaeology has been implicated in the development of a modern world. The case that I have tried to make is that archaeology as it is currently practised is not simply a product of modern technologies and social relations. Rather, archaeology relies upon a series of the central ideas of modernity, without which it could not have come into being. The first of these is the notion that humanity is the subject of history. Over the past two millennia, a universe structured around a creating deity has been replaced by one whose reality is guaranteed by human consciousness. This process is related to a second, in which the world has changed from being seen as an eternal and dynamic manifestation of divinity to being a set of material resources that is at the disposal of humankind. Together, these views have given rise to a linear and unidirectional conception of history in which the growth of reason and knowledge lead to the mastery of nature. It follows from this that the past, present and future of humanity will be different in character, and since technology is one of the principal means by which nature is subdued, that the progress of consciousness will be reflected in changes in the form of artefacts. The identification of human beings as conscious subjects, and of the material world as an arrangement of objects, led to the increasing separation of mind from body, as well as of culture from nature. The material world of nature performed according to the physical laws that science was increasingly identifying, yet the separate domain of consciousness was where free will was able to operate. Free will was to be associated with reason, and reason was the source of the moral law. So both nature and consciousness were potentially domains of order, and the utopia that the Enlightenment sought was one in which the moral law was observed, because people acted in a reasonable manner.

However, by the nineteenth century, the natural world and the world of conscious reason both came to be seen as subject to developmental change, in which their fundamental structures were repeatedly transformed. Human beings came to be seen as a combination of biological, social and cultural attributes, each of which was subject to long-term processes of change. Thus, while the thinkers of the seventeenth and eighteenth centuries had imagined that each individual 'blank slate' was capable of perfectibility, those of the nineteenth saw humans as finite, and limited by their bodies, their language, and their material culture. The new concept that linked together the continuities of biological, social and cultural evolution was that of Man, or Mankind.

Archaeology concerns itself with these long-term sequences of change, which spin themselves into a series of universal narratives. While archaeology is the study of the past, there is generally an implication that what is being studied is significant because it has contributed in some way to the present state of affairs. Like all science, archaeology legitimates itself by positioning its activities within a series of metanarratives. Very often, it has involved itself in the construction of the kinds of narratives that provide foundations for the nation-state, political institutions that do not have recourse to the narrative resources of traditional societies. But at the same time, archaeology is also distinctively modern because it asserts that new knowledge can be created from the observation of material things. Technology is the manifestation of the development of consciousness, and can be classified and ordered to provide information in the same way as the species of plants and animals. So just as the new science of the seventeenth century believed itself capable of producing a knowledge of creation that went beyond that which had been imparted in scripture, so archaeology uses material things to address aspects of the past that are not referred to in any written text.

The case that I have made is that archaeology has been made possible by modernity, and also that it has contributed to the formation of the modern world. Consequentially, the failings of the modern outlook, and the possibility that the modern era is coming to an end, should be of some concern to archaeologists. Modernity has promoted rigid order and instrumental reason, wilfulness and the separation of knowledge from social and ethical concerns. It has facilitated social inequality, genocide and environmental degradation. In the next part of this book we will investigate some of the more specific ways in which modern thought has provided the conceptual apparatus with which archaeology has been conducted.

3
THE TYRANNY OF METHOD

Descartes and the idea of method

One of the most significant ways in which archaeology finds itself embedded in modernity lies in its adherence to a conception of knowledge that privileges method. Throughout the twentieth century, archaeologists sought to establish abstract methodologies which might later be brought to bear upon material evidence. Effectively, a hierarchy was in place whereby universal and decontextualised logic was valued over the particular, the historical and the tangible. Indeed, it was often claimed that the evidence could only be rendered intelligible when a foolproof and already perfected methodology was applied to it. Even Ian Hodder (1997: 691) lamented the lack of a discussion of 'post-processual methodology' in the final years of the century. In this chapter I will hope to trace the emergence of this predisposition towards formal method in early modern philosophical thought, and demonstrate the ways in which it has affected the practice of archaeology.

Throughout its history, modern thinking has attempted to establish a definitive method that would guarantee the truth of any knowledge simply by virtue of rigorous adherence to a defined procedure (Bauman 1992: 129). This imperative is particularly closely associated with René Descartes, whose *Discourse on Method* ([1637] 1912) laid out a programme that might be followed in the pursuit of rational understanding. As we have already seen, Descartes was writing at a time when the possibility of universal knowledge appeared to be in crisis, following the upheavals of the Reformation. New scientific discoveries, and encounters with non-Western societies following mercantile expansion, were also threatening established frameworks of understanding (Guignon 1983: 210). Faced with endemic uncertainty, Descartes sought to reposition epistemology as first philosophy, a form of inquiry upon which all knowledge would henceforth be grounded. Ironically, given that the problem that Descartes sought to overcome was the tide of relativism and scepticism that was afflicting Europe, it was in scepticism that he proceeded to ground his method. Radical doubt was to be a means of overcoming prejudice, by cutting away any form of understanding that could not be substantiated.

Descartes began by questioning even whether knowledge itself was possible. Using the device of an imagined agent of the devil, a 'deceiving demon' who could cause a person to believe in falsehoods, he argued that while one could be encouraged to accept an untruth, one could not be made to think that one was thinking (Sorell 1987: 54). It was by making the human subject's certainty of its own thought the cornerstone of his approach that Descartes was able to award epistemology a primacy that it had not previously held, while simultaneously placing the subject at the centre of the question of knowledge. He suggested that reason provides the means by which the thinking subject can achieve understanding in an orderly fashion, working outward from the certitude of its own existence. Having used the *cogito* as a means of countering scepticism, Descartes had effectively argued that all things exist in relation to the subject. Human beings were the creatures who were capable of knowing the world, and they did so by representing it in their minds (Guignon 1983: 17). This meant that while methodology came to be seen as fundamental to the regulated operation of the intellect, nature and history were increasingly understood as simply the objects of knowledge, the raw material that the mind works upon (Heidegger 1977: 126). Descartes' influence on the Enlightenment was such that by the eighteenth century it was common for any investigation of the world to be equally concerned with the conditions of its own possibility (Cassirer 1951: 93). This in itself is no bad thing, but it tends to suggest that there is a single legitimate linear procedure for the acquisition of knowledge.

To a great extent, the enhanced importance of epistemology in the modern era can be connected with the growing distinction between subject and object. That is to say, where an observing person is considered to have a mind which is categorically different from the material objects that it is attempting to apprehend, the relationship between the two will increasingly come to be seen as problematic. It is in the attempt to overcome the gulf between subject and object that epistemology is constituted (Critchley 1999: 56). As soon as the mind is understood as something that inhabits a realm which is separate from the material world, the issue of how it 'gets out' and grasps physical things becomes *the* question that has priority over all others. This means that 'knowing' comes to be understood as an operation of some kind, consciously performed, and as the principal means by which human beings deal with the material things that surround them (Guignon 1983: 39). In the process, people are presumed to *give meaning* to physical things, which are meaningless entities distinguished merely by their extension and velocity. Thus epistemology has gained further prestige in the period since Descartes, because it has come to be recognised as addressing the process by which the world is rendered meaningful. Equally importantly, Descartes' vision of method has a quite specific conception of humanity built into it. He maintained that the working of reason is the action of an autonomous free agent, who dissolves complex problems down into their constituent elements and reconstructs them in his or her mind (Cassirer 1951: 14). In the process, the use of reason frees the subject from prejudice and tradition, yielding mastery over nature and material progress (Schouls 1989: 13). However, Descartes' consideration of the knowing subject went little further than establishing the reality of their consciousness. He failed to go beyond this to address the existential conditions that made knowing possible, and this means that his arguments remain metaphysical (Guignon 1983: 40).

It follows that Descartes' privileging of method not only places the human subject and their self-certainty at the centre of the creation of knowledge, but also implies a particular kind of humanity (Zimmerman 1990: 171). It is the rational modern subject who uses the combination of free will and method to overcome prejudice, particularly through doubting received ideas. Both the decision to use the rational method and the operation of the method itself are exercises of free will (Schouls 1989: 31). This means that human beings can identify themselves as the source of their own truth, a truth distinct from that of revelation, which was understood as the prerogative of God. Truth, the unhindered access to the order of creation, is now recognised as a product of human agency, and this is fundamental to the emergence of a distinctively modern form of subjectivity (Heidegger 1977: 128). However, while the decision to use rational method is an act of individual will, according to Descartes the successful outcome of rational procedure will always be the same, because reason is universal. Reason does not vary from person to person, and truth is absolute and objective. Descartes' method relied upon the notion that reason and the means of putting it into practice could be written down and conveyed from one person to another. Although each person had to work on their own use of reason, in the end unanimity would be arrived at on all matters, since any disagreements were purely attributable to prejudice and poorly exercised reason.

Analysis and experiment

The modern view of the importance of epistemology rests on a suspicion of experience, which leads to the conclusion that the gathering of knowledge from the world needs to be carefully regulated. This suspicion can in part be attributed to the subject/object dichotomy, which condemns us to scepticism, as our knowledge is always understood as a reflection or representation of worldly things. Nevertheless, the concern over experience took radically different forms in the empiricist and rationalist traditions. For Bacon it was the intellect that was not to be trusted, since it could fall under the spell of the 'idols' of received opinion and theory (Jones 1961: 47). These preconceptions had to be swept aside to enable the mind to be focused on the sensuous experience of material reality. Yet Bacon also argued that the senses themselves were dull and imperfect, so that their apprehensions need to be harnessed

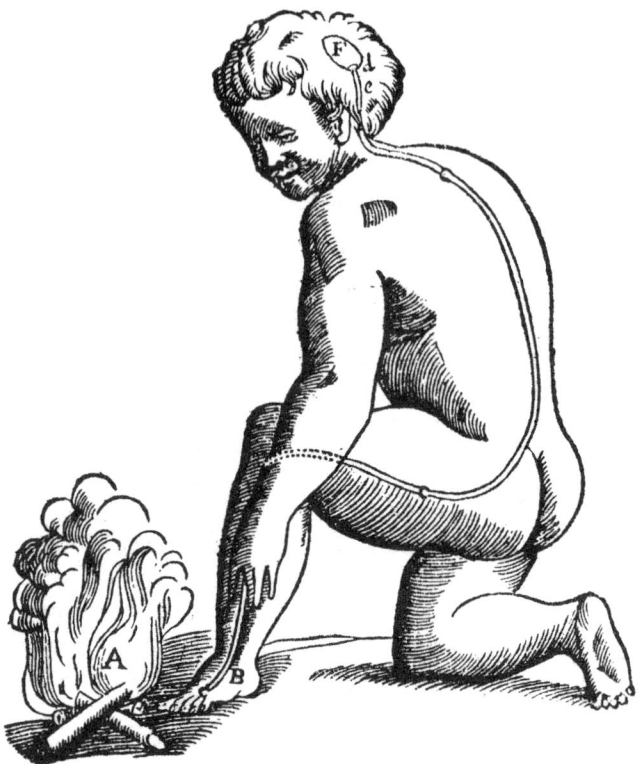

Figure 3.1 Descartes' representation of the human sensory apparatus – pain conveyed to the mind by the nervous system (from *Traite de l'Homme*, 1664)

through the meticulous construction of experiments. Descartes, by contrast, set more store in the development of conceptual systems, arguing that our sense experience was not to be taken at face value. It might be, for instance, that we are all dreaming, and the evidence of our senses does not derive from reality at all (Sorell 1987: 63). Indeed, for Descartes the only reason we have to believe that our experience of material things bears any connection with reality lies in the faith that a supremely good God would not allow us to be deceived in the sincere pursuit of truth. Humanity and its sensory apparatus are fallible, yet it is to be presumed that if we take every possible precaution against error it will be possible to distil something from our worldly experience (Figure 3.1). So for Descartes it was not the raw substance of sense experience that was to be trusted, but the essence drawn out of it through the mind's use of reason. This essence took the form of geometry and mathematical physics, in which material objects had been reduced to their most fundamental natures, and any extraneous and potentially misleading detail removed (ibid.: 58).

In their different ways, then, both Bacon and Descartes arrived at a position in which the volatile processes of experience had to be controlled through strict analytical procedure and experiment. For both of them, reality had to be refined or simplified in order to extract the kernels of truth from the confusion of human existence. Bacon's natural history was intended to be built up from precise and accurate observations wrenched out from the tissue of illusions in which human beings find themselves, while Descartes sought to reveal the hidden order that God had vested in the cosmos. Together, these opposed strands created the urge to strip physical events down to their barest components, enacted under controlled conditions so that they might be understood in the abstract terms of extension, density and velocity (Heidegger 1977: 121). Scientific experiment, as it had been envisaged by Bacon, actually fulfilled the requirements of Descartes' rational method of resolution and composition. This method stipulated that wherever one finds a complex situation, one should attempt to resolve it down, step by step, into a series of simple propositions (Descartes [1637] 1912). In a general sense this has served as a model of analytical enquiry ever since: it presumes that all phenomena naturally split themselves down into smaller autonomous and bounded entities (organs, individuals, sub-systems) which can be understood separately and then recombined to reveal the motion of the overall system. In this belief that the universe resolves itself into a series of basic units, the method amounts to a form of atomism (although a form that must be distinguished from corpuscularianism, or the belief in fundamental particles).

The Cartesian method sought to explain natural phenomena by separating them from human prejudices and interests. This required a recognition of our own common-sense image of ourselves as embedded in a complex social world, which could be challenged by the counter-intuitive conception of humans as minds which contain thoughts or representations of the world. It is this recognition of ourselves as mental substance in opposition to physical substance that enables us to stand apart from things and identify the causal relations between them. In this respect, Cartesianism fails to grasp the complexity of human existence in the world, for it presumes that our everyday dealings with physical things always take the form of a relationship between a subject and an object, in which we can maintain a dispassionate yet analytical attitude (Guignon 1983: 147). Any relationship that we might have with a material entity (ownership, sentimental attachment, symbolic meaning, avaricious desire) is thus built 'on top of' the object/subject relation. Yet we might argue that we exist in the first instance not as subjects amongst objects but in a state of Being-in-the-world, in which we find ourselves embedded in the midst of things. Under these conditions, we are likely to encounter entities as doors that we open and pass through, cups that we drink out of, or pens that we write with, rather than as objects that we focus on conceptually. Thus we can draw a distinction between things that are 'ready-to-hand' (engaged with without necessarily 'thinking' about them at all) and ones that are 'present-at-hand' (merely subject to contemplative looking and identification) (Heidegger 1962: 98–9). Of course, Cartesianism is incapable of making this distinction, and would have all things as continuously present-at-hand. For Descartes, we are continuously surrounded by things that are 'just there', like laboratory specimens or museum exhibits.

Unable to distinguish between distanced observation and everyday engagement with things, Cartesianism imagines that the subject/object relation sums up the way that human beings always deal with materiality, whether mowing a field of corn or making observations on a chemical compound in a test tube. This neglects the point that science, and experiment, involves a rather specialised attunement to things in which they are severed from their everyday horizon of meaning and conceptually framed in order to identify their behaviour as isolated objects. This is not to say that the procedures of science are in any way illegitimate. Rather, they represent a specialised way of dealing with things in order to find out very particular things about them. Indeed, it is undeniable that these procedures have been outstandingly successful in identifying the workings of physical, chemical and biological entities. However, this success is based upon the process of abstracting things from the world in which they are intelligible as meaningful things, useful things, tools or artworks, and rendering them as meaningless lumps of matter. They can then be given meaning of a quite different kind, within the operational 'worlds' of physics, chemistry and biology. Where Cartesianism goes wrong is in failing to recognise that the world of meaning, of everyday human engagement, actually has priority over the world of science. Science, in other words, is a 'founded mode of Being' (Guignon 1983: 150). It is not that meaning is added to a world of things that obey the laws of science; it is stripped from things in order to make them amenable to science. Cartesianism makes the mistake of imagining that the unusual and specialised way in which we relate to things in a scientific experiment can provide a basis for understanding the everyday world.

The stripping of knowledge back to its bare bones in modern experimental science and analysis is related to the search for epistemological foundations. Descartes argues that each person must learn the method for themselves, so that they establish the conditions for rational knowledge within themselves. One must know for oneself, and this can only be achieved by having direct access to unshakeable truth. Yet as we have seen already, this theme of foundation is linked with that of universality, for the method and the rationality that it employs are singular. By implication, Descartes' stress on a universal method that produces a single truth seeks to de-legitimate any other form of knowledge (Bauman 1993: 8). And as we have argued, Descartes was seeking a foundation for universal knowledge in the Platonic conception of worldly things as permanently present forms. Rather than consider the processes by which things are continually coming into Being, he presents existence as a matter of persistence in which geometrical entities are related to one another through chains of causality (Zimmerman 1990: 170). The production of entities is an issue of the transformation of matter, and this like movement can be attributed to the action of one body upon another. Such a view predisposes one to an *explanatory* form of analysis, whose objective is the identification of a pattern of causal relations between entities, as opposed to an understanding of their meaning or significance.

Descartes' methodology ultimately rests on a metaphysics, for his analytical approach relies on the notion that the universe as a whole can be grasped conceptually. This is because God has divided reality into distinct and classifiable entities, with characteristic forms of motion (Sorell 1987: 33). Descartes asserted that mechanics, medicine and morals all formed a 'rational scheme', which relied upon the a priori mental capabilities embodied in geometry. Others like Locke would deny the existence of such a priori knowledge, yet the view that the universe has an invariant and systemic structure that is amenable to formal analysis was retained in the Newtonian synthesis, which is arguably embedded in much modern thought. As we saw in Chapter 1, the mathematical physics of Descartes and Newton forms a major element of the 'ground-plan' of modernity, a set of assumptions which is taken for granted in our investigation of the material world. The conviction that a coherent and uniform methodology must be defined before we begin to address material things, and that it is through the application of method that we give meaning to our observations (which are 'without meaning' up to this point), is an aspect of this 'ground-plan'. This means that any research that we undertake into issues of nature or history is immediately located within a horizon that has been defined by a modern metaphysics (Heidegger 1977: 125).

Method, order and classification

In Chapter 1 it was argued that order and classification were distinctive aspects of modernity, and both are clearly linked to the development of rigorous and prescriptive methodologies. For thinkers like Hobbes the hallmark of human consciousness was the ability to perceive order in nature, and method was a means of regulating and refining this ability. Epistemology was valued from the seventeenth century onwards as a means of exterminating error, and thereby of eradicating ambivalence. We have suggested already that the philosophical ideas of the seventeenth and eighteenth centuries had a profound social and political significance, and this partially explains why the perfection of a system to guarantee the acquisition of truth was considered so important. It was social order that was at stake, as well as the order of nature. Bacon, Descartes and Newton had all promoted a view of the universe that was atomistic in the general sense, composed of sutured entities that could not only be linked together in systems and causal chains but could also be fitted into classificatory structures on the basis of their characteristics. We have seen already that Foucault (1970: 131) suggested that natural history provided the models for forms of classification that were increasingly employed in other areas of scholarship as the eighteenth century progressed. The categorisation of plants and animals gave rise to a series of practices that facilitated the emergence of archives, inventories, catalogues, indexes and filing systems. In this development we can recognise a process whereby history and society came to be identified as legitimate domains for the operation of modern analytical methodologies.

During this period it was increasingly accepted that all worldly phenomena can be compared, on the basis of measurements and the presence and absence of particular attributes, and thereby arranged into ordered series. This means that a universal ordering can be imposed on material things (ibid.: 54), which is understood to a greater or lesser degree to correspond with the real order of nature. The aim of science was increasingly presented as the reconstruction of this overarching order in representation. However, John Locke proposed a more sceptical approach to classification. Locke rejected the Aristotelian argument that the real essences of things in the world could be directly conveyed in language. For him, classificatory entities like species and genera were human constructs, which could never fully equate with the real essences of things (Ayers 1997: 58). The reason for this was that the true nature of any phenomenon was given by its 'microstructural organisation', something that was ultimately unknowable (Lowe 1995: 79). If the true essence of a thing cannot be known it cannot serve as the basis for any classification. The perceptible attributes of a thing do not give transparent access to its essence, even though they are caused by it and in some senses reflect it. Locke advised that scholars should devise their classifications in whatever way they found most useful for making sense of their observations, in the awareness that such divisions of phenomena into categories were ultimately arbitrary (Ayers 1997: 58). Analytical investigation might never reveal the real order of things, but the best approximation would be achieved through careful experiment and documentation. So again, while Locke was less optimistic than Descartes or Newton concerning the possibility of disclosing the true pattern of nature, his prescription for achieving the most satisfactory result involved the application of a rigorous methodology.

What should now be obvious is that many of the intellectual procedures of archaeology are wholly dependent on these historical developments. Artefact typology, seriation, numerical taxonomy, the establishment of chronological sequences, the definition of 'culture groups', and the plotting of spatial distributions of artefact types are all practices that would be unthinkable without the abstract notion of a methodology that fragments the world into discrete entities in order to render it malleable (Bauman 1991: 12). Obviously, these have all proved to be useful tools in making sense of the past, but it is undeniably disturbing that the means through which we address alien cultural contexts are ones that are so intimately tied to our own historical conditions. Indeed, we might go so far as to say that these are procedures that are meaningless outside of a modern context. In taking part in the modern 'war against chaos', archaeology seeks to establish an order amongst the things of the past. This may be an order that would be entirely unfamiliar to past people.

Decontextualisation and objectivity

From Descartes onward, method was understood as the correct application of reason. Reason was considered to be universal and homogeneous amongst human beings, and in its perfected form was imagined to exist in symmetry with the created world (Cassirer 1951: 95). The contents of the mind and of the material realm can be in harmony, because they are manifestations of the same underlying totality. Reason attempts to express in clear and distinct concepts the discrete and bounded things of the world. Descartes had maintained that it was the subject's certainty of itself that was the key to a knowledge of material reality, and Newton also argued that there was a connection between the problem of human knowledge and that of nature (ibid.: 44). Ultimately, the philosophies of the seventeenth century presented the mind and the material world as complementary structures whose relation to one another was symmetrical. Just as reason was a constant, so too the laws of nature were fixed and invariant. Consequently, from about 1640 onwards the claim began to be made that real philosophical questions (whether ontological or epistemological) must be of universal significance: they must be equally relevant to any cultural context, and addressed using methods that are universally applicable (Toulmin 1990: 36).

Two related demands were being made here. First, the aim of rational scholarship was to re-present the order of the universe within the mind, and the purpose of methodology was to ensure that this reconstruction was achieved without the distorting effects of prejudice and superstition. These sources of error arose from the subject's personal and historical conditions, their 'subjectivity', and so part of the role of methodology was to ensure that rule of universal reason was followed. That is, in place of the particular and the contingent, reason was intended to promote objectivity. Second, the rational method was now clearly targeted towards the establishment of universal laws, which should apply to all things at all times. As we have seen, Newton's vision of the universe was of a temporally invariant mechanism. The laws that governed its motion were fixed, and did not change across either space or time. The decontextualisation of knowledge in the seventeenth century thus applied to both the mode of its acquisition, which should be untainted by circumstance, and to its substantive content, which should be universally valid. The context-freedom of the thinking subject and the universality of their knowledge were intimately linked. However, the position that valid knowledge must be absolutely universal could not be maintained for any amount of time. The emergence of historical geology in the eighteenth century relied upon the notion that particular rock formations were the outcome of unique sequences of events, even if the forces involved obeyed universal laws (Toulmin 1990: 148; Schnapp 1996: 285; Hutton [1788] 1795). Therefore, there was demonstrably a value to contingent and specific forms of knowledge. Since this time, science has edged away from the demand for a set of invariant laws of nature, and has increasingly become interested in the historical and the particular. However, this means that it is less easy to insist that the conditions under which knowledge is produced are unimportant, and can only provide distortions to a true understanding of things. Can we have a universal method if the object of our investigation is a material reality which is not simply governed by stable, atemporal laws?

This problem is especially pertinent to archaeology, where the demand for universal laws, and standardised methods to evaluate these laws, would appear to be at odds with an interest in the historically changing conditions of human existence. We can identify this tension at work in Albert Spaulding's seemingly contradictory arguments concerning the objectives of anthropology. Spaulding (1968: 36) claims that there is only one form of explanation in science – the covering law. He suggests that the purpose of anthropology (and by implication archaeology) is to frame laws of human behaviour. However, he also notes that the weakness of traditional, culture-historic archaeology is that it operates on the basis of presumed and unproven human characteristics: a particular relationship between material culture and group identity, the manifestation of cognitive norms in material culture patterning, and so on. Spaulding's point is that anthropology exists to find out what human beings are like, so it should not take any human attribute for granted. Nonetheless, it is evident that he imagines that there *are* human universals to be discovered, even if none has yet been substantiated to the degree necessary to serve as a baseline for further investigations. This means that Spaulding's demand that anthropologists should search for laws of human behaviour is metaphysical: he is attempting to find something whose existence is at best hypothetical. It is at least arguable that there may be no human universals to find, and that human beings are infinitely plastic, their modes of behaviour being entirely contingent and historically variable.

Objectivity and universality have long been the criteria that have been used to distinguish science from 'inferior' forms of knowledge. Galileo, for instance, separated 'true science' from rhetoric, while Descartes argued that there can be no rational knowledge but science (Schouls 1989: 19). However, sociologists of science like Bruno Latour (1987: 33) have been at pains to demonstrate that science is successful not because it proceeds in abstraction from the real world but because scientists recruit allies, forms of authority and networks of association to support their arguments. Science works because it forges connections between heterogeneous entities. The dream of an infallible and universal method threatens to sever scientific inquiry from material reality, and promotes a kind of knowledge which is reduced to formal abstractions. Descartes had hoped that in time all forms of scholarship could be boiled down to such a calculus, and the eighteenth-century Enlightenment was based upon the notion that analytical science could provide the model for all knowledge (Gray 1995: 161). While this approach may be entirely appropriate for some forms of mathematics and physics, it is problematic when applied to other kinds of inquiry. Ethics, law or aesthetics are difficult to reduce to pure rationality, and this means that in order to comply with the demands of the Enlightenment they must either be emptied of their content or be declared to be non-scientific (Toulmin 1990: 20). What this means is that human knowledge must take a form that can be addressed using an abstract and formal epistemology, or it must be relegated to a lesser category of thinking, alongside rhetoric, superstition and fantasy. One reaction to this state of affairs is to reject the call for a universal method altogether, and to suggest that epistemology should be contextual and opportunistic, exploiting the richness of the empirical materials available to us by establishing disparate and unexpected connections between different realms of knowledge (see, for example, Feyerabend 1976). Yet in archaeology the demand for an absolute separation of science from other forms of knowledge is still sometimes heard. Fekri Hassan (1997: 1021), for example, has recently argued that science can appeal to 'epistemological canons of plausibility and veracity', and can be kept entirely separate from political, moral and ethical issues.

Ultimately, though, such arguments for the distinctiveness and superiority of scientific knowledge are based upon the supposed priority of the analytic mode of apprehending the world, which we discussed above. In these terms, ethical, rhetorical and political matters would be 'additions' to the bare materiality of things in the world. However, Latour's arguments concerning the status of science as a social activity have some further implications. Science takes place within the everyday world, and generally takes the form of a research project directed towards a particular outcome. Those who are familiar with the forms that need to be completed in order to apply for research funding will know that explicit aims and objectives are a priority in science. But along with these explicit goals, there will always be a less thoroughly articulated conception of what we are doing, and of why particular phenomena and procedures are significant (Guignon 1983: 152). This is an aspect of our more general pre-understanding of the situation that we find ourselves in, which in turn is a feature of the hermeneutical character of everyday life. If 'objective' scientific inquiry is a derived mode of

Being, which develops out of our mundane existence in the process of decontextualising the things that we propose to study, a very important transformation overcomes our relationship with those things. In everyday life, we encounter things through the hermeneutic 'as'-structure: things are always already-understood-as something. In scientific analysis, this is transformed into the apophantic 'as'-structure, in which a subject isolates objects and attributes properties to them (ibid.: 153). The objects-with-properties that result are always secondary to the scientist's general horizon of understanding, within which things reveal themselves hermeneutically. Consequentially, the foundational status that is often claimed for the objects of science is hard to sustain. In the remainder of this chapter I will seek to identify some of the problems that archaeology has created for itself through its demand for an epistemology that floats free from material engagement.

Classification and method in archaeology

Although philosophers like Locke had cautioned scholars against imagining that their classifications mapped directly onto the underlying order of reality, in antiquarian studies and archaeology the tendency has been to assume that rigorous method will lead to the disclosure of real patterns. The forms of classification applied to material culture were in the first instance derived from natural history. Just as the ordering of genera and species was hoped to reveal the 'tree of life', the grouping of artefacts according to shared traits has often been understood as a means of access to a hidden reality. In the case of the evolutionary typology of Pitt Rivers and others in the late nineteenth century, Gavin Lucas has argued that the objective of classification was to position objects within a universal sequence that was congruent with the real order of the past (Lucas 2001: 74). Unilinear evolution proposed that artefacts were directly representative of distinct stages in human development, so that their apparent sophistication was both an index of social (or cognitive) complexity and an indicator of chronological position (see, for example, Morgan 1877: 43). In its crudest form this is the rationale behind the three-age system: the skills necessary for the production of bronze are characteristic of a developmental epoch that we call the 'Bronze Age'.

While the theme of universal evolution declined with the growing interest in cultural diffusion in the early twentieth century, one critical aspect of the metaphysics of archaeology remained the same. The meticulous construction of artefact typologies, and their elaboration into chronological schemes and regional sequences, was now understood as a means of identifying cultural entities, and of observing their behaviour in time and space (Willey and Sabloff 1980: 83). The influence of post-Cartesian thought on this practice is absolutely clear. The crucial element of good scholarship in culture-historic archaeology lay in constructing and following a rigid method for defining archaeological phenomena: traits, phases, components, complexes, culture groups, and so on. If the method was rigorous and objective, then the patterns that it generated might be expected to have a real and empirical significance. Indeed, Willey and Phillips ([1958] 2001: 5) presented 'culture-historical integration' as a largely *descriptive* exercise. Processual interpretation was a later stage in the archaeological enterprise, once the culture groups had been defined and installed in their spatio-temporal slots. Moreover, culture-historic sequence building was understood as a scientific practice, because the results that it produced (temporal and spatial distributions of artefact types) were testable (Lyman and O'Brien 2001: 12). Another archaeologist could always re-evaluate the potsherds and their affinities. However, this kind of sequence building and testing always took place within a particular conceptual horizon, defined by a set of assumptions or prejudices concerning the relationship between the forms of material culture and human identity.

Normative culture-history aspired to an abstract methodology that placed the identification of patterned regularities in the evidence before their interpretation. Yet it was always already interpreting before it began to define its traits and sequences, because the culture-historic archaeologist had a clear idea of what he or she was looking for in any artefactual assemblage. Diagnostic traits of artefact form and decoration, shared by appreciable numbers of objects, were sought as the means of establishing typochronologies (Figure 3.2). The construction of a regional sequence is not simply a neutral means of organising a set of evidence according to an objective methodology: it reveals that evidence to us in a very particular way. The full significance of these procedures will become clearer later in this book.

In the wake of the professionalisation of American archaeology that followed the massive expansion of public works associated with Roosevelt's New Deal, the epistemology of culture-history underwent critical evaluation (Patterson 1995: 77). While we have argued that culture-historic method is embedded in modernist philosophies of science, Walter Taylor (1948) suggested that it was often understood by its practitioners as simple common sense. There was, he maintained, a lack of theoretical reflection in archaeology, yet the quality of archaeological work should be judged on the adequacy of the concepts that it employed (ibid.: 1). However, Taylor's own conclusion was that archaeology was *nothing but* a method. 'Archaeology *per se* is no more than a method and a set of specialised techniques for the gathering of cultural information. The archaeologist, as archaeologist, is really nothing but a technician' (ibid.: 43). Comparing archaeology with anthropology and history, he concluded that archaeological evidence could be used to pursue the goals of *either* discipline: it was not inherently anthropological or historical. In effect, Taylor's argument reinforces the Cartesianism of archaeological epistemology: archaeology merely extracts and orders data, which are then passed on to be given meaning. Implicitly, these data are assumed to be disengaged from the context of their production, for they can

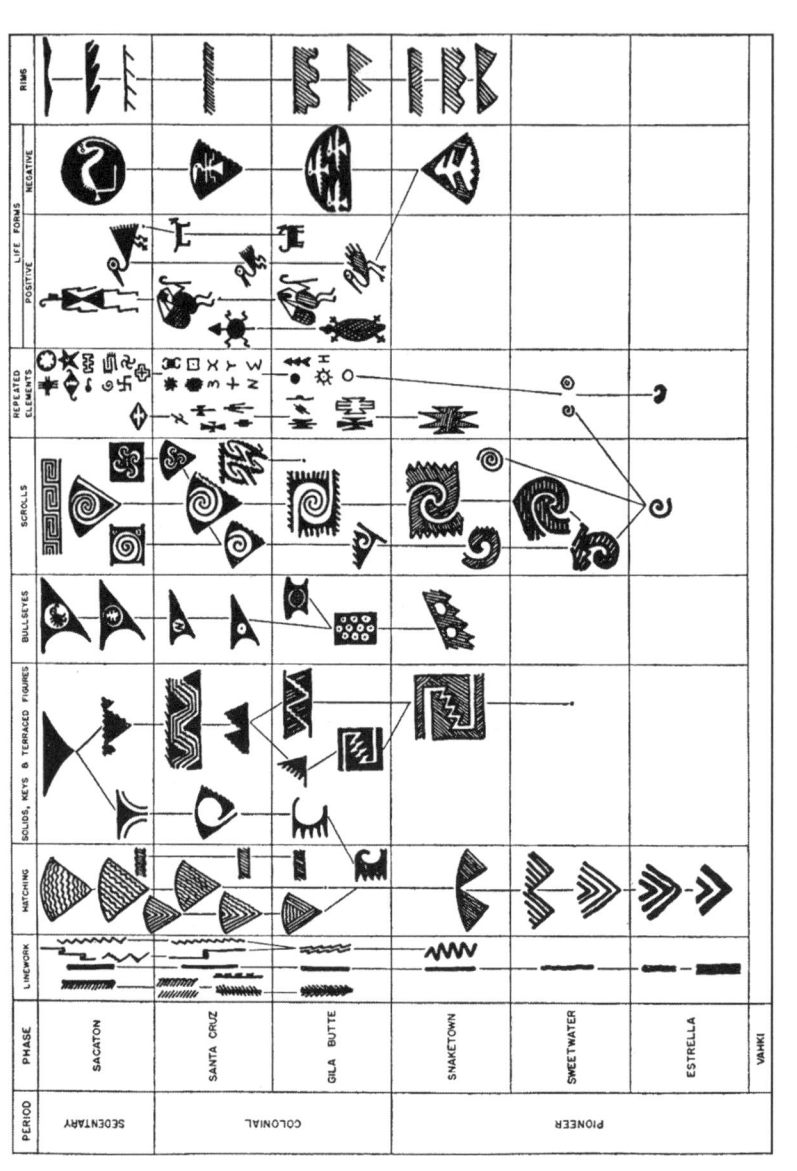

Figure 3.2 Pottery design change through time at Snaketown, Arizona (from H.S. Gladwin, *Excavations at Snaketown: Material Culture*, Medallion Papers 25, Globe, 1937)

be employed equally well by a variety of different scholars. Interestingly enough, when Taylor comes to discuss the work that a historian might perform on archaeological evidence, he suggests that 'thought about past actuality becomes historiography only when facts are related to one another and a picture is created from them by the efforts of the historian' (ibid.: 34). In other words, it is the agency of the historian that renders archaeological facts meaningful. Taylor's analysis of archaeological procedure ends up by restating the case for a formal sequence of analysis: data are produced using rigorous methods, represent autonomous units of information, and are given significance through an interpretation that comes at the end of the process.

The New Archaeology, positivism and method

The work of Walter Taylor, and others like J.W. Bennett and Albert Spaulding, can best be understood in the broader context of twentieth-century intellectual culture. The 1920s and 1930s saw a return to the philosophical outlook of the seventeenth century, which was if anything more extreme than its antecedents (Bryant 1985: 109). Logical positivism restated the case for a universal rational epistemology based on that of natural science (Toulmin 1990: 159). In so doing, it argued that science should be refounded from first principles. New foundations had to be established for intellectual inquiry, and this had to be achieved by constructing a more robust methodology. This reveals one of the recurring themes in modern discourse: that each time the practices of science and government have been found to be imperfect, calls have been made to rebuild the foundations of thought from scratch (ibid.). Rather than entertain the possibility that formal method cannot automatically guarantee truth and objectivity, the assumption has always been made that the method is simply in need of perfection. This phenomenon was evident in American archaeology in the years immediately after the Second World War, and again in the 1960s with the emergence of the New Archaeology.

The claim that was initially made for the New Archaeology was that it represented not just new ideas but a new epistemological position within the discipline (Binford 1972a: 90). Following the lead of logical positivism, the New Archaeologists separated scientific discovery from its evaluation, and argued that it was the responsibility of scholars to test their ideas once they had proposed them (Binford 1982: 126; Binford and Sabloff 1982: 137; Wylie 2002: 14–15). This meant that archaeology was being provided with new methodological foundations, provided by the hypothetico-deductive approach. Culture-historic archaeology, it was argued, lacked such rigorous procedures, and simply mapped its observations of the archaeological record onto a set of assumptions about how human beings operated in the past (Binford 1977: 6). Like Descartes before him, Lewis Binford wanted to take the responsibility for the objective truth of statements about the past out of the hands of the individual archaeologist. This would be achieved by having clear and distinct ideas to evaluate, and robust intellectual procedures that were distinct from those ideas. Objectivity was to be achieved through the careful design of the methodology (Binford 1982: 128). So, previous forms of archaeology had been inadequate because of their lack of epistemological sophistication, and a new start could be made by constructing a new method. The method should remove subjectivity from the process of evaluating archaeological claims about the past, and yet it was acknowledged that it was human ingenuity that would give the method its infallibility. This is precisely the ambivalence over the role of the human agent in the creation of knowledge that we find in Descartes: objectivity is ultimately assured by the subject's relation with itself.

Initially, the New Archaeologists were optimistic that almost any aspect of the past could be addressed archaeologically, provided that the question concerned could be phrased as an explicit hypothesis and tested on appropriate evidence. The limitations of a hypothesis-testing approach were demonstrated by a series of analyses conducted by James Hill, James Deetz and William Longacre on ceramic assemblages from pueblo sites in the southwest of the United States (Deetz 1968; Hill 1970, 1972; Longacre 1964). In each case the objective of the study was to substantiate whether presently existing patterns of residence and descent had originated in the prehistoric past. Many pueblo societies are matrilineal and matrilocal, and pottery is manufactured by women, who pass the relevant skills on to their daughters. It follows that micro-traditions of pottery decoration, associated with particular matrilineages, would be maintained over time within particular sets of rooms inside a given pueblo, assuming that they had been continuously occupied by the same kin group. Longacre's work at the Carter Ranch Site (Figure 3.3) tested for the presence of discrete clusters of design attributes in different areas of the pueblo, and contrasted pottery variation with a series of other artefact types. The hypothesis of matrilineality and matrilocality appeared to have been confirmed by the tests performed on the material evidence, which produced very much the predicted pattern. However, later work cast doubt on these results. A complex series of assumptions was built into the test hypothesis: all pottery was presumed to have been made within the pueblo, rather than traded; the location of potsherds was assumed to have been related to their places of production and use, rather than post-depositional processes; relations of kinship, descent, residence and skill-acquisition were imagined to have been relatively homogeneous (Plog 1978; Stanislawski 1973). But more seriously still, Binford was to point out that the major error of the early New Archaeology had been that it had attempted to establish statements about the past, and test them on archaeological evidence existing in the present (Binford and Sabloff 1982). The past was not available for testing – only the archaeological record was. Once

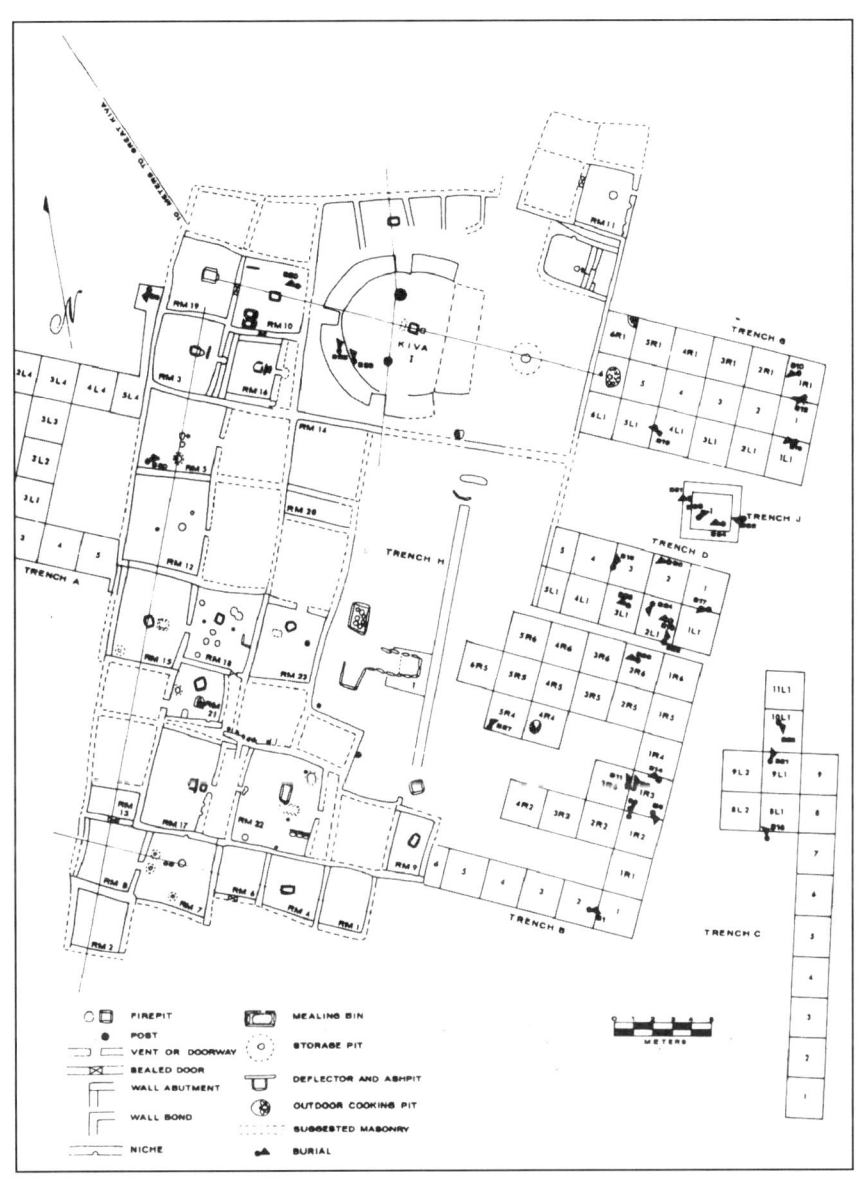

Figure 3.3 The Carter Ranch site (from W. Longacre, Archaeology as anthropology: a case study, in M.P. Leone (ed.) *Contemporary Archaeology: A Guide to Theory and Contributions*, 316–19. Carbondale: Southern Illinois University Press, 1972)

more, Binford's argument is deeply Cartesian here: the New Archaeology had failed as a result of the imperfect application of reason and method. Again, a new foundation and a more foolproof methodology was required.

Middle Range Theory as Cartesian epistemology

In his subsequent career, Binford has sought to overcome the apparent gulf between static remains in the present and dynamic processes in the past by establishing unambiguous connections between material signatures and the forces that generated them. These are conventions 'that guarantee when X is observed in the archaeological record, it means Y in terms of the past' (Binford 2001: 674). By this means it is suggested that the ambiguity of the evidence can be reduced. Yet if ambivalence cannot be resolved, he advises that aspects of the evidence should be set aside, 'not because the ambiguous facts are not interesting, but because of the limitations of our present knowledge to resolve the ambiguity' (Binford 1985: 297). For this reason, Binford is suspicious of 'interpretive' arguments which seek to link pieces of observable evidence with events or processes in the past. Indeed, he advises that even our research questions should be generated by abstract pattern-recognition exercises on dimensionalised data, cross-correlating numerical archaeological information with other classes of data (climatic, temporal, associational) (Binford 2001: 674) so that we are not guided by contemporary political or ethical agendas. In all of these ways, Binford appears to have been trying to refine the Cartesian project of creating an archaeological methodology that leads us automatically to the truth about the past, eliminating any human prejudice or error along the way.

The critical element of this methodological programme lay in the problem of how to accurately give meaning to archaeological observations (Binford 1989: 50). Binford insists that there are no cultural meanings to be found in the archaeological record. Our evidence is composed simply of patterns and arrangements of matter. Like Descartes, Binford understands material things to be first and foremost lumps of substance with particular properties, which are entirely without meaning once they have been severed from their original cultural context by the elapse of time. We cannot make history out of the dead things that we find in the archaeological record: we must *give* them meaning before they can be turned into concepts and arguments (Binford 1983a: 413). This meaning-giving is to be achieved through what Binford calls Middle Range Theory. In passing, it is worth noting that while Binford is often dismissive of what he describes as 'humanistic' research programmes (e.g. 2001), he actually adheres to a classically humanist outlook by presenting meaning as the outcome of human action (in this case, scientific procedure).

Middle Range Theory is conceived as a body of theory which is entirely separate from our ideas concerning what happened in the past, and which focuses exclusively on the relationship between past dynamics and presently existing static conditions. It sets up a series of connections between actions (flint-knapping, butchering animals, scavenging of carcasses) and their material consequences (flake-scars, butchery marks, patterns of bone representation). Middle Range Theory concerns itself with the ways in which the material world is organised and structured, and has to be meticulously assembled using the procedures of experimental science (Binford 1983a: 415). Once again, Binford presented his new way of working as a re-establishment of the foundations of the discipline: 'archaeology had to become a science concerned with understanding the significance of patterning observed in the archaeological record' (Binford 1989: 56). However, he acknowledged that the whole enterprise of Middle Range Theory rested upon a set of uniformitarian assumptions (Binford 1977: 7; 1983a: 412). For this reason, testing was essential before observations made in the present could be applied to materials deriving from the past. However, the belief that dynamic processes that can be observed today are identical in their outcomes to those that have taken place throughout human history remains a metaphysical aspect of Binford's programme. It is ultimately untestable for the very reason that Middle Range Theory exists in the first place: we cannot directly observe the distant past.

The notion of constructing a middle range 'science of the archaeological record' is distinctively modern in that it presumes that human actions can be reduced to context-free events (Lucas 2001: 182). The supposed separation of Middle Range Theory from our narratives about the past assumes that acts have a logical priority over the social relations in which they are embedded, or their meanings. This has the effect that the status of observations that are translated from one context to another as analogies is occluded. Archaeologists who make use of Middle Range Theory are actually doing what all scholars do when they construct arguments: drawing together elements from diverse sources in order to make a coherent case. This generally involves both rhetoric and analogy. The problem is that a spurious infallibility is claimed for Middle Range Theory, on the basis that it is separate from both ideas about the past and contemporary values and meanings. This is entirely characteristic of Cartesianism, which always hopes to create for itself a position of objectivity from which it can encounter evidence in a way that is entirely free of prejudice (Guignon 1983: 168). Binford claims to achieve this by separating our observations in the present from our accounts of the past, but in practice he cannot abstract his observations from his horizon of inquiry. We may wish to reduce material things to a series of signatures, relating to mechanical processes in the past, but this is an example of the operation of the apophantic 'as'-structure. The properties of the archaeological record are always enumerated once we have already identified certain material things as significant and relevant to what we want to know about the past. This recognition may not be explicit, and may be embedded in our pre-understanding. We always come to any inquiry with a set of assumptions and opinions, which stand behind our identification and selection of evidence. If we were sufficiently objective and disinterested to have no prior motivation in conducting our research, we would presumably undertake no investigation in the first place (ibid.: 173). Prejudice may colour our interpretations, but it also provides the inspiration for our research.

We can illustrate these points by looking at an example of the way that Binford puts his Middle Range methodology into practice, in addressing the role of faunal remains in studying the behaviour of human ancestors. Binford noted that Raymond Dart's work at the site of Makapansgat in South Africa had stimulated a series of arguments concerning the role of hunting in human evolution, and the innate aggressiveness of humans (1983b: 36). Dart had recognised that the representation of anatomical parts of ungulates at Makapansgat was uneven, and had inferred that carcasses had been brought back to the cave after initial butchery at the kill-site. Some bones were discarded during butchery, while others were selected for tool-making. Years later, C.K. Brain observed that leopards often consume their prey in trees overlooking limestone fissures similar to many of the South African hominid sites, producing characteristic patterns of bone alteration and body-part representation. This evidence, together with information on the scavenging of predator kills by dogs and the bone-accumulating activities of hyenas, porcupines and owls, led Brain to suggest that such sites had not been the living-places of Australopithecenes at all. Instead, he argued that ungulate bones had built up in these contexts as a result of the actions of various animals and other natural agencies, and that any hominid remains found could be attributed to their having been eaten there.

Independently, Binford had been studying sheep-bone frequencies in rubbish heaps at the winter and summer camps of Navajo people in New Mexico. The observed patterns were the outcome of a complex combination of seasonal death-rates, selective culling, and the density of bone in animals of different ages, which resulted in differential survival after gnawing by dogs (Binford 1983b: 54). As a Middle Range methodology, Binford placed these results alongside data from predator kill-sites, hyena dens and wolf dens, to establish characteristic ranges of bone representation and modification. These patterns had been generated in the present, and were judged to be independent of the past situations with which they would be compared. Binford's objective was to evaluate the faunal assemblages from the open hominid sites at Olduvai in East Africa, which had been recovered by Louis and Mary Leakey. Could these collections, too, be attributed to the actions of animal predators and scavengers? Binford proceeded to compare the Olduvai samples with his modern spectra, using a variety of mathematical and statistical techniques. The outcome was that while he believed that the majority of the bones had accumulated as a result of carnivore and scavenger activity, a residual fraction remained. Interestingly enough, this atypical material tended to occur on sites that also contained large numbers of stone tools. These 'Oldowan' tools were generally choppers and pounders rather than flake-tools, and Binford's interpretation was that early hominids had found a niche as scavengers, recovering bones from carnivore kills and extracting the marrow from them (ibid.: 57).

The way that Binford uses his contemporary observations to reassess the significance of archaeological assemblages is ingenious and informative, but it is hard to claim that this has been achieved in isolation from past and present contexts of meaning. On the contrary, Binford's inquiry proceeded within a particular interpretive horizon. As he noted, Dart's work had been recruited by Robert Ardrey to substantiate an argument concerning the evolutionary significance of aggression, which had been based upon the ideas of Konrad Lorenz (1963). Ardrey suggested that 'whatever environment's iron hand . . . every being will challenge such rule, will seek to achieve non-identicality and to fulfil its diverse genetic potential through an aggressiveness inborn' (1970: 39). This vitalist approach is quite distinct from the forms of evolutionary theory for which Binford has expressed enthusiasm, which connect with systems theory and ecology (1972b: 105). He is quite explicit that Brain's work was superior to Dart's because he had addressed the formation processes of the South African sites at an ecosystem level, rather than concentrating exclusively on the activities of a single species (Australopithecenes) (Binford 1983b: 48). It was Binford's interpretive horizon, which inclined him to address archaeological problems from an ecological point of view, that revealed certain classes of evidence to him as significant. Particular attributes and variables would suggest themselves to him at a common-sense level. He then strove to make his analysis objective and value-free by collecting modern data on bone representation. Yet he had already chosen to look at bones, and was asking research questions that could be answered through the analysis of bones. This was the outcome of a structure of pre-understanding, within which bones were already meaningful and were already linked to the activities of hominids in the past and archaeologists in the present. They had already been interpreted as something significant, and it was then Binford's intellectual labour that transformed them into objects addressed through the apophantic-'as'.

Furthermore, having recontextualised the objects of his analysis and given them new meanings as the bearers of attributes, Binford was able to recognise the disparity between the archaeological bone samples and the predicted signatures of predation and scavenging. But his eventual interpretation, which cast early hominids as marrow-scavengers, was effectively a *post hoc* rationalisation of the residual element in his data. This inductive argument itself harmonised with his general hermeneutic horizon, which predisposed him against the 'man the mighty hunter' model and towards seeing the diminutive Australopithecenes as niche-bound within a Plio-Pleistocene ecosystem.

Conclusion

The debate over Middle Range Theory has prompted an explicit consideration of the role of methodology in archaeology. By contrast, the influence of modernist epistemology on field archaeology has been more implicit, and as such it demonstrates the pervasiveness of these ideas in contemporary society. Manuals of excavation conventionally treat field methodology as a series of abstract skills that can be applied irrespective of the period or type of site under investigation (Wheeler 1954; Barker 1977). Not only are methods devised in abstraction, but their application in the field is presented as a means of acquiring evidence which is void of any historical meaning. This implies that data collection can be pursued as an end in itself (Tilley 1989a: 276), and that synthesis and interpretation are entirely distinct activities that constitute a later stage in a linear process (Andrews *et al.* 2000: 525; Lucas 2001: 11). In the British case this view proved to be politically expedient during the 1960s and 1970s, when the pressure of development resulted in an expansion of 'rescue' or salvage archaeology (Thomas 1974; Jones 1984). The doctrine of 'preservation by record' that emerged at this time held that if an archaeological site was to be destroyed, the information that it contained should be saved by preparing a complete inventory of the features and artefacts present on site. However, in many cases the budgets made available for rescue archaeology only covered the excavation stage, and the excavated materials and descriptive evidence were simply archived in the hope that they would eventually be brought to publication at a later date. The assumption that was made was that so long as a complete record of what was found on site has been compiled, any trained archaeologist will be capable of synthesising and interpreting the results. This is simply because the modern conception of method plays down the imbrication of observation and interpretation, so that the experience of having taken part in the excavation process is neglected. Ian Hodder (1997: 693) has recently argued that interpretation takes place 'at the trowel's edge', and the implication of this is that the way in which we physically engage with the materiality of archaeological evidence has direct consequences for the way in which it reveals itself to us. Archaeological sites and their contents are not simply sets of alienated objects that can be described in a distanced and abstract way. The production of knowledge about the past on an archaeological site is a collective interpretive labour, which involves the 'working' of a set of social relationships between people and things.

The legacy of the 'rescue era' in British archaeology is a huge volume of artefacts, field drawings, site notebooks and context sheets mouldering in museums and archives, placed there in the expectation that one day someone will have the time and inclination to make sense of them (Rahtz 1974). My contention is that this situation is the direct consequence of the modern condition, which involves the separation of ontology from epistemology. In the modern world, mind and body have come to be understood as occupying separate realms: the material world is addressed by the sensory organs and recreated in consciousness. It follows that the mind can create rational methodologies in abstraction, and then impose these upon the object world. When we approach an archaeological site in these terms, it appears to be an assemblage of objects addressed by a subject. Our principal objective lies in trying to describe these objects accurately. Later, we may wish to explain how they came to take on their present configuration, and to identify the causal agencies involved.

I would suggest that this approach is deeply unsatisfactory for it seeks to understand the archaeological evidence as if it were something separate from humanity and social relations, in both the past and the present. Yet this material is meaningful precisely because it was integral to a past human world, and is now revealed as intelligible through our actions in the present. Archaeological evidence does not in the first place exist in a purely material state, waiting for meaning to be applied to it. It is revealed to us in its meaningfulness. Abstract, rational method seeks to provide us with a set of objective and value-free data to work with. Yet simply performing a predetermined method that removes the responsibility for making ethical or political judgements is more likely to maintain the established order of thought than to produce novel re-descriptions (Feyerabend 1976: 26). In the seventeenth century the Cartesian method was part of the enterprise that enabled extensive new scientific discoveries to be made. However, any framework of inquiry has the dual effect of opening up new possibilities for investigation while foreclosing others (Guignon 1983: 16). By now, the absolute distinction between object and subject has come to limit what we can know about the world. It is, surely, preferable to accept that both the artefacts that we study and the ideas that we work with are thoroughly bound in to complex social networks (Latour 1987: 79). By attempting to understand the many contexts in which our efforts to understand the past are embedded, and in seeking continually to shift the perspective from which we frame our arguments, we stand a better chance of opening up a more interesting sphere in which to operate (Heidegger 1977: 118).

4

HISTORY AND NATURE

The objectification of history

Archaeology concerns itself with the changing character of human societies through time as it is manifested in material culture. This enterprise has proved possible because we in the modern West conceive of time as linear and irreversible, and understand particular aspects of human existence to be temporally variable. Moreover, it is conventional to imagine the linear process of human development to have issued from an origin at some point in the distant past, where history and culture emerged out of nature. Yet this picture is complicated, and to some extent compromised, by the way that nature itself has been for the past century and a half understood as dynamic and changing. It is arguable that without this particular configuration of ideas archaeology would never have developed, and moreover it is evident that until comparatively recently the notions of history and nature were viewed in quite different ways. For the early Greeks, for instance, nature was not the object of science but a colossal living being, with its own intelligence (Collingwood 1945: 111). Similarly, while Lucretius and Hesiod both presented human history as divisible into stages or phases, it was with the early Christians that the conception of an epoch defined by a critical event or process was first considered (Collingwood 1961: 51). Nonetheless, the events and processes that were central to this vision of history were those of divine purpose, and throughout the Middle Ages the principal diachronic process that was generally imagined to be taking place was the coming of the Last Judgement. Human acts were only understood to bring about decisive change where they enacted the will of God, through grace. By contrast, a preoccupation with time and temporal change has been identified as one of the defining characteristics of modernity, arguably replaced by the domination of space over a post-modern epoch (Jameson 1984: 64).

In the medieval world, nature was largely understood as creation — that which had been made by God. Yet creation was not so much a collection of things as the domain of potential human knowledge. That which God had created, humans could come to understand through perception, yet God himself could only be known through grace. A major change in this conception of the cosmos came with the Renaissance, and Giordano Bruno's account of God as immanent in nature as its internal principle of motion (Cassirer 1951: 40). However, this vision of nature as divine was relatively short-lived, replaced in the sixteenth century by Copernicus's view of nature as a machine. Christianity had replaced the image of an eternal world with a perishable nature that had been created by a divine being, and now that creation was increasingly seen as a made thing or entity. While Leonardo da Vinci, in the late fifteenth century, had talked of humanity's struggle to master nature, this had still been the mastery of one being over another (Collingwood 1945: 96). Copernicus's account of a universe in which laws of motion and gravity applied equally from one place to another introduced a world that had no centre, and to which God was external. Both Galileo and Newton were to build upon this cosmology by distinguishing a world that is knowable through being measurable from a God who transcends nature. For Galileo, both God and humanity are outside of nature, in that humans have minds while the rest of creation behaves in an entirely law-like and mechanical fashion. As Collingwood put it, this growing separation of a material world addressed by science and a transcendent realm of divinity and mind lay behind the 'huge outbreak of dualisms' in the seventeenth century, which would be formalised by Descartes (ibid.: 100).

The natural science of Copernicus, Galileo, Newton and Kepler presented nature as a mechanism with internal cycles and movements, but which did not change in fundamental ways over time. The laws of nature were conceived as fixed and immutable. This emphasis on the fixity of nature was emerging at much the same time as human history was coming to be seen as directional and non-reversible. As the dualisms of mind and matter and of culture and nature began to crystallise, so history came to be identified as a sphere of human agency and consciousness quite distinct from the operation of the laws of nature. However, this picture was cross-cut by the changing conception of the relationship between past and present. As the past came to be understood as qualitatively different from the present, so it was constituted as an object of knowledge. In this sense, history *was* similar to nature: it could be studied, and discourse about it could be generated (McVicar 1984: 55). Lyotard has identified this objectification of the past as a characteristic of modernity. While oral communities have a past that is embedded in social relationships and performed in the reiteration of tradition, modern societies relocate the past as an externality (Lyotard 1984: 22). Taking this argument to its logical conclusion, only modern people would have an interest in 'finding' the past, for in a traditional society the only past that matters is that which is recalled as myth. Elements of a past that are not already part of tradition are superfluous. Lyotard implies that this is partly attributable to the social role of knowledge: in oral cultures, the retelling of traditional narratives and origin myths is in itself a source of authority (ibid.: 23). By contrast, the objectified, external past of modernity serves as a source of legitimation through precedent and citation. The objective reality of the past, substantiated by material evidence, authorises institutions and social relationships that might otherwise be identified as arbitrary. All of this is only possible because the past is seen as categorically different from the present, yet linked to it by a linear trajectory.

This objectification of history was facilitated by the rejection of Aristotelian scholasticism in the sixteenth and seventeenth centuries. We have noted that Aristotelianism involved a theory of teleology, in which all phenomena were conceived as struggling to achieve a form that does not yet exist. In its stead, the new philosophy of natural science placed a theory of efficient causes, in which processes of change observable in the world should be explained in terms of relations between definable entities (Collingwood 1945: 94). As a result, historical processes could now be addressed within a framework of cause and effect, rather than immanent tendencies. This in turn enhanced the sense in which history could be viewed as composed of chains of contingency, irreversible and directional changes caused by human action. At the start of the seventeenth century Francis Bacon argued that the chief virtue in studying history lay as a source of examples of the appropriate or inadequate application of reason (Strauss 1952: 93). Bacon, clearly, understood history to be a mere catalogue of isolated events. The full implications of history as a directional process were only to be appreciated by his student Thomas Hobbes.

Historicity and the state of nature

For Hobbes, historical process was of cardinal importance for it leads towards the ideal state of the future. The past is worthy of consideration because it demonstrates that real progress has already been achieved, and this substantiates the belief that further progress is yet to come. Hobbes wanted to demonstrate that human reason was not constrained by any transcendental order. On the contrary, any order that could be detected in history was a product of human ordering capacities. Hobbes implied that Bacon's use of history as example betrayed a relict Aristotelianism because it concentrated on past people's success or failure in keeping the eternal law. While such an unchanging order might be found in nature, humanity is not bound by any such suprahuman structure, as continuous progress requires fundamental change (Strauss 1952: 107). With this move, Hobbes definitively separated history from nature, and changed the whole significance of the study of the past.

However, if human history is progressive, and proceeding towards a state of perfection, it is logically necessary for it to have begun somewhere. If the culmination of historical process is to be the ideal state, then humanity must have emerged out of a state of nature. Nature therefore had both a historical and a conceptual priority over society, and the social world of human beings emerged out of nature rather than having been directly created by God (Taylor 1985: 190). This notion of a state of nature was extremely pervasive in seventeenth- and eighteenth-century thought, and has exerted a considerable (if implicit) influence ever since. The logical necessity of such a condition to the philosophical histories of the Enlightenment perhaps explains why so little effort was expended in corroborating its existence with material evidence. However, the precise form that the state of nature was imagined to have taken varied somewhat, with Hobbes describing a primordial 'war of all on all', and Locke concentrating on the atomisation of the human individual and their labour (Strauss 1952: 104). A more concerted attempt to theorise the state of nature is found in the work of Rousseau, which expands on the ideas of Locke and Hobbes to speculate at length on the characteristics of primitive human society. For Rousseau, 'natural' human beings were no different from other animals, except that they had the *potential* to develop culture and society. This potential lay in the exercise of free agency, yet primitive society existed in a condition of static equilibrium, in which no social relationships existed beyond the immediate family (Horowitz 1987: 98). Consequentially, the development of human civilisation must have begun with the disruption of the state of nature by some external factor. For Rousseau, such factors could be found in agriculture, metallurgy and exchange, which established the market, and in the process created a realm of social relationships beyond the household.

Where Rousseau diverged somewhat from Locke and Hobbes, and indeed from his Enlightenment contemporaries, was in seeing human nature as possessing some degree of historicity. Locke and Hobbes had stressed that progress simply involved the achievement of human potential, for humans when born represented a 'clean slate' upon which anything might be written. However, Rousseau imagined categorical changes in the transformation of 'savage man' into 'civilised man', and this indicates a slightly different view of human perfectibility. It was the perfectibility of humankind that allowed them to pass through a historical threshold and develop a cultural existence. This was achieved through the development of language, labour and social relationships, and the harnessing of instinctual desires. For this reason, 'savage man' is not conceived entirely in the negative as a creature without redeeming features. Rousseau's 'savage man' is free, happy and independent, and entering into the social contract that leads to civilisation involves a loss as well as a gain. The freedom of 'savage man' is connected with his solitary existence, unbound by social relations, yet embedded in nature (Horowitz 1987: 67). Savage humans are delivered over to their drives and instincts, and yet unlike other animals they have the potential for elevation from this condition. Reason and free will can build a different kind of being onto the physical infrastructure of the savage. This implies a layering of one aspect of humanity onto another, for Rousseau connects free will with spirit, which is distinct from the biological constitution of the person (ibid.: 62).

Historical process therefore involves the progressive construction of a 'rational animal', and by implication a change in human nature.

Of course, part of the background to Locke's, Hobbes's and Rousseau's writing was the steadily increasing contact between Europeans and the indigenous peoples of the Americas, Africa and southern Asia. Just as this interaction revolutionised antiquarian conceptions of the ancient populations of Europe, which had hitherto been based upon the works of the classical authors, so it had an impact on philosophical notions of the savage and the primitive (Hodgen 1964: 354). The greater public awareness of societies with diverse economic regimes, systems of belief, customs and mores may have had some influence on Rousseau's view that the development of civilisation out of savagery had not been an exclusively positive process. Rousseau maintained the view that asocial, 'natural' humans had come together to forge a social contract, and had presented the emergence of civilisation as a linear narrative. However, he was much more willing than his predecessors to suggest that something had been lost in the process, and that bourgeois society was in some sense impoverished. The nobility of the 'noble savage' had been exchanged for the security of life in the state. In this respect, Rousseau's particular version of human history's emergence out of the state of nature was partially responsible for the construction of a romantic and nostalgic attunement to the distant past, which was fundamental to the development of archaeology.

Nature and culture

The view of history as being composed of rational acts of free will which contribute to the progressive development of human society was very much connected with the conceptual separation of nature from culture. As we have seen, the new science presented nature as a stable mechanism established by God and ruled by fixed laws, composed of inert matter that had spatial extension but which did not think (Toulmin 1990: 109). Yet human beings were defined by their capacity for rational thought, and reason did not follow the same rules as causality amongst material things. Although human beings were biological animals, and their rationality could be confounded by emotion and prejudice, many of their actions and products stood outside of the mechanical processes of nature. While nature was changeless, having been fixed by God at the creation, the notion of progress implied that human achievements were cumulative and incremental. While the human mind was entirely separate from the material realm, the reasoned instructions of the mind could have material consequences in the physical world. Thus human beings had a dual existence, capable of thought in the mental realm, and yet causing actions through their corporeal presence. Increasingly, from around 1700, it became necessary to distinguish human knowledge and its products from the static world of nature. This required a change in language, and the word 'culture' was recruited to cover those aspects of human existence that they themselves had created. 'Culture' had hitherto been a term that was connected with the cultivation of plants and the tending of animals, but it brought with it the connotation of progress and development (Jordanova 1989: 37). Culture was therefore that which human beings had achieved through the operation of rational thought in the world, and which contributed to the progressive historical change in the conditions of human existence. To a great extent, the term was associated with science, technology, and abstract knowledge.

However, once the distinction between culture and nature had been established, the conception of nature itself became more constrained. If culture included the products of conscious human action, then humans could take raw materials out of nature and transform them into culture. Material culture, effectively, was composed of physical substance that had been abstracted from nature and formed into cultural things, which had a role in the narrative of historical progress while natural things did not. So, while the scientific revolution had looked on nature as a kind of complex orrery, composed of many mechanical and cyclical processes instantiated by God, it was the aspect of nature as dead matter that was now increasingly emphasised. Nature was now seen as the object of human action: both the entity that humans render intelligible through scientific labour and the store of raw materials that they can quarry and transform into cultural things (Jordanova 1989: 41). On the one hand, this had the effect of encouraging modern westerners to think of the world as a set of resources that lay at their disposal to consume as they wished (Heidegger 1977). On the other, the passivity of nature was contrasted with willed human action. As a number of feminist authors have pointed out, it was the connections between the oppositions of mind and body, culture and nature, and action and passivity that enabled gender relations to be inserted into an emerging cosmology (Rose 1993: 65). Active, mental, male culture was contrasted with passive, female, physical nature, enabling different aspects of existence to be mutually evaluated within an overarching scheme. Gender relations both authorised this evaluation and were naturalised by it. Increasingly, a scheme in which men actively used culture to address a passive and physical nature to which women were more closely attached became the accepted order of things.

While Newton had argued that the universe was periodically 'corrected' by the creator, as if keeping the mechanism running true, by the eighteenth century many accepted the deist view that God had simply constructed the cosmos and left it to its own devices. This merely enhanced the distinction between culture and nature, for nature was now utterly timeless and unchanging, while the achievements of humanity had been arrived at without any divine involvement. Amongst these achievements were ethics, morality, and legal codes. Kant, for instance, argued that while the things of nature abide by natural laws, which can be identified by science, humans are exempt.

The freedom to act rationally that distinguishes humans is exactly this freedom from the laws of nature. It follows that the codes that human beings must follow have to be found elsewhere than in nature: our morality must be founded in reason (Burnham 2000: 23). One of the senses in which history can be understood as the progress of reason, then, lies in the gradual development of legal and moral systems.

However, if neither the regularities of nature nor the prescriptions of a divine being could be relied upon as a basis for moral conduct, Enlightenment thought sought its foundations in an understanding of the being who deploys reason. From the eighteenth century onwards there was therefore an interest in defining human nature as a means of resolving the problems of statecraft and governance. It was widely held that if people were to act freely and rationally an ideal society would emerge. From this time onwards, much of the business of creating laws in the modern West was concerned with encouraging or coercing people to act *as if* they were behaving rationally. Knowing human nature was understood as a means of achieving a rational society, and, as Foucault (1970: 349) has argued, this is one of the reasons why a series of 'sciences of man' began to develop in the eighteenth century. However, while some saw human nature as something that should be as fixed and invariant as the laws of nature, others, like Rousseau, argued that human nature, the state and politics were all produced in history (Horowitz 1987: 87). It would follow that a knowledge of human nature would itself have to be historical in character.

Paradoxically, though, the law-like character of nature was often presented by Enlightenment thinkers as a model to which human society should aspire (Appleby *et al.* 1996a: 17). So nature itself was understood in contradictory ways: sometimes as a structure possessing an immanent order which assured its homeostasis, but sometimes also as wild, raw and disorganised, needing the intervention of humankind to master it (Horowitz 1987: 37; Bauman 1991: 7). The implication of this ambivalence is that order is a quality imposed onto nature by God, but that human reason can construct new forms of order. As long as nature was conceived as fixed and timeless, divine order held a certain pre-eminence. However, once nature came to be seen as unstable, chaotic and changing, the rational ordering activity of humanity could supplant that of the creator. In the Enlightenment, the ordered character of nature was presented as superior to the arrangements that could be achieved by the Church or the absolutist state. This provided substance to the claims of natural science as a privileged form of knowledge. Only later did the arguments shift so that nature could be subordinated to the human will.

Philosophical histories

From Hobbes onwards, history was increasingly understood as a grand narrative which could be expressed as the unfolding or maturation of some underlying process. Very often, the directional movement of history was seen as progressive. Progress was especially important to the Enlightenment. The deist conception of a world that was no longer directly subject to the attentions of the creator left open the problem of evil. If salvation was not to be had from an interventionist God, greater rationality might result in the reduction of wickedness. Through progress, humans would overcome their own darker instincts (Horowitz 1987: 40). The effect of this is that Enlightenment histories sometimes read like narratives of personal salvation, applied to the whole human race (Gray 1995: 159). As with Hobbes, the objective of Enlightenment history was to demonstrate that this progress of reason had already taken place, when looked at over the long term. Enlightenment histories therefore tended to be general and totalising, concerned with the broad sweep of human development rather than with fine detail (Ayer 1986: 95). The classic example would be Voltaire's *Essai sur L'Histoire Générale et sur les Moers et l'esprit des Nations* ([1745] 1829), which makes a virtue of not dwelling on the particular, preferring to identify the 'spirit of the times'. Voltaire wanted to write a cultural history in which different ages were identified by their customs. Consequentially, he focused on the development of institutions and traditions, rather than concerning himself with events or personages (Harris 1968: 36). These phenomena were taken as manifestations of the stages that human communities have to pass through in order to achieve enlightenment. Voltaire argued that human nature is homogeneous and universal, but that it has to fulfil its potential gradually through the operation of reason. History is therefore not preordained, even if it involves a degree of teleology, in the coming-into-being of reason and human potential (Cassirer 1951: 220). Yet while humanity advances from the state of nature to civilisation, Voltaire presents reason as eternal and changeless, both part of the human constitution and in some sense separate from it.

Another example of a 'philosophical history' that was perhaps more significant from an archaeological point of view was Montesquieu's *The Spirit of the Laws* ([1748] 1750). Montesquieu was rather less concerned with the development of reason than other Enlightenment historiographers, and took a particular interest in the influence of geographical and climatic forces on the emergence of different systems of government (Collingwood 1945: 78–9). However, his innovation was to present what was effectively an evolutionary typology of different kinds of society, each with its own form of government. Although Montesquieu concentrated on monarchies, republics, aristocracies and despotisms, he also described the societies of 'savages', characterised by clan organisation, and of barbarians with their 'small nations'. The significance of Montesquieu's approach was that he saw each successive stage of human development as being underlain by a deeper structure of relationships or principles. Thus each form of human government was distinguished by a particular set of determining factors: despotisms gained their particular character because they were run on fear;

republics relied upon civic virtue; monarchies were based upon honour (Cassirer 1951: 210).

From Montesquieu onwards, Enlightenment historiography was dominated by the notion that human societies progress through a series of distinct stages which can be identified with ideal social types. Rousseau, for instance, implicitly pointed to primitive, traditional and bourgeois societies as historically distinct forms, with different kinds of governance (Horowitz 1987: 91). William Robertson, in his *History of America* (1777), identified savagery, barbarism and civilisation, while various thinkers associated with the Scottish Enlightenment preferred a scheme based on hunting, pastoralism, agriculture, and commerce (Appleby *et al.* 1996a: 7). Adam Ferguson's *An Essay on the History of Civil Society* ([1767] 1819) combined a model of successive stages with the view that these followed on from an escape from the state of nature. Most of these developmental schemes proposed that the intellectual, spiritual and material progress of humankind proceeded in tandem, following Voltaire's argument that history had seen a series of 'golden ages' of universal advancement. This view is particularly characterised by Condorcet's *Outline of the Intellectual Progress of Mankind* ([1795] 1822), which portrayed the gradual triumph of reason as a series of ten stages leading to a future utopia. Consequentially, the material products of a particular society could now be identified as an index of economic, social, and intellectual progress. This much is suggested by Robertson's statement that

> It is only by tradition, or by digging up some rude instruments of our forefathers, that we learn that mankind were originally unacquainted with the use of metals, and endeavoured to supply the want of them by employing flints, shells, bones, and other hard substances, for the same purposes which metals serve among polished nations.
>
> (Robertson 1777: 652)

It would not be until the nineteenth century that the metanarrative of social development from uniform simplicity to diversified complexity took on its final form, associated with the imperial aspirations of the Western nations (Rowlands 1989: 29). However, Enlightenment history first established the notion that societies progress through a series of stages of material and organisational elaboration as a result of the increasing freedom of reason. Increasingly, history was conceived as a directional movement between two stable states: the state of nature, and the utopia of the future, once human perfection had been achieved. Effectively, history was understood as a passing phase, which would have an end. The evidence that progress had been accomplished in the past was an indication to some Enlightenment thinkers that achievement of the perfect future would be relatively unproblematic, once religion, superstition and authoritarianism were overcome. That this has not proved so easy has sometimes been a cause for dissatisfaction: the modern West has often appeared impatient with the present, restlessly pushing forward into a future in which a universal civilisation has been created (Bauman 1991: 11). However, the question of how directional change had broken free from the state of nature was more difficult. These considerations have conditioned a concern with 'origins' that has been influential in Western thought ever since. In archaeology, the search for the 'origins' of a series of phenomena ('modern humans', agriculture, metallurgy, writing, urbanism, the state) has been especially pervasive. It is worth pointing out the extent to which this concern with origins is a feature of a particular understanding of history and nature.

This is not to suggest that all historical thought in the seventeenth and eighteenth centuries contributed to a uniform theory of the progress of reason. Vico, in *The New Science* ([1725] 1948), attempted something rather different in creating a systematic philosophy of history that aspired to the kind of law-like understanding that the natural sciences achieved, and yet focused on the autonomous creative activity of humans (Collingwood 1961: 66). In this sense, Vico could be said to have resisted the new form of teleology that had been adopted by most of his contemporaries: the teleology of the metanarrative as opposed to that of the ideal forms. By contrast, there has often been a desire to collapse history into nature, and to insist that human beings and their societies behave in ways that are just as lawlike and predictable as physical, chemical and biological processes. Gassendi's materialism was an example of a perspective so entranced by the elegance of Galileo's account of the universe that it held the human mind also to be a mechanical entity. Similarly, Mattrie, in *Man a Machine* ([1748] 1994), introduced a biological determinism that attracted contemporaries such as Diderot. What these examples demonstrate is that although modern thought has established a complex series of dichotomies which separate humanity from nature, there is a persistent temptation to achieve a unified conception of the universe by asserting that humanity abides by the laws of nature. These kinds of approaches can make themselves attractive by eschewing metaphysics, and denouncing any concern with the particularities of human existence as anthropocentric.

'Life' and diachronic nature

We have seen that the absolute separation between nature and history relied on the understanding that nature was static and changeless. This 'fixist' view of nature began to be challenged during the later eighteenth century. While Linnaeus based his classification of species on synchronic relationships between unchanging entities, other natural historians like Buffon entertained the possibility that 'varieties' of creatures did change – as a result of selective breeding for example (Horowitz 1987: 59). Consequentially, it became

Figure 4.1 Georges Cuvier (from R. Lee, *Mémoires sur le baron Georges Cuvier/publiés en anglais par Mistress Lee*. Paris: H. Fournier, 1933)

possible to think of natural history as a history of nature, rather than a tabulation and description of creatures (Toulmin 1990: 145). This view was encouraged by the deism of the Enlightenment. If God had simply established the structure of nature at the creation, it might be expected that this pattern would elaborate itself over time (Horowitz 1987: 56). It was the consideration of such a process that paved the way for the emergence of the concept of 'life' at the start of the nineteenth century, and with it the science of biology (Collingwood 1945: 133). Eighteenth-century natural history had been concerned with the description of entities and their distribution in the classificatory space of the table (Foucault 1970: 128). This meant that plants and animals had been understood on the basis of their outward appearance, which identified them as representatives of a type.

With the notion of life came a concern with what creatures did, as opposed to what they looked like. So the ordering of nature ceased to be a function of the visible character of the surfaces of things and became a matter of the hidden depths of living systems (Sheridan 1980: 73). Foucault (1979a) has emphasised the pivotal role of Georges Cuvier in the formulation of the idea of life (Figure 4.1). Cuvier, although a 'fixist', pioneered the study of the comparative anatomy of mammals, including that of extinct animals recovered from the 'diluvium'. By dissecting animals and seeking to understand how their bodies worked, he came to see nature as discontinuous, composed of creatures that did different things in different ways, rather than as a continuous field of classificatory boxes into which species could be slotted. Understood as functioning organisms, creatures could no longer be place-holders in taxonomic schemes but became the living connection between an internal anatomy and an external environment. Interestingly, the conceptual articulation of the relationship between surface appearance and the hidden depths of the processes of life was directly connected with the investigation of muscles, ligaments and organs through anatomical dissection. This is a theme to which we will return in Chapter 7.

Cuvier created biology by discovering life in the bodies of dead animals. Once species were understood in terms of their habits and bodily functions, the possibility that they might change over time could be considered. In this sense, Cuvier's contribution was more revolutionary than Lamarck's. The animal kingdom was no longer a grid of species, either fixed in position or marching forward in locked relationships, but a collection of separate entities, each of which was best explained by the way in which it operated. It was a small step now for the relationships between species to be given a narrative structure. Whether or not this might involve natural selection is not of immediate significance. More important is that models of evolution and ecology involve the understanding that nature changes, whether in directional or reversible ways. So we can have a metanarrative of nature, involving the diversification of species and their colonisation of the earth, and their continual struggles one against another.

The important point here is that by the start of the nineteenth century the basis for the division between nature and history had effectively collapsed. Both history and nature now involved diachrony. It is interesting that the Enlightenment philosophical histories, which effectively introduced schemes of unilinear social evolution, were relatively uncontentious in their time. Biological evolution, in its Darwinian form, caused a public outcry, ostensibly because it questioned the role of God as the creator of all things. But it is worth considering whether a more fundamental kind of ontological distress was caused by the notion of a changing and unstable nature. What was at stake was the possibility that the modern Western cosmology might be utterly compromised. Consequentially, the processes of nature had to be presented as a history that was actually non-historical. If human history was concerned with irreversibility, contingency and particularity, evolution and environmental change were governed by laws that were not context-specific. We can therefore argue that since the nineteenth century *history* and *process* have served as alternative conceptions of change through time, thereby maintaining the separation of culture and nature.

Positivism and naturalism

We have seen that one recurring pattern in modern thought has been the temptation to erase the distinction between history and nature, and to assert that a single set of laws and principles can be applied to the physical and social world. Generally, this has involved some form of reductionism, as with the extreme materialism of the eighteenth century. Another outbreak of this kind of thinking occurred with the development of logical positivism in the 1920s and 1930s. It is arguable that the emergence of a dynamic conception of nature during the nineteenth century was a contributory factor in the rise of positivism. Yet rather than concede that the vision of a natural world that was continually in flux did any damage to law-building natural science, positivism restated the case for a universal rationality and a universal method (Toulmin 1990: 159). If both natural systems and human cultures could now be understood as undergoing change over time, both could be addressed, using the same approach, as patterned sets of variables. Positivism achieved this by a radical rejection of all metaphysics, so that only knowledge that was derived directly from experience was admissible (Giddens 1974: 2). Ideas about human motivations and understandings of the world were considered to be empty and meaningless, with the effect that human existence could be reduced to observable behaviour. In this way, Carnap and Neurath argued that psychology and sociology should be reconfigured as behavioural science, founded in biology (Lloyd 1986: 46). With these limitations placed on the study of human beings, the human sciences become entirely compatible with the study of animals, plants and physical processes. Using a similar argument, Carl Hempel was to suggest that there was no difference between the forms of explanation that were appropriate in history and natural science, for causal connections between variables existed in both (Hempel 1966).

In the context of archaeology, Shanks and Tilley (1987: 31) have drawn attention to the way that the introduction of positivism in the 1960s enabled the discipline to aspire to the high status of natural science. This was achieved by adopting a *naturalist* outlook, where a knowledge of the human past is ideally mathematical and law-like in character, and similar in form to explanations in the natural sciences. For the New Archaeology the explanation of cultural processes was explicitly favoured over historical interpretation. History was rejected because it implied a concern with specificity and particularity, rather than law and generalisation (Flannery 1972: 106). While Binford was quite right to point out that culture-historic archaeology relied upon a presumed understanding of the psychological dispositions of people in the past, it was equally the insistence upon the distinctiveness of cultural contexts that outraged the New Archaeologists (Binford 1968: 269; 1989: 51). One of the hallmarks of positivist and naturalist approaches, then, is a denial of the contingent character of human action: everything can be subsumed under a covering law, and all events are manifestations of more general processes.

Narratives of agricultural origins

We have seen that modern thought presents time as linear, and modern societies understand themselves as standing at the end of sequences of development that can be expressed in narrative fashion. To begin with, the historical transformation of human communities was contrasted with the fixed and static character of nature, requiring that history must ultimately have emerged out of nature. By the nineteenth century, though, nature began to be seen as dynamic and changing, so that it was possible to devise 'narratives of nature'. The potential undoing of the modern cosmology that this threatened was sometimes overcome by distinguishing historical development from natural process. Yet at other times the separation of history and nature was collapsed, but only where it was to be asserted that *everything* could be explained by science, because the whole universe behaved according to predictable laws. Nonetheless, even in this scheme of things the essentially biblical narrative that stretches from an origin to a culmination (the Kingdom of Heaven; human perfection; Utopia) remained. These various possibilities for understanding the past have provided the context within which archaeology has developed. Archaeology has its own concern with origins, its own grand narratives, and its own debates over the relationship between history and nature. One area of inquiry where this much is especially clear lies in the study of the inception of agriculture.

From the Enlightenment onwards, agriculture has been identified as a central element in the development of civilisation, and has often been explicitly connected with particular stages of social evolution. One reason for this is doubtless that once modern thought had established a distinction between culture and nature, the end of 'natural' food-gathering and the start of cultivation retrospectively took on an epochal significance. An interesting example is Grafton Elliot Smith's account of the foundation of ancient Egyptian civilisation, which he held to be responsible for the rise of complex societies world-wide. As a diffusionist, Smith was opposed to the view that 'natural laws' could be applied to human beings, who have unique capacities for thought and language (Smith 1937: 15). Instead, he urged attention to the empirical detail of historical developments, for the particularities of tradition and the acquisition of knowledge would mean that no two cultural contexts could be directly compared. Nonetheless, Smith's discussion of the beginnings of food production is a characteristically modern historical narrative, and effectively presents agriculture as the means by which humanity escaped the state of nature. His description of 'Natural Man', the form of humanity who inhabited the earth prior to the inception of herding and cultivation, is strikingly redolent of Rousseau:

> We can form a very clear picture of the behaviour of all mankind more than sixty centuries ago, when even the foundations of civilisation had not been laid. Natural Man is thus revealed as a naked, harmless, truthful child, good-natured, honest, and considerate, with an aptitude for pictorial art and craftsmanship.
> (Smith 1937: 21)

This is very much the image of the 'noble savage': happy with a simple way of life, cognitively equipped for culture, but displaying 'no innate desire to build houses or to make clothes, to till the soil or to domesticate animals' (ibid.: 22). The life of 'Natural Man' is presented as comparable to that of the higher apes, and its transformation was by no means inevitable, or conditioned by steadily increasing mental powers (ibid.: 25). So the state of nature is, as it was for Rousseau, stagnant and changeless, and it requires some form of external agency to instigate the process that leads to civilisation. Smith argues that only one group of people in world history have achieved the momentous leap from a 'natural' existence to food production, and this can be attributed to the unique circumstances in which the prehistoric Egyptians found themselves. It was the presence of stands of wild barley on the banks of the Nile that was the 'predisposing factor' that encouraged the development of a sedentary life. So it was the environment that provided the determining element in activating the innate human capacity for culture. The need to store grain from the harvest to feed people through the winter would have encouraged people to make pots and build granaries, and these technologies would gradually have been put to other uses, such as the construction of houses. Furthermore, the stored grain from wild harvests would eventually have been used as seed-corn, extending the crop into areas that were rain-fed or irrigated, and beginning true cultivation. Ultimately, the different aspects of agrarian culture (cultivation, irrigation, a cow divinity associated with the moon, divine kingship) came to be integrated and held together by Egyptian religion (ibid.: 40) (Figure 4.2).

Figure 4.2 'The Divine Cow providing life-giving milk for the sustenance of Queen Hapshepsut and the prolongation of her life which was the essence of her divinity' (from Grafton Elliot Smith's *In the Beginning*, 1932)

This in turn enabled the whole civilising structure to be transmitted by diffusion to human groups throughout the world, including the Americas. For this reason, aspects of Egyptian religious practice could be identified in locations as widely spread as India and North America (ibid.: 90). Given that Natural Man had a near-universal character (that universality itself amounting to an indication of 'naturalness'), and was always and everywhere mired in a static existence, then the growth of civilisation in different areas must ultimately be attributable to Egyptian influence. For if Egyptian agriculture was the product of a unique set of circumstances, it was inconceivable that food production should emerge independently in other parts of the world.

A slightly different kind of narrative to explain the beginnings of agriculture is represented by V. Gordon Childe's 'oasis theory'. Childe presents the cultivation of plants and the herding of animals as a 'revolution', the most significant change that had overtaken humanity since the mastery of fire (Childe 1957: 23). Childe's conception of prehistory as involving a series of revolutionary upheavals (urbanism, metallurgy, etc.) is doubtless a reflection of his Marxist views. However, he shared with Smith the belief that some external factor must have initiated the shift to agriculture, and this suggests that he also saw mesolithic hunters and gatherers as a manifestation of humanity in the state of nature. Childe argued that the origins of agriculture in the Near East could be attributed to climatic changes in the immediate post-glacial. Increasing dryness led to desertification, with the effect that humans and animals found themselves more and more concentrated around streams and springs. In these conditions of enforced juxtaposition, closer relationships between people, plants and animals would develop (ibid.: 15). Becoming more familiar with the attributes and life-cycles of various species, human beings would gradually have come to influence and ultimately control their reproduction. Like Smith, Childe held that such a process might only have been possible under very particular conditions, and argued that the combination of the appropriate wild species and climatic circumstances would have been limited to the area where Africa and Asia met. Unlike Smith, he saw the development of agriculture in the New World as an entirely separate process from that in the Old, which followed a quite different trajectory. These separate phenomena were contingent upon different sets of circumstances, and could not have been explained by a universalising set of laws.

Different again was Robert Braidwood's account of the beginning of food production as a manifestation of human evolution through a series of 'cultural levels' (Bender 1975: 25). Braidwood pointed out that humanity had lived through a series of inter-glacials in which conditions had been similar to the post-glacial, without having adopted agriculture on any previous occasion. His explanation was that prior to the Holocene human culture had not been elaborated to the degree required to establish control over nature (Braidwood 1952). In other words, the process of human development was one of the unfolding of a design that was not influenced by the natural world. So Braidwood's narrative is not concerned with the escape from the state of nature. Nonetheless, his argument is close in spirit to Voltaire or Condorcet in that it is what eighteenth-century thinkers would have described as the gradual perfection of human reason that enables a transformation of the material conditions of existence.

All of these authors treat the beginnings of agriculture as something deeply serious, because it marks a boundary between the human occupation of a 'natural' world and a world in which humans have gained control over the material conditions of their own existence. It is instructive to contrast this point of view with that of the Cambridge 'Palaeoeconomy' school of the 1960s and 1970s. The palaeoeconomists argued that the basis for human existence lies in biology and subsistence economics. Indeed, simple economics and the factors governing the behaviour of animals could be seen as much the same (Higgs and Jarman 1975: 4). Although 'short-term factors' such as social organisation, religious belief and symbolism might exist, over the long timescale on which archaeology operates their effects would be negligible, and their consideration could be avoided (ibid.: 6). In these terms, human beings could be studied in much the same way as any other kind of living creature, and they might be expected to behave according to laws. They should therefore be studied scientifically, using the same concepts and methods as are appropriate to animal ethology. In particular, palaeoeconomic archaeology should concentrate on the relationships between population, technology and resources, which are all factors that have the benefit of being readily addressed through the archaeological record. Stress is always present in the relationship between population and resources, and technology allows the rise to higher levels of population (ibid.: 6).

The similarity of these arguments to those propounded by early economists like Thomas Malthus is obvious, but it is another aspect of palaeoeconomy that I want to emphasise. Higgs and Jarman were making very much the same move as the early twentieth-century positivists in arguing that if particular aspects of human existence were not readily accessible through direct experience they should be discounted. Just as Carnap and Neurath demanded that all metaphysics should be rejected, so palaeoeconomy turned the coarse grain of the archaeological record into a criterion for assessing the relative significance of human actions and their material traces. Similarly, both the early positivists and the palaeoeconomists argued that human behaviour conformed to natural laws, and could be addressed through the methods of natural science. Like nineteenth-century biology, palaeoeconomy broke down the distinction between history and nature, but only by reducing everything to the 'nature' of natural science within which there is no room for meaning. Consequentially, the account of the domestication of plants and animals that Higgs and Jarman presented was radically different from the accounts of Smith, Childe and Braidwood. They pointed out that over the course of history there had been many different relationships between humans and other species – herd-following, symbiosis, predation – of which domestication was only one (Higgs and Jarman 1972: 5). Osteologists and ethnobotanists had pointed to the morphological changes that had overtaken certain species since the last Ice Age, and had attributed these to domestication (Higgs and Jarman 1969: 35). However, such changes were a result of changes in the selective pressures affecting the plants and animals concerned, and there was no reason to draw a categorical distinction between those selective pressures that were imposed by human beings and those that were 'natural'.

This meant that morphological changes in animals and plants might indicate that domestication had taken place, but might equally be attributable to some other factor such as climatic change. Moreover, if domestication did not materially affect the selective pressures operating on a species, it might have no visible effect on the plants or animals concerned. Equally, zoological or botanical techniques cannot definitively tell us whether an archaeological site was occupied by cultivators and herders or by hunters and gatherers (Higgs and Jarman 1972: 8). The faunal assemblage left behind by a hunting band who specialised in taking a single species might be indistinguishable from that produced by a pastoralist community. Nor are food production and sedentism universally mutually associated, for neither pastoralists nor slash-and-burn horticulturalists need permanent settlements. Given the imprecision of the archaeological identification of domestication, Higgs and Jarman argued that it was probably not something that began definitively at a single place and time. Instead, domestication should be seen as one form of intensification in the relationships between humans and other species which had probably happened many times during the past 30,000 years or so. Intensification would have happened when it conferred a selective advantage on particular human groups, and would have declined when circumstances changed. Some species might have been domesticated on a number of different occasions. Not all domestication need have been post-glacial, nor need it have led in all cases to sedentism, craft specialisation, urbanisation and civilisation.

The important point about Higgs and Jarman's view of domestication is that, having denied the distinction between history and nature, they were obliged to take the origin of agriculture out of history. Indeed, domestication could have no 'origin' because it could have no historical contingency. Domestication was just 'something that happened', a natural process rather than a historical event. Domestication was a relationship between species that came and went, and as such it could not be invented nor passed from one community to another by diffusion. By merging history into nature, Higgs and Jarman placed themselves in the position of having to replace a historical narrative with a narrative of natural process. As such, they illustrate the ambivalence with which modern thought has treated 'natural history' and its relationship to human agency since the discovery of the dynamism of the non-human world.

5
NATION-STATES

Introduction: the rise of the nation-states

There were doubtless both states and nations in the pre-modern world. Abstract discussions of the state go back at least as far as Plato, and the Greek city-states were plainly the model for his arguments. Yet the city-states were primarily political entities, which claimed no pre-political origin in race or ethnicity (Taylor 1988: 202). Conversely, some medieval kingdoms could be claimed to have been 'nations' (Smith 1995: 22). However, the nation-state has been modernity's characteristic form of political organisation, combining national identity and a bounded territory with the organisational characteristics of the state. A number of authors have pointed out the significant connection between archaeology and nationalism (e.g. Kohl and Fawcett 1995; Díaz-Andreu and Champion 1996), but in this chapter my intention is to show that both nationalism and our archaeological conceptions of past social entities owe much to the formation of the nation-state.

Prior to the sixteenth century, political relations in Europe were based on loyalty to a dynastic ruler rather than to a national community. Feudal societies had a pyramidal form, with the king at the apex and the peasantry at the base: social relations rather than territorial relations. Consequentially the boundaries of the kingdom were much less distinct than those of the modern state. Events of death, succession and marriage amongst the royal houses could change which regions were ruled by whom overnight (Anderson 1983: 19). The legitimacy of rulership was vested in blood and descent, and had little to do with the will of the people. Kings were accountable only to God. The power of the ruling dynasties was widely accepted as being part of the natural order of things, to the extent that the king was often held to enjoy a closer relationship with the deity than the rest of the population. This pattern of authority was certainly focused on the past, in that the genealogies of monarchs were the guarantee of their authenticity and right to rule. However, the notion of a 'national past', shared by a national community, was virtually non-existent.

As well as dynastic rulership, medieval Europe was characterised by the power of the Church. Virtually all people held religious beliefs, and, with the exception of the occasional heresy, these were relatively uniform over very wide areas. Western Catholicism in particular promoted the view that fundamental religious truths were expressed in scripture written in a single language, Latin. One of the principal effects of the Reformation was to break down the uniformity of religious practice, creating numerous sects and churches worshipping in many different languages (Anderson 1983: 18). This development was corrosive of the notion of Christendom and contributed to the growing emergence of bounded national communities. It was the growth of religious diversity which represented one of the central problems of governance in the early modern period.

Just how far patterns of authority shifted in Europe with the emergence of modernity is demonstrated in Foucault's discussion of the changing historical reception of Machiavelli's early sixteenth-century text on the exercise of power, *The Prince* (Foucault 1979b: 6). When *The Prince* came to be re-read in the nineteenth century its contents were considered to be scandalous, because it portrays the business of the ruler as being entirely concerned with self-interest. However, this reading was anachronistic. The Machiavellian Prince may have stood at the apex of a structure of privilege and obligation, but he was also in some senses external to his domain. It was only later in the sixteenth century that sovereignty began to be associated with government, where government is a matter of the management of people and resources (McNay 1994: 115). The appearance of government as an issue was to have far-reaching effects. Where the medieval sovereign had exercised the power of life and death over his or her subjects, this power was relatively remote and sporadic in its impact. By contrast, the government of states involved the continuous administration of the lives of entire populations (Foucault 1978: 138). At the same time, the ruler began to become less the personification of sovereign power than a focal representative or embodiment of the nation (Mouffe 1993: 11). As we shall see, this more closely defined relationship between the sovereign and the subject population was connected with a growing sense that the will of the people was a significant element in government.

The decline of feudalism and the rise of the administered state were congruent with the growth of the national community. Ernest Gellner has argued that in feudal societies the aristocracy and clergy were utterly separate from the peasantry, maintaining a social distance from them and even speaking court and liturgical languages (Gellner 1983: 11). Medieval domains were thus fragmented into a series of in-turned and exclusive communities: merchants, guildsmen, clerics and aristocracy. While modern societies remain intensely hierarchical, the adoption of vernacular languages in public and religious life and the sharing of a common culture facilitated a more complex administrative structure and promoted a sense that all of the people belonging to a given nation shared more with each other than with the inhabitants of other nations. Arguably, the history of the period between the mid-sixteenth century and the earlier twentieth in Europe can be read in terms of the gradual decline of the authority of dynastic rulers, matched by the increasing legitimacy of the administrative nation-state (Anderson 1983: 113). Within the nation-state the subject became a citizen, who behaved according to an instituted code of laws rather than the dictates of a sovereign (Peters 1956: 186). This kind of citizenship is closely related to the modern Western notion of individuality, for the citizen is an autonomous political agent. At the same time, personal authority came to be a matter of holding office within a bureaucracy, instead of inheriting or being granted an aristocratic title. As with so many other aspects of modernity, the hallmark of the emergent form of government was its deployment of reason and logic in establishing legal foundations for social order.

The nation-states that started to develop in the sixteenth and seventeenth centuries combined a territorially bounded national community with a state apparatus which included institutions and agencies that were primarily concerned with maintaining social order (Gellner 1983: 4). These included courts of law, systems of taxation and duty, police, standing armies and fleets. It is important to note, though, that the early nation-states like England, France, Sweden and the Netherlands existed before any sentiment or set of beliefs that could be defined as 'nationalism' had come into being (Smith 1995: 37). It is clearly arguable that the European nation-states were the crucible of nationalism, rather than its product. These early modern nation-states developed out of existing monarchical domains, and can be distinguished from a separate wave of ethnic states that emerged in the nineteenth century. These 'smaller nations' were often created by independence struggles on the part of ethnic groups who were subsumed within larger empires (Hroch 1988: 94). Because these groups did not possess their own elite cultures or vernacular literatures the demand for independent statehood was generally prefigured by the formation of a 'national movement' spearheaded by the local intelligentsia (ibid.).

The notion of a social physics

The formation of the European nation-states was widely recognised as posing a series of problems for Western societies. There was an acknowledged growth in the importance of individuals, in which 'masterless men' were coming to identify themselves as political subjects. But there was equally a consolidation of centralised authority on the part of state governments, which were more and more concerned with the maintenance of stability and order (Peters 1956: 180). With the end of the Thirty Years War and the slow decline of the Holy Roman Empire the nation-states gained greater autonomy and territorial integrity. The power of the papacy had declined, and the possibility of restoring the empires of antiquity had evaporated, with the effect that each country was identified as a distinct entity, openly competing with every other (Foucault 2001: 409; Toulmin 1990: 90). In France and Spain absolutist regimes emerged, in which the state and its apparatus were entirely associated with the person of the ruler. But in England the relationship between the increasingly individualistic merchant class and the power of the monarchy was troubled and unresolved. State-formation and political instability in Europe coincided with the scientific revolution, and this resulted in the conviction that if society could be transformed by human action it could be remade for the better on rational lines. Just as nature could be reduced to its component elements, enabling it to be both understood and mastered, so the state could be redesigned and reconstructed. While utopian social thought had much earlier antecedents, the emergence of this kind of a 'social physics' is particularly associated with Hobbes and Locke.

The application of the new science to human relations resulted in a view of society as a system composed of distinct elements which could be understood in a relatively abstract and generalised way. This was the method of resolution and composition deployed in relation to humanity. A society could be broken down into a series of separate institutions, and more importantly the individual human subject came to be understood as the most basic unit of social analysis (Toulmin 1990: 77). The different parts of the social system were not fixed, but were in motion and influenced one another like the planets in the solar system, and could be affected by external factors like changes in the environment (Harris 1968: 12). The maintenance of order involved balance and harmony between the different parts of the social whole, and for Locke at least this was to be achieved through the state's guaranteeing the rights of individuals to life, freedom and property (Appleby *et al.* 1996b: 27). Once this way of thinking had been articulated, it is easy to see how Montesquieu's vision of the social as an 'artificial body' composed of a series of separate forces could develop, as well as the political economy of Adam Smith and David Ricardo (Cassirer 1951: 20). Moreover, while the image of society as a system whose internal elements could be rationally analysed and re-ordered was in some senses a reflection of the political developments of the seventeenth century, it nonetheless proved attractive to the elites who sought to manage and administer the developing nation-states.

One important aspect of the growth of an analytical approach to society was the more widespread recognition of the collective will of the people as a principle of political legitimacy. While medieval monarchs had justified their position through the combination of divine right and inheritance, a social order that is understood as a system of elements implies some kind of reciprocal relationship between the ruler and the ruled. The nation-state binds its subjects into much more intensive relationships than the feudal realm, yet this requires that they should give their consent to the political order, even if only tacitly. Modern societies require people continually to reaffirm their commitment to the state, by voting, paying taxes, using a passport or identity card, doing jury service, or being conscripted into the armed forces (Taylor 1988: 200). Moreover, it is characteristic of modernity that the state becomes a medium through which antagonisms and conflicts are expected to be resolved, resulting in the achievement of consensus (Mouffe 1996: 9). So individual subjects give their consent to the executive and the legal system, and social harmony is arrived at.

It follows from this that both the social philosophies of the seventeenth and eighteenth centuries, and the custom and practice of the European nation-states which both fostered and drew on these ideas, were highly atomistic. They presented individual human beings as the indivisible atoms from which the social sphere was created, so that social relations were secondary to the individual existence of human subjects (Strathern 1990: 8; Taylor 1985: 187). Society in general and the state in particular were seen as existing for the benefit of individuals who logically preceded them. Needless to say, this view conflicts with more recent accounts that stress the contextual, fragmented, and constructed character of human identity, so that rather than constituting the unshakeable ground of the social, human beings occupy a plurality of subject positions (Mouffe 1995: 33; A.M. Smith 1998: 88). The social physics of Hobbes and Locke had independent and autonomous individuals coming together to create the state as a kind of contract.

The idea of the social contract

It is this conception of society as a kind of contractual arrangement, freely entered into by autonomous individuals, that I will argue continues to exercise considerable influence in the Western world, and in archaeology in particular. It implies that human beings can exist independently before they enter into social relations with others, and sometimes also that they can have an essential identity (racial, ethnic or national) that precedes its political articulation (Taylor 1988: 198). While human identity is taken as a given, society and the state are presented as artificial, having to be brought into existence by human agency. In early modern Europe these ideas were often presented as a corrective against the autocratic rule of the monarchy. If civil society had to be summoned into being, the authority of the king was not primordial but stemmed from the will of those who came together to create it. Obviously, thinking of political allegiance as a kind of transaction was attractive to the burgeoning mercantile classes of the seventeenth century, who were often those who sought to limit the power of the ruler (Peters 1956: 184–6). For them, society could be compared to the market, and personal skills and abilities should lead to achievement and authority. However, the most thoroughly elaborated version of the theory of social contract, which came to be particularly influential, actually approved the absolute authority of the monarchy. In *Leviathan* ([1651] 1996), Thomas Hobbes argued that human beings had a natural tendency to fall into wicked and antagonistic ways. Yet their rational capacities allow them to construct a social order that restrains these impulses. This can best be achieved by giving the monarch the unrestricted ability to impose the rule of law.

Prior to Hobbes's intervention, two different versions of the social contract had already been articulated by philosophers. The first was the *pactum unionis*, where a group of persons come to a mutual agreement to live together in a civilised fashion, and the second the *pactum subjectionis*, where a community agree to submit to a certain kind of government (Peters 1956: 182). Hobbes developed the latter of these, arguing that submission to the rule of the king should be the criterion of belonging to a society. In his version of the social contract it is the agreement between autonomous agents that brings the artificial Leviathan of the state into being. Aware that without the state they are under the constant threat of violence, even the strongest people will pool their natural rights and set up a powerful ruler whose unquestioned legitimacy provides them with security. Ironically, it is the absolute coercive power of the sovereign that allows people to cease living in fear of one another. Because this is a conclusion that needs to be arrived at logically, Hobbes stresses the place of reason in bringing the social contract about. The monarch, as the embodiment of the state and the repository of the individual rights of the multitude, is not party to the contract so much as a product of it (Figure 5.1). Only the sovereign is in a position to make decisions that represent a distillation of the general will of the population, and as a consequence that population have no right to depose the sovereign (Tuck 1989: 67). The resonance of this conclusion, in a book published two years after the execution of Charles I, is obvious.

Hobbes's argument is that the social contract brings a very different social environment into being. As we saw in the previous chapter, society emerges from the 'state of nature' in which the institutions of the state are absent (Strauss 1952: 104). Rather than a 'multitude', the participants in the contract become a 'people' with a single will (Peters 1956: 192), and the implication is that the potential of an ethnic or national group is realised through the formation of the state. Furthermore, in gathering together the natural rights of the people and establishing a single point of view for the state, the sovereign is able to provide a definitive adjudication in areas of dispute (ibid.: 190). In other words, the modern nation-state is in a position to dispense justice, and the perspective of the dominant person or group is to be associated with right and truth. The legitimacy of the ruler is the ground of the legal system, and where the social contract is in operation promises and agreements can be expected to be honoured (Tuck 1989: 68).

While it is arguable that Hobbes's vision of the social contract has dominated modern thinking on states and nations, it is important to note that our understanding of the political community has also been influenced by a rival

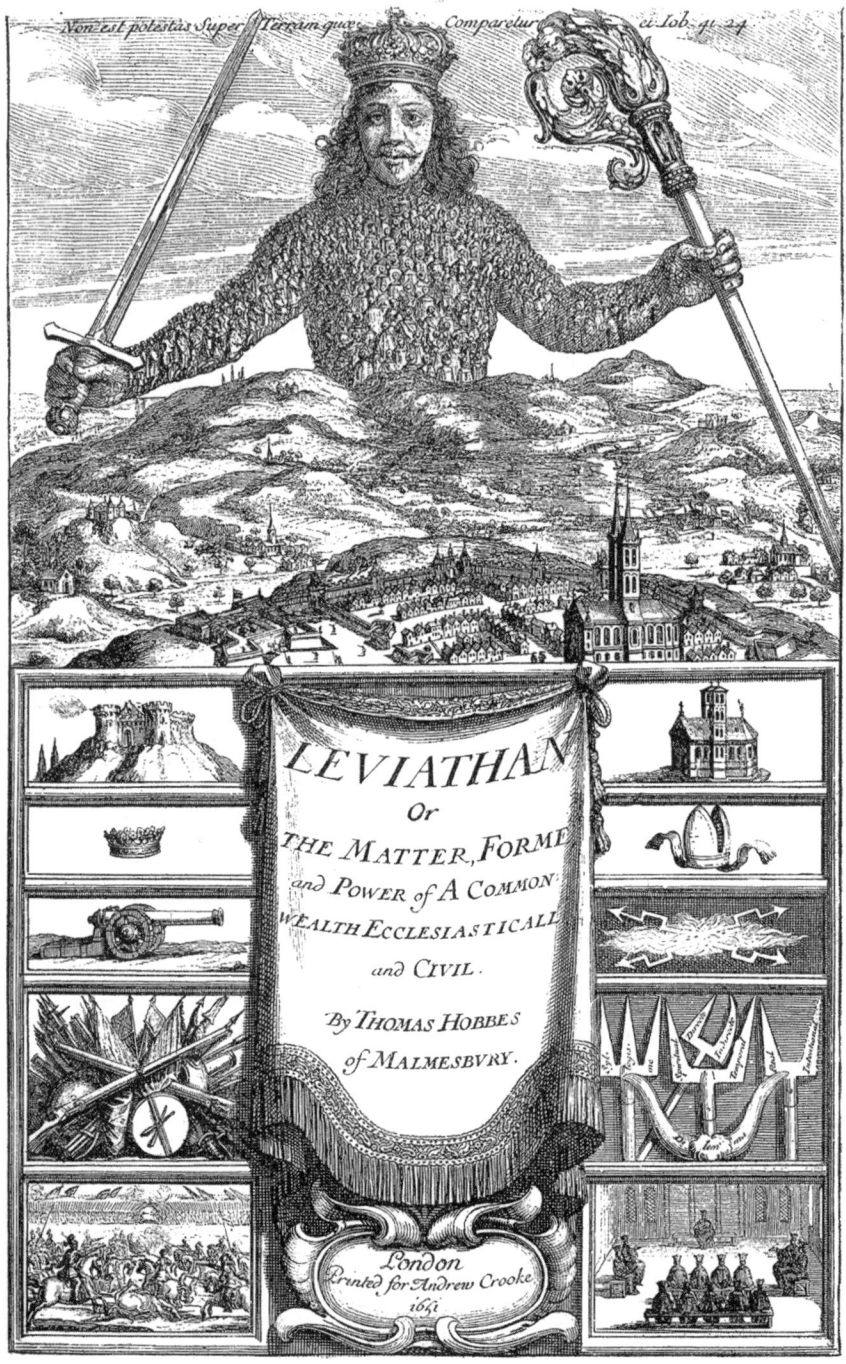

Figure 5.1 The title page to Thomas Hobbes's *Leviathan* of 1651, showing the 'great mechanical man' of the state, created by the will of the people

account presented in the following century by Jean-Jacques Rousseau. Hobbes had suggested that human beings are *naturally* individuals, and that the state of nature is the condition that obtains where individual motivation is unchecked. For Rousseau, though, individuality was a condition that had developed historically. In the ancient *polis* the conflict between the citizen and the community had not been so pronounced as in the modern era of enlightened reason and market relations (Horowitz 1987: 167). These forces had eroded the rule of custom and tradition, so that within bourgeois society there existed the danger of a return to the barbarism of absolute and unrestrained freedom. Reason had freed human beings from nature, but at the same time it had destroyed the possibility of any kind of traditional or instinctive sociality. New, artificial forms of social relations had to be created as a result. In identifying a degradation of the social fabric which needed to be overcome by institutional arrangements Rousseau defined one of the central themes of modern social theory, which would later be echoed in Ferdinand Tonnies's distinction between *Gemeinschaft* and *Gesellschaft*, as well as Emile Durkheim's notions of organic and mechanical solidarity.

As with Hobbes, Rousseau saw the state as an artificial construction that stemmed from the willed use of human reason. Where he differed was in arguing that the freedom of individual will cannot be renounced and subsumed by the sovereign (ibid.: 172). This was because the individual does not enter into a contract with either the social whole or the sovereign. On the contrary, it is the social contract that brings both the society and the ruler into being. The ruler cannot receive the individual will of the subject, for he or she has nothing to exchange for it; they are not a party to the transaction. For Rousseau, the social contract involves an alienation of sovereignty on the part of the state in order to allow coherent collective action, but each citizen retains their individual liberty. The contract then takes the form of an understanding between autonomous subjects to recognise each other's absolute right to freedom, in the process creating the corporate body of the state. This is quite distinct from Hobbes's emphasis on the need for a central coercive authority, for in Rousseau's version of the social contract sovereignty remains with the people, and it is their equality and freedom as much as their safety that is guaranteed by agreement. Where Hobbes presents a defence of absolutism, Rousseau constructs a blueprint for bourgeois liberal democracy, which is more often the form that modern Western societies have taken. Rousseau presents the modern state less as a body that is manifested in the person of the ruler and more as one that brings itself into being through the process of legislation (ibid.: 186).

Anatomy of the nation-state

Contract theory provided the intellectual legitimation for the state as a political community. But what is striking is that the early modern nation-states were not simply created *ex nihilo*: they also drew on a series of resources that granted them a particular identity. Each of the European nation-states understood itself as a 'people' with a homeland and a shared culture, including a historical or mythical tradition accounting for its origins (Smith 1995: 29). Importantly, while these myths and identifications were often of dubious authenticity the formation of the state generally resulted in their reification. The existence of a coherent political entity in the present encouraged the belief in unbroken traditions and uniform ethnic identities in the past. The sense of common identity that was fostered within the nation-state by these means was, however, distinctively modern rather than primordial. As Benedict Anderson (1983: 43) has argued, the modern nation exists in a horizon of simultaneous happenings that makes up an 'imagined community'. A nation-state is a bounded unit within which the majority population share a language. This means that since the Reformation they will have worshipped in the same vernacular, and since the advent of print capitalism they will have shared the same awareness of events through newspapers, posters, broadsheet ballads and other news media. The modern national community is one in which it is possible to imagine a multitude of other people, many of whom one has never met, all concurrently engaged in different activities and yet comprehensible as an articulated whole. The consequence of this is that the citizens of a nation are capable of thinking of themselves as a collective historical actor, in a way that would be quite impossible in the pre-modern world. Just as nations could be imagined as something like organisms struggling against each other in order to survive, so Anderson suggests that they were now understood as inhabiting a homogeneous temporal environment (ibid.: 69). Particularly once Europeans had started to come into contact with African and Amerindian societies, they increasingly imagined their nations progressing alongside others within the featureless 'container' of time. This is quite different to the conception of temporality that prevailed in the Middle Ages, where change through time was not a major issue and the only significant event to look forward to was the Last Judgement.

In post-medieval Europe the achievements of individual subjects were more and more understood as the consequence of their own personal efforts. The Reformation had emphasised each human being's individual responsibility to God for their own salvation, while mercantile capitalism was presented as enabling great wealth to be accumulated by industrious persons, irrespective of their social background. In the same way, the offices of state were increasingly devolved to those who demonstrated competence, merit and training, rather than descent from a noble line. Within this scheme of things the role of the sovereign was transformed into that of the chief executive of government (Peters 1956: 186). This chimes with the vision of a state in which authority is answerable to the people, and which exists to legislate for, administer and organise people and things. Where decisions are made by bureaucrats with the aim of redesigning society rationally, Bauman's metaphor of the 'gardening state' begins to apply: promoting some social trends and rooting out the 'weeds' (Bauman 1991: 20). We have seen already that the philosophy of the social contract fostered the idea that civil society had to be constructed by human effort. Increasingly, the state involved itself in the more and more detailed management of all aspects of the lives of the population. One consequence of this was that for the first time people were categorised according to 'norms' of behaviour, and delinquency, perversion or aberrance identified (Foucault 1978: 144). By the eighteenth century this process of increased management began to focus on public health and welfare, and it is arguable that the growing involvement of the state in organising the life of the population was paralleled by the administration of mass death in warfare (Foucault 2001: 404).

Through the eighteenth and nineteenth centuries the state took on a rationality and a momentum of its own, which was initially identified as 'reason of state'. Populations were increasingly policed, regulated and subjected to surveillance. However, while these developments could easily be portrayed under the rubric of 'social control', giving the impression of a synchronised and enveloping totalitarianism, in practice the organs of government have become more heterogeneous and uncoordinated through time (McNay 1994: 118). What Foucault called 'governmentality' is a paradoxical phenomenon, which at once aims to improve the health and welfare of the population while at the same time achieving greater knowledge and power over human subjects (ibid.: 121). It is neither wholly benign nor wholly coercive, while the more completely it imbricates itself in the social body the less it can amount to a single structure controlled from a single centre. The principal effect of this combination of regulation and pastoral care is the enhanced individualisation of human subjects.

While medieval societies were based around a hierarchical relationship between the ruler, the aristocracy, the guilds and the peasantry, modern states define both their own boundaries and the place of the subject much more precisely. If the rational state has to be artificially constructed then the subject has to be integrated within it, and as this came to be understood as a problem the state came to formalise its relationship with the person through the series of mechanisms that we have already mentioned. These mechanisms of care, classification and policing have had the side-effect of producing a more individuated kind of human being (Foucault 2001: 416). Just as market economics shifted the focus away from kin relations and towards economic autonomy, so the nation-state established relations with subjects that were categorical and analytical rather than based on social networks (Taylor 1988: 197). In tune with the theory of social contract, the key political relationship was now that between the individual and the state, unmediated by the feudal lord or the priest. One consequence of this is that modern societies are characterised by a single public sphere, within which the whole nation exchanges and communicates. Each member of the national community is equipped to 'do business' with each other (ibid.: 192). Rather than a series of mutually exclusive and self-reproducing castes or sub-cultures, modern Western societies are relatively generalised, and individual people are to some degree interchangeable. Although the modern West has become steadily more industrialised and technology-based, the education that has been increasingly provided by the state is much more universal in content than the kind of traditional learning that prepared medieval people for a specific profession (Gellner 1983: 27). This sense of a single cultural space inhabited by an entire population was enhanced by the science and philosophy of the seventeenth and eighteenth centuries, which emphasised the universality of logic and reason. The same laws and rules applied through society just as they applied throughout the cosmos.

National identity

The foundation of the European nation-states in the early modern period created for the first time a series of very large social entities that could understand and represent themselves as integrated communities possessing a distinctive shared identity (Anderson 1983: 4). By the end of the eighteenth century these national identities had been attributed a foundational character, recognised as the essence of the state and providing legitimacy for its independence. This growth of national identity within the nation-states was the precondition of the emergence of nationalism as a more or less coherent political outlook. This development depended to some extent upon the philosophical elaboration of ideas of nationhood that took place during the later eighteenth century, and which is particularly identified with the work of Johann Gottfried von Herder (1744–1803). However, while Herder is sometimes presented as a kind of 'prophet of nationalism', his views were more concerned with the particular value of the forms of life that grow up in and were sheltered by specific contexts than with atavistic chauvinism. Herder applauded the advances of natural science, yet he rejected the Enlightenment's attempts to apply them to human society and to reduce human diversity to a set of universal laws (Berlin 2000: 168–9). He argued that the multiplicity of cultures throughout the world all had their own value, and that they were incommensurate. It would not be possible for them all to merge into a single, ideal, rational society with a uniform set of values. On the contrary, it was good for people to feel that they belonged to and were nurtured by a particular tradition. Expressing the particularity of one's own culture, especially through art, was for Herder the essence of being human.

Herder's pluralism was opposed to narcissistic individualism, to the centralised power of the state, and to bellicose claims of national superiority. Most of all it rejected imperialism, in which one nation attempted to dominate or erase another (Berlin 2000: 182). For Herder, *nationalismus* involved trying to recognise what one is, as a means to achieving one's own potential by drawing on one's cultural inheritance. He imagined autonomous national communities finding their own way to fruition in harmony with one another. However, there can be little doubt that despite all of this some of his ideas resurfaced in later years as an element of a much more reactionary conservatism.

It was at much the same time that Herder was articulating his view of a nurturing, expressive national identity that images of a distant Gallic, ancient British or Germanic past were beginning to grip the popular imagination in Europe. This has sometimes been presented as a simple consequence of the growth of romanticism (e.g. Trigger 1995: 268), but it may also be pertinent to place the concern with national origins in the context of modernity and the nation-state. We have seen that in the medieval era political legitimacy was vested in the dynastic descent of the sovereign. The only past that was of significance to the European monarchies was that of genealogy, the lines of inheritance that built up the ruler's pedigree. But once sovereignty had given way to government, and once the political order had come to be conditional upon the will of the people, the authenticity of particular communities began to be at issue. As soon as the nation-state was identified as the natural political entity in Europe, the past of each nation started to be recognised as the source of that authenticity.

It is therefore revealing that long before the emergence of an explicit popular nationalism, antiquarian activities had been promoted by precisely those rulers who were attempting to rebuild their authority as the embodiment of the nation rather than bearer of the royal blood. In other words, the national past began to gain significance with the development of a constitutional, bureaucratic and managerial monarchy. This was most obviously the case in Scandinavia, where the creation of nation-states was combined with the organisation of centralised government on modern lines. Gustavus Adolphus of Sweden (1594–1632), for instance, created an army that represented the model of hierarchically structured discipline, while his chancellor, Count Axel Oxenstierna (1583–1654), carried out financial and administrative reforms and eventually authored a written constitution. Seventeenth-century Sweden amounted to an early paradigm of Foucauldian governmentality. It was in this context that Johan Bure (1568–1652) secured royal patronage for his antiquarian researches, including the study of rune-stones which documented the lives of the early medieval Swedes (Klindt-Jensen 1975: 15). Similarly, in Denmark Ole Worm (1588–1652) was supported by Christian IV in sending out a royal charter of 1626, requiring members of the clergy to record all of the antiquities in their parishes (ibid.: 19). John Aubrey's investigations of Avebury and Stonehenge on behalf of Charles II in England are somewhat comparable. In each case what was represented was not so much a precocious nationalism as the study of the past in the service of the state, substantiating the origins of the nation and, by implication, the legitimacy of the sovereign as the personification of the popular will.

Nationalism

We have argued that neither the existence of nationhood, nor the nation-state, nor national identity amounts to nationalism, which refers properly to a specific conception of the political implications of having and belonging to a nation. Nationalism holds that the freedom and autonomy of nations (or a particular nation) must be the overriding principle around which the world should be ordered. To achieve their liberty, the modern individual must belong to a nation, and that nation must be granted self-determination. The world is naturally divided into nations, and all members of a given nation (who might share an ethnic, racial or linguistic identity) should be contained within the borders of a single state. Above all, then, nationalism is the belief that natural justice is best served by the coincidence of ethnic, political, linguistic and territorial boundaries (Gellner 1983: 1; A.D. Smith 1998: 25). As Gellner points out, there are far more ethnic and linguistic groupings in the world than nation-states, and many of them show little desire to achieve statehood. Indeed, it is difficult to imagine a situation in which all the potential nation-stares had been realised. Nonetheless, it seems to be an implicit assumption of nationalism that it is normal for people to live within bounded and internally homogeneous communities, each of which has claim to its own lands, and that at some time in the immemorial past this was universally the case. It follows that nationalism generally legitimates itself by reference to the past, and looks forward to a future that involves a return to some aspects of past conditions.

The formulation of this perspective at the end of the eighteenth century and the start of the nineteenth took place within the nation-states of Western Europe. As we have seen, it then later provided the inspiration for national movements in Central and Eastern Europe. While the implication of my argument is that nationalism is a product of Western modernity, it has proved to be a set of ideas that can be transferred into other contexts, so that in the past half-century in the Near East and East Asia it has formed an element of movements that seek to resist Western 'modernisation' (Taylor 1988: 207). Wherever nationalism establishes itself, though, it seeks some raw material to work with in the form of a past identity to essentialise. So although nationalism can grow up in societies that are self-consciously anti-modern, it tends to bring with it at least one aspect of modernity: the search for foundations on which to build the present. Because nationalism is generally fixated with the image of a harmonious and uniform community within its own borders, it often gives rise to phenomena such as racism and anti-Semitism, which involve the rejection or annihilation of elements that are believed to disrupt homogeneity (Bauman 1991: 35). While thinkers like Herder had sought to stress the possible coexistence of nations, nationalism generally advocates an identity politics that requires the repudiation of the Other, whether within the boundaries of the nation-state or outside. In the late nineteenth-century geographical writings of Friedrich Ratzel, for instance, each nation was presumed to have the right to form its own state, but these states were then imagined competing against each other for space in which to live (Bassin 1987: 474; Wanklyn 1961: 42).

In some of the recent archaeological literature, attempts have been made to align nationalism with relativism (e.g. Anthony 1995; Kohl and Fawcett 1995; Trigger 1995). This is curious, given that the most obviously defining feature of nationalism is its essentialism. Nationalism relies on the supposed existence of a latent reservoir of national authenticity, with which it hopes to re-connect. It seeks a return to a 'golden age' of ethnic and linguistic uniformity, and promotes the folk culture of those supposedly still connected with the past, in preference over cosmopolitan hybridity (Gellner 1983: 57). In short, nationalism presents itself as traditional and anti-modern, where in reality it is a profoundly modern phenomenon. The relationship with the past that nationalism nurtures is itself distinctively modernist. While we have seen that the rulers of the early nation-states showed an interest in national origins, this gained new impetus with the rise of nationalism. This much is evident in the development of national museums from the start of the nineteenth century (Schnapp and Kristiansen 1999: 29). In Denmark, for instance, Fredrik III had created a *kunstkammer* or cabinet of artworks in 1663, collecting together objects of artistic merit or historical significance which had been collected under treasure trove law, and which hitherto would have been melted down to fill the royal coffers (Kristiansen 1985: 12). Yet the significance of this royal collection was transformed in 1802 when a pair of fifth-century AD golden horns from Gallehus in Jutland were stolen and melted down (Klindt-Jensen 1975: 46). Significantly, this was popularly interpreted not as an affront against the king but as a crime against the national heritage. Danish nationalist sentiments were at that time very strong, following the defeat at the Battle of Copenhagen in April 1801, which had been received as a national calamity. The public outcry that followed the Gallehus theft created the necessary support for Rasmus Nyrup's proposal for the foundation of a national museum, the curatorship of which provided the context within which Christian Thomsen was first to apply the three-age system to prehistoric artefacts. Such national museums and displayed sites and monuments are of the greatest importance since they gave the national past a visibility and a material presence (Anderson 1983: 182).

Broadly speaking, the rise of nationalism in Europe coincided with the transformation of antiquarianism into archaeology. The development of a discipline with a more rigorous methodology was at least in part a consequence of the greater weight of public expectation and curiosity now vested in the study of the past. As J.J. Worsaae put it, 'with a greater respect for the political rights of the people, there awakened in the nations themselves a deeper interest in their own history, language and nationality' (quoted in Daniel 1950: 52). In particular, archaeology held out the possibility of identifying the traces of the long-distant inhabitation of particular territories by specific national groups (Díaz-Andreu and Champion 1996: 19). By the earlier twentieth century the explicit aim of much archaeology was the characterisation of artefact types as the products of distinct ethnic communities, and thereby plotting the spatial extent and migratory movements of particular populations in prehistory. Perhaps because the period that was documented by the earliest written sources in Europe was dominated by population movements (particularly those occasioned by the collapse of the Roman Empire), the distant past was often imagined to have been characterised by almost continuous invasions, wanderings and migrations. In the climate of increasing nationalism, the origins of nations were often thought through in spatial terms, borrowing the predilection of philology to explain linguistic relatedness in terms of the comings and goings of population groups.

These debates had real political implications. After the First World War, the Versailles peace conference made use of distribution maps of the speakers of different languages in order to establish the borders of new nations in Eastern Europe, carving up the remains of the German, Habsburg and Ottoman empires (Herb 1989: 291). In the particular case of the border between Germany and Poland, the archaeological evidence for the distribution of prehistoric and Dark Age tribes was understood as having considerable bearing on the outcome of these negotiations (Wiwjorra 1996: 175). It is well known that prehistoric archaeology was promoted by the Nazi regime in Germany, as it purported to be able to identify the achievements and territorial extent of the Aryan Germans in the distant past (Arnold 1990; Arnold and Hassman 1995: 76; McCann 1987). However, Nazi archaeology did not represent a radical departure from the kind of ultra-nationalist anthropogeography associated with Gustaf Kossinna in the early part of the twentieth century (Veit 1989: 37). While it might be comforting to imagine that an essentially apolitical empiricist archaeology was co-opted by Fascism in the 1930s, it is more probable that Kossinna's and Ludwig Wilser's ideas (concerning the relationship between racial genius and cultural superiority, and the racial purity of the Germanic tribes who had remained continuously in the Baltic area for millennia) actually contributed to the formation of the Nazi world-view (Wiwjorra 1996: 172; Härke 1995). Although many archaeologists are agreed that the nationalist politics articulated through the discipline has been extremely harmful, it appears that for some it represents a layer of distortion or bias imposed by practitioners with an atavistic agenda (Kohl and Fawcett 1995: 5). The alternative is to argue that archaeology is irreducibly political, and that nationalist discourse permeates the practice of the discipline at even a methodological level (Jones 1997: 11). I would suggest that this is because the emergence of archaeology is so thoroughly implicated in the development of modernity and the nation-state.

Culture-history and ethnic entities in the past

Culture-history, which dominated archaeology during the first half of the twentieth century, drew upon approaches to the classification and typology of artefacts that had been developed in the nineteenth century. These approaches, as refined by Oscar Montelius, relied on the notion that human beings elaborate and perfect their material technology, as time progresses, through the application of the intellect (Trigger 1989: 157). That is to say, the temporal development of material culture was attributable to the same process by which Hobbes and Locke had imagined civil society emerging from the state of nature: the realisation of human reason. Montelius focused on the potential of material culture variation to disclose change through time, enabling him to establish a series of distinct 'periods' within the Scandinavian Bronze Age. His explanations for stylistic change in metal artefacts were concerned with successive waves of cultural influence making their way northward from the Mediterranean. Gustaf Kossinna was firmly opposed to the diffusionist aspect of Montelius's work, yet his own 'settlement archaeological method' effectively complemented the typochronology of the Scandinavian tradition by emphasising the geographical distribution of artefact types. As he put it in his *Herkunft der Germanen* of 1911, 'sharply defined culture areas correspond unquestionably with the areas of particular peoples or tribes' (cited in Veit 1989: 37). The fusion of these two mutually antagonistic schools of thought created a culture-historic time–space systematics which enabled entities known as 'cultures' or 'culture groups' to be defined on the basis of the ordering of artefactual assemblages. Culture-history concentrated its efforts on the construction of ordering chronological charts. These charts were understood as the foundation of the archaeological knowledge of any region of the world, and any other kind of analysis was considered to be secondary to the imposition of a certain kind of order on the material (Willey and Sabloff 1980: 110).

Binford and Sabloff (1982) have made an important distinction between Old World and New World traditions of culture-history, where the former imagined a 'culture' to be the material manifestation of the 'spirit' or essence of a people, while the latter saw a particular community's set of material traits as the outcome of environmental utility and historical happenstance. In other words, European archaeologists were more likely to follow Kossinna (and indeed Herder) in seeing the material assemblage used by a population as a reflection of their collective personality. They were also more disposed to identify particular assemblages with the progenitors of specific contemporary

European nations (Jones 1997: 19). Nonetheless, even in American culture-historic archaeology it was generally assumed that the sharing of material traits between populations was an indication of a shared history and heritage (Trigger 1989: 191). We might suggest that this difference between the European and American traditions of culture-history was to some extent connected with the relative political utility of archaeology in these two parts of the world. We have seen that in Europe the ability to document the existence of a particular people in the distant past served as a means of substantiating their authenticity, innate superiority, or right to self-determination in the present. In the Americas, the prehistoric peoples under study were patently not the ancestors of the dominant (white) community, who conducted virtually all archaeological research (although sporadic attempts were made to identify particular pre-Columbian cultures as one of the lost tribes of Israel [Fagan 1977: 80]). Consequentially, throughout the nineteenth century there was less of a political imperative to link past and present identities in the New World, and the ascendancy of European Americans was legitimated instead by the notion of their 'manifest destiny' to extend the 'boundaries of freedom'.

In organising materials in space and time, and identifying them as 'cultures', culture-history was employing a distinctively modern set of assumptions. The development of material culture through time was presumed to reflect the gradual emergence of human rationality, while also expressing the essential character of a people. More importantly, discrete distributions of artefacts were expected to correlate with spatially bounded human populations. The coincidence of ethnic identity, political borders and cultural expression that had come into being with the European nation-states was here being imposed on the past. The nationalist myth of a golden age of uniform ethnic and linguistic identities was now given a kind of solidity by informing the expectations with which archaeologists addressed their evidence.

In the European context these ideas were most thoroughly explored in the work of Vere Gordon Childe. Childe's vision of culture-history was one that emphasised the significance of tradition in that material culture could be understood as a concrete manifestation of a social tradition (Childe 1942: 16). An assemblage of artefacts is therefore the outcome of the operation of standardised and reproduced customs of manufacture, and the coherence of the assemblage is a consequence of its production by a single group of actors at a single historical time (Childe 1956: 111). This group, which Childe identifies as a 'people', need not necessarily have been members of a single race, but they were clearly understood as having some form of social solidarity and representing a distinct population. Their shared cultural tradition was the principal determinant of their material expression, although this might also have been influenced by environment and climate (Childe 1950: 1–5). As well as being distinguished by a coherent tradition, a people would always inhabit a definite territory, and for this reason cultures might be expected to exhibit mutually exclusive distributions (Childe 1956: 115–18).

So while Childe's was a more sophisticated version of culture-history than much of the archaeology of his era, it is plain that it embodied a series of expectations about past societies that are characteristically modern. This is important, because although culture-history has been eclipsed within the explicitly theoretical discourse of archaeology, it still retains much of its influence. As Jones (1997: 24) points out, culture-history has often been able to represent itself as an atheoretical methodology: simply an efficient way of rendering archaeological material comprehensible. Yet as I have hopefully demonstrated, culture-history is not merely a theoretical perspective (as articulated by Childe and others), it also contains a series of less explicit suppositions about the past. It is worrying, then, that Hodder and Preucel (1996: 7) describe the time–space systematics of culture-history as 'an essential building block for research in a new region'. This suggests that culture-historic methodologies are merely neutral tools of analysis, which must be applied as a first step in the archaeological investigation of any part of the world. The implication is that each region's archaeology must pass through a series of 'necessary stages' which replicate the history of the discipline. Yet if we always begin with culture-history, we will always end up with an archaeology that is mired in the social-historical vision of Western modernity.

This point is very well demonstrated by Siân Jones and Colin Richards's discussion of the recent history of research into the neolithic archaeology of the Orkney islands (2000). Neolithic Orkney presents an unusually rich array of material evidence which has long been subject to typological analysis with the aim of identifying discrete archaeological cultures (e.g. Childe 1940: 81–90). The megalithic chambered tombs of the area have been classed into an Orkney–Cromarty group (including bipartite and tripartite chambers, stalled cairns and horned cairns) and a Maes Howe group of passage tombs (Davidson and Henshall 1989: 19–51). Decorated pottery is separated into an Unstan and a Grooved Ware tradition, while there is also a variety of undecorated vessels of less certain attribution. Furthermore, Orkney is unusual within the British Isles in having a number of neolithic settlements of stone-built houses. Sometimes, these have been divided into Unstan Ware-using farmsteads like the Knap of Howar, and Grooved Ware-using villages of cellular houses such as Skara Brae (Clarke and Sharples 1985: 58) (see Figures 5.2, 5.3). Because routine forms of analysis still seek to identify artefacts and monuments as examples of types and styles, the tendency has been to continue thinking of neolithic Orkney as having been occupied by distinct population groups with mutually exclusive material assemblages, long after an explicit adherence to culture-historic explanation has been abandoned. For instance, Hedges (1984: 117) suggested that the islands had been divided up into the territories of sub-cultural groups (Figure 5.4).

Figure 5.2 The neolithic settlement at the Knap of Howar, Orkney (photo: author)

Figure 5.3 The late neolithic 'village' at Skara Brae, Orkney (photo: author)

More recently, opinion has tended to favour the idea that some of the artefactual and monumental styles of neolithic Orkney were not contemporary, but sequentially ordered (Hunter and MacSween 1991; Renfrew 1979: 207). Yet as Jones and Richards point out (2000: 102), the notion of a change from one cultural package to another merely puts off the problem of interpretation. For the culture-historic model of communities which adhere to established norms in the manufacture and decoration of material culture remains in place, and it has now to be explained how one set of norms gave way to another. Moreover, it is highly likely that the evidence supports neither of the two alternative neat interpretations: of a series of coexisting

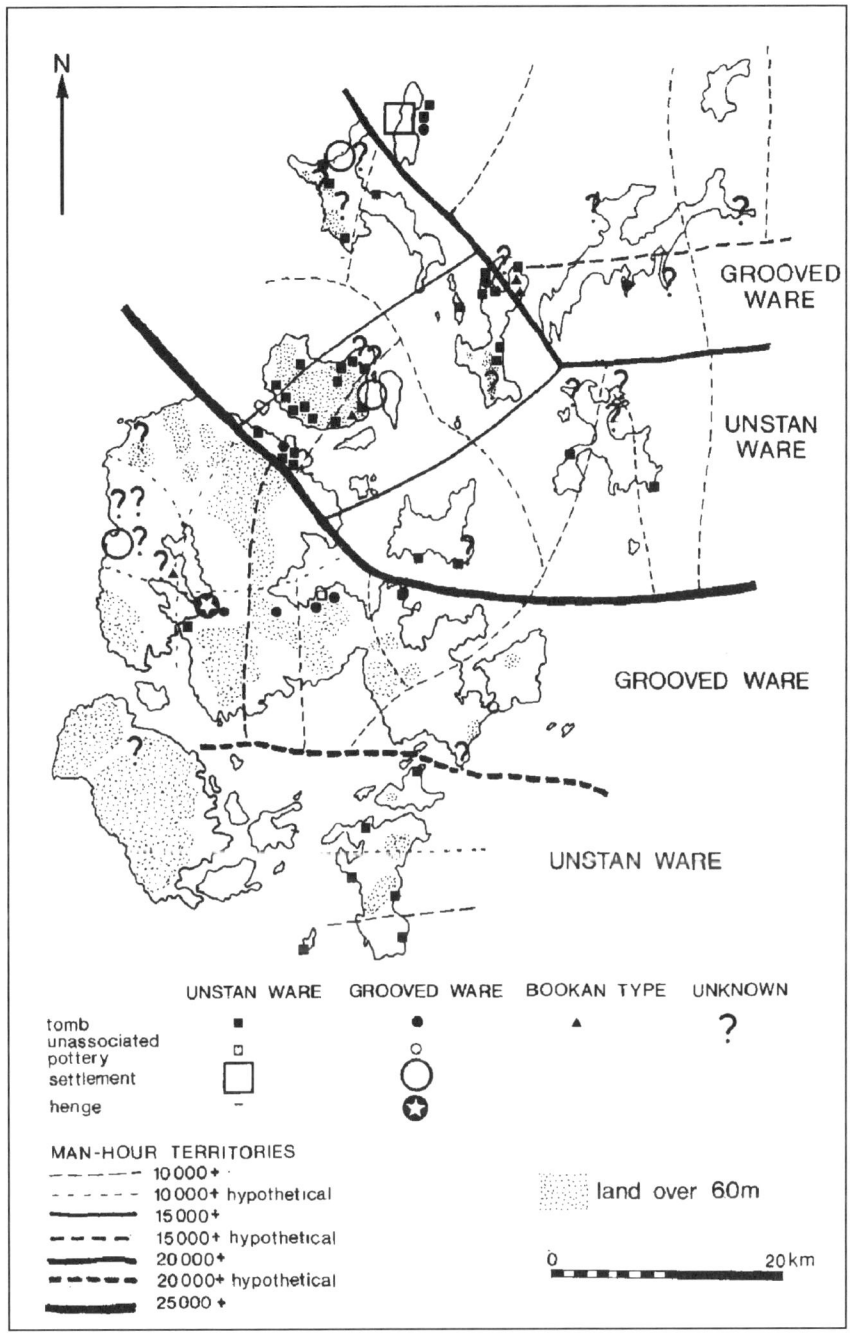

Figure 5.4 Map of hypothetical tribal areas in neolithic Orkney, based on the distribution of artefact and monument types (from J.W. Hedges, *Tomb of the Eagles*, John Murray, 1984)

sub-cultures or an orderly chest-of-drawers succession of one culture to another (Jones 2000: 128). The real pattern may have been a much messier one, characterised by overlaps, lags in the adoption of new forms by particular kinds of people, or by the use of different material forms in different practices. As Jones and Richards imply, as long as we continue to see the typological methods of culture-history as neutral heuristic tools, we are likely to assume implicitly a homogeneity of cultural norms and social practices in the past.

The idea of a social archaeology

It is, perhaps, a little less than revelatory to suggest that culture-historic archaeology was underwritten by aspects of nineteenth-century nationalism. However, we can extend the argument by addressing the project of a 'social archaeology' that has formed one aspect of processualism from the 1960s onwards. Echoing the social physics of the seventeenth and eighteenth centuries, processual archaeology rejected particularized historical interpretations, and sought to generalise about social organisation (Spaulding 1968: 35). The notion of culture groups that equated with peoples in the past was largely abandoned, and culture (including material culture) came to be viewed as a set of strategies that were participated in differentially (Binford 1965: 206). Nonetheless, *societies* were still presented as bounded entities which are constituted through the actions of individuals. Indeed, as in the work of Locke and Hobbes, society was explicitly understood as a system, or more precisely a sub-system within a larger ecological system (Flannery 1972: 103). And like the thinkers of the seventeenth century, processual archaeology was preoccupied with questions of centralised administration, organisation and redistribution. Just as the theory of social contract dwelt on how the sovereign achieved the legitimacy that enabled them to act on behalf of the community, so processual archaeology focused on the relationship between social organisation and decision-making (Johnson 1978).

Moreover, 'social archaeology' was distinctly atomistic in tenor. Colin Renfrew, for instance, very commendably debated the issue of exactly how a social group might be defined. His answer was that 'it is precisely when a number of individuals do interact fairly strongly in a number of different ways, and less strongly with others outside that number, that we can begin to speak in terms of a social group' (Renfrew 1977: 98). In a language that is redolent of the social contract, sociality is addressed in terms of the *interaction* of *individuals* who would seem logically to precede this interaction:

> A human society is conveniently regarded as a system, whose components are the human individuals within that society, the artefacts they use, and the elements of the environment with which the men and artefacts interact.
>
> (Renfrew 1977: 108)

Elsewhere, Renfrew again invites comparison with contract theory by arguing that social relations can be understood as being analogous to economic transactions:

> Sociologists like to analyse all exchanges or transfers in terms of social behaviour, reducing economics to sociology. I would like to suggest the converse, expressing sociology as economics, that we can analyse most social behaviour in terms of exchange.
> (Renfrew 1973b: 14)

Now this statement is ambiguous because it could be taken as approving a view of the social as a relational network articulated through (amongst other things) gift exchange, in which relationality provides the context for the production of human subjects (e.g. Strathern 1988). However, the remainder of Renfrew's discussion suggests that what he has in mind is a social world made up of reciprocal transactions between autonomous individuals. Renfrew is at pains to stress the spatial aspects of social life, so that a social unit can be defined by 'the habitual association of persons within a territory' (1977: 102). So although he is not attempting to interpret bounded distributions of artefacts as discrete population groups, his expectation is that a defining aspect of any social entity is that it occupies a fixed spatial area, within which there will be a population that is more or less homogeneous. These social units may be multiple, and hierarchically nested, so that a person belongs to a number of groups of different orders of magnitude. The *polity* is the highest order social unit, and while 'the individual person has allegiance at a number of levels . . . he is a member of each, but he is a *citizen* of the highest order polity' (Renfrew 1977: 105). Evidently, social archaeology concerns itself with a past in which territorially bounded social groups were formed by autonomous citizens: very like the modern nation-state.

Conclusion

Why should any of this matter? Why should modernity not create a past in its own image? The theory of social contract provided intellectual support for a new form of organisation in the shape of the nation-state, which came to dominate Europe from the Treaty of Westphalia in 1648 onwards. The modern state orders and administers a population by defining their position within both analytical and geographical space. People are classified and disciplined, while at the same time being given the freedom to act as political and economic agents. The definition of national communities from the eighteenth century onwards gave rise to nationalism, which sought origins and legitimacy for ethnic nations in the past. As a consequence the distant past has gained a political value. This is sometimes only too obvious: in the Caucasus, for instance, many of the leaders of the ethnic nationalist movements that have emerged since the collapse of the Soviet Union have been ancient historians or archaeologists (Chernykh 1995: 143). As a result of its intellectual debt to the social physics of the eighteenth century, archaeology tends to present a view of a prehistoric world occupied by internally undifferentiated ethnic groups, or social groups that amounted to bounded adaptive sub-systems composed of individual agents. The problem is that these interpretations tend to support the nationalist belief in a past of pristine communities, before miscegenation began.

Extreme nationalism today often demands a return to this imagined idyll. In the recent conflicts surrounding the collapse of the Yugoslav state, the practice of 'ethnic cleansing' was based upon the presumption that at some time there had been a uniformity of population that could be returned to through an extreme form of social engineering. Revealingly, the extreme violence and forced population movements were accompanied by the focused destruction of religious buildings, traditional architecture, museums, libraries and civil archives (Barakat *et al.* 2001; Hall 2002). The evidence for an ethnically diverse past, for mixed marriages, shared settlements, and mosques cheek-by-jowl with churches was systematically eradicated. In its desire for a structured, ordered, readily comprehensible prehistory, archaeology runs the risk of giving legitimacy to nationalist fantasy. This is clearly not the intention of processual archaeology, but it seems that this kind of social archaeology is not well placed to overcome the intellectual legacies of the age of nation-states.

6

HUMANISM AND 'THE INDIVIDUAL'

Introduction

In the previous chapter we argued that as a consequence of its intimate relationship with the modern nation-state, archaeology has tended to construct an image of the past that is dominated by bounded and internally homogeneous social entities. This tendency was most pronounced in the culture-historic and processual archaeologies of the early and mid-twentieth century. In more recent years, in reaction against this totalisation, an emphasis on the 'archaeology of the individual' has begun to emerge. While there are many positive aspects to this development, I will argue in this chapter that stressing the individual and subjectivity as against the social and objectivity merely reinforces the modernist dichotomies that these terms imply. More importantly, I will suggest that 'the individual' refers to a very particular understanding of what it is to be a human being, which is specific to Western modernity and is both anachronistic and ethnocentric when applied to the distant past. In other words, the assumption is that there is only one legitimate way to be human, and it is *ours*. This viewpoint originates in a philosophical humanism, which posits a fixed and universal human nature as the basis for the dignity and natural rights of all human beings. However, as I will hope to show, the attempt to base a moral perspective on supposed human universals is doomed to failure, while the notion of the free and autonomous human agent actually sustains the divisive politics of the New Right.

During the 1960s and 1970s, much of American and European archaeology was dominated by the ecological functionalism of processual archaeology. This approach rejected the view that human history was determined by the actions of 'great men' and 'great women', preferring to investigate the interactions of population, environment, resources, technology and climate over the long term. Taking the long view, the acts of particular persons within these great processes were considered to be inconsequential. As Leslie White once memorably put it, the general trend of events in ancient Egypt 'would have been the same had Ikhnaton been but a sack of sawdust' (White

1949: 279). In its most extreme formulations, ecological archaeology maintained not only that human beings in the past were best studied as collectivites but also that they should be approached using much the same conceptual apparatus as any other living system (Higgs and Jarman 1975: 2). More moderate thinkers also rejected any concern with the acts or intentions of particular persons in the past, because human development was to be understood in terms of universal 'laws of culture' rather than 'individual psychology' (Binford 1965: 206; 1981: 202). Culture-historic archaeology had embroidered its accounts of the past with isolated illustrations of past lifeways of uncertain significance, drawn from sites with unusually good preservation, and had explained the incidence of cultural phenomena in terms of ideas held in the mind. Both of these practices were now to be rejected. However, as numerous authors have pointed out, the single-minded pursuit of system-level generalisations about cultural process had the effect of reducing gender, class, faction and ethnicity to the status of mere 'ethnographic variables' that could be neglected by the archaeologist (Brumfiel 1992; Wylie 1991: 34). The resulting 'prehistory of genderless, faceless blobs' (Tringham 1991: 97) was clearly unsatisfactory. Moreover, the functionalist emphasis on the long-term survival of social systems as totalities gave the impression that human beings only existed to realise the goals of the social whole, and that material culture was simply a reflection of the operation of the social system (Hodder 1986: 7). As a result, processual archaeology took on a distinctly conservative tinge, valuing equilibrium and changelessness, and seeing any form of change that was generated *within* a society as pathological (Hodder 1982a: 2).

This is not to say that the role of the person was entirely neglected within processual archaeology. Stephen Plog, for instance, argued that an evolutionary perspective required a consideration of variation at the level of the organism (Plog 1977: 14). The behaviour of single human organisms might be varied, but not infinitely so, and it should not be written off as random 'noise'. Instead, behaviour will be patterned as a result of the situations that humans find themselves in, their perception of their circumstances, their motivation, and their capacity to respond to change (ibid.: 16). Consequentially, it should be possible to identify behavioural variability at the level of the organism in the archaeological record. One attempt to achieve this was undertaken by Hill and Gunn (1977), who suggested that human individuals could be recognised through the artefacts that they made and used. Their argument was that individuals are always different from one another in their motor habits and motor performances, and that as a result there should be minor stylistic differences in terms of execution and use-wear between artefacts that had been made or used by different people. Two points are significant here. First, the kind of variation that Hill and Gunn were attempting to identify seems to be understood as something unconscious, so that the 'individuality' being sought appears to reside in the central nervous system, and might easily be biological in character. Second, the various chapters in Hill and Gunn's edited volume propose a series of mathematical or statistical techniques for identifying individuals through material culture variation. Each individual is therefore presumed to possess the same degree of motor-habit variation, and the methodologies are transferable because the individual is presumed to be the same thing in all cultural and chronological contexts. Each individual is precisely as 'individual' as each other, across time and space.

With the development of a critique of processual archaeology in the early 1980s, a concern with 'the individual' was promoted as a means of challenging some of the shortcomings of ecological functionalism. If group-level analysis gave the impression that the behaviour of human beings was determined by systemic pressures beyond their own control, focusing on the individual introduced a concern with purposive action and creativity (Hodder 2000: 22). The acts of individuals were not predetermined, and could not be predicted by systems models. Furthermore, material culture was presented as being created and manipulated in idiosyncratic ways, amounting to a medium through which human beings could negotiate their own roles and identities. This emphasised the volatile and indeterminate character of social life (Hodder 1986: 8). Indeed, social relations were now understood as being made and remade through innumerable interventions in the material world, rather than being dictated by ecological circumstances or innate cultural codes. In his singularly important review of the state of archaeological theory in 1982, Ian Hodder pointed to the work of 'practice theorists' like Anthony Giddens and Pierre Bourdieu, who addressed the relationship between willed action and social structure (Hodder 1982a: 6). Unfortunately, there has been a tendency for Hodder and those who followed him to conflate agency with 'the individual' and structure with 'society'. Thus Hodder writes of the need for 'an adequate consideration of the ways in which individuals act within societies' (1986: 149), Knapp and Meskell complain that 'archaeology has tended to ignore the relationship of the individual to society' (1997: 189), and Wilkie and Bartoy emphasise 'the dialectical relationship between the individual and society' (2000: 755). The consequence of this has been that 'individual' and 'society' have become reified as distinct entities, and individuals are presented either as 'drawing on' social structure (which somehow exists in some other space to be 'drawn on'), or as having a 'relationship' *with* society, or as being contained *within* society, as one object inside another. In his study of the place of agency theory in archaeology, Matthew Johnson (1989: 189) identified this sense that social structure was being presented as something extrinsic to the person, but refrained from attempting to overcome the difficulty.

Arguably, Hodder's preoccupation with agency and indeterminacy suggests a concern with freedom of choice in human affairs, and the threat to human dignity and value that ecological functionalism posed in its denial of this freedom. In this sense the archaeological use of 'practice' or 'agency theory' has always been at something of a tangent to their role in sociology and anthropology, which was perhaps more concerned with overcoming the ahistorical character of structuralism and functionalism. Hodder's more recent work has gone on to imply that the human individual can be associated with the individual event (or at least the short term) and the small scale (Hodder 2000: 21). While he is entirely correct in pointing to the way that successive generations of archaeologists have concentrated on 'top-down' explanations of the past that privilege population movements, climatic changes, or global shifts in relations of production, it is questionable whether setting up an opposition between individual/agency/event/small-scale and society/structure/process/large-scale is entirely helpful. In each case the construction of absolute, opposed categories suggests distinct objects that interact in some fashion, thereby reiterating some of the problems of systems theory and functionalism.

The growing stress on freely willed action as the prerogative of an agent whose motivations cannot be reduced to those of classes, groups or factions eventually led on to another development: an interest in 'accessing individuals in the past' (Meskell 1998: 363). This actually involves a significant change of emphasis, from the individual as an abstract analytical category, the social atom, to distinct personalities and their biographies. Hodder presents this as a shift of focus from the construction of social beings to 'subjectivity and self as constructed by individual agents' (2000: 25). Taking the argument a stage further, Lynn Meskell (1998: 377) suggests that the discipline's traditional concern with objectivity has resulted in a neglect of the subjective experiences and emotional lives of people in the past. Both Hodder and Meskell affirm that this interest in past experience should encompass the lived and embodied experiences of individual people, located within contingent historical contexts (Hodder 1999: 137). The kind of human being who should be the focus of a post-processual archaeology is conveniently summed up by Meskell when she states that

> I use the terms 'individual' and 'individuality' to refer to a single person as the fount of agency, consciousness, interpretation and creativity in cultural and social life, by virtue of his or her sole ownership of discrete, corporeal, sense-making apparatuses ... the skin-bound mortal human being.
>
> (1999: 9, 32)

The important points to note here are that the individual is a self-contained entity, is distinguished by its consciousness, and is a centre from which agency is emitted (see Fowler 2000: 109). I will argue that in all of these respects 'the individual' is particular to the modern Western experience.

Ethnographies of the person

One place where we might begin to address the question of the specificity of the concept of 'the individual' is in social anthropology, where the diversity of personhood has been explored in recent years. Put simply, the important finding has been that many people in the world today do not understand themselves as individuals in the Western sense, and do not act in ways commensurate with 'individuality'. Meskell produces a series of arguments for being wary of the accounts of ethnographers:

> Anthropologists have often made ethnocentric claims that 'primitives' have no real concept of the individual separate from their social roles and no morally universal idea of the person . . . in our unconscious ethnocentrism, we accord the possibilities of self-awareness or detachment to ourselves, but seldom to others.
>
> (Meskell 1999: 10, 20)

She goes on to claim that opinion in social anthropology is split between two schools of thought: universalists who believe that there could never have been a society that lacked a concern with the human individual, and relativists 'who believe traditional societies thought of people as an undifferentiated mass' (ibid.: 11). This is a curious argument, for it seems to propose that there are no other alternatives besides being an autonomous, bounded free agent, and being part of an 'undifferentiated mass'. Moreover, it suggests that ethnographers routinely equate 'difference' with 'primitiveness', and that modern Western individuality is inherently superior to any other way of being human that we might conceive. As self-aware, detached individuals we are conscious of the infinite value of our own mode of existence, and presumably we should be magnanimous enough to recognise the universality of this individuality amongst humankind. Yet as I will hope to show, there is a strong case to be made that 'individuality' is in some senses an impoverished kind of humanity. To be fair, Meskell is prepared to accept that selfhood, and the character of the embodied individual, varies from one culture to another (Meskell 1999: 11; Knapp and Meskell 1997: 189). However, this is some way from an acknowledgement of the culturally specific character of individuality.

One of the most thoroughly articulated demonstrations of non-individual humanity is to be found in Marilyn Strathern's *The Gender of the Gift* (1988). Strathern addresses Melanesian societies from the point of view of exchange relations, and uses this framework as a means of explicating a form of human existence that is very difficult for westerners to comprehend. For many Melanesian societies goods pass from hand to hand as gifts: not exchanged for a universal equivalent (money) but given in such a way that they are never really separated from their previous owners. Exchanges are embedded in existing social relations, and serve to create new social relations. To the Western observer these exchanges might appear as isolated events, but in reality they are always implicated in broader networks of relationships and patterns of reproduction. Each exchange acknowledges old debts and creates new ones, referencing both the past and the future. In these societies, goods are not alienable, and neither is labour. The objective of economic activity is not the accumulation of wealth but the reconfiguration of social relations in a favourable manner. Thus people do not ever act in isolation: they always act in relation to others, so that another person could always be said to be the cause of an agent's act (Strathern 1988: 172). Moreover, the distinction between persons and things is not recognised (Strathern 1996: 518). An axe cannot ever be separated from its owner because it is like a part of their body. And in the same way, human beings are understood as partible, composed of body parts that have come together like an assemblage of artefacts. Hence Strathern refers to Melanesians as 'dividuals' rather than 'individuals', for the notion that a person is a sutured entity containing a distinct consciousness is simply incomprehensible in this context. These body parts are differently gendered, so that the gender of a person is understood as a performance facilitated by their bodily substance. People conceive of themselves as cross-sex, and their gendering may be transient and unstable. Just as the goods that a person holds at any given time are a function of the changing state of exchange relations, and at a more fundamental level are a reflection of the overall system of circulation of things between persons, so persons themselves are understood as manifestations of sets of relations which precede them and extend beyond them – in particular, kinship. There is no sense here of an individual self who is the initiator of actions and who creates relationships with others at will, sitting at the centre of their own world (Strathern 1988: 269).

In the modern West, human beings are what Strathern calls 'possessive individuals', the proprietors of their own goods and their own selves. So both persons and objects are alienated and thing-like. In Melanesia this is not the case, and relationships are more like entities since they are the objective of social conduct. It is because both things and persons are embedded in relationships, and can only be recognised as facets of relationships, that no conceptual polarity can be established between them. Indeed, persons are understood as hybrids or amalgams, constituted by relationships and substances and not separable from either. As Strathern (1996) puts it, the problem of living in such a 'relational world' is not one of maintaining relationships over time but of limiting them. This is clearly the case in Nancy Munn's study of funerary rituals in Gawa, where the objective of mortuary practice is to generate a forgetting of the network of connections that is condensed within the person of the deceased (Munn 1986: 164).

Commenting on Strathern's research, Edward LiPuma points out that the 'dividual' personhood of Melanesians is not simply difficult for westerners to understand, it is also incompatible with the nation-state, liberal democracy, civil rights and electoral politics, all features of modernity that are increasingly encroaching on Papua New Guinea (LiPuma 1998: 53). As a result, globalisation is bound to have a serious impact on the Melanesian sense of selfhood, given that the desires excited by modernity are ones that are specific to individuality. However, LiPuma goes on to suggest that the distinction between individual and dividual may be too categorical, and that aspects of both may be present (in differing degrees) in all societies (ibid.: 56). This seems to me to be overly schematic, and to neglect the possibility that not all human beings can be placed on a continuum between 'individual' and 'dividual', as well as neglecting the specificity of the modern West. Nonetheless, LiPuma has a very important point to make: it is vital that we should not take the Western notion of absolute individuality at face value and merely oppose any other kind of personhood to it as an exotic Other. On the contrary, I will hope to show that 'the individual' is actually an ideal image, a cultural fiction of modernity, which may dominate our conception of how we are but which is never actually lived up to.

Quite how diverse the experience of being human can be is eloquently demonstrated by Cecilia Busby's study of personhood in south India, which she explicitly contrasts with Strathern's work in Melanesia. South Indian people do not understand themselves to be partible, but they are equally not individuals in the modern Western sense (Busby 1997: 269). Indian bodies may be integral wholes, but their boundaries are permeable, and substances and energies flow through and between them. This is most evident in the relationship between marriage partners, who are conceived as a single body. There is a continual exchange of substances between husband and wife, in the forms of sexual intercourse and the serving and eating of food. As Busby puts it, south Indian people are most clearly gendered in their cross-sex relations, for men need women in order to be men, and women need men in order to be women. Their bodies might be sexually dimorphic, but this is simply a manifestation or symptom of the presence of gendered substances (milk and semen) flowing within and between bodies (ibid.: 270).

Modernity and 'the individual'

These ethnographic examples demonstrate that all human beings do not conceive of themselves as autonomous intelligences enclosed in bounded bodies. Consequentially, it is an unwarranted assumption that the past people whom we study in archaeology were 'individuals' in any sense that we would recognise. Surely the forms of personhood that existed in the past should be something that we seek to investigate rather than take for granted. There is no reason to assume that the kinds of humanity that existed in the prehistoric world were directly comparable with those in the contemporary West (or Melanesia, or India). However, I wish to argue that individuality is a way of being a person that has emerged as part of the development of modernity, as it has been discussed elsewhere in this book. It is a form of human existence which is in some senses aberrant or even pathological when looked at critically. In order to delegitimise and denaturalise individuality as a universal form of personhood, it is important to consider its historical emergence within the modern world. Meskell (1999: 15) rejects the attempt to present a history of the modern individual on the grounds that it represents an 'evolutionary paradigm' that simply reflects the West's narratives of identity, beginning with the Greeks and excluding non-Western peoples as 'Other' or exotic. However, I suggest that it is essential to recognise the particularity of the Western experience if we are to relativise our own mode of existence. This need not involve anything remotely similar to Victorian evolutionary schemes that presented the white male European individual as the pinnacle of creation. On the contrary, the historical descent of individuality is better conceived as a genealogy or pathology, which directs us to the heart of the question of how Europeans and North Americans have been able to construct other peoples as 'different' from themselves. To trace such a genealogy back to the Greeks is not to reiterate a triumphalist 'story of civilisation' but to identify a series of fateful turns that contributed to a contemporary predicament.

One good reason to begin with the ancient Greeks is because some aspects of the Greek understanding of the person are so distinct from our own. As Charles Taylor has argued, one of the critical aspects of this difference lies in the way that the source of human dignity and virtue was to be found not deep within the self but in an encompassing cosmological order. Mortal humans were not thought of as containing an inward sphere of thought and reflection, and indeed the Homeric texts can be read as relating to a 'mind' and a 'body' that are fragmented and dispersed rather than localised around a centre (Taylor 1989: 118). In arguing that ancient Egyptians possessed an individuality comparable with our own, Meskell is anxious to demonstrate that many of the cultural traits associated with modern personal identity (diaries, portraits, biographies) actually existed in the ancient world: 'all such discourses were present in antiquity and . . . only cultural chauvinism stands in the way of our recognising this' (Meskell 1999: 13). However, it is arguable whether the significance of these media was really the same in the ancient world as it is today. For the Greeks at least, meaning was found in the *telos* and the world at large rather than the inner self. Thus Plato was much concerned with reason, but rather than identifying rationality with the operation of the mind (as Descartes would later do) he was concerned with the rational order of the universe. According to this scheme of things, living the good life was a matter of orderliness and restraint, in which one accommodated oneself to the cosmic order (Taylor 1989: 20).

It is in similar terms to these that Foucault (1987, 1988a) has discussed the role of sexuality and the 'care of the self' in the classical world. Thus for the ancient Greeks, sexual conduct was an art of the erotic rather than a matter of deeply hidden desires. Sexual impulses did not need to be monitored and scrutinised as there was no obscure wellspring of inchoate desire within the person (Poster 1986: 211). Likewise, the Roman preoccupation with the 'government of the self' was not concerned with disciplining a wayward unconscious. On the contrary, this was more an aesthetic practice by which the person constituted her- or himself within the framework of accepted conduct (Bernauer 1988: 62). It is in this context that the writing of personal documents such as journals and notebooks should be evaluated. In the modern West the diary is the epitome of individualised writing: a private record of reflection on one's 'innermost thoughts' and emotions, or on the condition of one's soul. By contrast, personal writing in the ancient would was part of an array of techniques that contributed to the cultivation of a self of a socially presentable kind. This might include notes and reflections on things read, overheard or brought up in conversation. But there is no attempt to dissect or uncover the true nature of a hidden self or soul. As Foucault puts it, 'we are still very far from what would be a hermeneutic of the subject' (1997: 102). This lack of the notion of a deep truth about the self has often proved perplexing to a modern sensibility, and Burckhardt ([1860] 1995: 113) points out that as early as the Renaissance there was a fashion for rewriting the classical past in such a way as to attribute the features of modern personality to the 'great men of antiquity'.

While ancient philosophy often asserted the idea that there were obscure and profound aspects of the universe that needed to be uncovered, it generally did not locate these inside the person. In this respect the widespread adoption of Christianity in Europe brought about a critical change. According to Christian doctrine, mortals were constantly subject to temptation. The desires and lusts of the flesh were for ever threatening, and this meant that instead of something to be worked on and perfected the self needed to be examined and (to some extent) renounced (Foucault 1988b: 49). The self became less of an aesthetic creation and more of a burden. While the Greeks had believed that it was possible to stray from the path of reasonableness and self-restraint, Christianity introduced an opposition between good and evil, and emphasised the need to apply the will in order to achieve goodness. Moreover, attentiveness towards the self now took a form that was interpretive, seeking to uncover deep truths and to decipher them (Bernauer 1988: 52). Moreover, through the institution of the confessional, Christianity encouraged the objectification and verbalisation of transgression and desire. What had been found hidden inside the person had to be brought out into the light and made explicit. This sense of a division between inside and outside is entirely new, and is notable for the connection now established between sexuality and the interior. As a number of authors have pointed out, human 'interiority' is a necessary precondition for the emergence of some of the characteristic discourses of modernity, most notably Freudian psychoanalysis (Hutton 1988: 131).

Christian interiority was most explicitly theorised by St Augustine. Augustine maintained that we live in a world of physicality and transience, yet our souls share with God the qualities of being immaterial, transcendental and eternal (Taylor 1989: 127). Human beings therefore have a dual existence: the 'outer man' has a body that is very like that of an animal, but the 'inner man' is the soul, which can be approached through introspection. By turning inward we confront our sinfulness, but in the process we become aware of our own thoughts and perceptions. Hence we confront ourselves, we become aware of ourselves in a more acute way: a 'radical reflexivity' (ibid.: 130). For Augustine the lesson of the inward turn is that as we become conscious of our own consciousness, and apprehend our own eternal soul, we inevitably gain a recognition of our own dependence upon a supreme being beyond ourselves. By turning inwards we eventually reach God (ibid.: 134). However, in historical terms the significant element of Augustine's argument is that truth is now located inside the self, and that by meditating on our own hidden depths we can achieve a deeper level of understanding. Furthermore, this act of knowing is both willed and intensely personal: we are not crafting a self to present in public, but struggling to purify our soul and achieve a relationship with God.

Augustinian interiority and the Christian focus on the willed renunciation of sin together contributed to the identification of human beings as moral agents. This was elaborated at the start of the modern epoch by two opposed movements: the Renaissance and the Protestant Reformation. Renaissance humanism, as we have seen, was built around free will and reason. Erasmus, for example, argued that God endowed human beings with free will so that they should have moral responsibility (Carroll 1993: 49). In contrast, Luther stressed guilt and faith: it was for God to decide who will be saved, not humans. All that one can do is to put absolute faith in God and live a blameless and industrious life. Nonetheless, Protestantism also rejected the role of the clergy as an intermediary between the lay person and God. The total guilt of humanity also implied total personal responsibility (Lukes 1973: 53). So although Luther and Erasmus were ostensibly on different sides of a fierce doctrinal argument, they were both effectively present at the inception of the modern individual as a morally responsible subject. Where they would have differed is over the humanist interest in the diversity of human character. Medieval Christianity had maintained that there was only a single path to salvation, so that any deviation in personal conduct was not so much intriguing as reprehensible. But with the Renaissance another aspect of 'individuality' began to be celebrated: the particularity and distinctiveness of personal identity. In time, what was most individual and creative about a person would come to be identified with an inner essence. Now, it has often been argued that the novel is the diagnostic literary form of modernity (Kristeva 1984). But it is difficult to imagine that the tradition of novel-writing would have developed as it has if the unique motivations, aspirations, concerns and sense of selfhood of the person had not come to be localised in an 'inner world' (Toulmin 1990: 27). Still less could the 'stream of consciousness' writing of James Joyce, Virginia Woolf and others, which represents the hallmark of literary modernism, have emerged in any other historical and cultural context.

Philosophical humanism

The emergence of the modern individual was deeply connected with the growth of philosophical humanism. Being an individual suggests that one is entirely distinct and separate from each other individual. But at the same time it requires that everyone is different *in the same way*. Individuals are individual to the same degree as each other. Difference is therefore built upon sameness, and the distinctiveness of the characteristics of the individual rests on their universality. Humanism is, simply, the belief that certain characteristics of humankind are invariant and transcendental, are broadly already established, and can be used as a basis for our discussion of human beings (Heidegger 1993b: 225). Humanism is therefore metaphysical, making a series of debates of the greatest difficulty appear to be straightforward and settled. Human beings are understood in a particular way, but only because they are addressed from the perspective of modernity, and this perspective is itself occluded. To be more specific, the modern conception of humanity is as the 'rational animal', to use a phrase coined by Aristotle. This view is based upon the supposition that the world is composed of free-standing, isolated entities, or things. Some of these things are animate, and some of these animate creatures are human beings. So we are objects or animals alongside others in the world, and yet we understand ourselves to be in some important sense different. This difference is conceived as a supplement, something added 'on top' of our animal-like physicality. Thus Locke speaks of the difference between 'Man', a particular kind of body, and 'the person', who is distinguished by their individual consciousness (Lowe 1995: 106). So the supplement that makes a beast into a human is the mind or the soul or the consciousness (Glendinning 1998: 45; Heidegger 1993b: 226). As we will see below (pp. 171–6), the mind/soul is classically understood as being immaterial or 'otherworldly', and although it is added to the body it also has a kind of conceptual priority over it. That is to say, the individuality of the person is associated with their immaterial essence, and this essence is considered capable of existing prior to and outside of their fleshly embodiment (Falzon 1998: 26).

While humanism in some form or other had been in existence since classical times, it came to dominate Western thought with the coming of modernity. This was largely because of the more fundamental place that humanity had come to hold in the prevailing model of the universe. Rather than being one kind of creature amongst others occupying the world, humans were increasingly the foundation upon which the order of the world was based. As we have already argued, the modern era saw the demise of a teleological cosmology held together by an objective and rational order. In its place came the belief that order had to be created by the human mind (Foucault 1970: 313). Thus for nominalists like Hobbes and Locke the world is only composed of particular things, which we group together and give structure to by giving them names (Morris 1991: 35). It follows from this that humankind, as the bringers of orderliness into the world, occupy a central position in creation. The world is laid out before them, so that it becomes what Heidegger refers to as a 'world-picture'. If the world is at humanity's disposal, and has become an object, then people have become 'subjects' in a new and important way (Heidegger 1977: 134; Ricoeur 1974: 229). Tellingly, the modern philosophical use of the term 'subject' relates not just to 'that which lies under' the ruler of a state but also to a foundation on which other things can be built (Critchley 1999: 51). Once humanity had taken on this focal position in relation to knowledge and order, the 'Archimedean point' of the modern world-view, humanness inevitably had to be seen as invariant. Humanism simultaneously insisted on the fixity of 'human nature' and created the imperative for its investigation, so that humans became at once the object as well as the subject of knowledge.

As we have argued in Chapter 3, it was Descartes who most explicitly defined the foundational character of the human subject. Like Augustine, Descartes sought truth in inward reflection, but found it in the certainty of his own consciousness rather than the certainty of God. Importantly, Descartes argued that the growth of knowledge required that the individual should not simply be endowed with reason but should use it through free will. Our reason is constrained by prejudice and oppression, and it requires an effort of will to liberate it through systematically doubting all received notions (Schouls 1989: 39). Again, this view echoes Augustine's emphasis on the struggle required to approach the divine. Free will and autonomy would become one of the central themes of modern philosophy. Locke, for instance, distinguished between the 'simple' ideas that the mind thinks without effort, and the complex ideas that are formed through its active engagement (Morris 1991: 33). Spinoza went further and linked the active exercise of thought with human freedom (Lukes 1973: 54). Here freedom is concerned with the search for truth, but also with the ability to make choices, and it would be freedom of choice that came to be identified with the autonomy of the individual. Eventually, autonomy and choice would take on an ethical implication, rather than simply an epistemological one. By the eighteenth century, both Rousseau and Adam Smith would come to argue that the mutual dependence of human beings could have a degrading effect (Berry 1989: 115). Smith, indeed, developed an evolutionary account of the rise of 'commercial society' in which the reciprocal independence of individuals promoted emotional restraint and mutual respect. While human beings had originally been free, the development of the tribe had suppressed autonomy, as only dominant persons had full self-command and kin relationships encouraged familiarity and disrespect. Commerce, however, drew on people's natural proclivity to barter and exchange to increase the wealth and well-being of all. Provided that individuals were not interfered with by political forces, commercial society would combine personal autonomy with justice and the rule of law (ibid.: 119). By creating a society of strangers, whose only relationship with each other was an economic one, Smith believed that capitalism would lay the foundations for order and reciprocal deference.

From Descartes onward, the 'problem' of knowledge was seen as the relationship between the subject and the object: the human being and the material thing that they apprehend. Both of these entities had a physical existence in the world, and yet one was capable of perceiving the other. It is the unequal relationship between subject and object that necessitates the humanist logic of supplementarity discussed above, and which led Descartes to institute a radical separation between mind and body. If the body is simply a biological machine it cannot think, and the thing that is doing the thinking must transcend the body. Yet our experience of the world is generated through the body's sensory apparatus, so the mind must exist outside of the physical world, and it must be fully formed before it gains any worldly experience (Olafson 1995: 7). What this means is that sensory impressions accumulated in the physical world must transfer themselves into the separate space of the mind. By implication, all of our experiences are transformed into representations in order to render them comprehensible (ibid.: 30). If sense data are collected, comprehended and 'worked on' within the mind, then it follows that ideas have come to be understood as the *contents* of the mind (Taylor 1989: 145). This is clearly a major change from the Platonic conception of ideas as components of an eternal cosmic order, but it also relegates thinking to the status of an 'otherworldly' pursuit rather than any kind of engagement (Heidegger 1993b: 217).

Descartes presents the mind and the body as both distinct and occupying separate locations, although they are nonetheless 'joined'. The individual identity of the person is encapsulated in the mind rather than the body, and indeed the mind could exist without a body. Yet as we have seen, the 'whole assembly of bodily organs' is the only means by which the mind can gain access to material things (Cottingham 1992: 236). So while the mind could exist and be conscious in abstraction it could not acquire information about the world. A mind without a body would therefore have a consciousness that only contained the innate ideas (Morris 1991: 12). Rejecting Descartes' rationalism, Locke nonetheless agreed with his characterisation of the mind or the soul as a thing without physical extension, a point of consciousness. Locke also agreed that the mind could be separated from the body, and toyed with the notion that the minds of two persons could be 'swapped' between bodies (Lowe 1995: 106). Where they differed was over the question of whether the bodiless mind would have any innate content. This degree of convergence between Descartes and Locke highlights one of the dominant themes of modern thought: it is the mind, not the body, that is the essence of humankind. What distinguishes a human being is rationality, consciousness, morality, and being a subject of perception and action (Cottingham 1992: 244). The body is simply a container, or an executive apparatus, for the mind.

Two immediate sets of difficulties have been identified with this prioritisation of the mind over the body. First, it suggests that people have an 'inner life' of thought and reflection, and that in a sense all of the significant events (or at least the comprehension of those events) take place in a space that is not accessible to others. This gives rise to the philosophical debate over 'the question of other minds'. I know that I am thinking, and I can experience my own thoughts and emotions. But when I observe another person, all that I can see is their physical *behaviour*. How am I to know that there is another mind in there somewhere, and that the actions that I can observe have been caused by a consciousness, as mine have? How am I to know that I am not surrounded by biological robots, whose mode of existence is entirely different from my own? As Glendinning (1998: 28) argues, this line of thought can cause us to become sceptical about other humans, and solipsistic. The mind/body dichotomy leads to ethical difficulties, which he holds can only be overcome by recognising other persons in their actions as well as their thoughts. Second, both Descartes and Locke neglect the question of the gender or sex of the mind. Implicitly, they suggest that the mind is neutrally gendered, and thus that only the body has a sex. However, Descartes is specific that the passions of the body afflict the mind, and cause lapses in reason. On this basis, the gender-order of modernity has built a series of connections between rationality, the mind and masculinity, as opposed to irrational, emotional, corporeal femininity (Butler 1990: 12; Gatens 1996: 50).

While Descartes is unspecific about where the mind or soul is to be located – and given that it has no physical location the logic is that it is nowhere at all – his pursuit of introspection in search of truth adds to the Western concern with inwardness. The idea that a more profound level of understanding is to be achieved by going beneath the surface of the self has become pervasive in the modern West, while we conventionally speak of our thoughts and emotions as being 'within' us (Taylor 1989: 111). Furthermore, a growing aspect of individualism has been an imperative for people to seek 'meaning' in their own lives, on a personal basis. If the order of the universe is no longer to be found in an eternal cosmology, but is a product of our own ordering capacities, then we often feel that we can give our existence a structure by searching out and reconfiguring something inside of ourselves. This strand of thought is particularly associated with Michel de

Montaigne, whose essays established a form of personal reflection which sought to identify the essential truth about a particular person, rather than individuals in general (ibid.: 181). Yet the creation of a human interior concerned with personal identity, meaning and truth also coincided with the creation of the body interior: the notion that one could 'open up' the body surgically and identify its functioning and pathologies (Foucault 1973: 124). The result is that human beings have two 'insides', a physical and a mental one, and the body comes to mediate between an inner and an outer life in two senses (Olafson 1995: 23) (see Chapter 7 for further discussion).

According to Descartes, the mind directs the body, and orders the outside world. The mind is singular and autonomous, and is the source of agency. Just as the body is simply a biological mechanism, so the physical universe is a set of objects that obey mechanical laws, containing no inherent meaning. In either case, it is the rational application of free will that humans must use to prevail over the physical realm. We can overcome the passions of the body, and direct them to their proper functions, and we can gain instrumental control over nature (Taylor 1989: 149). Taylor points out that the implication of all this is that 'the good' can no longer be identified with the cosmic order, the *telos*. Instead, it is human nature and human reason that must serve as the basis for morality (ibid.: 144). Moreover, if the creation of order in the physical world is to be attributed to the autonomous exercise of will, then a post-Cartesian ethics would have to be concerned with the rational conduct of individuals and their dignity as free agents. This new ethics involved not only laws to guide the moral conduct of others but a new kind of self-responsibility that secularised the Christian monitoring of the inner self. If the mind could order the world, then the will could also be turned to the refashioning or rehabilitation of the self. Self-discipline involved working on one's own desires and habits in an instrumental fashion, so that the self became a kind of object of analysis (ibid.: 159–60).

The growing distinction between interior and exterior would also have its consequences for the understanding of the social world. We have seen that both Descartes and Locke considered the mind to be 'detachable' from the body, and to have a conceptual priority over it. This can be taken as evidence that the individual consciousness also exists prior to the social, a key aspect of the theories of social contract discussed in Chapter 5. So an individual can exist in the first instance as a biological being, who later enters into relations with others and acquires a common culture. If this culture is shared and 'public', then it is to be distinguished from another sphere, which is pre-social and 'private'. As Strathern (1988: 94) has argued, the tendency has been for this new dichotomy to be explicitly gendered, so that the public world is constructed by male reason while the private realm is concerned with biological reproduction and is female. If the public domain is the space of politics, then the private is a world that should be immune from political interference (Lukes 1973: 62).

The individual and the rational justification of morality

We have seen that there are deep connections between the form that personhood takes in a given social setting and the character of morality. By the seventeenth century the notion of the 'individual' was well established in Europe and its colonies, but the full ethical implications of individuality would only be worked out during the Enlightenment. Indeed, one could say that the central project of the Enlightenment was to construct a workable morality based around a form of reason that had been shorn of faith and tradition (MacIntyre 1981: 51). For such a morality to be workable, human nature must be understood as fixed, for the rules that it puts in place must be equally applicable to all persons. As we have seen in Chapter 2, the most thoroughly elaborated discussion of morality inspired by the Enlightenment was that proposed by Immanuel Kant. Kant, of course, had a conception of the human subject that was considerably more sophisticated than that of Descartes. Yet he echoed Descartes in arguing that the world is only ordered because the human mind had ordering capabilities. Rather than innate ideas, Kant suggested that the mind has categories of understanding, and these allow us to organise our sense impressions, thus rendering our perceptions of the world comprehensible. This means that we only ever apprehend the world from our own standpoint, and in a form that has already been ordered by our mental faculties (Falzon 1998: 22). This may not be the same as knowing things as they 'really are', but such a perspective is inaccessible: we cannot know the thing in itself. Kant rejected the Cartesian notion of a soul that has no physical extension, but nonetheless found himself arguing for a dualistic conception of the subject. This was because he accepted that all material things obeyed the laws of nature, and were subject to causality, yet he wanted to see human beings exempted from such laws. In turn, this arose from Kant's identification of free will as being essential to morality: human actions could not simply be determined like physical or chemical processes. He therefore resorted to the humanist image of a person with a dual nature. On the one hand there was the phenomenal or empirical self which operated according to physical laws. But on the other there was the 'noumenal self', which had the character of the 'thing in itself', which is to say that it could not be apprehended by the human sense-making apparatus. The noumenal self was the moral agent, which exercised free will (Morris 1991: 56).

Kant's moral theory is one that concerns the relations between reciprocally independent individuals, and which seeks to demonstrate that it is rational for them to treat each other with respect and mutual empathy. He professes that this morality is not actually based on human nature, but the rationality that is his foundation is presented as a human universal. All humans are endowed with free will, and this means both that they are in a position to obey the moral law and that they are worthy of its protection.

All human beings should be treated as ends rather than means, and this requires that the will of no person should be subjugated to the will of any other (MacIntyre 1981: 46). It is a duty for people to seek their own perfection, but it is also a duty to strive for the happiness of others, and to show active sympathy for their sufferings even if we cannot actually share them (Kant [1797] 1998: 457). People must be free to be themselves and to exercise their wills, but they must also follow universal maxims that are a genuine expression of the moral law. Acting morally is rational, but it is not automatically determined, and one must willingly choose to follow the ethical path.

Kant's problem, and that of the Enlightenment in general, was that of securing an ethical framework for autonomous individuals who inhabit a world of isolated objects, rather than a relational cosmos. In Chapter 4 we discussed the tension between Enlightenment metanarratives and the classical teleological view of history. The latter had posited that while humanity was flawed, it was moving towards an ideal state that would eventually be achieved. Rejecting the notion of a teleological order, the Enlightenment nonetheless followed Locke in arguing that the application of reason could lead to human perfection. Yet the character of this perfection was indeterminate. Alasdair MacIntyre has pointed out the discrepancy between the acknowledged failings of 'human nature as it is' and moral rules which sought to institute a perfection that was difficult to envisage (MacIntyre 1981: 55). At the same time, universal moral laws were increasingly difficult to reconcile with the identification of the individual as both a sovereign moral agent *and* a unique creative intelligence. That is, individuals were at once endowed with ethical equivalence and unrepeatable difference. The Enlightenment insisted that individuals were now free from inherited moral structures and religious prohibitions, but it had to identify a universal foundation for ethical conduct. That the free agent will act rationally is effectively a metaphysical proposition, and the danger is that the removal of tradition and prejudice will simply produce amoral perspectives like those of the Marquis de Sade, or Aleister Crowley, who held that 'do what thou wilt shall be the whole of the law'.

The individual, society and natural rights

The ways in which Europeans had come to understand themselves as persons by the seventeenth and eighteenth centuries, as articulated by Descartes, Locke and Kant, do much to clarify the theories of social contract that we discussed in Chapter 5. It is the notion of the individual as a free rational agent whose essence lies in their consciousness that underpins atomism, the belief that societies are constituted by individuals for their own benefit (Taylor 1985: 187). If the conscious mind can exist independently from and prior to the body, so the individual essence of the person precedes their introduction into social relationships with others. While few would now argue that the mind is an immaterial essence, much of archaeology is still dominated by the view that the mind is a distinct entity, distinguishable from the outside world (Taylor 1993: 320). Much of the evolutionary and ecological archaeology of early humans, for instance, relies on a picture of agents who input sense data from their environment and then 'process' them cognitively (e.g. Donald 1998: 10). This is in part a consequence of the self-fulfilling prophecy of artificial intelligence studies: having created a simulacrum of what 'the mind' does it is possible to argue that human beings operate in much the same way as computers. Necessarily, this requires that all humans are 'hard-wired' to negotiate their environments in a particular way, and this capacity is presumed to precede society and culture, even if it is installed by the evolutionary process (these issues are discussed in more detail in Chapter 8). Where an absolute priority is afforded to the individual, society almost inevitably comes to be seen as contract-like. In this vein, Meskell claims that 'many social anthropologists now propose that it is in individuality that the roots of the social and cultural lie' (1999: 9). The individual is present before the social.

If the individual is 'detachable' from society, and has a range of characteristics that are not conferred on him or her by society, then it is often claimed that they must have a series of natural 'rights' that are inalienable and inviolable. Natural rights are generally considered to be universal, vested in a person simply because they are human. Moreover, they are very much a feature of modern thought: MacIntyre claims that the concept of a 'right' did not exist before AD 1400 (1981: 69). These rights are something like the property of the individual, and are another indication that the worth and dignity of the person are to be associated with their autonomy and uniqueness, rather than their place in the cosmic order (Taylor 1989: 11–12). Just as the individual's autonomous existence precedes that of society, so the rights of the individual have precedence over the demands of society. This means that issues of social obligation and community belonging tend to be devalued, and indeed come to be associated with tradition and prejudice as undesirable. The ethical value of rights is considered to lie in curtailing the power of a despot, since one can appeal and protest against the infringement of one's natural rights.

Modern ethical systems therefore depend upon the universality of human reason, or the universality of human rights, both of which are the prerogative of the individual rather than society. The drawback of such systems is that while liberal humanism enjoins us to show respect, sympathy and empathy for others, the same intellectual resources can be used to support an agenda that combines freedom of choice and the absolute value of rights in support of *laissez-faire* capitalism. That is to say, the neo-liberalism of the New Right. In his book *Anarchy, State and Utopia* (1974), Robert Nozick proposes that:

individuals have rights, and there are things no person or group may do to them (without violating their rights). So strong and far-reaching are these rights that they raise the question of what, if anything, the state and its officials may do.

(Nozick 1974: ix)

Nozick proposes a version of the social contract in which individuals band together in a mutual protection organisation, in order to support each other when their rights are in danger of infringement. He describes this as an 'ultraminimal state', which has no powers of redistribution; it maintains a monopoly of force, but it provides protection and enforcement services only for those who 'buy in' to the system. According to Nozick, any more extensive state than this necessarily violates people's rights (ibid.: 26). So the danger is that once we prioritise the individual over society the questions of how we provide for the welfare of all, and of what happens when one individual wants to use their freedom to exploit another, become secondary and, in a sense, negotiable. Worse still, the Kantian argument that we are all the same in our difference, and that we should all therefore be afforded the same rights, is hostage to being undermined by the counter-argument that some persons are *not fully human*, and thus exempt from the moral law. This is precisely the logic that allowed the Nuremberg Laws to discriminate against the Jews in Nazi Germany, within the framework of legality. I would suggest that an ethics based around responsibility to the other in their difference rather than the universal rights of the individual will be more robust in this respect (e.g. Levinas 1998). We will return to these issues in the concluding chapter.

The phantom individual

The modern individual combines uniqueness with universality. Everyone is different, but they are equipped to be different with a universal set of attributes. Modern discourses of public life – politics and morality – emphasise the abstract, universal individual. Indeed, Kant argued that acting as a moral agent required one to put aside the particular, the bodily and the passions (Falzon 1998: 28). Works of modern political theory, like Hobbes's *Leviathan* ([1651] 1996), have tended to pronounce on how society should be ordered according to the needs and capabilities of abstract agents. So the idea of the social contract implies that individuals come together on a basis of reciprocal independence *and* relative equality to found their community. All individuals are knowledgeable political agents, and consequentially are equally able to take part in public life and give their consent to whatever form of government is instituted. This picture of individuals consenting to the existence of the state, but resisting its incursions into economic and domestic matters, is the basis of classical liberalism. In more recent forms of liberalism the consent of the population to the continued existence of the institutions of government is regularly renewed through voting in elections (Lukes 1973: 79). Of course, such a conception of political life is entirely at odds with arguments which propose that individuals are differentially equipped to understand the social circumstances in which they find themselves, such as the Marxist theory of ideology.

Now, I have been arguing that individuality dominates the treatment of human beings in the modern philosophical tradition, and also characterises the way in which contemporary Europeans and North Americans understand themselves most of the time. It is 'common sense' to think of oneself as an individual, and I do not exclude myself from this generalisation. It requires a counter-intuitive effort to think anything else. This does not mean that in the period since the fifteenth century AD or so the inhabitants of the West have actually *become individuals*. The point is more subtle than that: modern westerners have become a form of humanity that recognises itself as an individual. For reasons that we will discuss in more detail below (see pp. 140–3), no one is ever actually an individual. No one really has a conscious identity that precedes their physical embodiment, their placement in a world, their existence alongside other human beings, and their acquisition of a language and concepts to think with. So, while there are serious problems with the concept of ideology (see Foucault 1980, for example), it might be helpful to describe individuality as 'ideological' in one of the senses suggested by Althusser. That is, understanding oneself as an individual involves a real, lived relationship with conditions of existence that are imagined (Althusser 1971: 152). 'The individual' is a cultural fiction of modernity, but one that nonetheless provides the ground for our day-to-day existence.

The individual is a spectral identity that we identify with, and achieve greater or lesser success in approximating, even if we can never actually *be* 'the individual'. The individual is what we aspire to be. In practice, this means that some persons are better able to pass as individuals than others. Being an autonomous political subject and bearer of reason, the individual is implicitly gendered male: it is harder for a woman to recognise herself in the public individual (Caverero 1996: 192). It follows from this that liberal political institutions and modern legal codes are so constructed as to assume a male subject (Gatens 1992: 124; Hekman 1990: 64). Thus, the image of the universal individual serves as a principal of exclusion, and post-Enlightenment Western society has been able to profess its egalitarianism while limiting the opportunities of women, blacks, homosexuals, Jews and the disabled to participate in public life. Perhaps the most startling example of this was the United States Declaration of Independence (dating to 4 July 1776), which initiated a nation that has to a great extent embodied the ideals of the Enlightenment. It states: 'we hold these truths to be self-evident, that all men are created equal, that they are endowed by their

Creator with certain unalienable Rights, that among these are Life, Liberty and the pursuit of Happiness'. This document was written by a group of people who were all male, all white, and the majority of whom were the owners of slaves.

More recent political thought has provided further reasons for being critical of the idea of the individual as a universal political subject. We have seen that Locke offered an account of a 'punctual' self, an individual who occupied a single point in space. In the same way, we often imagine that individuals have a single point of view, and that their ideas, values and opinions are abstract and invariant. In reality, people take a stand on issues and on themselves in different ways dependent on context. Different aspects of their personalities are elicited in their interactions with different people. When we talk with someone about an acquaintance, we can sometimes feel that we are talking about a different person. And so we are, for who we are is contingent and contextual, rather than held stable by an inner essence of irreducible individuality. Chantal Mouffe (1993: 12; 1995: 33) describes this situation rather well by saying that 'we occupy multiple subject positions'. Enlightenment thought assumes that the distinctive arguments of different individuals can be brought into dialogue, and thereby resolved. But in reality the human subject is not a 'closed system of differences'. We can be self-contradictory without being duplicitous, and we cannot be reduced to a unified perspective. Our identities are multiple and precarious, and conventional liberal politics is poorly placed to cope with this (Schrift 1995: 39; A.M. Smith 1998: 88).

The individual and individualism

It is only fair to point out that archaeologists who have sought to identify 'individuals in the past' have not neglected the distinctiveness of the forms of personal identity that exist in the modern West. For the most part, these authors have drawn a distinction between 'individuals' and 'individualism' (Meskell 1999: 9–10; Tarlow 2002: 26–7; Wilkie and Bartoy 2000: 771). According to this view, the former refers to the universal condition of being a single mortal human being possessed of agency and creativity, while the latter is concerned with the more specific Western conception of the autonomous sovereign individual. I do not find this distinction satisfactory, and not simply because I would deny that the term 'individual' has a universal cross-cultural validity. For while *being an individual* (or rather, aspiring to that condition) is a mode of human existence that has prevailed in the West for the past five or six hundred years, *individualism* properly refers to a discourse that celebrates and valorises the individual, and which is much more recent in date. Individualism was largely a nineteenth-century phenomenon, and the word was first used in France in the period immediately after the Revolution of 1789 (Lukes 1973: 1–10). In the first instance the term had a pejorative implication, for it was used by right-wing critics of the Revolution who feared the social dislocation and instability that might be brought about by the adoption of the ideas of the Enlightenment. In Germany, however, the early nineteenth-century development of individualism was connected with Romanticism. The German Romantics approved of individuality, for they associated it with creativity, self-realisation and uniqueness, all of which they saw as challenging the universalising views of the Enlightenment (ibid.: 17). In this respect, German Romanticism was a precursor of the hermeneutics of Schliermacher and Dilthey, which was much concerned with the relationship between part and whole, individual and society (Gadamer 1975: 173).

In the United States individualism reached a higher degree of elaboration, and indeed became central to some visions of national identity. Thus Herbert Hoover, for instance, described the 'American system of rugged individualism' in his campaign for election as president in 1928, and distinguished it from the paternalism and state socialism of Europe (Lukes 1973: 26). Individualism was here connected with equality of opportunity, enterprise, self-reliance and ordered liberty. It was grounded in the 'frontier spirit' of those who had left Europe in search of a wilderness from which they could carve out a future untroubled by state intervention. Similar sentiments were expressed by Social Darwinists like William Graham Sumner, who declared 'that all men should be alike or equal, by any standard whatever, is contrary to all the facts of human nature and all the conditions of human life' (Sumner [1906] 1960: 53). Here the universality of individuality became less significant than uniqueness: the differences between individuals provided the basis for competition. A further development of this argument is found in Ayn Rand's linking of 'reason, individualism and capitalism' in the blueprint for a economic social order based on self-interest (Rand 1983). Individualism, then, takes as given that all persons are individuals and proceeds to argue for the greatest possible freedom for individual action. It does not simply acknowledge the existence of individuals, it identifies certain of their defining characteristics with the good.

Archaeologies of the individual

The preceding lengthy discussion of the variability of personhood and the particularity of individuality has prepared the ground for us to return to the question of an 'archaeology of the individual'. We have seen that within a particular strand of post-processual archaeology, the claim has been made that individuality is a universal feature of the human condition. It is generally argued that this individuality is an aspect of a 'core' of human essence, while the culturally relative aspects of personhood are presented as a supplement or addition which overlies this basic stratum. Thus we have the image of a person 'built in layers', as Knapp and Meskell explain:

> experiencing oneself as an individual entity is part of human nature ... layered upon this is a more culturally specific determination of what it is to be a person at a given time and place ... Overlaying this second stratum is a finer layer of interpretation, that of individually determined experience.
>
> (Knapp and Meskell 1997: 198)

If the contingent aspects of personhood are 'added' to individual human nature, the implication is that the latter is pre-social. Knapp and Meskell also appear to be claiming a similar status for the human body when they appeal to 'a new desire for groundedness, whereby we regard the body as a material, physical and biological phenomenon irreducible to immediate social processes or classifications' (ibid.: 188). So the universality of the individual and their body are vested in their primordiality, existing before culture and society come on the scene. This, of course, is an essentialist argument. Similar claims are made by Paul Treherne, in his study of the warrior identity in the European Bronze Age (1995). Treherne's is a rich and sophisticated line of reasoning, which suggests that 'warrior graves' represented more than simply a new ideology that presented personal wealth and authority as legitimate and necessary aspects of social existence. On the contrary, the identity of the warrior involved a new form of life and a new conception of personhood, focusing on 'individual and personal display' (ibid.: 107). This form of life was heavily aestheticised, so that the warrior both lived a beautiful life and died a beautiful death. Funerary rites that enhanced the warrior's beauty had a role to play in securing their personal fame, and in a sense their immortality (Figure 6.1). At the same time, creating a beautified image of the deceased had the effect of overcoming the horror and existential anxiety associated with death. Difficulties begin to emerge, though, when Treherne starts to reason that these practices were grounded in a materiality and identity of the body that escapes or precedes its cultural articulation:

> the insistence that the body and subjectivity are purely cultural-linguistic constructs ... is untenable in that it totally denies the organic existence of the body, the physicality by virtue of which it can actively resist social construction ... The body is an unfinished organism which is 'completed' by the individual within a particular socio-historical context.
>
> (Treherne 1995: 119–20)

What Treherne is arguing is that the body has a fixed and foundational character, and that all that culture and language ever do to it is to attach a series of culturally specific labels onto its surface. This is a point of view that has been heavily debated in the recent feminist literature. The central question that it raises is, simply, how could we have access to the body in

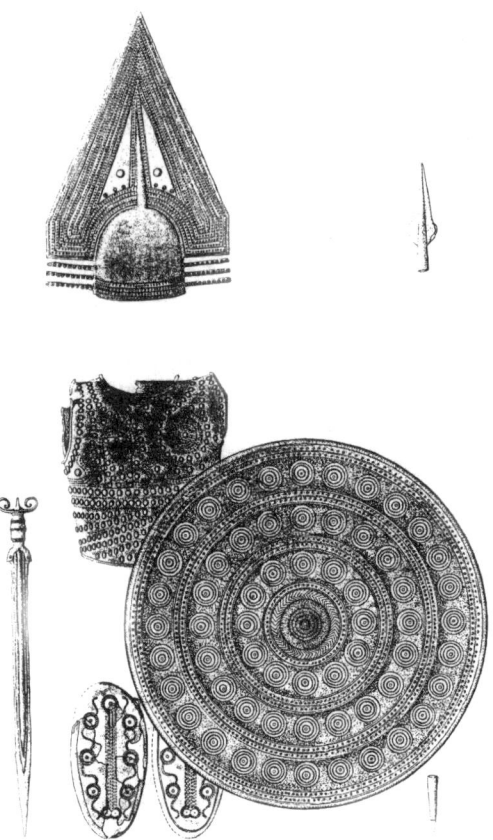

Figure 6.1 The beautiful Bronze Age warrior: Chiefly Urnfield equipment from northern Italy (from K. Kristiansen, *Europe Before History*, Cambridge University Press, 1998)

a pure, 'corporeal' state? (Shildrick 1997: 14). How could we gain an 'extra-linguistic' understanding of the body? This question is a legacy of the distinction that was made in 1960s–1970s feminist thought between 'sex' and 'gender', where the former was the biological 'truth' about bodily difference and the latter was its cultural interpretation. Only the latter was considered to vary cross-culturally. The flaw in this framework of thought is that its conception of biological sexual difference is indistinguishable from that identified by medical science. This in turn has been influential in forming the modern Western understanding of sexed bodies. As a result, the sex/gender distinction is irredeemably ethnocentric: 'sex' is the reality of the body, known to westerners, 'gender' is the exotic recasting of bodily identity by 'others'. At best, the distinction is between a 'natural' sexual difference and a 'cultural' gender that is added to it. More recent work has questioned this viewpoint by pointing out that Western medical science is only one interpretation amongst others (Butler 1990: 7). It does not give access to a pre-discursive reality, because it is itself a discourse with a history and social context of its own.

Contrary to Treherne's argument, there are other options besides asserting the existence of a directly accessible material body or seeing the body as a 'purely cultural-linguistic construct'. The world is not made of discourse, and we do not bring it into existence by talking about it. We live in a physical world, but we never access that world in its raw materiality as pure sensory inputs. On the contrary, the world *reveals* itself to us, and language and culture are instrumental in this process. We do not first see a thing in the world, and then discuss it: perception and interpretation are coextensive. Therefore, our experience of things in the world consists of understanding them 'as' something. Any notion of a pre-discursive materiality is incomprehensible, since we cannot articulate the pre-discursive other than in discursive concepts (A.M. Smith 1998: 88). This is not the same as saying that all existence is mediated through language. This would be to accept a Cartesian conception of language, in which 'facts' are transformed into words and transferred from one mind to another. Instead, what we are saying is that language, and being an embodied human being, and existing at a given time and place in a given cultural context are all aspects of the 'background' that enables material things to 'show up' to us, to register as culturally intelligible. This is the process that Judith Butler refers to as 'materialisation' (1993: 31). As she points out, language never simply refers to a materiality that is already fully seen and comprehended, it is integral to the process through which material things emerge and register as comprehensible. The body is not constructed in language, but it is revealed and articulated in a process in which language is thoroughly implicated. We can have no other access to the body because we are mortal human beings.

These points begin to reveal some of the difficulties with Treherne's point of view. If the body is an 'incomplete organism ... completed by the individual' in a particular context, where exactly does the body reside in its pristine and incomplete state? I would suggest that human beings exist in a condition that Heidegger (1962: 174) refers to as 'thrownness': they are always-already within a society of other persons, always-already understanding themselves through an inherited cultural framework. They never live as mere organisms, awaiting the stamp of culture. It is telling, too, that Treherne falls back into the modernist language of interior and exterior in order to describe human experience. The lived body, he says, is 'known from within', while he criticises my own focus on subjectification as being concerned with an 'external process' (Treherne 1995: 120). It would seem that whenever the attempt is made to insist on the primordiality of the individual this dichotomy between the transcendental yet unique self *inside* and the cultural world *outside* will recur.

The Ice Man cometh

Those archaeologists who have advocated a focus on the embodied individual have broadly been critical of attempts to investigate prehistoric landscapes and monuments through the framework of bodily experience (e.g. Barrett 1994; Richards 1993; Tilley 1994; Thomas 1993). The criticisms that these authors raise are that the experiences of walking through a landscape or entering a megalithic tomb are not addressed from the point of view of a particular individual; the lives of specific individuals are not explored, and the bodies involved are implicitly universalised (Hodder 1999: 136; Meskell 1996: 6; 2000: 16). This is not entirely accurate, for the intention of many of these studies was not to empathise with the experiences of past people, but to use one's own embodiment (real or imagined) as a medium for thinking through an unfamiliar materiality (Fowler 2000: 114). The bodies concerned, then, were not universal, so much as the modern bodies of contemporary archaeologists transposed into situations in which they could appreciate the alterity of a past material world. The implication is that while one can never enter into the mental life of a past person, one can use one's body as an analogue for a past body as a means of addressing the physical world, *because that physical world has a history* and is not homogeneous across time.

What Hodder's and Meskell's criticisms imply is that an experience is only valid if it is the experience of an individual. This is troubling, because it could easily harmonise with the late modern fixation with self and subjective experience. The attempt to identify all of the people of the past as individuals 'just like us' raises the spectre of a prehistory that has been rendered familiar and comfortable. Similarly, insisting that an experiential archaeology should be exclusively focused on the lives of particular individuals rather than the alterity of past worlds and forms of human existence suggests a reduction of history to the concerns of self and subjectivity. The early twenty-first century is a time of hyper-individualism, self-absorption and emotivism. Recent years have seen such phenomena as growing apathy towards democratic politics; the rise of 'reality' and 'confessional' television; an increasing fear of crime and investment in personal security; the incursion of the market into areas of public service and the omnipresence of the language of management and marketing; a growing preoccupation with the personal lives of celebrities (epitomised by the public outpouring of emotion following the death of Princess Diana – overwhelmingly expressed in the language of personal relationships); and the increased popularity of the 'psychobabble' literature of self-help (Figure 6.2). This suggests a world in which the embeddedness of people in community and tradition has withered away, and the possibilities for collective political action and shared experience have been undermined. In their place, we have a public culture that valorises personal gratification, intense emotional experience, insatiable material consumption, and individual economic enterprise. The misfortunes of the poor

HUMANISM AND 'THE INDIVIDUAL'

Figure 6.2 Memorial messages from the public at the Pont D'Alma following the death of Diana, Princess of Wales, 1997 (photo: Jennifer Vickers)

and the needy are put down to their personal failings or lack of motivation, rather than connected with social or economic conditions. We should be very concerned about the dangers of constructing a past that simply mirrors these preoccupations.

Archaeologies of the individual do not provide us with a theory of the subject, and assume the universality of the individual. This is ironic, given the claim that experiential archaeologies deploy a universal body. What is suggested instead is that the lives of past individuals can be addressed through a process of 'thick description'. Hodder, for example, argues that we can build a picture of individual lives by focusing on the micro scale and identifying sequences of events on archaeological sites (2000: 26). The example that he gives is that of the 'Ice Man' from the late Neolithic found preserved in the Italian/Swiss Alps (Figure 6.3). The Ice Man is presented as an example of a 'window into deep time', a fortuitous case of exceptional preservation in which the details of an individual life allow the evaluation of the consequences of long-term change. The Ice Man lived at a time of profound social and technological change: the decline of large, kin-based social units; the growing importance of male violence, hunting and warfare; the introduction of metals.

> These new developments ushered in a life of independence, harshness and individual opportunity. The Ice Man found individual

145

Figure 6.3 The 'Ice Man' in the Alps (illustration by Mike Pringle)

solutions. He found a way of carrying embers in a birch bark container. He had his own 'medicine kit' in the form of two pieces of birch fungus attached to his left wrist. He got someone to make tattoos on him to protect him or heal a strain or wound. We see in all this the intentional creation of a new world, breaking away from but dependent upon the corporate.

(Hodder 2000: 27)

But the question of what *kind* of a human being the Ice Man was is not asked. He may have died a lonely death in the mountains, but most of the features that Hodder points to speak to us of social relationships. The glowing embers in their birch bark and the 'medicine kit' are arguably evidence not of 'individual solutions' but of shared traditions of knowledge, practice, and arcane lore. That 'he got someone to make tattoos on him' tells us of a relationship with *some other person*. Was this simply an instrumental relationship? What kinds of debts and obligations would be accrued in the process of tattooing another person's body? Particularly if this act was recognised as one of healing, drawing out malign influences from the body? Hodder presents the Ice Man as a kind of Neolithic rugged individualist, but we could equally argue that his materialisation on the Alps was the outcome of a network of relationships that together constituted him as a specific kind of person, able to act and understand the world in a particular way.

This is not to say that the potential for addressing the diversity of past forms of humanity has been altogether neglected by archaeologists. For instance, Joanna Brück has suggested that in the British Middle and Late Bronze Age the life-cycles of people, houses and artefacts such as pottery vessels, quernstones and metalwork were linked within a common cosmological framework. In being cremated after death, human bodies were subject to processes of burning and crushing that were analogous to cooking, metal-smelting and pottery manufacture. Brück argues that human existence was understood as a cycle of birth, death and regeneration, mediated by transformative events shared by other aspects of the material world (2001a: 157). A human body that could be repeatedly broken down into fragments and reconstituted, and which was knitted in to the transformational cycles of the tangible world, evidently suggests a conception of personal identity that was quite remote from modern individuality. In a more explicit way, Brück (1998; 2001b: 653) has also indicated that addressing alternative conceptions of personhood might enrich our understanding of the ways in which prehistoric monuments were used and experienced. Similarly, Chris Fowler (2001; 2002) has evaluated the forms of personal identity that may have prevailed in the British neolithic. Fowler argues that the dismembering, rearticulation and partial representation of human bodies in funerary contexts on the Isle of Man indicate a set of practices that cited and reiterated forms of personhood that were not bounded and individuated. Instead, in life and death Neolithic people were immersed in a world of relations between persons, places, animals and artefacts.

Conclusion

'The individual' is an idea constructed by modern philosophical humanism. It is not a description of how we actually are, but it condenses a series of aspects of the way that westerners imagine themselves to be. We think of ourselves as unique and unrepeatable, yet possessing a series of attributes that are common to all individuals. We are at once a thing, an object amongst other objects, and an essence, a mind that is a source of volition, creativity and agency. This mind is pre-social, able to operate in abstraction from the world, and when placed in a body it extracts information from the world and re-presents it to itself. What the notion of the individual most evidently neglects is relationality. We cannot be human at all without others: we cannot articulate the world without a language, or make sense of it without a culture. Our agency is not a force that issues out of the body interior: we act in relation to others, and we act from a position that is socially constituted. Furthermore, if a morality cannot be based upon the universal attributes of the individual and their rationality, we must seek an ethics based in the relationship with the other person. This means that the alterity of the other is much more significant than the selfness of the self (Critchley 1999: 75). All of this indicates that to impose the concept of the individual on the distant past is a dangerous and potentially narcissistic exercise. A respect for the other demands that we should allow that other to be itself, rather than reflect our own image back to us. If personhood is relational, we should explore the relationships that enabled humanity to create and sustain itself in the past, and attempt to distinguish what that humanity was like, rather than presume that the transcendental individual has always stood at the centre of everything.

7

DEPTHS AND SURFACES

Introduction: archaeology as metaphor

In previous chapters I have been seeking to demonstrate that archaeology took shape within the conceptual framework of Western modernity, and that distinctively modern ways of thinking are still fundamental to the discipline and its practices. However, we should not imagine that this has been a one-way process, in which archaeological thought has simply come to embrace the main currents of modern philosophy. On the contrary, archaeology occupies a significant place in the modern imagination because it has provided a series of extremely potent metaphors that have been employed in a very diverse range of contexts. Archaeology is widely understood as being concerned with the recovery of knowledge about the past, by uncovering and revealing structures and artefacts that have been hidden for centuries. As such, it evokes notions of the repressed, the lost and the forgotten, and of the drama of discovery, which are often spatialised in terms of the relationship between depth and surface. While I have argued that the emergence of archaeology depended on ideas of historical time, nature, method and sociality that came into being from the Renaissance onwards, in this chapter I will suggest that the more specific transformation of antiquarianism into archaeology was bound up with significant changes in the character of modern thought at the end of the eighteenth century. Broadly speaking, this was the period in which a view of the world as composed of isolated entities (which were best understood through classification) began to be compromised by the notion that hidden structures underlay perceptible reality. My suggestion will be that archaeology itself has continued to embody a conflict between the search for hidden depths and the urge to classify objects and deny the existence of the insensible. Addressing these themes will require some recapitulation of ideas that have already been discussed in this book. Hopefully it will be clear that the intention is to open up some quite different implications of this material.

For as long as it has been recognised as a discipline, the word 'archaeology' has been drawn on to describe forms of analysis that address origins, hidden realities, or fragments. Interestingly, one of the earliest examples was that of Kant, in the *Critique of Judgement* ([1790] 1988), discussing the idea of an 'archaeology of nature' in which the world itself could be understood as a set of archives that could be consulted in order to understand the past (Cassirer 1951: 79). What Kant was perhaps accentuating here was the sense of archaeology as a meticulously descriptive exercise. He was seeking in particular to distinguish the empirical natural science of Buffon from the more mathematical approach of physics. This is probably the aspect of archaeology that has been least often employed metaphorically, although it is interesting that Kant's usage bears some similarity to what Michel Foucault had in mind when he wrote of *The Archaeology of Knowledge* (1972). For Foucault, 'archaeology' is a way of analysing written and spoken discourse that is to be distinguished from the history of ideas. While the latter attempts to identify the true content of texts or enunciations, archaeology concerns itself with how discourse operates as a system for creating authoritative statements. The history of ideas sets out to construct a continuous narrative of the development of thought; archaeology is interested in the specific, the particular, difference and temporal rupture. Archaeology does not try to recover whatever people were thinking when they spoke or wrote particular statements in the past, it seeks the mechanisms that allowed them to speak and be taken seriously (Foucault 1972: 138–9). Strikingly, Foucault claims that his archaeology of discourse is 'not a return to the innermost secret of the origin' (ibid.: 140). In this respect he is almost unique, for as we will see the cultural significance of archaeology in the modern West is more commonly connected with the idea of the recovery of lost truths. Perhaps because his work attempted to avoid the search for 'deep meaning' in past utterances, the development of human interiority was a persistent if not always explicit theme in his analyses of modern Western thought. This chapter will be heavily indebted to that work, while attempting to draw out of it a more coherent picture of how the notion of a human being with an 'inside' and an 'outside' came to transfigure the Western conception of knowledge.

The inner self and the depths of 'Man'

In the previous chapter we discussed the creation of the modern individual, the autonomous moral and political subject. One of the principal themes in this development was the gradual construction of a sense of human interiority. As we have seen, from the time of St Augustine the search for truth came to be associated with introspection, leading to a radical reflexivity in which the inward gaze came to focus on the experience of one's own self (Taylor 1989: 129). With the emergence of Cartesian rationalism, meaning ceased to be found in the resemblances and harmonies between things in the world, and was exclusively associated with the activities of the mind. Ideas were now identified as the contents of the mind rather than the abstract forms of worldly things, and the human subject was isolated as the giver of meaning. As the inner self came to be understood as the source of value and worth, an 'instrumental' stance in relation to the self began to develop. This involved the belief that it was possible for a person to renew or rehabilitate her- or himself by working on their own deepest desires, thoughts and feelings (Taylor 1989: 160). This kind of 'work on the self' is to be distinguished from practices of self-care and self-realisation in the ancient world, which worked on the person as an aesthetic creation rather than seeking to transfigure any hidden, inner essence (Foucault 1988a). But while the policing of the inner self became widespread in the seventeenth century, it was only at the end of the eighteenth century that this was complemented by the notion that one can act on the inner self of another to bring about change. This was the basis of the fundamental changes in penal practice that Foucault documents in *Discipline and Punish* (1977). Up to the middle of the eighteenth century the infringement of legal codes was often met with by severe physical punishment, such as torture or public execution. However, by the end of that century torture as a public spectacle had declined in the West, and a new regime of penal justice was coming into being. This regime worked through the disciplining of the incarcerated body to effect the correction of the soul. The complex machinery of enclosure, segmentation, regulated exercise, surveillance and timetabling indicates nothing so much as that the inner person had now been identified as an analytical object, to be worked upon from outside.

While the institutionalisation of the notion of the inner self has proved expedient for authority in some ways, the growing idea that human beings have an inside and an outside has also served as a means of expressing social fragmentation and dislocation. For a society of autonomous individuals has often become one of alienation and anomie. Frederic Jameson (1984: 61) presents Edvard Munch's painting *The Scream* as a paradigmatic representation of the modern condition. The inner feelings of anxiety, isolation and loneliness experienced by the individual are projected outwards in a cathartic expression. Similar themes of interiority, personal isolation and the external release of inner tensions recur in the arts of high modernity, from stream of consciousness writing to rock and roll. Very often the implication is that oppressive or dislocating external conditions are the cause of inner turmoil, which in turn has to be turned outwards as a form of therapy. As we saw in the previous chapter, this expressive or therapeutic relationship between the inner person and the outside world was promoted in the early modern period through the institution of the Catholic confessional. This was especially the case after the Council of Trent and the establishment of the Counter-Reformation. During the medieval period confession was largely focused on sins that had been committed, and, as far as sexual matters were concerned, concentrated on the detail of physical acts that had taken place. Paradoxically, after the sixteenth century these particulars were dealt with more euphemistically. Rather than carnal acts, the confessional changed its emphasis towards the inner desires. Lustful thoughts and imaginings were now to be examined and policed, with the objective of externalising them as spoken words (Foucault 1978: 19–21).

As we have seen already, these changing conceptions of the person are intimately connected with views of the physical world, and of appropriate ways to study it. If the pre-modern world was understood through the idea of a cosmic order underwritten by the *telos* of archetypal forms or ideas, that of the seventeenth century was a collection of free-standing objects that could be grasped by consciousness and ordered within a classificatory grid. For those who sought a divine pattern in nature, it was to be found in the mind's ordering of perceptible things. In giving meaning to the outward appearances of things, one was effectively rethinking the thoughts of God. However, from the late eighteenth century onwards scholars in many different fields began to suggest that there were aspects of reality that were not immediately visible, but which served to explain the character of more readily accessible phenomena. The 'inward turn' had led rationalists to suggest that it was the inner world of the mind that made knowledge possible. Now interiority began to be associated with the *objects* of knowledge as well as the knowing subject. If humanity was already at the centre of the universe as the kind of being that gave things their meaning, it now became a centre with a centre of its own, and that centre needed to be known. According to Foucault (1970: 216), the culmination of this process was the creation of 'Man', a creature who was at once object and subject. If Cartesianism had allowed that it was consciousness that ordered the world, post-Enlightenment thought wanted to understand the being who was the bearer of that consciousness. This imperative was responsible for the formation of the 'human sciences', the sciences of Man, which charged themselves with understanding how humans come to be human, rather than studying them as one species amongst others. In practice, each avenue that led to an understanding of 'Man' did so by burrowing into structural depths rather than by describing surfaces. As a biological entity, the human organism was composed of organs that had functions; as a creator of wealth the human being was embedded in social relations of production; as a speaking subject the human being had access to the depths of language. In each case, understanding only arose from going beyond the superficial appearance of things.

As we have noted, several of Foucault's histories of modern systems of thought have some bearing on aspects of the emerging 'inner self'. For instance, in his work on the history of insanity, Foucault argues that for seventeenth-century rationalists like Descartes madness was not a matter of concern. For these thinkers, madness was 'unreason', and a person who possessed reason could not become insane. However, in the late eighteenth century madness changed its significance utterly, coming to be seen as an eruption of the fundamental animality that underlay human existence.

This in turn relates to a change in the conception of animals. For Descartes, animals were biological machines, lacking the consciousness that transformed human beings into agents. Yet by the end of the eighteenth century this had been replaced by the notion of the bestial, and with this came the fear of 'the beast inside' (Foucault 1967: 189). If we recall that the basic assumption of humanism is that human beings are animals to which a mind or soul has been added, this localisation of the bestial is very revealing. The civilised human being is the outer shell, while the beast lurks below and within, thereby expressing its primordial character.

If the mind had come to be seen as one aspect of the 'inside' of the human being, it is equally important that the eighteenth century also saw a renewed interest in the *body* interior. Ludmilla Jordanova has pointed out that for the Enlightenment the body, and particularly the female body, served as a metaphor for the dark and unknown nature that humanity sought to instrumentally control and understand. Thus eighteenth-century science and medicine made much use of a language of 'unveiling' and 'penetration' (Jordanova 1989: 24). This is significant, for it implies that the linguistic and conceptual resources on which archaeology depends are both sexualised and inherently violent. That dark interiors needed to be penetrated in order to yield knowledge was a sentiment that informed the changes in medical perception that Foucault documented in *The Birth of the Clinic* (1973). The early modern cosmology of resemblance and affinity had had its correlate in the medical theory of the humours – blood, phlegm, yellow bile and black bile – which did not so much *cause* illness as embody it. The four humours were all present in the body in various quantities, and all gave off vapours that rose to the brain. It was the imbalance between the humours, when one came to dominate within the body, that brought about sickness, as well as giving the person their characteristic temperament. Medical practice prior to the seventeenth century was therefore geared to maintaining the balance between the humours. The 'nosological' medicine that replaced this was inspired by the scientific revolution, and sought a systematic classification of diseases. Diseases were ordered into genera and species, and the human body was understood as a continuous surface on which these diseases were manifested: almost a canvas. The significant relationships in this nosology were the classificatory ones between diseases. Diseases revealed themselves as symptoms on bodily tissues, but this was understood as a matter of temporal development which lacked any spatial specificity (Foucault 1973: 136).

The new clinical medicine that developed towards the end of the eighteenth century was based upon the observation of the particular manifestations of disease in specific patients, and in particular parts of the body. This meant that physicians were more likely to learn their craft in the clinic and the teaching hospital, rather than in the classroom. But along with this shift from the abstract and general to the particular and empirical went a new desire to probe the body interior. In particular, there was a sudden revival of interest in pathological anatomy around 1800, a need to 'open up a few corpses' (ibid.: 124). Dissection and observation now became a means by which the functioning and spread of disease within the body could be assessed. Rather than being comparatively undifferentiated, the body had come to be seen as having depths that withheld secrets. Moreover, pathological anatomy transformed medicine into a 'science of Man', which investigated human beings as singular organisms and, in their finitude, as dead bodies (Sheridan 1980: 43).

Depth models

If the construction of human interiority created a human being whose 'truth' had to be sought in the depths of their body and their psyche, we have already suggested that this development was connected to a more general change in the character of knowledge, which we might call the 'discovery of structure'. Seventeenth-century thought had imagined the world as a multiplicity of facts that could be organised into a colossal classificatory table; phenomena were linked by physical forces and geometrical relations that could be rendered in mathematical terms. This vision of tabular order started to fragment as the suspicion of hidden structures underlying visible reality began to be taken seriously. The identification of organic functions, economic forces and linguistic structures was only the beginning of a proliferation of forms of knowledge that could not readily be reduced to mathematics (Foucault 1970: 349). Thus by the early nineteenth century, Hegel's historical idealism was to be based around the view that events in the physical world were the surface manifestations of thoughts in the mind (Collingwood 1961: 118). Frederic Jameson (1984: 62) argues that the relationship between depth and surface is the hallmark of high modernity, and takes a number of related forms. The first of these is the distinction between inside and outside, which he suggests is characteristic of hermeneutics. A clear example of this would be Collingwood's (1945: 215) distinction between the 'inside' and 'outside' of an event. Here the outside is the appearance of what happened, and the inside is its *meaning* to those involved. Obviously, such a meaning would be very difficult to express in algebraic form, but for Collingwood it is considerably more important than the external shape of things. A second form of the 'depth model' is the Marxist distinction between essence and appearance. In this variant, the real character of things is obscured by a shell of ideology, so that an effort of demystification is required if the subject is to penetrate and appreciate their own real interests. Third, Jameson points to the Freudian conception of latent and manifest thought, held in place by a repression. Indeed, Freud's ideas are built around a whole series of depth metaphors, which we will discuss in more detail below (see pp. 161–9). A fourth depth model is found in the existential opposition between the authentic and the inauthentic. While this is associated with a variety of forms of philosophy it articulates a more general unease in late modern society concerning the impoverishment of experience in an increasingly commercialised world. Everyday public existence is presented as 'superficial' or 'shallow', and people are enjoined to look for a deeper truth in a simple life, contemplation, religious experience or self-knowledge. Finally, there is the separation of the signifier and the signified, characteristic of structuralism.

In some ways structuralism represents the culmination of modern traditions of thought. Ferdinand de Saussure, and those who followed him, actually aspired to creating a universal science of signs and language, and claimed that certain principles applied to all forms of signification. Saussure's structural linguistics represents the clearest possible use of the image of depth and surface: speech is observable, but language is a hidden structure that has to be reconstructed on the basis of our observations. The analogy that Saussure draws is with a game of chess – we may not know the rules of the game, but we can reconstruct them by watching the players over a period of time. Similarly, by listening to people speaking, observing their marriage practices or collecting their myths, we can isolate the rules and syntax of language, kinship or mythology. In this respect the parallel with archaeology is a particularly obvious one: in order to gain access to the past we have to delve beneath the surface of things. However, other aspects of structuralism demonstrate something of a transformation of modern thinking. For while authors like Lévi-Strauss would effectively follow Kant in seeing the world being organised by cognitive structures, they did not attribute this organising to an individual consciousness (Falzon 1998: 47). And more than any other school of thought structuralism rejected atomism, the collection of facts as isolated entities (Sturrock 1993: 6). Structuralists held not simply that outward appearances were misleading, but also that the deep grammars beneath the surface were relational in character. The connection between the sign and its referent was arbitrary, and the relations between signs were more significant than the signs themselves. The implication of this is that the cause-and-effect universe of monadic entities that had been in place since the seventeenth century was merely a façade that occluded a more networked and interconnected reality. The things around us are linked, but the links are never visible for they operate at a deeper level of existence.

The separation of signifier and signified, speech and language had further implications. Saussure argued that while particular speech acts were the prerogative of individuals, they drew on linguistic structures that were embedded in 'collective consciousness' (Sturrock 1993: 8). Lévi-Strauss took this argument further, suggesting that ultimately the classificatory powers of the mind were human universals (Tilley 1989b). So all myths, kinship and totemic systems were in the final analysis manifestations of a universal mind. To some extent this conclusion parallels the attempt by psychoanalysis to identify shared and inherited structures in the deeper recesses of the mind. So while St Augustine had advocated a withdrawal into the inner self as a means of finding God, structuralism and psychoanalysis both indicated that beneath the surface of the individual the collective and the immemorial were to be found. Again, this sheds some light on the place that archaeology holds in late modern thought: in a world of alienation and groundlessness, a descent into the past signals the possibility of reconnecting with community, heritage, the instinctual life, and authenticity.

If structuralism was concerned with the deep grammars of culture, the interpretive tradition of hermeneutics and phenomenology was sometimes more preoccupied with deep, hidden meanings. This, at least, is Jameson's charge: that texts or artworks are treated as mere symptoms of a more significant truth that they can give access to (Jameson 1984: 59). This renders interpretation prey to Susan Sontag's criticism that it devalues the text and neglects the sensuous experience of art, always too impatient to move on to a deeper layer of analysis (Sontag 1967: 6). In the case of earlier, historical forms of hermeneutics this is accurate enough. Schliermacher's demand that one should put oneself into the position of the author in order to understand a text amounted to an attempt to assume the mental state of another (Johnsen and Olsen 1992: 421). Similarly, Dilthey's claim that hermeneutics should provide the basis for a methodology for the human sciences that would be quite distinct from that of natural science rests on the belief that human beings and their actions require interpretation because they are meaningful. In other words, the physical world is meaningless, and humans bring meaning into the world: effectively a reiteration of the Cartesian position. However, a quite different point of view emerges from the philosophical hermeneutics of Heidegger, Gadamer and Ricoeur, and this is one that actually points away from depth models. In *Being and Time* (1962) Heidegger conducts an analysis of human existence that challenges romantic and historical hermeneutics. For Heidegger, interpretation is not one task that human beings carry out alongside other activities. Rather, to be human is to be an interpreting being. Interpretation is not something we do, it is what we are; it is not restricted to literary or aesthetic scholars, it is the way that people continually make themselves at home in the world and make sense of their own existence. In this way of thinking, meaning is not the content of a mind that has to be recovered by plunging into the depths of consciousness. Instead, meaning is understood as the same thing as 'significance', by which I mean the way in which things achieve intelligibility by showing up within a world. For this significance to be possible, the world itself must provide a 'background' of sense and practices – a 'horizon of intelligibility'. This leads us away from 'deep meaning', and towards the connections and relationships *in the world* that render things meaningful. In their different ways, Gadamer and Ricoeur turned this conception back onto hermeneutics, arguing that cultural products should be understood in the context of their historical horizon. From this point of view, the objective of interpretation should be the revelation not of a meaning behind the text but of a world in front of text (Dreyfus and Rabinow 1982: xv; Outhwaite 1985: 25; Ricoeur 1974: 3). These arguments will be essential to the critique of the concept of mind that will be offered in the next chapter. For the moment they demonstrate that it is possible to overcome the depth/surface opposition. As we will see, this has fundamental significance for the way that we understand the practice of archaeology.

The growth of structural thought and depth models from the nineteenth century onwards helps to explain the significance of positivism, as discussed in Chapter 2. We have seen that logical positivism represented an attempt to return to the canons of reason, logic and epistemology of the scientific revolution (Toulmin 1990: 159). This 'born again' enthusiasm for pure facts was expressed through an absolute rejection of metaphysics. We can read this as a refusal of the notion of hidden structures: for positivism anything that cannot be directly observed has no explanatory value. Positivism wanted to reinstate mechanistic explanations, classification, and a form of knowledge that aspires to the condition of mathematics. Of course, this was difficult to achieve once the modern West had begun to entertain ideas of hidden thoughts and deep meanings. For this reason, positivism has always been seen as reductionist, even if this is sometimes portrayed as a virtue. In a predominantly humanist culture addicted to the notion of individual freedom of action, it could only have limited success, and the dominance that it achieved in some disciplines in the immediately post-war period is consequentially remarkable (Gouldner 1970: 168). Positivism wanted to transcend the subject/object dichotomy, but only by asserting the absolute objectivity of the scientist and denying the subjectivity of those that they studied. In archaeology the tension between 'structural' and (implicitly) positivist modes of knowledge has been a recurring theme. If there is a distinction to be made between antiquarianism and archaeology it is that the former largely restricted itself to the description of remains existing in the present, while the latter attempts to use those remains to address the past in a systematic way. But again and again the urge to describe, classify and to restrict inference has reasserted itself. Either it is asserted that we should limit ourselves to the detailed presentation and ordering of archaeological materials, in the belief that any knowledge about the past that is legitimate will simply reveal itself in the process, or analyses of the past are restricted to a series of readily addressed explanatory factors. Thus, for instance, it has been argued that we should study past people 'as if' they were simply biological organisms, and limit our investigations to issues of population, technology and ecology (e.g. Bailey 1981; Higgs and Jarman 1975). I would like to suggest that this recurring failure of nerve results from the way that archaeology has understood itself through a series of depth metaphors. Because the discipline conceives of itself as revealing a buried and hidden past, that past always seems to retain some of its inaccessibility.

Archaeology, stratigraphy and depth

According to Glyn Daniel (1950: 29) the 'revolution' that transformed antiquarianism into archaeology was attributable to the recognition of geological stratigraphy, and dated to the beginning of the nineteenth century. That is, it was precisely contemporary with the 'structural revolution' in Western thought – the transfiguration of the body interior in medicine, the emergence of the grammatical study of language, and the beginnings of political economy. As we saw in Chapter 2, the existence of distinct layers of soil and rock had long been recognised by excavators, but the significance of this variation was not fully appreciated until the publication of Hutton's *Theory of the Earth* ([1788] 1795) and Smith's *Strata Identified by Organised Fossils* (1816). Together, these volumes established that rocks could be generated by heat, pressure and weathering acting over long periods of time, and that different strata followed an orderly succession and could be distinguished by the fossils that they contained. Significantly, William Smith kept his collection of fossils and rock specimens in a cabinet that was organised stratigraphically (Harris 1989: 3). Already, the idea had taken root that vertical depth could be equated with chronological change, and that the division of spatio-temporal entities could be used as a principle for the ordering of objects. Charles Lyell's *Principles of Geology* (1830) was to add the concept of uniformitarianism to this framework, arguing that if geological processes could be observed in the world today it could be assumed that they were responsible for rock-forming in the past. Early nineteenth-century geology thus maintained that strata built up over time and were superimposed upon one another; that they were laid down by sedimentation in horizontal bands, which were originally whole without exposed edges; that the unconformities and interfaces between strata themselves represented periods of time; and that the chronological succession of layers was paralleled by the changing morphology of the fossils that they contained (Harris 1989: 5). It seems highly likely that Smith's observations in the canal cuttings were to some extent informed by the more general belief that the forces responsible for the appearance of things could be found below the surface. In this case, scenery and topography were the outcome of geological processes that could be understood through stratigraphy, which opened a window into the distant past.

Initially, these geological findings were most important to archaeology in respect of the finds of stone tools stratified alongside the remains of extinct animals in geological deposits. This was critical to the establishment of human antiquity. However, Thomsen's archaeological application of the three-age system also dated to the start of the nineteenth century, and just as clearly as Smith's cabinet expressed the idea of slices of time-depth serving as a basis for the ordering of objects. Thomsen's concern with 'closed finds' is not dissimilar to Smith's and Lyell's ideas concerning fossil assemblages,

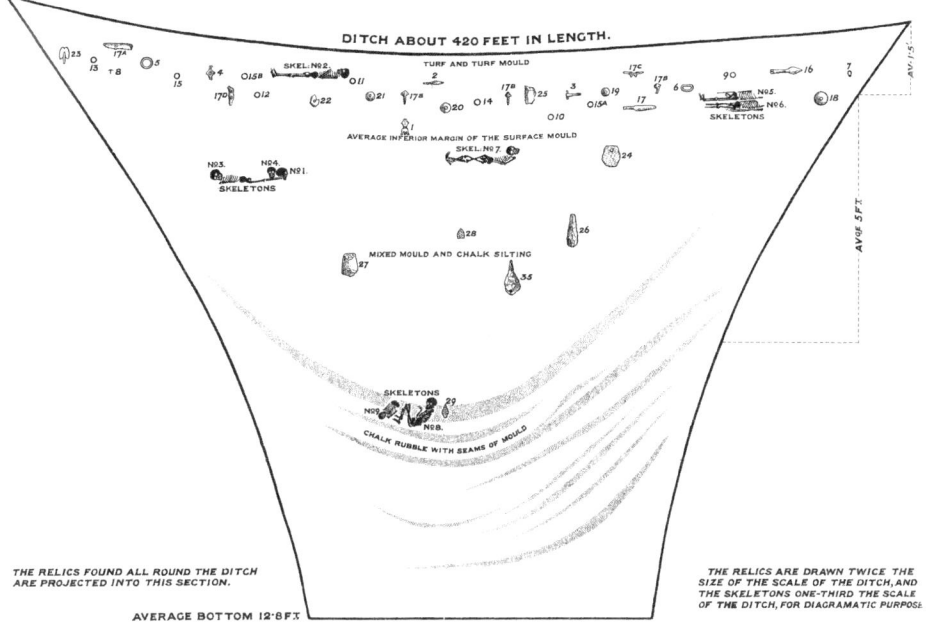

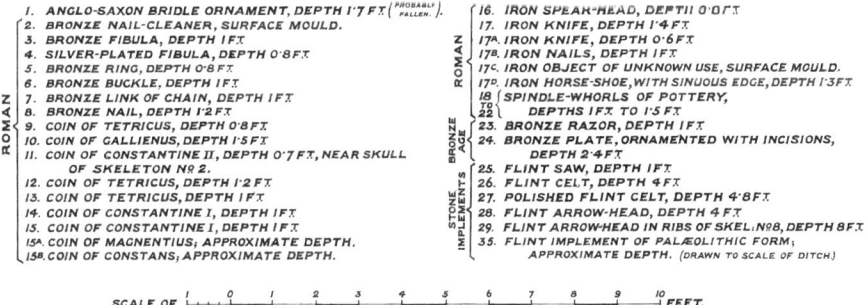

Figure 7.1 Pitt Rivers's ditch section from the Wor Barrow neolithic long mound, Dorset (from A.L.F. Pitt Rivers, *Excavations in Cranbourne Chase near Rushmore*, Vol. IV. Privately printed, 1898)

which collectively typify a vertical block of time. Significantly, Thomsen's work was followed up by Worsaae's demonstration that finds of different periods were vertically stratified within the Danish bogs. As Lucas (2001: 32) points out, for Worsaae, and others like Pitt Rivers and Petrie, the principal importance of stratigraphy was that it placed artefacts in temporal succession (Figure 7.1). This was largely a consequence of developing ideas of cultural evolution and technological progress, and it meant that the use of stratigraphy as a record of sequences of depositional events on sites took second place to the sequencing of artefacts. Even in the work of Wheeler and Kenyon in the mid-twentieth century, stratigraphy was still presented as a series of layers, best recorded in section, which provide a surrogate form of relative dating for material culture (ibid.: 41). In contrast to geology, interfaces were of relatively little concern in archaeology, for the narrative that was pursued through prehistoric time was that of technological and stylistic change, rather than the formation of landscape. For this reason, approaches to archaeological stratigraphy that emphasise the vertical sequence of discrete layers are closely associated with culture-history. Just as the spatial distribution of artefact styles identified the extent of bounded social or cultural entities in the past, so vertical stratigraphy demonstrated their succession, as migrations, invasions, diffusion and cultural drift took place.

The radical changes that overtook the study of archaeological stratification in the 1960s and 1970s have often been connected with the growth of large-scale urban rescue projects, in which thousands of distinct depositional entities might need to be recorded. However, it is also significant that this development coincided with the increasingly widespread use of scientific forms of direct dating, principally radiocarbon. Under these circumstances the conception of stratigraphy as a series of vertically nested containers for artefacts, the temporal counterpart of the distribution map, became redundant. The new pattern that emerged by the middle of the 1970s (at least in Britain) was one of large, open-area excavations that were often machine-stripped, within which both vertical and horizontal variability were judged significant. Each distinct stratigraphic entity on a site was understood as the consequence of a separate action in the past, and each was recorded separately, often on a unique context sheet. The stratigraphic relationships between these entities were then explicated using a Harris matrix. It barely needs stating that this context-and-matrix system is absolutely characteristic of modern Western thought. Stratigraphic units are first defined as free-standing entities, their attributes (texture, colour, inclusions) are identified, and their relationships are then distinguished. These relations are, of course, secondary to the entities themselves, which are monadic. Causal logic is then invoked to connect each unit with a discrete event or act. These actions are not presented as engaged in a flow of conduct. Rather, they are seen as isolated events: 'bursts' of intentionality. Consequentially, the whole scheme is overwhelmingly atomistic.

While post-1960s field archaeology is very much concerned with the plan view, and within single-context recording systems may even replace section drawings with a series of superimposed plans of individual units, stratigraphy is still understood as primarily a matter of sequence. Roskams (2001: 155), for instance, draws a distinction between *physical* and *stratigraphic* relationships, the former representing a simple juxtaposition while the latter necessarily involves a chronological sequence. Equally, Harris (1989: 33) argues that archaeological sites contain 'complex multilinear sequences'. In other words, a site can be understood as a series of parallel threads of events, crossing over and interconnecting at various points. The stratigraphic sequence of the site is the order in which these events took place, so that the overall objective of stratigraphic analysis is a non-reversible chain of acts. Indeed, Harris goes on to distinguish between geological and archaeological stratigraphy (ibid.: 42). Clearly, he is invoking the culture/nature dichotomy in this respect: the agencies that create geological stratigraphy are cyclical in character, while those that contribute to archaeological stratigraphy are linear. That is, archaeological deposits are historical and directional, while geology may contribute to the evolution of landscape, but is essentially reversible. Our view of stratification in archaeology is thus something of a throwback to the seventeenth century. Moreover, it appears to be predicated upon a *descent* into a depth, which seeks a point of origin that combines the lowest with the earliest, the most profound. This recalls Jacques Derrida's claim that any archaeology will attempt to explore depths and interiors, and in the process will attempt to order them (1978: 279). If nineteenth-century thought had displaced the classificatory table, the archaeological imperative appears to be to fix and organise structures. In doing this, it tries to reduce structures (which are characterised by play and relationality) by ordering them about a centre, and bringing the hidden into full presence. In the case of stratigraphy, the centre that is established is the origin, the start of the sequence.

Freud: the archaeology of the mind

Archaeology uncovers hidden depths and reveals the truth of the past; or such is the popular understanding of the discipline. The historical emergence of archaeology was connected with the development of the structural thought of late modernity, but it also provided a metaphor through which that thought could articulate itself. This is particularly evident in the case of the psychoanalysis of Sigmund Freud. Freud's own lifetime (1856–1939) spanned a period during which archaeology became a more coherent and professionalised pursuit, and gained greater public interest (Armstrong 1999: 19). Freud himself was fascinated by archaeology, reading extensively about Heinrich Schliemann's excavations at Troy and closely following the progress of Arthur Evans's work at Knossos. Over a period of decades he gathered a large collection of prehistoric and classical artefacts, particularly figurines, which he kept in his study and often used for didactic purposes during consultations (Gamwell 1989; D'Agata 1994; Ucko 2001) (Figure 7.2). Some of these objects had direct connections with Freud's theories, such as sphinxes, other human/animal hybrids, a Greek vase with an image of Oedipus, and a

Figure 7.2 Sigmund Freud with his private collection of antiquities (etching by Max Pollack, 1914. Freud Museum, London)

figure of Eros (MacCannell 1996: 42; Gamwell 1996: 2). As a whole, though, the collection elicits a more general sense of the distant past, the archetypal and the mythic.

Of all of the new strands of Western thinking that developed in the nineteenth and twentieth centuries, psychoanalysis was perhaps the one that made most play on the relationship between depth and surface, and explicitly drew on the language of archaeology in doing so. Freud writes of 'the deepest strata of the mind' (1927: 53), and makes distinctions between the manifest and the latent, civilised and uncivilised, historic and prehistoric, adult and infantile, and fact and fantasy (Kuspit 1989: 135). These different evocations of depth are often mutually correlated in his work.

The key insight that psychoanalysis grew from was effectively a negation of Cartesian and Kantian theories of knowledge and ethics. Seventeenth- and eighteenth-century philosophy had emphasised reason and consciousness as the foundation of the good life. Freud pointed out in contrast that consciousness was only one aspect of mental activity, rather than its core element (Freud 1927: 9). He argued that ideas do not stay constantly within our conscious minds. Something that we are thinking about at one moment can slip from consciousness the next. Furthermore, thoughts that have seeped away and become latent can be recalled at a later time. This much might have been accepted by thinkers like Locke, who held that all thoughts in the mind must at some time have been subject to awareness (Gardiner 1991: 144). However, Freud went on to argue that while in some cases the return of latent ideas to consciousness is fluid and unrestrained, at other times they cannot be brought to the surface because some force is opposed to them and holds them in place. This is what Freud refers to as repression. Obviously, this picture of an accessible consciousness and an unconscious that is out of reach is readily spatialised in terms of an 'above' and a 'below' or an 'inside' and an 'outside' (Ricoeur 1974: 238). The notion of repression builds on the picture of human interiority that had been emerging through the modern period by suggesting that people are never fully capable of expressing their own motivations. The apparently orderly surface of the person may hide internal chaos, and it is the prerogative of a particular kind of professional (the psychologist or psychoanalyst) to mediate between inside and outside in order to bring about therapy (Bauman 1991: 9; 1992: 125). In contrast with the Catholic confessional, the person is now understood as being so alienated from her- or himself that the intercession of another is required in order to articulate the inner self. In this respect psychoanalysis shares with the 'hermeneutics of suspicion' and the critical theory of the Frankfurt School a belief that superficial reality 'covers over' darker aspects of existence. This is arguably the element of structural thinking that has been added during the late nineteenth and earlier twentieth centuries.

Freud suggested a parallel between psychoanalysis and archaeology in a number of different ways. From Rousseau he drew the social evolutionary argument that prehistory was the 'childhood of mankind' (Bernfeld 1951: 107). But he turned this back on itself, and claimed that childhood was the 'prehistory' of the adult human being, both providing a mythic past for the person and recapitulating the development of humankind. It was for this reason that Freud developed an interest in ethnography. Evolutionists like General Pitt Rivers had long argued that the study of non-Western peoples was of help to archaeology, because these societies were at a stage of cultural development equivalent to the prehistoric inhabitants of Europe (Bowden 1991: 55; Bradley 1983). For J.G. Frazer the behaviour of contemporary 'primitive' people amounted to a recapitulation of prehistory, and therefore provided a more reliable source of information concerning the distant past than archaeology (Ucko 2001: 273). Freud took this train of thought further, by suggesting that the mental lives of 'primitive peoples' might prove informative about those of children and neurotics as well:

> Primitive man is known to us by the stages of development through which he has passed: that is, through the inanimate monuments and

implements which he has left behind for us; through our knowledge of his art, his religion, and his attitude towards life, which we have received either directly or through the medium of legends, myths, and fairy tales; and through the remnants of his ways of thinking that survive in our own manners and customs . . . their psychic life assumes a particular interest for us, for we can recognise in their psychic life a well-preserved, early stage of our own development.

(Freud [1919] 1938: 15)

In Freud's work, then, there is a conflation of archaeology, ethnology and mythology, as each potentially provided access to a primordial realm of experience. This was also germane to the early lives of modern subjects, and to their subsequent development. In part, this explains his use of the language of Greek mythology as a source of terms for psychological archetypes, most notably the 'Oedipus complex'. All of this meant that he identified archaeology not only with the recovery of the ancient past but also with the reclaiming of the lost mythic happiness of childhood. These themes were brought together in Freud's fascination with Schliemann's work at Troy. Schliemann professed in print to having been inspired by the works of Homer as a child; Freud opined that he must have gained the greatest possible joy in using archaeological excavation to materially retrieve his boyhood dream (Kuspit 1989). This sentiment indicates why he saw a close affinity between the work of the psychoanalyst and that of the archaeologist:

I had no choice but to follow those discoverers whose good fortune it is to bring to the light of day after their burial, the priceless though mutilated relics of antiquity.

(Freud 1946: 74–5)

Because childhood memories are hidden by repression, psychoanalysis is like archaeology in that it seeks to uncover a lost reality (Kuspit 1989: 134). Like archaeology, it begins with the known and the visible and clears away the debris to reveal the fragments of an earlier time. In the process, it demonstrates that what appears to be dead and lost is actually ancestral to the reality that we experience. Bernfeld (1951) argues that the archaeological metaphor had a more personal significance for Freud, in that he developed an interest in classical literature and ancient art in his youth. This happened at a time when his family had moved from the countryside to Vienna, separating him from an old nurse who had introduced him to Christian religious ideas. Denied the consolations of religion, Freud turned to archaeology, which taught him that things that had been lost and buried could be brought back to the present and reanimated. Bernfeld takes this to mean that archaeology assumed for him the place of an alternative religion, a means of overcoming the finality of death. However, it seems that Freud's interest in archaeology greatly increased during the 1890s, when he was professionally isolated and Vienna was subject to an upsurge of anti-Semitism and Catholic nationalism. It was at this time that he formed a close friendship with the classical archaeologist Emmanuel Löwy, and began his collection of antiquities in earnest (Schorske 1991: 18). Gamwell (1996: 7) suggests that the specific group of figurines that Freud now placed facing him on his desk may have served as symbolic colleagues and friends: warriors and deities drawn from a timeless realm of power and truth.

Whether we choose to follow Bernfeld or Gamwell, it seems that for Freud, as for many others, archaeology served as a source of ontological security. We have seen that a central concern with stratification in archaeology lies in the attempt to identify a point of origin from which the present descends. It may be that in some cases this is connected to the need to recover and substantiate the foundations of our own civilisation. In any case, the theme of a return from the realm of death was particularly important to Freud. In showing some of his antiquities to the 'Rat Man', he pointed out that a specific group of objects had come from an Etruscan tomb, and that it was because they had been purposefully buried that they had survived into the present (Bernfeld 1951: 110). In the same way, the contents of the psyche were preserved in the mental depths, covered over by the force of repression. In one respect, though, memories differ from archaeological finds: they are preserved whole, and never fragmented. This point is exemplified in an elaborate metaphor that Freud develops in *Civilisation and its Discontents*, in which he compares the mind to the archaeology of the city of Rome:

> With the best information about Rome of the republican era, the utmost he [an archaeologist] could achieve would be to indicate the sites where the temples and public buildings of that period stood. These places are now occupied by ruins, but the ruins are not those of the early buildings themselves but restorations of them in later times after fires and demolitions.
>
> (Freud 1930: 16)

If the city were a mind, however, all of the buildings from all phases of its development would still be standing alongside each other, crossing and interpenetrating. For this reason, the psychoanalyst has an advantage over the archaeologist, for in excavating the mind he or she is able to recover a lost world that is preserved in its entirety. Nonetheless, Freud found a further parallel between the psyche and archaeological deposits in the way that both mental objects and ancient artefacts are made susceptible to damage by being brought to the surface. He noted that the streets and buildings of Pompeii had been preserved by the layers of ash from the eruption of Vesuvius, and that now the site had been excavated its destruction had really begun (Reinhard 1996: 65). This suggests a relatively sophisticated understanding on Freud's part of the character of excavation as destructive as well as disclosive.

The stratification of the mind

Freud's talk of the depths of the mind was not purely metaphorical, although there is little doubt that his interest in archaeology gave him a language to discuss the different elements of the psychic apparatus. When he writes that the unconscious is 'deeper' than the conscious mind he is actually making a quasi-physiological claim. This is partly because he understood consciousness to be connected with visual perception and body ego, and partly because he considered that the structure of the mind as a whole had literally been formed through a process of stratification (Kuspit 1989: 140). Bowdler (1996: 425) makes the important point that Freud was attracted to theories of biological recapitulation that were current in the earlier part of the twentieth century. These maintained that the morphological changes that an organism goes through in its growth to maturity involve its passing through the physical forms of the creatures from which it had evolved. Thus each animal recapitulated in microcosm the process of descent that had given rise to its species. In a similar way, Freud argued that the formation of the mind of any individual human being reiterated the psychic history of the human race (Paul 1991: 271). The building up of the layers of the psyche from childhood reflected cognitive evolution.

Elaborating this topographic theory of the mind led Freud to introduce a series of terms that built on the conscious/unconscious distinction: Ego, Id, Preconscious and Ego-Ideal. The Ego is the source of the sense of selfhood, and is the part of the mind that directs motility. It is also the source of the repressions that keep the Unconscious submerged, and is an aspect of the 'deeper' mind that has been modified by its 'contact' with the external world through the perceptual systems (Freud 1927: 15–16). While the Unconscious is held in check by repression, latent ideas and memories that can readily be returned to consciousness are attributed to the Preconscious, which is closer to the 'surface'. The spatial idiom in which Freud discusses the relationships between these various mental entities is particularly striking:

> The Preconscious is presumably a great deal closer to the Conscious than the Unconscious, and since we have called the Unconscious mental we shall with even less hesitation call the latent Preconscious mental.
>
> (Freud 1927: 12–13)

All of these 'superficial' aspects of the mind, though, are simply a 'façade' for the Id, the remaining element of the psyche (Freud 1930: 10). While the

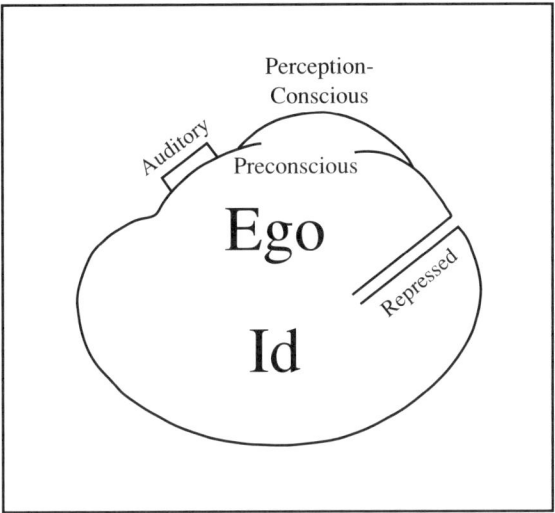

Figure 7.3 Freud's 'topographic' model of the psyche (redrawn after Freud 1927)

Conscious is connected with visual perception, and the Preconscious is linked to the auditory system (as verbal images are the raw stuff of memory residues), the Id is tied in to the instincts, which Freud clearly considered to be hereditary, and physical rather than mental. Like the structuralists, then, Freud seems to associate the individual Ego with the surface and the collective (in this case the species) with depth. The Ego, containing the Conscious and the Preconscious, rests on the surface of the Id 'like the rider on a horse' (Freud 1927: 30), and actually develops out of it (Figure 7.3). However, there is a further element of the Ego that is less firmly connected with perception and consciousness. This is the Ego-Ideal or Super-Ego. Freud argued that as the mind develops, the Id makes a series of object-cathexes, or identifications with sexual objects, which are sequentially abandoned. The process of abandonment is facilitated by an 'energetic reaction-formation' within the Ego, which brings about the formation of the Ego-Ideal as the Oedipus complex is repressed (ibid.: 45). The Ego-Ideal is therefore composed of a precipitate of identifications, primarily ideal images of the parents. As the child's relationship with the mother and father is transfigured, the feelings of admiration and fear for the parents are taken into the Ego as the Ego-Ideal and provide the basis for the 'higher values' to which human beings aspire (ibid.: 47). These include the conscience, and in Freud's later work the Super-Ego becomes the agent of morality within the personality, the means by which anti-social aggression is drawn off at the cost of personal suffering and guilt (Deigh 1991: 299).

The important point here is that Freud believed that the personal psychic drama of the suppression of sexual feelings (and aggression) towards the parents and the formation of the Ego-Ideal recapitulated actual historical events that the human race had experienced in the distant past:

> The differentiation of the Super-Ego is no matter of chance; it stands as the representative of the most important events in the development both of the individual and of the race . . . Through the formation of the Ideal, all the traces left behind in the Id by biological developments and the vicissitudes gone through by the human race are taken over by the Ego and lived through again by each individual.
>
> (Freud 1927: 46–8)

So, collective experiences inherited and laid down in the Id are relived as part of achieving human maturity, and the Id represents the deep past as well as species being. The stratified topography of the mind is temporal, in terms of both the personal history of the individual and the shared experience of humanity.

The particular experience that Freud is thinking of as responsible for the creation of the Ego-Ideal is the so-called 'primal crime'. Because the division between the Ego and the Id is based upon the perception of the outside world, Freud argues that it must date to a very early stage in evolution, and must apply to even very simple forms of life. However, the formation of the Ego-Ideal is much more recent, and is connected with both the origin of the incest taboo and the development of totemism. Following Darwin, Freud reasoned that at some time in the far past human beings had lived as a patriarchal horde, presided over by a jealous primal father (Paul 1991: 275). This patriarch monopolised the women of the tribe, and cast out his sons from the community during a period of hardship which followed the Ice Age (Ucko 2001: 277). These brothers consequentially had extremely ambivalent feelings towards the father: they at once loved, feared and resented him. Eventually, 'one fine day', they banded together to kill and devour their father, taking on his authority in the process (Freud [1919] 1938: 189). Immediately, however, they were seized with remorse. Although the patriarchal horde was destroyed for ever, the brothers had developed a conception of crime, and in their guilt created the fundamental elements of human society.

In order to dispel some of this guilt, the brothers substituted a totemic animal for the father, and declared the killing of the totem illegal, just as father-killing would henceforth be forbidden. Similarly, they renounced sexual relations with their mothers, the women whom they had taken from the dead father, thereby creating the incest taboo. In seeking not to gain from their crime, the men laid down the conditions that would ensure that it would not be repeated (ibid.: 210). The two great wishes of the Oedipus complex, killing one's father and having sex with one's mother, were now repressed (Paul 1991: 274; Simon and Blass 1991: 164). Yet Freud also argued that the prohibition on killing and eating the totemic animal could be violated in the case of a *totemic feast*, in which the totem is both consumed and mourned, with the effect of increasing the identification between the members of the community and their totemic creature. Thus the solidarity of human society is reaffirmed through totemism and exogamy.

It is clear from Freud's account of the primal crime that he considered that the differentiation of the different elements of the psyche was attributable to a specific event or series of events in the human past. The stages of psychological development that a child underwent in growing to adulthood effectively recapitulated these events, as collective memories were drawn up from the Id. By implication, the stratification of the mind was formed through a kind of sedimentation in which the deeper elements could be attributed to the more distant past of the person or the species.

Conclusion: depth, surface and archaeology

In this chapter I have argued that one of the contributory factors in the formation of contemporary archaeological thinking has been the modern emphasis on a distinction between depth and surface. This dichotomy is ultimately attributable to changing conceptions of the person, and a growing concern with human interiority in the post-Reformation era. The same separation of above and below, inside and outside can also be recognised in the increasing interest in the body interior, and the 'structural' view of language and society that would culminate in twentieth-century structuralism. However, while structuralism proposes a very specific relationship between signifier and signified, speech and language, the modern use of depth models is very much more widespread. These ideas emerged at very much the same time as notions of stratification in geology and archaeology. In both disciplines it came to be recognised that layers of rock and sediment were laid down over long periods of time, and that descent into the depths of the earth corresponded in some way to descent into the depths of linear time. However, of the two archaeology is more connected with the investigation of the human past, and thus with historical time. Moreover, it is archaeology that is connected with the practice of stripping back the layers of sediment in order to reveal the traces of the past – a geologist is more likely to record a section.

For this reason, archaeology has found itself with the burden of being the source of many of the metaphors through which the modern imagination has sought to understand the world. For our culture, archaeology is firmly connected with a movement from the present to the past, from superficiality to profundity, from the individual to the mythic, from the known to the mysterious. As we have seen in the case of Freud, these different oppositions tend to become conflated with one another. The past is automatically connected with stratigraphic depth, and needs to be drawn back from darkness and obscurity if it is to be a source of significant knowledge. This creates some serious problems for the discipline, and for how it understands itself. Recently, Thomas Dowson (2001: 314) has pointed to the way that rock art research is often derided as not being 'proper archaeology'. As he suggests, this dismissal can be attributed to the lack of excavation in the study of petroglyphs. Of course, much of our disciplinary culture is based around the social experience of excavation, but I think that there is something else at work here. Rock art is generally visible in the contemporary landscape. In some cases turf or moss has to be cleared away to reveal the decorated surface, but for the most part rock art research involves survey to locate decorated stones, followed by the tracing of designs. Arguably, then, the comparative lack of professional legitimacy afforded to the archaeology of rock art arises from the contemporary accessibility of its object. It does not have to recover its source material from the depths through excavation. And because we conflate depth with the past and the truth, we assume that anything that is already visible cannot be a source of significant knowledge about the past.

The same argument could be applied to other forms of archaeology that do not involve excavation: standing buildings recording, or industrial archaeology, or the experiential analysis of prehistoric monuments, for instance. Indeed, the one exception to the general disregard for rock art studies lies in the case of palaeolithic cave art, where the images concerned are hidden deep underground, and much effort is invested in the folklore surrounding their discovery by dogs and small children (Dowson, pers. comm.). It could be argued that this disciplinary orientation towards depth, concealment, mystery and revelation is quite obstructive, for it enhances the belief that the past is entirely separate from the present: it is 'somewhere else' that has to be accessed in a particular way. This essentialist view of the past could be compared with the post-Cartesian view of the mind, hidden away in the interior of the person. In the same way, it is unhelpful to imagine that the past is a substance that is secreted in dark places awaiting its recovery. The remains of the past are all around us, and we *inhabit* the past in important ways.

8
MIND, PERCEPTION AND KNOWLEDGE

Rationalists, empiricists, and the birth of the concept of mind

We have seen in earlier chapters of this book that sixteenth- and seventeenth-century philosophical and scientific developments were responsible for engendering a conception of knowledge as a representation of the world, and one of mind as being distinct from matter. These views have been singularly influential in the modern world, and have had a critical role in the development of archaeology. This is increasingly the case at present, when evolutionary psychology and computer-based approaches to the perception of past landscapes (Virtual Reality Modelling (VRM) and Geographical Information Systems (GIS)) are enjoying growing popularity within the discipline. In this chapter I will seek to demonstrate that these perspectives embody a blend of Cartesian and empiricist views of mental functioning, and that this inhibits our understanding of the past in serious ways.

The categorical separation of mind from body owes much to the epistemological imperatives of early modern science. Both Galileo and Bacon framed the problem of knowledge in terms of a relationship between material things in the world and the contents of a mind. Indeed, for Galileo minds exist outside of nature, and true knowledge is to be achieved by harmonising the appearance in the mind with the outward reality of things (Collingwood 1945: 103; Taylor 1989: 144). While rationalists and empiricists differed very considerably over the character of the mind and how it works, they were nevertheless united in distinguishing the mental from the physical. Descartes adhered to a view of the mind as having no physical extension or density, and representing a kind of substance that was defined simply by what it does – thinking (Cottingham 1988: 116). Although separate from the body, the mind 'communicated' with it by way of the pineal gland (Figure 8.1). This was itself characteristic of the way that the body was divided into parts which have different functions, but the same was not true of the mind. The mind is internally undifferentiated: the same mind exercises will, discrimination and understanding, and receives information from the senses (ibid.: 117).

MIND, PERCEPTION AND KNOWLEDGE

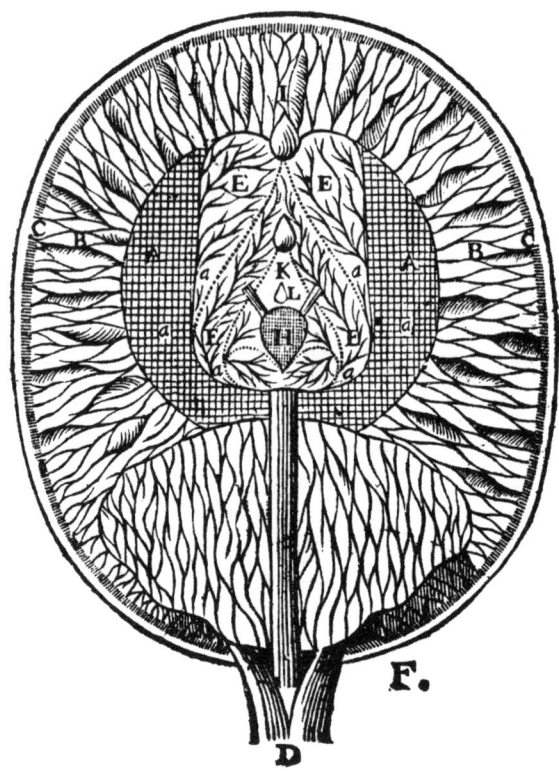

Figure 8.1 Descartes' illustration of the brain, showing the pineal gland (H), the 'seat of the soul' (from *Traite de l'Homme*, 1664)

That mind and body were separate was confirmed for Descartes by the Christian vision of the judgement and afterlife, which implies that the soul can continue to exist in the absence of the body. Furthermore, mind and body are utterly unalike in that it is possible to doubt that one has a body (in the conventional formulation, it is possible to imagine oneself as a brain floating in a tank on Mars, which is deluded into thinking itself to be connected to a body) but not to doubt that one is thinking. It follows from this that the body is not essential to human existence; no body is required in order to recognise oneself as a thinking thing. Only the mind is diagnostically human, for animals have bodies but only humans have reason and ethical powers (Cottingham 1992: 244; Olafson 1995: 2). By implication, consciousness also has a logical priority over physical existence, and the structure of the mind itself is the basis for any epistemological certainty. It was on this point that both Locke and Newton differed from Descartes, arguing that it was the experience of material things that provided the guarantee of secure knowledge. For Locke, ideas in the mind were happenings caused by worldly entities, while Newton saw mental experience as being fed by sensory impulses transmitted by the nervous system (Ayers 1997: 108). Thus, whilst there was debate over the relative importance of logic and experience, rationalists and empiricists both understood the mind to be a space within which representations are generated. If cognition is to be identified with representation, it follows that it is distinct from the worldly objects and processes that it re-presents. As we will see, it is this notion of a distinction between the physical world and its mental representation that has allowed the notion of 'artificial intelligence' to develop, and with it the belief that what goes on inside a computer is in some sense equivalent to what happens inside a human head (Taylor 1985: 201). This suggests that a digital intelligence does not require a body in order to do what a human being does.

Separating thought from its material objects has the immediate effect of drawing attention to perception, which is now understood as mediating between the two realms. In the empiricist tradition the mind was presented as acquiring its ideas through perception, but even Descartes saw experience as a means by which a person built up a conception of the world around them, however much their perceptions were to be regarded with suspicion. Indeed, he used the image of the mind as a 'store-house' of accumulated ideas, not all of which would be in the forefront of consciousness at any one time. Locke's empiricism was qualified by the suggestion that our mental representation of a thing that we experience in the world may be different from the way that the thing is in itself, but he nonetheless afforded that representation (or 'sense-impression') the status of a causal entity (Ayers 1997: 27; Smith 2002: 54). So an idea is an event of sensing, in the mind, whose instantiation can generate human actions. Thus while Descartes held that certain ideas were already present in the mind by virtue of its inherent reason, and empiricists insisted that all ideas were introduced from outside, both understood thoughts to be bounded entities contained within an equally bounded inner world. Even Hobbes, who believed thought to be no more than a particular kind of movement within the brain, distinguished the mind as an arena within which a very specific range of happenings could take place, such as dreams and the recognition of images (Peters 1956: 77). Hobbes's conception of thought may have been entirely mechanistic, but he still understood thinking to be something that went on within an encapsulated space that was entirely separate from any context of engagement. That he saw the worlds of thought and action as the inside and outside of the body did not make his version of the mind–body relation any less dualistic. Furthermore, in presenting thought as a series of events that were occasioned by the mechanical workings of the body, Hobbes could be argued to prefigure aspects of contemporary cognitive psychology.

Mind, matter and meaning

In a sense, the full force of the mind–body dichotomy would not be felt for so long as Christian theology retained its influence within Western thought. In Descartes' conceptual framework, mind and body were ultimately united by God, as they formed complementary aspects of creation. Similarly, Locke held that thought and matter were conceptually distinct, but that God was capable of adding a mind to a material thing in order to produce a unified rational creature (Cottingham 1988: 123). It was only when the Enlightenment established a secular version of the new philosophy that the cognitive and the physical came to be understood as utterly irreconcilable (Cassirer 1951: 97). In this view, the mind is not the same kind of substance as the physical world, but is composed of thought itself (Olafson 1995: 7). Irrespective of whether the mind had any innate content, or whether it was simply a 'blank slate' that could be filled by experience, it had come to be seen as transcendental, existing prior to its insertion into the material and social world. For if mind and body are separate, then the ability to think rationally is anterior to one's having any physical world to think *about*. One consequence of this formulation was that language began to be understood in a very particular way. This involved the transformation of the ideas inside human heads into utterances or inscriptions in the external world, before they could be internalised by another mind. This gives language a somewhat ambivalent character, composed of encapsulated ideas in communicative form which are distinct from any material thing that they might represent or discuss.

The issue of language raises in acute form the inner–outer dichotomy that we discussed in Chapter 7, and which seems to attend any separation of mind from matter. In Descartes' view the mind or soul has no spatial extent, and so in a sense cannot be said to 'be' anywhere, yet he clearly also understands it to constitute an inner realm within the person (Smith 2002: 52). Just as language is believed to convey thoughts from the inside into the outer world, so the problem of knowledge comes to be seen as one of *correspondence* between mental representations and physical reality (Taylor 2000: 119). Cartesian rationalism is grounded in a sceptical attitude towards what we experience, and while empiricism presents materiality as an absolute guarantee of being, it is no better placed to cope with the 'problem of other minds', already raised in Chapter 6. As the reader will recall, we may be content not to doubt that we ourselves are thinking, or even the physical existence of other persons. Yet if we adhere to the mind–body duality we may be reluctant to admit that those other persons are thinking beings like ourselves. Our own inner workings and mental states seem to be transparent to us, and it is self-evident to us that we ourselves have a mind (Glendinning 1998: 9). But if the minds of others cannot be directly observed, and we can only see their behaviour, we may conclude that they are some elaborate form of automaton, programmed to act as if thinking. Modern notions of mind can consequentially have the unfortunate effect of leaving us in some uncertainty over the humanness of those who surround us.

Modern epistemology has attempted to find certainty in the irrefutability of our thinking, or in the absolute character of our experience of material things. In either case the thinking mind is separated completely from the objects that it apprehends. In Descartes' formulation the external world has only extension and velocity, qualities that can be expressed in mathematical terms. Physical matter cannot think, but can be represented in the mind. Mind thinks, and renders the physical world meaningful. So human beings find their essential being as creatures who bring meaning into an inherently meaningless world. Moreover, humans are understood as rational and ethical agents, who cause change in the world through deliberate decisions that they make, while worldly objects are determined by causal necessity (Toulmin 1990: 107). This distinction was to prove persuasive for many decades: even Kant would argue that the natural world could be understood through mathematics, but that thought was exempt from mechanistic explanations (ibid.: 114). Later still, Husserl was to argue that the universe was composed of meaningless things that were rendered meaningful by the human mind (Andler 2000: 146). These developments form a part of the process described at the start of this book, in which the Aristotelian teleological vision of the world was eclipsed by a cosmology that was focused on humanity, and particularly on consciousness. Meaning was evicted from the world, and limited to the contents of the mind. If the world can be identified as amounting to nothing but meaningless matter before human beings involve themselves with it, then it can be rendered as simply a set of resources that is at their disposal.

Both rationalism and empiricism presented the existence of material objects as relatively unproblematic. Things simply exist in the world, prior to being given meaning by humanity (see Chapter 9). Cartesianism admits to scepticism over the existence of the physical world as a first principle, but goes on to suggest that if we can be sure that we are thinking then our reason can confirm the character of the physical world for us. Through reason, the knower knows the world, reciprocally guaranteeing their own existence (Marion 1996: 77). Descartes argues that we should come to know things through reason and mathematics, while the empiricists demanded that we should gain knowledge by encountering things in their brute physicality. But in either case things are seen as essentially 'present-at-hand'. That is, they are free-standing and isolated objects that can be addressed in the first instance through distanced, analytical observation (Heidegger 1962: 129). In this sense, objects are taken as givens by modern thought. They can be measured and weighed, and their attributes can be catalogued. Accordingly, the mind of the human subject comes to be seen as not merely conceptually distinct from the object world but also disengaged from the world in which it operates.

We have seen that modern thought defines the essence of humanity in terms of consciousness, rationality and ethical action. Despite this, modern westerners often conceive of themselves as things or entities, as a 'what' as much as a 'who'. There are two elements to this paradox. First, although the mind is understood as the source of our humanness, the mind–body distinction enables us to think of it as having been conferred upon a pre-existing physical entity. Thus our existence is conceived as substance-plus-thought, and we have two 'natures': as a thinking subject and a material object (ibid.: 123). This enables us to slip into the way of thinking where we find ourselves as an object amongst other worldly objects. But more importantly, the object–subject relationship is one between a thinking thing and a substantial thing. The mind, although a metaphysical concept, is always understood as an entity.

Innate ideas

The central issue that divided empiricists and rationalists was that of whether the mind had any innate content, a debate that directly prefigured contemporary arguments over 'nativism' in psychology. During the medieval era it had broadly been agreed that one could only know that which had been directly experienced by the senses. Descartes' distrust of sense data effectively recalled Plato, who had argued that the physical world was complex and confused, and that real knowledge consequentially had to be developed in abstraction (Lowe 1995: 15). Descartes was content that the senses conveyed information about material things to the mind, which then represented them. However, he also claimed that the mind was complete and able to think without recourse to a world. This is because the mind contains certain innate ideas, which have been placed there by God (Sorell 1987: 72). Indeed, for Descartes the human mind is similar in structure to that of God, and contains all the necessary equipment to enable thought to take place. This means that at birth a person will already have an awareness of God, a recognition of causation, an understanding of physical substance, an appreciation of the principles of geometry, and so on.

The challenge to Descartes' view was presented in Locke's *Essay Concerning Human Understanding* ([1690] 1998). Locke took very seriously the view that ideas were the contents of the mind, claiming that at birth the mind was 'an empty cabinet'. For this reason, his work proved influential in the study of education, and in those areas of social thought that emphasise the conditioning effect of the environment (Harris 1968: 11). The publication of the *Essay* is sometimes taken as the single event that started the Enlightenment, for Locke's advocacy of the view that the mind is a 'clean slate' underwrote the pursuit of human perfection through knowledge and reason. Locke argued that all knowledge comes ultimately from experience, but that complex ideas can be put together in the mind from simple ones. He believed any notion of innate knowledge to be nonsensical (Atherton 1998: 50). This was because it required ideas to already be in the mind without having been consciously considered. For Locke, a person could not agree with some statement if they had not ever been consciously aware of it. Locke compared innate ideas, which must logically have been in the mind since birth, with memories. The latter might have to be brought back to consciousness by a deliberate effort, but did relate to something that had been consciously experienced at some time in the past. He did not deny that the mind might have certain fixed abilities or principles of operation, but he rejected any notion of a pre-given content (ibid.: 54). Descartes professed to see consciousness as characteristic of human thought, and Locke objected that this conflicted with the proposition that a person could have ideas of which they had never been conscious.

For Descartes the innate ideas of the mind served to render sensory experiences intelligible, but Locke suggested that the senses directly introduced information into the mind, and that this did not need to be qualified by thought. Experience in the world caused ideas to enter the head (Ayers 1997: 17; Lowe 1995: 36). Hence Locke's image of the empty cabinet is especially apt: he simply imagines ideas being lodged into an enclosed space. It would only be once these ideas had been internalised that they would form raw materials that could be 'processed' by reason. For Locke, the reason why the ideas in our minds might not correspond with things in the outside world was not related to interpretation but was a consequence of perception itself. Our perceptions can be inaccurate. The different senses apprehend different aspects of any phenomenon, thereby disaggregating it. So in the mind a thing registers as a series of simple ideas generated by its various qualities: motion, figure, extension, density, and so on (Ayers 1997: 9).

However, Locke's intervention did not settle the issue of innate ideas for good. In the later eighteenth century Kant was to argue that although objects are always encountered in the world, they are rendered comprehensible by concepts which are a priori. The human mind has certain cognitive powers, which include reason, judgement and understanding. The understanding is able to provide principles and categories which pre-exist any experience of the world, and which organise our sense impressions. When we experience worldly things, we discover that we already know how to make sense of them, and in the process come to recognise that we already have certain a priori understandings (Burnham 2000: 20). In this way, Kant seeks to overcome Locke's arguments against innate ideas by suggesting that it is through our perception and ordering of nature that we come to recognise understandings that we have always already had. This is subtly different from Locke's characterisation of innate ideas as being like memories of experiences that we have never had.

Vision, perception and objectivity

The relationship between the subject and the object which characterises modern conceptions of knowledge is often identified with visual perception. Early modern philosophy was much preoccupied with optics (see Figure 8.2), while the telescope and the microscope were of fundamental significance to the scientific revolution (Jardine 1999: 95). As human beings came to be understood as autonomous individuals, their relationship with the world was increasingly expressed in terms of vision. Seeing was prioritised over the other senses, as sight came to be regarded as the principal means by which knowledge was acquired by the mind. Vision presented itself as a paradigm of cognition, for the mind was understood as re-presenting in visual form the entities encountered in the external world. The 'mind's eye' *reflected* the appearances of physical things (Jay 1986: 176). In Cartesian terms, sight is fundamental to human identity, for the subject is the bearer of the gaze while we conceive of other persons principally as visual objects (de Bolla 1996: 68). Moreover, privileging vision supported Descartes' view of the world as a series of planes and surfaces, which could be consumed from a distance. That these shapes can be apprehended by the mind has come to be seen as a consequence of intensities of light that intersect with and are reflected by objects (Barceló 2000: 21). Consequentially, realism in representation has come to be widely associated with the ways in which light falls upon geometric figures. Reality is thus connected with the outward appearance of things.

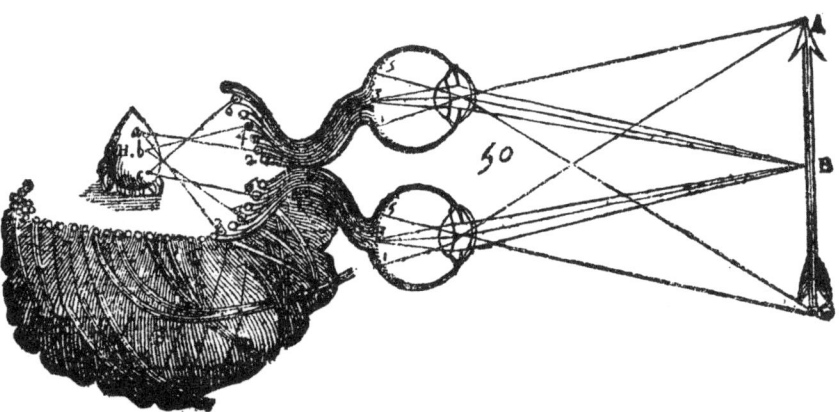

Figure 8.2 Descartes' image of visual information being conveyed to the mind by way of the optic nerve (from *Traite de l'Homme*, 1664)

It is no coincidence, then, that the coming of the modern era was connected with the emergence of new ways of looking at the world, which emphasised the realism and objectivity of the distanced gaze. Linear perspective in art, which emerged in northern Italy in the fifteenth century, enabled a 'realistic' rendition of the three-dimensional world to be achieved on a two-dimensional canvas (Cosgrove 1984: 20). Significantly, Alberti and Brunelleschi achieved this through the geometrical construction of lines converging at a 'vanishing point' on the horizon, enhancing the impression that the external world was ordered according to the laws of mathematics. From this time onwards, landscape art reproduced and legitimised an understanding of the world as having a uniform spatial order that could be apprehended visually by a dispassionate observer (Jay 1993: 118). Worldly objects – including people – were enclosed within the geometrical order of perspective art, yet the artist as viewer occupied the singular position outside of the frame from which the scene could be consumed. This location might be illusory, yet it was understood as one of godlike objectivity from which the scene as a whole could be rendered intelligible (Pollock 1988: 64). So a relationship of externality with the observed world seems to allow a simultaneous rather than a narrative perception, which makes the whole comprehensible in its totality. As Cosgrove (1984: 24) points out, landscape art was produced for the benefit of the landowning classes, who now thought of land as something that could be bought and sold, from a position of externality. Landscape art, then, embodies a series of related developments in early modern Europe: the alienation of land as wealth, objectivity, geometry and measurement, and the disengagement of autonomous individuals from social and environmental relations.

In landscape art, visuality is connected with order, just as in the observational science of the seventeenth century the structure of nature was apprehended through visual perception. In both cases, nature takes on the passive role of the object, while the observer is both active and rational. The painter is removed from any emotional entanglement with the landscape and those who live within it, just as the scientist maintains an objective distance from their experiment. In short, the ocularcentrism of the early modern West created a position of privilege for a subject who was disengaged and distanced from social life, and who could use their reason to identify or impose order on the world (Jay 1993: 118).

By the eighteenth century this emphasis on the visual sense had taken on a moral dimension. Adam Smith, for instance, argued that it is our ability to observe others that enables us to empathise with them, thereby tempering our self-interest. Equally, we are constantly aware that we may be watched by others, and this serves as a source of restraint. If we always act as if observed, we will be likely to act in an ethical manner. Finally, one aspect of our sympathy for others arises from our recognition that if we were in their position we would be seen in our distress, just as we now see them (de Bolla 1996: 75). So to a far greater extent than the other senses, vision had come to be recognised as instrumental in promoting moral behaviour. This view was given an instrumental value in Jeremy Bentham's design for the 'Panopticon', a circular prison in which the inmates could at any point be observed by warders in a central tower. Unable to be sure whether they were being watched or not, the prisoners' behaviour would be regulated accordingly (Foucault 1977: 201).

In a different way, Immanuel Kant more explicitly linked the moral complexion of visual perception to a consideration of the mental apparatus. His treatment of the mind and its functions is distinctly hierarchical in character, arguing that the capacities of thought transcend the mere functions of the brain (Burnham 2000: 8). Cognitive mechanisms enable the mental faculties to operate, and these are concerned with the ability to think about things, to have feelings, and to have desires. Thought, feeling and desire all have higher and lower forms, where in each case the lower is embedded in the physical world while the higher transcends it. It follows from this that the ability to observe freely and think about things is a superior form of cognition, while 'subjective associations', habitual practices and bodily desires are inferior (ibid.: 11). Kant clearly considered distanced, objective perception and thought to have an ethical significance.

Cognitive archaeology

Over the past four decades, extensive debates have taken place over the possibility of a 'cognitive archaeology'. My contention is that these have proceeded entirely within the metaphysical framework of mind and body that had been established in the seventeenth and eighteenth centuries. Many processual archaeologists have rejected the notion of an archaeology of mind on the grounds that 'these minds are gone, and their mental contents are not recoverable' (Hill 1994: 83). Most notably, Lewis Binford has railed against any attempt to conduct a 'palaeopsychology', since informants are not available to provide us with information concerning past norms and values (Binford 1965: 205). For Binford, archaeology is concerned with the development of culture as an extrasomatic means of adaptation, which cannot be reduced to a single feature such as thought. Yet his argument against palaeopsychology is revealing, for it relies on the view that ideas are the contents of minds, which are encapsulated in human heads. Because we do not have access to the mental worlds of past people we cannot know about past ideas. I take this to mean that Binford's point of view is as thoroughly embedded in a view of mind inherited from Cartesianism and classical empiricism as those that he seeks to criticise.

Most forms of cognitive archaeology are grounded in cognitive psychology, which understands human beings as intelligent, decision-making creatures who achieve their goals through 'complex hierarchical systems of information processing' (Segal 1994: 23). As such, they harmonise with approaches to culture as an information-processing system which have an established history in the discipline (e.g. Clarke 1968; Johnson 1978; van der Leeuw 1981). Cognitive archaeologies understand material culture as the manifestation or outcome of cognitive processes, so that each stone axe, house form or burial practice can be regarded as the end-point of a problem-solving exercise. The kind of analysis that this view promotes is one in which the problems, skills and procedures involved in achieving a change in the physical world are identified (Segal 1994: 25). These are then related to human cognitive processing abilities. It follows that whatever we can learn about human neural physiology and computational abilities can enhance our ability to comprehend the archaeological record, and conversely that the archaeological record may illuminate the evolution of the human mind. Renfrew and Bahn (1991: 342) suggest that archaeological materials that can provide evidence of human cognitive abilities in the past include living floors, traces of raw material procurement, lithic assemblages, deliberate burials, graphic representations, and indications of food sharing and time planning. Furthermore, they suggest that these issues can be addressed by assuming a universal cognitive structure in which all human beings have an individual perspective on the world, an interpretive framework, and a cognitive map of their lived world.

A classic example of how a cognitive archaeology might be put into practice is found in Colin Renfrew's study of the cubic weights of coloured stone from Mohenjo-Daro in the Indus Valley, dating to *c.* 2000 BC (Renfrew 1985). These objects represent multiples of a standard unit of weight of 0.836 grams. Renfrew argues that they can be taken as evidence for a series of ideas that must have been current within the Indus Valley civilisation: a notion of equivalence, a system of numeration, a rate of exchange between commodities of different kinds, and so on. There are few objections that can be made to what Renfrew is suggesting, but the case of the Indus Valley weights raises the question of whether an archaeology of *ideas* is necessarily the same thing as a cognitive archaeology. The concepts that Renfrew derives from the weights (units of measure, equivalence) are social ones, deployed in material practices and transactions between persons in public. Whether Renfrew has succeeded in accessing the contents of the minds of ancient Indus Valley people is at once more arguable, and even inessential to the broader thrust of his argument. Perhaps more directly relevant to the project of accessing past minds is Thomas Wynn's use of the degrees of symmetry identifiable in Acheulean hand-axes and upper palaeolithic cave art as an index of developments in human cognition (Wynn 2000: 130). By this means, Wynn seeks to demonstrate that artefacts can directly inform us about the organisation and functioning of human minds. However, it is notable that in order for Wynn's arguments to hold one must accept a series of assumptions about the character of minds, in this case derived from

Piagetian psychology. This means that Wynn's project is inherently metaphysical. In this respect, cognitive archaeology itself can be regarded as a kind of metaphysics, for it always begins from the position that there is a thing called a mind, which is distinct from the outside physical world and which can only ever be observed through the consequences of its functioning.

Contemporary Cartesianism: mind, brain and information

Descartes used the terms 'mind', 'soul' and 'spirit' relatively indiscriminately, and it is plain that contemporary cognitive psychology rejects the latter two concepts. There is a more materialist edge to cognitive science, which emphasises that the brain is a physical organ that operates through electrical and chemical processes (Cottingham 1992: 252). Nonetheless, cognitivism continues to understand the mind as a closed system distinct from the outside world, and there is some ambiguity concerning the relationship between brain and mind. In the arena of cognitive evolution, Merlin Donald argues that the human mind 'coevolved' with brain and culture (Donald 1993: 737), suggesting that he at least considers it not to be quite the same thing as either. Much of the literature on evolutionary psychology is preoccupied with the notion of 'mental architecture', but again the way that this imagined spatiality is linked to that of the brain is often obscure. My impression is that the mind is sometimes understood as an entity which is immanent in the brain. It is not like the Aristotelian soul, which was conceived as something that is integral to the body. Instead it is brought into being by the operation of the brain, occupying the same space as it, but also a kind of virtual space of its own. Hence it is able to acquire an 'architecture' of its own which is only indirectly linked to the physical organisation of the brain. For instance, it is sometimes suggested that the peripheral systems are linked to specific parts of the brain, but that the central processing capacities of the mind are more distributed. In this way, cognitive science presents an image of the mind that implicitly draws on both Descartes and Kant: the mind is bounded and separate from the object world, while transcending the physical matter of the brain.

Where cognitive psychology is more explicit and unified is in its belief that the mind is an information-processing system, as mentioned above. It broadly adheres to the cybernetic theory of information defined by Claude Shannon in the 1940s (Guilbaud 1959). This holds that information is quite distinct from meaningful content, and can be reduced to a binary mathematical code which can be transmitted from an emitter to a receiver (Dreyfus 1992: 165). So information can be a representation without being meaningful. Such a view demands that information is always atomic in character, transmitted as a series of 'bits' that can be picked up by the receptors of the receiver. As an information-processing system, the mind takes in such messages and reorganises them, comparing, evaluating and storing units of information (Segal 1994: 23). Visual information, for instance, is accessed as patterns of light and rendered significant by comparison to representations that are held in the memory. This means that the intelligibility of things in the world is identified with their capacity to be processed (Taylor 1993: 324). In other words, the conception of the mind as an information-processing system demands that it operates according to heuristic rules in order to classify, compare and order information. This view has become entrenched over the past century, owing to the development of electronic computers. Computers have been created within the framework of modern thought, as a means of replicating and enhancing some of the tasks attributed to the human mind. Their overwhelming success at those tasks has tended to promote the circular argument that the computer therefore provides an analogue for what the mind is like. Artificial intelligence research, for instance, is based on the assumption that since minds do the same things as computers it is only a matter of time before a machine is successfully configured to achieve consciousness. Yet it is arguable whether the mind has an information-processing level of operation at all, which takes in bits of information as raw sense data bereft of meaning, and proceeds to organise, typify and compare them prior to giving them meaning (Dreyfus 1992: 164; Wrathmall 2000: 95). For the vision of the mind as an information-processor to be viable it would have to be able to explain how the ingestion and processing of bits of knowledge from the outside world could achieve an understanding of that world which is anything like our own. This proposition demands some explication.

First, the suggestion that human beings absorb information in an atomic form needs to be questioned. The scientific revolution had promoted a view of the world as composed of atomic particles that behaved in relation to one another according to a series of mechanical laws (Smith 2002: 36). This facilitated the derivation of mechanistic theories of physics, but in the process the procedures of science were 'ontologised', in the sense that they came to be identified as an accurate representation of the universe (ibid.: 54). If laws of nature could be defined in atomic terms, so could the operation of the mind, conceived as a container of ideas supplied with information by the neural system. This picture has been made more sophisticated by equating the intake of information with bursts of neural energy in the brain (Dreyfus 1992: 159). However, this implies that what goes on inside the mind is a straightforward series of distinct events, each linked causally to the next. In this conception our understanding of reality is pieced together from units of information that have been processed in this way before being subjected to some form of pattern recognition. The flaw in this is that it presumes that our awareness of the world takes such an accretional form, and is always the end product of the gathering of atoms of meaning-free information. This cannot explain why our understanding of our context is generally unthematised and inexplicit. The implicit character of our everyday, habitual dealings with our life-world suggests something very different from an internal representation generated from a heap of facts. Indeed, the alternative that I will suggest below is that we apprehend worldly things in their meaningfulness, and that the world constitutes a horizon of intelligibility which renders them significant. This intimate and imbricated relationship between phenomena and the world as background makes a nonsense of the idea that human beings pick up bits of information and process them as neural impulses that equate to binary machine code.

There are a variety of ways in which human activity is quite unlike the rule-based processing of atomised inputs that is characteristic of computers. Not only do we deal with significant phenomena in a world of meaning, but we are able to tolerate the ambiguity of things, which is not easily expressed in binary code. Phenomena may be 'neither one thing nor another', or they may only impinge on the fringes of our awareness. Furthermore, human beings are capable of distinguishing between those aspects of their surroundings that are relevant and irrelevant as they go along: they do not first process masses of data and then decide which of them are relevant (Dreyfus 1992: 206). The comparison between computers and human minds breaks down because, on the one hand, computers do some things (like calculation and storing raw information) much better and faster than humans, but on the other, no attempt to make a computer do the rest of what humans do has been remotely successful. Most importantly, a computer is always a 'what' and never a 'who'. It is most unlikely that any amount of increased processing power or memory storage will result in a device that, like HAL9000 in *2001: A Space Odyssey*, will suddenly blossom into self-awareness. A computer could not overnight find itself in a situation in which its own being had become an issue for it. One reason for this is that a computer is not an embodied social being, and does not have purposes of its own. A computer cannot care, or feel shame (Taylor 1985: 195). Moreover, the purpose of the computer is always relative to a being outside of itself, who operates it. A computer is composed of hardware (processors, memory, peripherals) and software, the former built by engineers and the latter written by programmers. But over and above this, when I sit at my computer and use my word-processing package to write, or use a graphics package to draw a diagram, it is *my* purpose that is being enacted not that of the computer.

My intentionality is engaged in directing the computer to carry out certain tasks which it is better placed to conduct than I am. This relationship demonstrates the difference between us. I can compute, although I cannot do it anything like as efficiently as the computer. But computation is only one of the things that I can do, and I do not do it all the time. Indeed, it is not even the only means that I have for coping with everyday problems: I won't always articulate my tasks in explicit terms and then seek to resolve them into a series of discrete steps (Taylor 1985: 188). Yet this is precisely what a computer would have to do were it to simulate the process by which my actions are arrived at. And a simulation is all that this could ever be, for in carrying out the same operations as I do the computer only achieves the outward semblance of the process, without the core of meaning, care and concern. Human action rarely involves any kind of explicit computation, and while it might be argued that we are simply unaware of the extent to which our own thought processes are calculative at a subliminal level, all our skilled performances rely upon forms of knowledge that we would struggle to spell out verbally.

Background, world and coping

The most thoroughly and explicitly articulated challenge to the model of mind that has emerged from early modern philosophy and which now manifests itself as cognitive psychology and artificial intelligence research is found in the work of Hubert Dreyfus (1992). Above all, Dreyfus contests the idea that a machine could ever become indistinguishable from a human being on the grounds that computers do not have a world, in the sense of a background against which phenomena are rendered intelligible, and they do not have coping skills. As I have already suggested, we do not consume raw information from the environment and then render it meaningful; things are always already meaningful to us as soon as we register their existence. This happens because things are always revealed to us as 'standing out' from a background, which is to say that nothing ever exists for us independently from its context. This background is composed of shared social practices, skills and activities (Wrathmall 2000: 93). These practices enable us to find our way around our world, to get on with our everyday lives without having to make everything explicit. Traditions of practical knowledge are inherited without needing to be made explicit, and are embodied and inhabited rather than articulated (Taylor 1993: 327). It is in the context of coping with our daily existence, knowing how to go on from one moment to the next while not having to stand back and think about it, that phenomena are revealed to us as things that we already understand.

The background is the context that renders things comprehensible, and the interwoven relationship between things and their context is such that it can only be understood in holistic terms. It is a totality of involvements, a network of relationships within which things are enmeshed. However, this is not to say that we could ever describe the background in its totality, still less that it is composed of a series of free-standing things that we could enumerate or list. The background is the context in which we human beings operate, and in which we are embedded. This is something that only an embodied human being can achieve, just as only a fleshly creature can have haptic skills. A background which is at once a totality and yet inexplicit – and incapable of being made explicit – is difficult to put into the terms of artificial intelligence. A computer is not able to inhabit such a background, or to 'have' a background, and it is still less possible for the background to be rendered in such a form that it could be input into a machine (Dreyfus 1992: 208). The background cannot be defined as a set of rules, and it cannot be represented in any way (Andler 2000: 141). Yet if we encounter things as meaningful rather than as meaningless sense data, the background is the condition of the possibility of anything registering as significant to us at all (ibid.: 144). This is how it is that we do not first process information and then decide what is important: things show up to us in their significance because of the place that they occupy within a relational totality.

To put this into more concrete terms: when we encounter a drinking glass on a table, cognitive psychology would say that our eyes register a pattern of light, which is conveyed to the brain via the optic nerve as a series of impulses. The mind then processes the raw information about the glass, working upward from meaning-free sense impressions to considerations of form and size, material substance, and design, finally comparing it with memory traces of other objects, which ultimately identify it as a drinking glass. I suggest that the process is quite different: we simply see a drinking glass. This 'seeing' is not built upon a pyramid of sense data, classification, processing and comparison, conducted inside the head. Rather, it is our worldly engagement with the thing itself, our skills and practices, that enables the thing to show up to us as a glass. It is the knowledge that containers hold liquid, the experience of thirst and its quenching, the habitual presence of glasses on tables in rooms of a particular kind, our familiarity with drinking vessels that have been made from a particular substance, and so on, which together form the web of intra-worldly relations from which the thing stands out as intelligible. Much of this knowledge takes the form of knowing about relations and conventions, rather than facts about things. The thing can be comprehended because it has a place in a cultural nexus within which it has a function, and is drawn into the purposes of human beings. And we can comprehend it because we ourselves are embedded in the same background, we inhabit a world of meaning that we have never had to enter from outside. We find ourselves 'thrown' into such a world, we are always already within it (Heidegger 1962: 174). This is another important distinction between a human being and a computer: a machine can never experience *throwness*.

This notion of a non-representable background begins to break down the dichotomy between the inside and outside of the person. It suggests that our understanding of things does not take a form in which it is represented within us. As Charles Taylor puts it, our grasp of the world is not to be distinguished from what it is a grasp of, which resides inside us, over and against the world (Taylor 2000: 118). This means that much of our knowledge is not mediated: it is a means of engagement in the world rather than abstracted reflection in preparation for action. My ability to cope with the drinking glass lies in its materiality and capacity to hold liquids, my embodied ability to raise it to my lips, my familiarity with this means of drinking, as opposed to a baby's feeding bottle. None of this can be expressed as a set of rules or codes, because it has been understood without ever having been made explicit. But it is only capable of operating in the context of a lived material world. Our skilled coping abilities are not contained in our heads to the extent that they could be extracted from a brain floating in a tank (Geertz 2000: 205).

The concept of a relational background also does damage to the belief that entities in our environment represent disengaged objects that can be readily grasped as atoms of information. Things always present themselves to us as parts of a world. The world that we inhabit is composed not of a pile of autonomous facts, but of a network of practical involvements, or states of affairs (Olafson 1995: 104). Being human is a matter not simply of having a body or a mind of a particular kind, so much as of having a world. As human beings, things show themselves to us as comprehensible, but they always do so in the first instance within a context of involvement. So to return to the glass: it announces itself to me in the context of my project of having a drink of water. My understanding of this particular glass emerges from a set of connections between my thirst, my habituated familiarity with the spatial layout of the kitchen, my awareness of the properties and behaviour of water, and my skilled ability to turn on a tap. As an isolated, freestanding object the glass does not exist as a given; it has to be made. Rather than seeing it first as an alienated object and then assessing its usefulness for my purpose, I may come to focus on it in an analytical way and transform it into an isolated entity, which I can reflect on, and whose attributes I can list. But this may not happen until I have already used it to quench my thirst. For the creation of an analytical object requires an act of 'unworlding', in which I have to strip the thing of the background context in which I first recognised it.

Human being and presencing

As we have seen, Cartesianism identifies being a conscious subject as the essence of humanity. Our discussion of background and everyday coping suggests something quite different: being human means being the kind of creature for whom things are 'there' (Critchley 2000: 106; Olafson 1995: 11). What this means is that it is only for human beings that the things of the world present themselves in a meaningful way, a process that we might refer to as 'presencing'. Humans inhabit a world within which things are intelligible. Presencing can occur because human beings are embodied and relational interpreting beings. It cannot be attributed to any isolated characteristic of the mind or the body. Nor can it be seen as the achievement of any single being: it can only happen because humans exist in a state of being-in-the-world, which involves being alongside others, and being an inheritor of cultural traditions of understanding. All of these things together form a 'horizon of disclosure', within which things present themselves. Furthermore, things are revealed to us whether we like it or not. We do not at any point choose whether we are going to allow or require them to show themselves – it just happens (Young 2002: 8). This is a matter not of consciousness, but of inconspicuous familiarity with a life-world.

Just how non-optional the disclosure of worldly things is can be demonstrated by the issue of mood. Just as we always find ourselves to be already in a world and embedded in many sets of relationships, we always find ourselves to be in a mood, whether it be one of joyfulness, elation, amusement, anxiety, indignation or equanimity. We do not choose this mood: we are 'delivered over' to it (Heidegger 1962: 173). Our moods reveal the world to us in different ways. Depending upon how we are feeling, some prospects for the future suggest themselves to us and others are closed off. So mood is not just a superficial shading that rests on the surface of our existence, it is instead a significant aspect of the way that different possibilities present themselves to us at any given time. Further, because things disclose themselves to us in relation to our projects and concerns, they will attract our notice or elicit our involvement in different ways depending upon our mood. Heidegger's classic example of this is the case of anxiety, which is a mood in which we are unable to cope with the world at all because we cannot project our future possibilities. We simply cannot see our way forward in life. Such a state discloses the world in a very particular way, such that our familiarity with our surroundings falls away, and our environment seems uncanny and distressing (ibid.: 233). The intelligibility of things has broken down, and we stare at them as they confront us with their weirdness. Needless to say, it is hard to imagine a computer that finds itself in a mood of any kind, let alone a mood of anxiety that threatens its ontological security. Yet for human beings mood is an integral part of the way in which the world is comprehensible.

Being human, then, is not a matter of being a physical organism to which a mind has been added, whether by God or by evolution. We are not conscious entities that look upon the outside world with disinterest, from within the interior of a person. Similarly, worldly things are not isolated entities that are given to us to be transformed into atoms of information. Instead, humans find themselves in a context of engagement in which their understanding of things emerges from their practical involvements. Our lived world is one of meaning, within which things reveal themselves in their significance. Cartesianism imagines that the world is first of all composed of bare objects that can be adequately described and explained by natural science, and to which meaning can be added by minds as a secondary issue. But the reverse is the case. Our world is inherently meaningful, and to arrive at a world of autonomous objects that can be grasped in purely scientific terms we must carry out an 'unworlding', and arrive at what is in some senses an impoverished and etiolated version of our environment. These considerations will now enable us to address the ways in which the concept of mind has been used in recent forms of archaeology.

Evolutionary psychology and mental modularity

We have been arguing that in a general sense the conception of mind that emerged with seventeenth-century rationalism and empiricism is one that still exerts a considerable influence over 'cognitive archaeology'. However, in recent years the more elaborate Cartesianism of cognitive psychology, and in particular evolutionary psychology, has begun to be drawn on in the study of the earliest periods of human existence (e.g. Mellars and Gibson 1996; Carruthers and Chamberlain 2000). Evolutionary psychology concerns itself with the changing structure and function of the human mind over time. This means that it asserts not only that there is a distinct and bounded entity that we can identify as a 'mind' but also that this has a particular form, which is subject to the process of natural selection. To be more specific, evolutionary psychology proposes that the mind is a system composed of a number of distinct sub-systems, which are referred to by cognitive psychologists as 'modules' (Fodor 1983: 7). These modules are special-purpose cognitive entities, which process information relevant to a series of distinct domains, and 'whose operations are largely independent of, and inaccessible to, the rest of the world' (Carruthers and Chamberlain 2000: 1). Needless to say, this is the Cartesian encapsulated mind, with bells on. According to evolutionary psychologists such as Cosmides and Tooby (1994: 87), these modules have been crafted by selective pressures in order to cope with the characteristic problems faced by hunters and foragers in the Pleistocene, during which much of the evolution of the mind took place.

Mental modules are relatively autonomous entities which access information in the form of representations (Samuels 2000: 19). Each module is connected to others, receives information from perception and from other modules, and in some cases may output the results of its own processing. Yet the processing itself takes place in isolation from any external influence. Samuels (ibid.: 14) draws attention to two different conceptions of mental modules current in cognitive psychology. In the first, associated with Chomskian linguistics, the module is simply understood as a cluster of mental representations that relate to a particular domain of knowledge. But in the second, which is more characteristic of evolutionary psychology, modules are domain-specific computational devices. The critical point here is that these 'computational modules' not only receive information as representations or codes but also transform them through the operation of sets of formal rules, or algorithms. This means that the computational module is more obviously comparable with (or based upon) the kinds of processes that take place within an electronic computer. Indeed, evolutionary psychology adheres to the understanding that the mind is 'a computer made out of organic compounds rather than silicon chips' (ibid.: 16).

Computational modules are 'designed' to carry out a distinct kind of manipulation, which is limited by the specific kind of data that they are fitted to input. This is argued to be highly efficient in evolutionary terms, because if the mind were like a computer that ran a single, general-purpose learning program, it would take a very long time to come up with a solution to immediate problems. If every aspect of the surrounding environment had to be input and assessed before a decision was made on how best to intercept a gazelle or to avoid a sabre-toothed cat, the survival chances of the Pleistocene hunter would be compromised. Yet if the appropriate information is quickly processed by a special-purpose module, the appropriate action can be arrived at almost instantly. This means that specialised mental modules would confer a selective advantage on particular human beings. However, this characterisation of the so-called 'frame problem' (Mithen 1996: 45) demonstrates that it is only a problem at all within the assumptions of cognitive psychology. For it relies upon the premise that actions are taken on the basis of cognitive deliberation, and that this deliberation takes the form of an encapsulated processing of explicit input information gathered by perception. Our discussion of background suggests that instead of the hunter's acts issuing out from their head, they are formulated within the world by an embodied being who has an implicit understanding of gazelle, cats, vegetation, spears, and their own ability to run away.

In addition to the distinction between 'Chomskian' and computational modules, there is a difference of opinion over the extent to which the whole of the mind is or is not composed of a series of modular units. Jerry Fodor, who pioneered the notion of mental modularity, insists that only the peripheral systems of the mind are modular: those that are concerned with perception and with other inputs and outputs. By contrast, the central processing systems are not modular, but more networked and connected, and are not related to the activities of any particular part of the brain (Fodor 1983). Similarly, Merlin Donald makes the case that consciousness is not modular because it involves the integration of information from many different domains. Consequentially, he argues that the evolution of the human mind in its present form could have involved the increasing processing power of the central systems, or the development of a series of more specialised modules, or some combination of the two (Donald 1998: 9). Others take the view that even the central systems of the mind are modular: this has become known as the 'massive modularity' hypothesis (Carruthers and Chamberlain 2000: 2). The implication is that the central part of the mind is composed of a series of elements that have distinct tasks, such as the generation of beliefs from information provided by the peripheral systems, probabilistic inference, and biological categorisation.

One such central processing module whose existence has been hypothesised is that which concerns itself with 'theory of mind'. The theory of mind module confers on a creature the ability to understand another's mental states, and to see the world from their point of view (Dunbar 2000: 238). The intuitive understanding that this generates allows creatures to predict each other's behaviour, while also facilitating co-operation. This relates directly to the problem of other minds, as discussed on p. 132. The notion of a theory of mind module is based on the assumption that, universally, primates first apprehend each other as behaving bodies, and may then be in a position to infer that the other creature has a mind like their own. That others are what they think, and that their doings are merely a surface manifestation of their cognition, is a very modern Western prejudice. As we have seen, the alternative view is that others are what they do, and that our everyday understanding of them as people emerges from our living alongside them (Glendinning 1998: 58). This demonstrates very effectively the extent to which the metaphysics of evolutionary psychology is riddled with contemporary presuppositions.

By definition, mental modules are specialised. For evolutionary psychology they are 'elegant machines' designed by natural selection to deal with specific problems. Moreover, they may be 'content rich', so that rather than simply amounting to a set of abstract algorithms for particular procedures they actually contain information relevant to specific projects and problems – a kind of hybrid between computational and Chomskian modules (Samuels 2000: 21). This means that, according to certain evolutionary psychologists, not just the structure but even some of the content of the mind is innate. Individual modules and their native information are hard-wired into the mind at birth, and lie dormant until a particular stage of development (Mithen 1996: 43). So, effectively, the concept of mental modularity has re-ignited the debate between Descartes and Locke. Evolutionary psychology claims that the architecture of the mind is the outcome of millions of years of natural selection, and that innovations that have served to solve adaptive problems have gradually become embedded in the genetic inheritance passed on to each new generation. The empirical justification for this is that children learn so much about their world so quickly that their minds must be programmed to do so at birth (ibid.: 44). Once again, such an argument only holds for so long as we accept that knowledge must take the form of atomised units held inside the head. Such units of knowledge either must be acquired in the outside world or must be innate in the mind. This view neglects both the role of background and implicit understanding, and that of social tradition.

One revealing characteristic of the literature of evolutionary psychology is the way that much of it is concerned with the choice of appropriate metaphors for the mind. This appears to amount to a tacit acceptance of the metaphysical nature of the concept of mind. The model of a computer running a general-purpose learning program is widely rejected, as modularity is connected with specialised forms of mentality. The alternative preferred by Tooby and Cosmides (1992) is to say that the mind is like a Swiss-army knife. By this they mean that the mind is a singular entity which has a series of special-purpose elements. This structure has arisen from the way that the evolutionary process has bolted a number of task-specific entities onto the mind as adaptations to particular sets of selective pressures. Nonetheless, if the mind is a Swiss-army knife, it appears to be one that inputs, processes and outputs information. So at a deeper level, the comparison between the mind and the computer is still active, and evolutionary psychology keeps returning to it. Mithen (1996: 33) expands on this point by suggesting that the brain is the fleshly computer hardware, and that the mind is the software that runs on it. This being the case, he argues that cognitive evolution has been a process analogous to the de-bugging of a program: first the software has to be made to run without crashing, and then more complex functions have gradually been added. So according to Mithen's metaphor, 'natural selection blindly wrote the software programs of the mind' (ibid.: 243). Thus natural selection is the software engineer, and the mind is a program, or perhaps more appropriately a software suite. However, this way of thinking falls foul of the problem of agency that we have already noted. A computer always has an external operator, who uses the software that the designer has created in order to perform a set of tasks. Mithen gives us no indication of how it is possible for the mind to be at once a tool that is used by an agent and a conscious subject who is directing a set of actions. This is the flipside of the question of how a computer could ever come to be a conscious social actor simply by becoming a more and more powerful processor of information. And all of the special-purpose mental modules in the world cannot serve to explain how a mind could come to define problems for itself, and to care about them.

Narratives of cognitive evolution

A series of competing accounts of cognitive evolution have emerged from different strands of evolutionary psychology as it has been applied to archaeology. To a greater or lesser extent these are somewhat teleological, in that the upper palaeolithic 'cultural explosion' of 35,000 years ago is taken as a fundamental horizon of change that requires explanation, and as a kind of denouement to the evolution of the mind. In particular, where the modular structure of the contemporary human mind is understood as a consequence of selective pressures specific to hunting and gathering in the Pleistocene, it is the cultural efflorescence of the end of the palaeolithic that appears to round the process off. This phase of cultural change was characterised by the emergence of a series of material innovations. Elaborate symbolism is demonstrated in cave painting, figurines, carvings on bone and antler and funerary

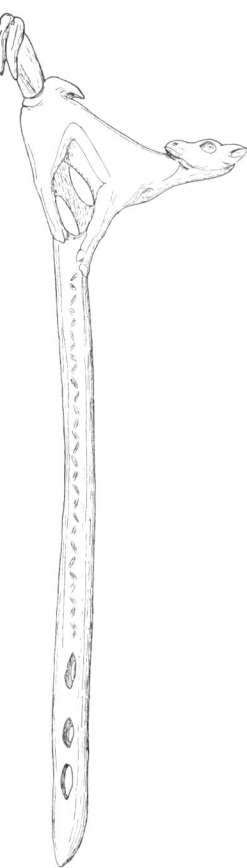

Figure 8.3 Upper palaeolithic art and hunting technology: spear-thrower from Mas d'Azil (from Dorothy Garrod, Palaeolithic spear-throwers, in G. Clark (ed.) *Contributions to Prehistoric Archaeology Offered to V. Gordon Childe*, Prehistoric Society 1956)

ritual (Carruthers and Chamberlain 2000: 6; Gamble 1986: 324). In addition, more complex forms of subsistence technology can be attributed to the same general period (Figure 8.3). All of this is taken as an indication that the upper palaeolithic saw the achievement of a human cognitive capacity equivalent to that of people now living. However, there is some debate over whether the changes in art and technology are a straightforward manifestation of a reorganisation of the mind, or whether they were built upon a cognitive capacity that had already been in place for some considerable while (Gibson 1996: 39).

One interpretation of the evolution of mind that draws heavily on the language of computers and artificial intelligence is that presented by Merlin

Donald in *Origins of the Modern Mind* (1991). For Donald, cognitive evolution was partly a matter of the increasing processing power of the brain. As in a computer, the growing capacity of the brain allowed qualitatively different functions to emerge. The human brain is, he argues, simply a larger version of the brains of other apes, and the mind that it supports has had certain new modules added which enable faculties such as language (Donald 1991: 100). However, Donald maintains that the critical process in transforming the mind has been the development of new forms of memory representation. He identifies three critical transitions in human evolution, each associated with changes in the representational structure of the mind: mimesis (non-linguistic representational acts), lexical invention (language, enabling the creation of a mythic culture) and the externalisation of memory. These new representational strategies are taken as indicating changes in the underlying 'neuropsychological architecture' (Donald 1993: 738). In particular, the new cognitive abilities involved in reading, writing and visual representation may have been made possible by the increased neocortical plasticity attributed to the most recent expansion of the human brain (ibid.: 746).

The extent to which Donald relies upon the atomist-computational view of cognition is demonstrated by his discussion of the mind's memory system, which he holds to be composed of an 'articulatory loop', a 'sketchpad' and a central executive (Donald 1991: 247). When we think, he argues, we either visualise or verbalise. Clearly, this view maintains the Cartesian separation between things in the world and representations of those things in the head. This impression is confirmed by the last of the hypothetical transitions in his evolutionary scheme, the introduction of external memory. This involves a series of increasingly powerful new representational devices in the period since the upper palaeolithic: visuosymbolic invention (drawing, painting, and eventually writing and number systems), external memory records, and theories (Donald 1993: 745). 'Exographic storage' is described as a 'hardware change' which had a colossal effect on human memory structure. This sounds very much like adding an external hard-drive to one's computer, enabling a greater volume of information (in the strictly cybernetic sense) to be retained and accessed. Such a storage device is certainly external to the computer, but in what sense are the art and writing that Donald is referring to external to human beings? Clearly, the relationship of exteriority only makes sense if one is again relying upon the Cartesian model of an encapsulated mind. The notion of 'external symbolic storage' implies that information from inside a human mind can be 'dumped' into the material world in such a way that it can be recovered at a later point:

> The items displayed in the external memory field are treated first as natural objects and events and second as memory representations that can externally program the user's brain.
>
> (Donald 1993: 747)

This indicates that Donald is drawing a distinction between material things as mere objects and material things that have been invested with retrievable information (like the distinction between the hard-drive as a mute lump of plastic and silicon and as a working peripheral device). So he echoes Descartes' view of the world as a meaningless geometrical space that is invested with meaning by human beings. Moreover, the suggestion that the introduction of such material storage devices represents a radical departure forces a separation between *cultural* memory aids and the mnemonic quality of moving and dwelling within the *natural* world. That is, Donald's argument suggests that only objects that have had information deliberately vested in them are significant for the purposes of remembering. We might object that memory is a matter not of the investment and retrieval of information but of the relationship between embodied subjects and their world. Remembering the past involves physical movement, bodily posture, taste and smell (Connerton 1989). Furthermore, the use of material things to trigger memories always involves interpretation. The very existence of literary theory demonstrates that reading a written text is never the equivalent of a computer's reading of a binary code.

Donald's concern with the internal mind and its external symbolic storage leads him to construct an evolutionary narrative that is strangely reminiscent of seventeenth-century views of the civilising process. He argues that non-human mammals have 'isolated minds' which are untouched by culture (Donald 1998: 11). Over time, humans who live in symbol-using communities have developed towards a 'collective mind', through a process of 'emergent enculturation'. As Donald puts it, 'collectivity depends ultimately on individual capacity' (ibid.). Through the use of gestures, language and symbols, separate minds gradually become embedded in an accumulating cultural tradition. Since the upper palaeolithic, with its horizon of representational acceleration, cognitive change has been driven by cultural innovation. All of this suggests a picture very like the change from the state of nature, in which human beings lived in isolation, to the social contract. The change is one from nature to culture, and from singularity to collectivity through the construction of relationships that extend beyond the person. Donald presents human beings as in the first instance unconnected and autonomous, like modern individuals, and only enabled to enter into relations with others through their achievement of cognitive maturity. That language and culture are inherently social, and not added to a pre-existing cognitive entity, appears not to figure in this version of human development.

Mithen: the making of the human mind

A rather different view of cognitive evolution is presented by Steven Mithen in *The Prehistory of the Mind* (1996). In this very impressive synthetic work, Mithen seeks to balance what he acknowledges as the advantages of the specialised intelligence of mental modules with the connectivity and flow of ideas facilitated by a general intelligence. For him, the evolution of the human mind has seen alternating phases in which either of the two forms of cognition has dominated. Amongst early hominids, minds were dominated by general intelligence. The 'programs' of these minds were composed of a suite of multi-purpose learning and decision-making rule-sets. Later, multiple specialised intelligences (or modules), each of which was connected with a particular domain of practical activity, were added on to the core of general intelligence. But these specialised intelligences operated in isolation from one another, so that Neanderthals (for example) were unable to transfer ideas relating to natural history into the domain of technological knowledge, and vice versa. Finally, the barriers between the several specialised intelligences were broken down, creating a new mental fluidity as knowledge began to flow between cognitive domains (Mithen 1996: 69). This collapse of separate cognitive spheres could be attributed to the increasing significance of language, which Mithen suggests was initially used to convey social information but which could eventually also refer to technology and nature. It is this cognitive fluidity, which enabled humans to mix ideas together and create art, religion and metaphor, that Mithen identifies as the source of the upper palaeolithic cultural revolution.

Mithen's view of the upper palaeolithic is not that it represented the signature of an increased cognitive capacity. Instead, it provides an indication of a restructuring of the mind and its internal flows of information. He attributes the expansion of culture at this time to the creative mixing of elements found in different cognitive domains. People and animals could be mixed together to produce supernatural beings that were then represented in art (Figure 8.4); the technical understanding of natural substances could be mixed with a knowledge of natural history to create complex hunting technologies, and so on (ibid.: 184). Conscious thought and language may have originated as means of coping with the social behaviour of others, but when they spread to the evaluation of nature and materiality the world as a whole became subject to introspection and cognitive manipulation.

Like Cosmides and Tooby, Mithen suggests that the specialised intelligences of early humans were 'content-rich', giving them an intuitive knowledge of four domains of activity: language, psychology, physics and biology (ibid.: 52). All are relevant to the hunting and gathering way of life, and all would become connected to each other by links of analogy and metaphor during the upper palaeolithic. Mithen argues that these connections result in a 'hunter-gatherer world-view' in which people and animals, culture and nature are not placed into separate classificatory spheres. However, we could argue that Mithen's different domains of knowledge ('natural history intelligence', 'technical intelligence', 'linguistic intelligence' and 'social intelligence') are not simply blurred together by hunter-gatherers. On the contrary, they are modern categories that Mithen is seeking to ontologise and naturalise.

MIND, PERCEPTION AND KNOWLEDGE

Figure 8.4 The 'Sorcerer' at the cave of Trois Frères (from Miles Burkett, *Prehistory*, Cambridge University Press, 1924)

'Nature' (distinct from 'society') is a concept that only emerged in its present form during the seventeenth and eighteenth centuries; 'technology' was unknown to the ancient Greeks. Mithen is arguing that a series of different domains of knowledge exist in the minds of all humans, processing kinds of information that are empirically distinct. The implication is that the categories of modern Western science are universal. Contemporary hunter-gatherers may be unaware of these separate domains of thought, but the suggestion is that they are present in their minds nonetheless. One could suggest that this is at once patronising and ethnocentric.

Furthermore, Mithen's conception of 'intuitive knowledge' is another example of the way that cognitivism fails to account for background understanding. His discussion of 'intuitive physics' is a case in point: 'concepts of solidity, gravity and inertia appear to be hard-wired into the child's mind' (ibid.: 57). But this is to presume that the child has a mind that operates over and against the world of physical things; that it must have the ideas of solidity, gravity and inertia in its head before it can respond to them. Surely, all of these are aspects of the world that the child finds itself amidst: it neither has to learn them explicitly, nor does it 'contain' them as innate, hard-wired representations. Mithen's characterisation of 'natural history intelligence' similarly relies upon an inside/outside dichotomy:

> It is simply impossible that people could generalise from the limited evidence available to them during development to the complex taxonomies universally adopted, unless they possessed a 'blueprint' for the structures of the living world hard-wired into their minds.
> (Mithen 1996: 54)

This is to claim that human beings must operate in their environments by having explicit structures of representation inside their minds. In reality people always exist amidst the 'structures of the living world', and what may appear to be 'complex taxonomies' are often generated by simple principles in engagement with the phenomenal world, as Bourdieu (1990: 210) has demonstrated.

Archaeologies of perception

Over the past decade, a series of new spatial information technologies have become increasingly significant within archaeology, and represent a very different instance of the influence of modern ideas of mind and perception within the discipline. Of these, perhaps the most important are Geographical Information Systems, and Virtual Reality Modelling. The former allows the storage, manipulation and analysis of spatial data in visual form, while the latter can reconstruct ancient buildings, monuments and landscapes in a digital environment. In both cases, the claim is that information technology can help us to transcend two-dimensional forms of representation, which are predominantly objectivist and experience-remote. Geographical Information Systems, for instance, allow the user to construct view-shed models, assessing the relative visibility of different locations within a landscape (Fisher 1999: 8; Lock and Harris 1992: 82). Similarly, VR models enable us to 'move through' structures and spaces that no longer exist in their original form (Barceló 2000: 9).

Consequently, these digital technologies are often understood as being connected with a more general growth of interest in experiential and phenomenological issues in archaeology. Rather than simply mapping the distribution of artefacts, there is now a growing imperative to understand past life-worlds, and the ways in which they were negotiated by past people. So it is obviously attractive to be able to reconstruct the 'spatial narratives' of people moving across prehistoric landscapes, and to investigate the ways in which topographic and built features would have presented themselves. Nonetheless, the arguments developed in the earlier part of this chapter must engender some scepticism concerning these approaches, and the view of the past that they promote. It may be that GIS and VRM are irreducibly embedded in ways of looking and thinking that are distinctively modern, and hence that they are anachronistic when applied to the distant past.

An obvious point of departure lies in the overwhelming (and sometimes exclusive) visuality of these approaches. Vision is often understood as a mode of perception that is self-evident, unproblematic, and unitary. Indeed, when something can be readily apprehended, we say that it is 'transparent'. This reflects the primacy that we have already noted is afforded to vision in the modern West, where sight has become the paradigm for the acquisition of information about the world. Nonetheless, vision has its drawbacks. *Language* allows us to use metaphor, to be allusive, and to be ambivalent, all of which are more difficult to do in an exclusively visual digital medium.

To recapitulate: we have seen that the isolation of vision from the other senses can be linked historically to the emergence of a modern world-view in which humans are conceived as observing subjects, while nature is cast as the inert object of the gaze. As object, the world becomes manipulable and controllable by disengaged reason. Space is now conceived as rectilinear, isotropic, gridded, and framed. In the separation of subject and object, mind and world, the conditions are established for distanced and dispassionate observation, unencumbered by haptic engagement. Disengaged rational procedure thus came to be seen as both the guarantee of scientific truth and of human goodness. At the same time, it is a commonplace that the distanced gaze is the gaze of the voyeur, a gendered way of looking that constructs the object of a desire that cannot be fulfilled (Pollock 1988: 67). Moreover, through objectification, vision disembeds and alienates material things, rendering them as resources and commodities that exist primarily for the satisfaction of human needs and desires. As a form of simultaneous perception, the gaze is presented as a universal. Yet as Merleau-Ponty (1962: 226) points out, looking is always a practice that is conducted from within a corporeal and social context. The gaze is embodied, and we always have to ask *who* is doing the looking. In the modern West the analytical, objectifying, penetrating gaze is a way of looking that is distinctively male, and we have to consider whether when we look at representations of the past on the computer screen we are not merely reproducing a dominant scopic regime (Best 1995: 184; Jay 1993: 114).

Much of the foregoing is familiar enough to practitioners of landscape archaeology (see Barrett 1999; Bender 1999), and in the past few years a number of authors have suggested that it may be possible to transcend the positivist origins of digital spatial technologies, creating sensuous, humanised computing (Witcher 1999: 15). The argument is that although these approaches tend to privilege distanced and objective perspectives it may be possible to simulate a landscape that is experienced from within. This would involve a focus on subjectivity and perception, and perhaps a supplementing of visual information by other sensory inputs. In particular, it is suggested that future digital technologies should be concerned with the role of the human body as a mediator between the physical world and the mind. So the question of who is doing the looking becomes embedded in the analysis.

However, it may be that this attempt to 'humanise' digital technologies is misguided, principally as a result of the way in which it deals with the concept of *perception*. Very often, 'perception' appears to involve a subjective experience of an objective world. That is to say, it is a layer of meaning that is draped over the surface of a material reality whose character is known, transparent, and non-problematic. In the case at hand, this implies that the representation of the world as a geometrical structure composed of points, lines, surfaces and solids, picked out by patterns of contrast and luminance, can be taken (for the sake of argument) as *what the world is really like*. Our task is then merely to comprehend how such a world might be perceived in culturally specific ways by people in the past.

The difficulty with such a formulation is not merely that it affords priority to the object world as a given, but that it leaves the modernist oppositions between object and subject and mind and matter in place, and unquestioned. It assumes first of all that the world we inhabit is just as Descartes imagined it, and then presumes a particular understanding of how human beings comport themselves to that world. For, as long as we accept that 'perception' involves giving meaning to an external physical world, we are hostage to the atomist-computational view of human functioning. This, as we have seen, is the belief that humans behave like computers, processing bits of information that they take in from the outside world, in order to put together a mental image. There is an obvious circularity of argument here, in which geometrical models of what things are like and artificial-intelligence models of how people operate are taken as the unquestionable grounds for digital reconstructions of past worlds. If we cast aside these assumptions, the whole enterprise of a virtual past begins to collapse.

To return to an earlier theme, the alternative to an atomist-computational view is to jettison the notion of perception outright, and to talk instead of the world being revealed or disclosed to us in its meaningfulness. We never just internalise raw sense data and then interpret them in order to render them meaningful. We hear birdsong, smell wood-smoke, and see sunlight, not sound-waves and patterns of illumination. Meaning is not added on top of what we experience, and this is because the world is a structure of intelligibility rather than a set of objects. Things are comprehensible to us because they are embedded in a background of meanings and practices, which serves as their context of legibility.

In order to see objects as geometrical forms, or to reduce experiences down to sensory stimuli, we have to take them out of their relational context and look at them in a rather unusual way. We have to translate them into the objects of natural science. The digital worlds of GIS and VRM are *simulacra* (Baudrillard 1988: 168). They are the appearances of things divorced from any context of human involvement. Indeed, as well as being desocialised in terms of their alienation from past contexts, computer models also systematically occlude their own conditions of manufacture in order to create an illusion of authenticity (Bateman 2000). The notion of humanising our relationship to these images suggests that it is possible to reverse the order of the process of unworlding, and generate a meaningful context for them *ex nihilo*. Digital technologies reduce the past to a pattern of pixels, viewed on the screen of modern rationalism. It may be that it is possible to develop a sensuous, experiential archaeology of place and landscape, which is sensitive to the relationality that renders things meaningful. But it is questionable how far this process can be facilitated by a microprocessor.

9

MATERIALITIES

Introduction: a history of materiality

Archaeology studies the past through the medium of material culture. This much appears to be self-evident. Yet the very idea that material things are entities that we can stand apart from, and employ as evidence for the actions of people in the past, is, while not exclusively modern, at least characteristic of a modern sensibility. This is a further important way in which modernity represents the condition of the possibility of archaeology as it is presently constituted. The sixteenth and seventeenth centuries saw fundamental changes in the way in which matter was understood, and these were critical for the development of the idea of the 'archaeological record'. However, these changes had their roots in the various ways in which people had sought to characterise the material world over many centuries. It is therefore appropriate to refer to a 'history of materiality', which charts the changing relationship between people and the material world. We have already dwelt at length on the dichotomy between mind and matter, whose emergence was central to this history. But equally significant is the complementary distinction between form and matter, which was introduced much earlier by Aristotle. He argued that form and matter together make up a substance, and such a substance will have a series of qualities. Following Aristotle, medieval scholasticism was to argue that the essential qualities of a thing were the key to its behaviour, as these would be refined and realised through time. While the form of a living creature might be intrinsic to it, that of an artefact is imposed upon it by humanity. Consequentially, the effect of opposing matter to form was to open up the possibility of a view of material things as passive recipients of labour, something that had not been present in the work of the pre-Socratic Greek philosophers. For the philosophers of the seventeenth century the notion of an ideal and immaterial form was risible (Shapin 1996: 54), yet the form/matter dyad survived as *design*, imposed on the material world by humanity. When this version of form as a source of coherence that was exterior to material things eventually collided with the Cartesian opposition between mind and body, a closed conceptual framework resulted which emphasised the role of the dynamic human subject acting upon the dead matter of the object (Cheah 1996: 131). This effect was enhanced by the Christian cosmology which presented the world as created and transient, in contrast to the eternal world of the Greeks. Like this world, the modern view identifies material things as having been made, created by human action as God created the cosmos (Heidegger 1971a: 27). Thus the imposition of form produces artefacts out of brute matter.

Prior to the seventeenth century, though, scholasticism presented an image of the universe in which the greater whole was of more significance than its parts, and where the overall motion toward the *telos* was of more import than the accidents of efficient causes. Therefore, the overall disposition of worldly things could be attributed to their tendency towards fruition, whether or not this was to be associated with a divine plan. That material objects might document historical events and irreversible processes would not have been denied, but might have been seen as relatively inconsequential. Things may have been formed by human acts, but they were also tending towards their *telos*, and this represented their destiny. For scholasticism, ideas in the mind were identical with qualities in physical things: things really have the attributes that we perceive in them. It was only with Duns Scotus in the thirteenth century that the idea began to develop that thought might have a different kind of being from nature (Frede 1993: 49). This is much more akin to a modern theory of representation, which distinguishes thoughts or words from things. As the internal and the external worlds were severed from one another, notions of sympathy and semblance declined, and a conception of nature ruled by causal relations began to crystallise. Rather than being composed of elements which have a natural motion immanent within them, matter would come to be seen as having an atomic microstructure, and as being governed by the force of inertia.

The view of a material world composed of inert entities that was fostered by the scientific revolution represented an epochal shift in cosmology, but in a sense Aristotelianism had already contained the seeds of its own destruction. In setting up his doctrine of substance, Aristotle had effectively denied the possibility of a category of Being *in general*. For Aristotle, each instance of formed matter was a substance, while all other conceivable entities are the qualities or attributes of substances – colour, quantity, time, and so on. Being is either 'being a substance of a particular kind' or 'being the attribute or quality of a substance', and these kinds of being cannot be reduced to each other. Similarly, the being of one kind of substance cannot be substituted for that of another, even if they are linked by resemblance or analogy. If the kind of existence attributable to one type of phenomenon is distinct from that of any other, then there can be no overarching sense of Being. In consequence, the inherent unity of the world that scholasticism promoted was fragile, and would eventually unravel into a vision of separate and free-standing entities (Frede 1993: 60). This is the source of our contemporary conviction that if we know about objects then we know about Being.

In the modern world the understanding that matter is dead was to cause the image of nature as an organism to be replaced by that of nature as a machine (Collingwood 1945: 95). The movements of worldly things ceased to be recognised as being occasioned by their intrinsic *anima* or vital energy, and came instead to be attributed to mechanistic forces. By the seventeenth century, the elements of nature were widely understood as being like the cogs in a mechanism rather than the parts of a living body. Indeed, bodies themselves were increasingly conceived as biological machines. The actions of units of dead matter within uniform and homogeneous space were reducible to mathematics, and the only qualitative distinction in creation was that between mind and matter (ibid.: 111). Once thought had been separated from materiality, substance was increasingly connected with irreducibility and givenness. Substance was what was 'just there' as the object of consciousness. As the irreducible, substance takes on a foundational role. Its etymology as sub-stance suggests something that lies beneath whatever is, the bearer of qualities and attributes (Guignon 2001: 36; Heidegger 1971a: 24).

Matter, mechanism and extension

The formation of a mechanistic world-view was already evident at the start of the seventeenth century when Bacon declared that nature was composed of isolated bodies performing discrete acts in accordance with universal laws (Jones 1961: 58). Accordingly, science was given the new task of identifying these laws, which when compiled would represent an exhaustive catalogue of whatever nature was capable of. This is not to say that such a cosmology immediately achieved pre-eminence. On the contrary, McCann (1994: 57) suggests that by the middle of the seventeenth century four distinct conceptions of matter were all current. Scholastic Aristotelians continued to adhere to the belief that all substance was made up of the four elements of earth, air, fire and water, which combined hotness, coldness, wetness and dryness. But there was also the alchemical tradition of Paracelsus with its Spagyric chemistry, and two new, rival views: the Cartesian philosophy of matter as extension, and corpuscularianism or mechanistic atomism.

Descartes' physics perhaps amounts to the most austere conception of matter imaginable. It holds that all matter is inert, and is distinguished by its occupation of a geometrical space. All of the qualities of matter, from volume and weight to cohesion and texture, can ultimately be reduced to physical extension. The combination of geometry and motion can explain the disposition of all natural phenomena, and the separation of mind and body means that sense impressions like colour and smell are only semblances of things (Cassirer 1951: 63; Cottingham 1988: 123; Sorell 1987: 3). These semblances must have a basis in reality, since they are delivered to the mind by our faculties, and this process has been sanctioned by God, who does not seek to deceive us. The reality of material things is therefore not to be doubted, although they may not be precisely as they seem to us in sensory terms. This means that a knowledge of things that is as abstract and mathematical as possible will be more secure than one based on experience. Extension, shape and movement sum up all that is really knowable about matter. These are what Descartes called the 'simple natures' (Marion 1992: 116). Since only human beings have minds, and mind is a different kind of substance from matter, the latter is not capable of thought. That which cannot think cannot put itself into motion, so matter is absolutely passive, and its processes are purely causal where humanity is rational.

Beyond this, the defining characteristic of matter is that it is divisible, and can be divided a limitless number of times for it has no fundamental particles. Adopting a primarily geometrical view of nature, Descartes insisted that only a point is indivisible, and a point is distinguished by having no extension in any dimension. If there are no particles or atoms, substance must be either fully present or absent, and nature will not tolerate a vacuum. If there is extension, there must also be substance: there can be no space that contains nothing. This means that for Descartes the universe is perfectly full. God has divided the universe into separate and individually knowable parts. These bodies of matter can be distinguished from each other on the basis of their different movements, but all movement is movement *through* a material of some kind, a plenum. For this reason, Descartes devised a theory of planetary motion in which the heavenly bodies were carried in a vortex around the sun. In a 'vulgar' sense the planets were in motion, but it was more correct to argue that they were stable in relation to one another within the fluid medium in which they were suspended (Disalle 2002: 37).

The corpuscularianism of Locke and Newton

The belief that matter is not homogeneous but composed of particles or atoms was closely connected with empiricism, but not exclusively so. The rationalist Leibniz, for instance, rejected the notion that matter was infinitely divisible, and held that it was composed of innumerable moving points (Cottingham 1988: 138). During the seventeenth century these 'corpuscles' were generally held to be indestructible and indivisible entities moving in void space. Because they are indivisible, particles could not penetrate each other or occupy the same space, and since they were in motion this meant that they could collide and change each other's direction (Collingwood 1945: 142). In John Locke's version of corpuscularianism the existence of atoms implies that matter must have physical as well as geometrical characteristics, solidity as well as extension. All matter is therefore comparable with all other matter, since all bodies are either single atoms or compounds of atoms. The size and character of atoms is fixed, but the arrangement of atoms within a body is variable and gives a body its particular texture. This texture can be transformed by the action of one body on another, principally through impact (McCann 1994: 56). That one body can impact on another at all is a consequence of their solidity and coherence, aspects of substance which are absent from empty space and which cannot be accounted for by geometrical extension or motion (Ayers 1997: 25).

Like Aristotle, Locke identified substance as a support or 'substratum' that stands behind the qualities of a thing and our experience of it. Even single atoms have qualities, although they are too small to be encountered through the senses (Lowe 1995: 75). Because the 'microstructural organisation' of bodies is atomic in scale it will necessarily be beyond our capabilities to identify their essence. This means that while our sensory experience of things is real, and is the only source of our knowledge of them, they may withhold something of their objective reality. Things may not be as we sense them to be, and just as something of their substance is unknowable so the notion of substance is itself somewhat obscure (McCann 1994: 76). All of this suggests that Locke was at once a little fatalistic and frustrated in his attempts to understand substance.

Despite this, Locke was able to elaborate a theory of the relationship between materiality and perception through his discussion of primary and secondary qualities. The primary qualities are those that are directly attributable to a body's having a finite, extended, solid substance. They include extension and solidity themselves, as well as texture, motion, shape and number. Secondary qualities, by contrast, are features of a body's capability to produce effects in us. So a thing can seem to us to have a particular taste or smell, to be a certain colour, to make a noise or to be hot or cold. These sensations are registered in our own physiology, yet they are occasioned by some feature of the object's microstructural constitution that we cannot identify, and may never be able to (McCann 1994: 60). What is most significant about Locke's account of materiality is that it enshrines a hierarchical relationship between substance, which simply exists, its primary qualities (which are a function of its physicality), and its secondary qualities (which arise from the way that the material affects us). Seemingly, matter is given and irreducible, while our experience of it is contingent. We can experience the secondary qualities of a thing if the light falls upon it, or if we lick it, sniff it, or run a hand across it. But none of these happenstances changes the way that the material is in itself.

Locke's philosophical articulation of the implications of atomic theory was complemented by Newton's work on a physics of forces and motion. Newton gave corpuscularianism a greater coherence by introducing new conceptions of gravity and inertia. Gravitational force was a notion that had been resisted by physics until Newton's time, for it had been regarded as axiomatic that action at a distance was impossible. Indeed, the notion of action at a distance was stigmatised by its association with Renaissance occult beliefs. However, Newton regarded the question as a purely empirical one. The idea of the gravitational pull of one body on another allowed him to develop a mathematically valid account of how curved or orbital motion could be generated, thus explaining how the planets could circulate around the sun in the absence of a plenum (Cohen 2002: 78; Disalle 2002: 52). These same ideas of force and motion enabled Newton to address some of the aspects of atomic theory that had appeared unsatisfactory since the time of the Romans; namely, how bodies composed of particles cohere, and how they transmit motion to one another. He considered atoms to be moving in a vacuum, to be capable of moving in any direction, and to change direction when they collided. Atoms also possess inertia. While inertia had always been understood as the tendency of objects to come to a halt, Newton argued instead that *stationary* bodies will remain stationary, while *moving* bodies will continue in motion until interfered with. So atoms are in constant motion and interaction, but this picture is complicated by the attractive gravitational force that each exerts on the others, proportionate to their masses and relative distance from each other (Cohen and Smith 2002).

In defining his laws of motion, Newton introduced the concept of mass, a quality which combines density and volume. The effect of this is to provide a means of measuring matter which is context-free. For while the weight of an object varies with its latitude on earth, its mass remains constant. Equally, while the volume of a substance can expand or contract with temperature, its mass does not change (Cohen 2002: 59). Newton was attempting to create a physics within which space and time were absolute and universal, and in tune with this project he found a way of asserting that matter is essentially the same wherever it occurs within the universe. The physics of the heavens was the same as that of the earth. From a more empiricist point of view, Newton had reached a measure of agreement with Descartes: matter obeyed a set of laws that was utterly invariant.

Productionist and consumptionist metaphysics

Seventeenth-century physics and philosophy had thus put together a schema in which matter was connected with nature rather than consciousness, and represented an irreducible given substance that might be moulded by human agency. Matter was the always already existing stage on which culture was built, directed by the mind. This framework has proved to be influential within subsequent social thought, perhaps because this has had to grapple with the conception of matter-as-resource that appears to be built in to capitalist economics. It is arguable, though, that in attempting to understand the social conditions of modernity, theorists have overlooked aspects of the metaphysical ones. The labour theory of value, for instance, proposes that the worth of commodities is derived from the human effort that has been expended in their production. Thus artefacts can be identified as 'congealed' masses of human labour (Marx 1970: 39). The alienation that takes place within capitalism is a consequence of the process in which workers sell their labour power in return for a monetary wage, with the result that they become estranged from the things that they produce (Miller 1987: 44). When those products then circulate in the market and are bought and sold, their relationships with their producers have effectively been erased. The source of their value has been annihilated, and they appear to stand free from (and opposed to) the people who made them. This reification of produced objects is the 'fetishism of commodities' in which the whole character of reality comes to be misunderstood. Objects seem to have an identity and an efficacy that is intrinsic to them, and as private property they achieve an importance that is as great as that of human beings (Dant 1999: 41). Isolated from the reality of the collective activity of production, people instead find themselves engaged in the individualised appropriation of goods (Love 1986: 3).

However, we could argue that this whole argument rests on the inter-related distinctions between object and subject, mind and matter, nature and culture, and form and matter. Matter here represents a raw material, a substance that is given form by the process of production. Matter appears to be extrinsic to society, and only the labour that is invested in the substance renders it social. By being formed and valorised, matter is transformed into 'material culture'. This implies that the social is a sphere that is constituted by inter-subjective relations, whose willed action draws material substance out of abject nature and renders it formed and meaningful. While it is practical, bodily labour that brings this change about, the material is nonetheless conceived as an object that exists in opposition to a collective subject (Cheah 1996: 131). Indeed, Marx's argument is that capitalism obscures the productive relationships between people and substitutes a relationship amongst things, which should properly be understood as the products of labour.

In identifying the alienation of human beings from the products of their labour power, Marx made an unparalleled contribution to the recognition of the conditions under which people exist under capitalism. But it may be that this alienation builds upon the more fundamental estrangement of human beings from their material world manifested in the object/subject dichotomy. While Marx points to the way that fetishised commodities can take on a role very like that of a human personality, it may only be because matter has already been rendered meaningless that artefacts can become foci of projection and social construction. That is, materiality has become substance. This much is suggested by Simmel's argument that the increasing distance between subject and object creates a space that comes to be filled by desire (Miller 1987: 70). For Simmel, the circulation of commodities in exchange for money is an indication of a more abstract set of relationships between people and things, yet the acquisition of goods has mysteriously come to be identified as a source of human fulfilment. While this would be crude in the extreme, we could go so far as to suggest a developmental process of abstraction in which human beings first separated themselves from the material world, rendering matter as the meaningless raw material on which human agency operates in order to create formed objects. These objects were initially understood as having been socialised through craft and labour, but with the advent of capitalism they would have gradually become more alienated commodities. This process would have been enhanced by industrialisation and mass consumption. As a result, the primary relationship between people and things may have shifted again, from the sphere of production to that of consumption. No longer able to think of themselves as vesting meaning into objects that they form and craft, people seek instead to create a sense of meaning and personal identity through their choices of commodities to buy and use (Baudrillard 1988: 12).

In the contemporary West, people increasingly define and actualise themselves through their relationships with consumer products, which may enable them to identify with a particular 'lifestyle' or 'demographic'. But as Baudrillard points out, in using categories of object to construct themselves as categories of person, people are actually establishing relationships with the abstracted ideas of objects rather than the things themselves. This is one reason why the desire that Simmel refers to remains forever unfulfilled: acquiring more alienated things can never assuage the ontological disquiet that arises from the severance of object and subject. One of the central paradoxes of contemporary life is that although such effort has been invested in separating human beings from objects in conceptual terms, the things that we use and own continue to proliferate (Latour 1993: 30). In the past century, developments in plastics, electronics, textiles and precision engineering have surrounded us with a hitherto unimaginable diversity of artefacts. Computers, mobile phones, cars, compact discs, televisions, new forms of clothing and new building materials have changed the texture of our existence in very significant ways. This is to say nothing of a variety of forms of prostheses, from pacemakers and spectacles to contraceptive devices and hip replacements, which means that we are ever more closely bound into relationships with material things. But if we turn this argument around, it seems that simply because our lives are lived in and through a multiplicity of artefacts, we have achieved no reintegration into the material world. This, presumably, is what Heidegger is referring to when he states that the frenzied abolition of distance in modern life brings us no *nearness* (Heidegger 1971b: 165). We can talk to our friends on our mobile phones irrespective of where we find ourselves, or fly to the other side of the world in a few hours, because we have developed the technology that enables us to do these things. But we remain 'homeless' amongst this mass of things that stand opposed to us.

'Stamped on these lifeless things': the materiality of archaeological evidence

Our understanding of archaeological evidence has been constituted by the notion that matter is a dead substance that bears qualities, and that artefacts are matter that has been given form by human action. However, I want to emphasise that this should not be seen as an entirely negative outcome. For while our modern understanding of matter encourages us to think about the traces of the past in ways that are anachronistic and objectifying, if we were not inclined to think of those traces *as* evidence, there might be no archaeology at all. So this is a double bind, but it is one that is enabling as well as constraining. The existence of archaeology is grounded in a modern attitude to the physical world, and it must be an open question whether the adoption of a radically different engagement with materiality would be compatible with anything that we could still recognise as archaeology. This is a theme that we will return to in the concluding chapter.

As Linda Patrik has argued (1985: 33), the predominant rubric under which material evidence is discussed within the discipline is as 'the archaeological record'. Stone tools, pottery sherds, post-holes, burials and midden deposits have been collectively described as a 'record' in two distinct senses. First, the archaeological record can be seen as the equivalent of the fossil record, so that the process of recording is a natural one governed by the law-bound operations of physical and chemical agencies. Alternatively, the record may be considered to be a textual one, which has been generated by acts of inscription and is capable of signification. These different understandings of the record each suggest different forms of interpretation that are appropriate for addressing archaeological evidence. However, they both partake of a substance ontology, in which the materiality (and by implication the 'recordness') of the record is taken as a given. Matter is simply stuff in each case. To those who believe that they are addressing a fossil-type record, archaeology is a matter of identifying the physical transformations that have overtaken material things. Some of these transformations may have been purely natural in character, such as the action of wind and weather on structures and deposits, or the gnawing of animal bones by dogs or hyenas. Others are the outcome of human actions, such as the knapping of a flint nodule or the digging of a post-hole. But in either case chains of cause-and-effect intervene between the initial state of the raw material and the condition in which it is encountered by the archaeologist. Similarly, where the archaeological record is understood as a text that must be read by the archaeologist, the assumption is that matter provides a kind of substrate that is altered and rendered meaningful by the act of inscription. Both frameworks accept matter as substance, a formless and meaningless platform for physical impacts or events of encoding.

This conviction that the record is formed out of primal and irreducible matter has manifested itself in a variety of different ways. Gordon Childe, for example, took the view that archaeological materials only constituted a record at all once they had been classified and ordered. Indeed, Childe only recognised material things as archaeological data if they were located within a determinate context (Childe 1956: 30). An archaeological type or assemblage was a 'message' from the past, but our ability to comprehend that message depends upon our reconstructing the order or structure that has been generated in the material by human action. In grouping traits to form industries and cultures, and plotting them as distributions, the archaeologist was overcoming the seeming disorder of ancient fragments. This ordering activity in the present echoed that of people in the past, whose social traditions had encouraged them to manufacture artefacts in distinctive ways that reflected their collective identity. Without the classification and typologising of the archaeologist, the evidence is not evidence at all but formless matter, just as the 'message' component of the assemblage has been placed in it by the productive labour of past people.

Childe's conception of the archaeological record as formed matter whose structure needed to be reconstituted by the archaeologist makes an interesting comparison with Lewis Binford's view. For Binford the most significant point about the archaeological record is that it exists in the present, and has no necessary relationship with social processes in the past. The archaeological record is static, and composed of structured arrangements of matter (Binford 1983b: 416). The patterned nature of archaeological deposits is such that they contain potential information, but Binford distinguishes between such information and meaning. The data that archaeologists create through excavation, survey and laboratory analysis are representations of events of observation that take place in the present, not of events of social life that took place in the past (Binford 1987: 392). Yet it is possible to link our observations to the processes that caused the evidence to take on its present configuration (see Chapter 3). The presently existing matter of the archaeological record takes the form that it does as the result of a concatenation of physical actions: impacts, abrasion, gnawing, trampling, collapse, water-flow and wind-blow. These processes are all mechanical ones, whose causal structure is universal, so that the relationship between an action and its physical trace is unaltered across time and space. Like Newton, Binford believes that matter has the same characteristics throughout the universe, and obeys general laws. The archaeological record has been formed by the actions of forces on matter. These are not social forces, are not meaningful, and can be explicated without reference to past societies. Indeed, we should fully understand the formation of the record before we even address past social relations. Because the archaeological record is inert and contains no social information, archaeologists should be able to agree on criteria on which to identify formation processes, and this should always precede any form of interpretation (Binford 1977: 2).

One corollary of the static and contemporary character of the archaeological record was that for Binford the conceptual frameworks of the social sciences were inappropriate to archaeology, at least at a procedural level (1983b: 21). As we cannot observe the dynamic actions that took place in the past, we should restrict ourselves to addressing the material facts of the record, which are the preserve of the natural sciences. Assuming that Binford is still happy that social theory should inform our analyses at what he insists must be the later, interpretive stage, it seems that he has succeeded in forcing a division between the analytical frameworks appropriate for matter (nature) and society (culture). He therefore establishes a hierarchical sequence for archaeological procedure which is built upon raw materiality: we encounter the record, and give meaning to our observations before addressing the dynamics of the past (Binford 1983b: 22). The outstanding requirement for a mature archaeology is therefore an observational language in which we can render arrangements of matter meaningful, quite distinct from the language that we use to discuss concepts and interpretive arguments (Binford 1983a: 413; 1989: 50). It will be apparent that, in their quite different ways, both Childe and Binford have erected inferential structures that rest on the primordial givenness of matter. In both cases, matter is substance, whose qualities and meaning are imposed upon it by natural forces and human actions. It seems that in relation to the formed matter of the record, archaeology can understand its task in a number of ways: as a reconstitutive activity which reconstructs the order vested in the material; as a 'reading' that renders its elements meaningful; as a stripping of extraneous material to reveal the formed pattern. But in all cases, the matter that these actions rest upon appears to be both inert and irreducible.

Form, style and meaning

If the notion of 'the archaeological record' in general terms suggests dead matter that has been interfered with by people and nature, a more specific example is provided by the concept of style. In culture-historic archaeology it was often argued that while different communities might have artefacts that were functionally equivalent, their stylistic variation provided an indication of distinct social traditions of manufacture. These traditions amounted to non-discursive social norms, passed from generation to generation as a by-product of the process of learning everyday craft skills. Style, as the residuum of formal variation that cannot be accounted for in functional terms, provided a means of defining 'types' of artefacts, which in turn served to distinguish the social groups who were hosts to particular traditions. Immediately, it is clear that style is concerned with the form that has been imposed on matter, that this is expressed in terms of qualities or 'traits', and that it arises from the investment of human labour in the object. Moreover, as Conkey argues, a preoccupation with style suggests an approach to material culture which privileges a visual knowledge of things (1990: 5).

In the archaeology of the 1960s and 1970s it was increasingly maintained that culture was not automatically shared by whole communities but was participated in strategically. This led to a series of attempts to reconceptualise style. Yet all of these remained wedded to the view that style represents the imposition of form on meaningless substance. For instance, Martin Wobst (1977) proposed that style amounted to a means of transmitting information between groups of people. Stylistic variation in dress, ornaments and personal artefacts was for Wobst a way of signalling status and identity to a target population beyond the immediate household or community. This implies that information that reflects personal affiliation or standing can be readily condensed into a material form that allows its transmission. In other words, artefacts represent a passive medium through which identities that have already been established in some other arena are conveyed between persons. By implication, material things are extrinsic to society, and social meaning is imprinted upon them to enable its transfer to the minds of other people.

Similarly, the debate in the literature over style between James Sackett and Polly Wiessner in the 1980s did not question the fundamentally static character of materiality. Sackett (1986: 266) argued that artefactual style was isochrestic, which is to say that objects that are 'equivalent in use' may vary in form as a result of implicit traditions of habitual practice. Style is thus a side-effect of the manufacture of functional objects, which can nonetheless be used by archaeologists as a means of identifying distinct communities of artisans. By contrast, Wiessner (1984: 195) suggested that stylistic variation may sometimes be encoded in things. Style can serve as a means of establishing identity through comparison, and this may take a form that is either *emblemic* (where objects identify affiliation to a group of some sort) or *assertive* (where dress or artefacts make more personal but less precise statements about a person). The difference is seemingly that Sackett sees style as predominantly the unconsidered outcome of manufacture, while Wiessner holds that it can often be a deliberate and strategic means of negotiating social identity. Yet in either case, regardless of whether style is active or passive, form is the consequence of human action and material is the recipient of human design. This seems to confirm Robin Boast's arguments regarding the redundancy of the concept of style. Boast suggests that style is conventionally understood as a social or meaningful aspect that is added to the functional object world as a kind of 'embellishment' (Boast 1997: 174). It will be evident that this 'supplementarity' of style is attributable to the modern separation of form and meaning from materiality.

Ostensibly, the contextual and symbolic approach to material culture that was pioneered by Ian Hodder in the 1980s represents a break with earlier archaeologies which had relegated artefacts to the status of a reflection of society. Hodder argued that 'material symbolism is not a passive process, because objects and activities actively represent and act back upon society'

(1982a: 10). So material culture has a dynamic presence in society, and Hodder does not neglect its physicality. But despite this he seems to suggest that the efficacy of artefacts lies in their meaning, in the sense of their role as material *symbols*. For Hodder, material culture is *meaningfully constituted*, which is to say that it has had meaning vested in it by human beings (1992: 12). Hodder's original inspiration for developing a contextual archaeology lay in structuralism, and his approach to archaeological evidence suggests a search for patterns and structures which can be traced back to ideas in the heads of past people. So it is the search for past minds and the meanings they contained that informs the contextual examination of material culture (ibid.: 16). Material culture may be meaningful, but this evidently does not apply to material things in general. Instead, formless matter has been made meaningful in the course of its transformation into material culture by meaning-giving subjects. Human beings do not inhabit a world of meaning, according to this way of thinking. On the contrary, they introduce meaning into a Cartesian world of inert substance. Thereafter, material culture is distinguished as that aspect of the material world that communicates, and is meaningful. While Hodder emphasises the structural order and contextual disposition of material things, rather than their production, he nonetheless appears to maintain the distinction between the mind as a realm of meaning and dead matter.

Beyond the substance ontology

We have argued that archaeology recognises material things as evidence for past events by adopting a view of substance that draws on Newtonian physics and Cartesian metaphysics. This has enabled positive contributions to be made to the understanding of prehistoric societies, but it may be that a more subtle conception of materiality might enable us to develop richer interpretations of past material worlds. It is worth pointing out that although the everyday common-sense view of matter held by most people in the contemporary West is that of inert substance, this has actually been undermined by the past 200 years of science. While Newton had held that atoms were fundamental and indivisible particles, the chemistry of John Dalton was to show that the various elements of the periodic table were distinguished by their having atoms of different mass and weight (Patterson 1970). This was eventually explained by J.J. Thomson's inference of the existence of sub-atomic particles, or electrons, on the basis of his cathode ray tube experiments. Thus a new image of the atom emerged, not as a particle but as a system of electrons, where atoms of different mass possessed different numbers of electrons (Collingwood 1945: 146). Eventually, still more complex models of atoms, involving nucleii, protons and quarks, would develop. All of this meant that one element could be transformed into another, by the emission of particles of different kinds, as happens in the process of radioactive decay. Furthermore, electrons are constantly moving in a rhythmical fashion. The implication of this is that every element is what it is not by simply having a fixed constitution but through a process of movement that takes place over time. So time and motion are not external conditions that impose themselves on matter, they are intrinsic to the existence of matter. No substance can be itself within an instant moment; time is constitutive of material being, and matter is kinetic rather than inert. In this respect, contemporary physics provides an interesting parallel with Heidegger's (1962) account of human existence. For Heidegger, our Being is time, for we are what we are by having a past that hands possibilities for existence down to us, by being alongside others in a present, and by projecting our possibilities and aspirations into the future. We, too, cannot be understood as existing in the moment, but only as 'stretched' across time.

Philosophy, too, has made efforts to question the character of materiality. One area in which the issue has proved critical has been in feminist thought, where a rejoinder to the argument that 'biology is destiny' has been found in questioning the fixity and universality of human physicality (Gatens 1996: 61). Judith Butler has pointed to the way that the distinction between sex and gender has actually reinforced a belief in biological determination. For while it is readily accepted that gender roles are culturally variable and socially constructed, it is nonetheless implied that sexual difference is the point of departure for any such construction. Sexual anatomy is understood to be foundational, and Butler considers that this is because of a propensity to identify the body with matter, and to see matter as irreducible. Materiality is thus exempt from any cultural construction, and is the platform upon which constructions are built (Butler 1993: 28). Materiality and constructedness are thus opposed to one another. But if the production of gender identities takes place in discourse, this would require materiality to exist prior to language. And yet, our supposed knowledge of the irreducibility of matter is itself always constructed in language. The medical science that tells us what human bodies are like is itself a discourse, created under particular historical and cultural conditions. Butler suggests that we need to address the discursive practices by which matter is awarded its primordial, extra-linguistic status, and which turn the biological determination of sex into something ontological. These, she suggests, will always be bound up with power (ibid.: 29). Power forms a matrix within which materiality becomes intelligible.

Importantly, Butler is not claiming that material things are 'made out of discourse'. This is not some form of idealism that gives ideas and language priority over matter. What she argues is that our knowledge of things is always discursively articulated, and that this articulation is always finite. It may well be that bodies and other entities have a physical existence that lies outside of human knowledge: but we cannot know them except as knowledge. This knowledge is created in our engagement with the world, through which things 'materialise' and become intelligible. Language can never simply refer to a materiality that we already understand. On the contrary, language is the condition under which materiality can be said to appear (ibid.: 31).

Now, while Butler's critique of the modern Western understanding of matter is cogent and helpful it arguably has the drawback of being anthropocentric. Butler argues that it is in the citation and performance of gender norms that the human body secures its recognition as something that is culturally intelligible. Referring back to Freud, she suggests that the embodied human subject is formed in relation to the psychical body image. But as Cheah (1996: 113) points out, this model of incarnation simply has the effect of making human bodies cultural, while maintaining the division between culture and nature. The line is redrawn, but non-human matter remains inert and immutable. This is because for Butler the Freudian body image takes on the role of the Aristotelian form, and it is this that gives the body its dynamism. We could argue that what would be more useful is a framework which recognises that materialisation is always a dynamic process.

From substance to the event of disclosure

The 'substance ontology' of Western modernity is metaphysical in that it fails to distinguish between Being in general and the specific existence of particular entities (the 'being of beings') (Young 2002: 26). As we have seen, this is an error that goes back as far as Aristotle, although it has been compounded by the Cartesian vision of material things as self-evident. If we believe that objects are just 'occurrent', lying around in the world, we will fail to ask what Heidegger considers to be the most fundamental of all questions, 'why are there beings at all instead of just nothing?' (2001: 1). In very much the same way as we have seen in Butler's account of the materiality of the body, it is possible to accept that material things have a 'raw' physical existence without affording this primary significance within a human world. For what is more important is how things come to be part of a structure of intelligibility that is constituted by, but not controlled by, human beings. If there were no human beings, there would still be mountains, and streams, and rocks, and trees. But they would not exist *as* mountains, *as* streams, *as* rocks, and *as* trees, for there would be no one to recognise them as such. And they would not exist in relation to one another, within a structure that we call a 'world'. So what a substance ontology misses out is the phenomenon of *disclosure*, by which things 'announce themselves', and show up as intelligible within a world (as addressed in Chapter 8). This involves a great deal more than our simply 'seeing' them. For disclosure is a horizonal phenomenon. Things show up in the way that they do, and take the particular place that they do in a world, under conditions that are finite. The ways in which things present themselves are neither eternal nor universal.

Disclosure is an event, or more accurately an unfolding process, in which the world gradually reveals itself to us (Guignon 2001: 36). It is finite because disclosure always takes place in relation to human beings, who are themselves finite beings. How we recognise and understand physical things is a consequence of the finitude of our past, present and future. Our past has happened, and has provided us with a restricted set of possibilities. In the present, we exist alongside other people and things, and yet none of these provides the foundation for an understanding of reality that transcends our social and cultural positioning. And our future is finite in that we must choose between a number of possibilities that present themselves to us, in the awareness that those possibilities are ultimately limited by our mortality (Polt 2001: 69). All of this forms the context within which things become recognisable and salient to us. We occupy a horizon of disclosure, which we have no option but to find ourselves within. Living in a particular time and place a particular range of phenomena are revealed to us, but other things are unavoidably concealed, so that human existence is surrounded by a 'dark penumbra of unintelligibility' (Young 2002: 9).

This is why the Cartesian view of things as being in the first instance meaningless matter, to which we latterly append meanings, is so utterly mistaken. As we saw in the previous chapter, things reveal themselves to us in their meaningfulness: they announce themselves *as* rocks, or flowers, or whatever. For something to *be* means for it to be understood-*as* (Frede 1993: 57). Once we have become aware of things in this fashion we can measure them, describe them and represent them in various ways. In other words, we can consider them as indifferently occurring objects, which are free-standing and detached. But we do this on the basis of our already having understood them in a certain way. Identifying things as 'just' dead matter actually involves subtracting their meaning from them, rendering them as pure objective substance. By contrast, we cannot unfold the meaning of something out of a technical or scientific description of it. Once a thing has been severed from the relational context that enables it to present itself meaningfully, its meaning cannot be reconstituted.

If the conditions that enable us to recognise worldly things are finite, historical and relational, it is evident that this Heideggerian perspective converges with the views of Butler and Foucault, who argue that power is the condition of the intelligibility of bodies. In a recent article, Ziarek (2002: 177) has suggested that Heidegger's discussion of power in many ways prefigured that of Foucault. Both Foucault and Heidegger saw power as productive and constitutive rather than a purely negative phenomenon, and as something that was immanent in other relationships. Yet Ziarek argues that Heidegger is referring to power in the sense of *machenschaft*, the productionist making of things that uses up the material world as a resource. Power here is the mobilisation of labour and substance in order to create a modern world of constructed objects, and to subject nature to the human will. It would seem on this reading that Heidegger is identifying power with *Gestell*, or enframing, the horizon of disclosure that is particular to modernity. *Gestell* is a mode of disclosing in which people and things show up only as means, not as ends. However, it may be that Ziarek's interpretation is too restrictive. For Heidegger does not only refer to power in terms of nihilistic force; indeed, he writes of 'the saving power' (Young 2002: 124). This notion is connected with caring for things, and releasing them to be themselves. Yet such a mode of disclosure is nonetheless facilitated by relationality, and where there is relationality there is power. This would be a form of power that involves the renunciation of force and control, a democratic power relation.

Modes of disclosure

We have seen that rather than occupying a world in which everything is equally and continually accessible to us, things show up to us in ways that are specific to our time and culture. This means that some things, or at least some aspects of things, always remain concealed from us. Being involves presence and intelligibility, but also unintelligibility (Young 2002: 12). At different times, different modes of disclosure have revealed the world in different ways. We have argued that *Gestell*, enframing, is one such mode, in which the world and its contents are reduced to the objects of instrumental reason. If this is the characteristic way in which things present themselves in modernity, one of the challenges to archaeology lies in attempting to recognise the entirely different relationships between people and materiality that may have existed in the distant past. This is saying more than that past people may have had different perceptions of reality from ourselves, for the world-revealing relationship is a constitutive one, while disclosure is non-optional for human beings. Humans *have* a world, in much the same way as they have a past and a future. There would be neither time nor world without humans, although this is not to say that they wilfully *make* either of these things.

Relationships between people and with the material world enable things to register with us as intelligible. To demonstrate how different this phenomenon might have been at other times in human history Heidegger repeatedly resorted to the example of ancient Greece. For the Greeks, the continuous coming-forth of the world was *physis*, a process in which the cosmos was understood as burgeoning and pressing forward dynamically. Within this dynamic world, the activity of human beings in crafting things was *poeisis*. *Poeisis* did not involve the oppositional relationship with nature that characterises *Gestell*, in which the world is 'challenged' to bring forth resources that will simply be expended (Heidegger 1977: 10). Instead, *poeisis* was a kind of extension of *physis*, in which materiality was brought forth by humans and fashioned to show itself in a way that was true to its nature. In

Heidegger's thought this bringing-forth of things to show themselves as they are is closely related to a reconceptualisation of truth as *altheia* or unconcealment, in contrast with correspondence theories of truth. This is truth in the sense of 'being true to one's principles', as opposed to the successful representation of a state of affairs in words. When a material is crafted poetically, it appears on the scene not as a dead object, with a series of attributes or qualities attached to it, but as a happening. Thus in Heidegger's example of the Greek temple the crafting of the marble allowed the material to reveal its character, while the architecture itself crystallised the elements of an emerging world. Rather than being a reflection of a Hegelian spirit or world-view, the building of the temple provided the context for a realisation of the potential for a relationship between people and their world (Guignon 2001: 42). The temple was not the product of the Greek genius but the occasion for its coming into being. Where *Gestell* opposes humankind against nature in order to extract and transform raw materials, *poeisis* was a kind of building that did not confront nature. Indeed, it could be understood as an extension of the continuous blossoming forth of the natural world (Young 2002: 41). For the Greeks, the crafting of artefacts and architecture was a way of entering into the process by which the world at once reveals and conceals itself.

Now, it is entirely arguable that Heidegger's view of the ancient Greeks was idealised or romanticised, and much the same has been said of his idyllic accounts of the Black Forest peasants. However, the historical accuracy of a particular interpretation of classical antiquity is less important than the hypothetical argument that at different times in the past people have enjoyed different kinds of engagement with the material world. In other words, different communities have inhabited different materialities, and this is something that archaeologists need to address. As inhabitants of the modern West, the tendency will be for us to understand past societies through the lens of an ontology that stresses the production of things as formed matter, transforming dead substance by imbuing it with meaning. Prehistoric archaeology has provided numerous indications that this has not always been the case. For instance, Gabriel Cooney (2002: 95) has discussed the way in which the working of prehistoric stone axes in Ireland and Britain, by grinding, polishing and wetness, changed the colour of the stone. The lustrous surface of the stone was enforced, and the veins in some of the axes were emphasised, drawing attention to the particularity of their geological origin. This suggests that the material may not have been simply 'made into' products in a modern sense, but that the crafting of the axe was a way of releasing and enhancing the character of the rock. These axes would therefore have been more than functional tools, or even 'prestige items' with an enhanced exchange value, for in 'freeing' the rock to reveal its materiality, the stoneworker was responsible for the increased 'eloquence' of the artefact. Knapping and polishing did not bring anything to the stone that was not already there, and while the imposition of the axe form gave the object a certain functional capability, much of its social efficacy lay in the relationships, places, people and qualities that it evoked.

Another example can be found in the upper palaeolithic cave paintings of France and Spain. As these are an aspect of a relatively sudden cultural efflorescence (discussed in the previous chapter) which has few clear precursors, there has been a tendency to identify the images of bison, horse, mammoth and other animals at sites like Lascaux and Altamira as the progenitors of the entire Western tradition of representational art. But this has the result of reducing the cave walls on which they were executed to a mere canvas, devoid of any significance in themselves. Making art is then a matter of imposing meaningful images on a meaningless substance, whose only role is as a bearer of those images. The work of Leroi-Gourhan (1982) had the important effect of drawing attention to the locations in which images were deployed, emphasising the structural relationships between different creatures. But even this was a somewhat formalist approach, which paid limited attention to the physical character of the paintings' locations. More successful in this respect was Bender's (1989: 87) discussion of the role that painted images in secluded places may have had in rituals and initiations. Another significant aspect of cave art and its material situation is the way in which paintings and engravings make attentive use of the undulating surface of the rock. At sites like Font-de-Gaume and Bernifal, animal images achieve a strikingly lifelike quality by having been painted onto slight, rounded protuberances in the cave wall (Figure 9.1). From a modern point of view,

Figure 9.1 Upper palaeolithic image of a mammoth on a raised rock surface at the cave of Bernifal, France (photo: Thomas Dowson)

Figure 9.2 Garnwnda chambered tomb, south-west Wales (photo: author)

this seems an ingenious but opportunist way of creating representations. But we could equally argue that this art is not 'representational' at all. Instead of invoking creatures that were understood to be distant from the cave, whether as a means of instruction or as sympathetic magic, it may be that the artists were elaborating something that they considered to be already present in the rock. Whether this amounted to some kind of life force, animal deities, or ancestral creatures is unclear.

Finally, we could point to the materiality of megalithic monuments in neolithic Europe. Recently, Vicki Cummings (2002: 112) has drawn attention to the similarities between many chambered tombs and natural geological features in south-west Wales and south-west Scotland (Figure 9.2). As she points out, it is not simply that it is now difficult to discern which is a megalith and which is an outcrop, it may be that neolithic people did not distinguish between the two. If one recognised no fundamental separation between culture and nature, the question of whether a given structure was 'natural', or whether it had been created by past generations of people, or by the deities, might not occur. Similarly, the issue of whether a structure was fundamentally different as a result of having been 'made' by human labour might not have been a consideration. This means that we need to question the view that prehistoric monuments should principally be understood as the manifestations of human labour power (Renfrew 1973a; Startin and Bradley 1981). That a particular amount of effort had been invested in an arrangement of stones might be relatively inconsequential if no distinction was acknowledged between those 'monuments' that had been built and those that were of natural origin. Both might equally be understood to embody spiritual forces, and both might equally serve as foci for collective memory. To neolithic people, the material world may have revealed itself in ways that would be quite unfamiliar to ourselves.

10

TOWARDS A COUNTER-MODERN ARCHAEOLOGY

Difference, ethics, dialogue, finitude

Introduction

This book has sought to demonstrate that, in a variety of ways, archaeology is bound in to the modern condition. Yet as we noted in the first chapter, there are many who would now hold that the world has entered a 'postmodern' era, in which many of the principal features of modernity are withering away. Where does this leave archaeology if its very existence is tied to a set of historical conditions that are presently vanishing? This is an issue that has already been raised by a number of authors. Hodder (1999: 179), for instance, has pointed to the decline of the national identities that were often legitimised by archaeology, together with a loss of faith in universal origin stories and a general commodification of the past. Similarly, Olsen (2001: 42) suggests that globalisation and changing relationships with place and locality are promoting a new and different kind of identity politics, which archaeology may be less well placed to engage with in its present form. More generally, if archaeology were only to be conceivable within the scaffolding of modern thought, and necessarily relied upon an epistemology, an ontology, and a relationship to ethics that was uniquely modern, it might be that the discipline was one that had outlived its usefulness. We have maintained that archaeology appears to be wedded to notions of materiality, mind, personal identity, nature and history that have characterised the modern era. Is it possible to imagine what the subject might become if it were to relinquish these ideas? Would it still be recognisable as archaeology?

Shanks and Tilley (1987: 28) argued persuasively that archaeology was in a state of crisis as it neared the end of the twentieth century. It may be that by focusing on the relationship between archaeology and modernity we will be able to define this crisis with greater precision. However, in this chapter my strategy will not be one of simply rejecting modern thought and the archaeology that has been fed by it. We have seen that modernity itself has repeatedly sought to overcome problems by clearing the slate, rejecting all that has gone before, and starting again from new foundations. It would contradict my own argument if I were to attempt to do the same here, to call for another new paradigm, yet another new archaeology. The answer cannot be this simple, for without modernity there would have been no archaeology at all. The existing traditions of the discipline need not be cast aside; indeed, it is arguable that one could not possibly erase archaeology's existing practices and prejudices. Instead, we might seek to transform archaeology for the twenty-first century by enriching it with new and complementary ideas and ways of working. As much as anything, modern thought was characterised by the attempt to reduce all forms of knowledge to their simplest and purest terms. The richly interconnected world of meaning that prevailed during the Renaissance was stripped down to the austere geometry and calculus of the seventeenth century, and it is this vision of knowledge as atomised, purified and unencumbered that archaeology has inherited. We can reinvigorate archaeology not by going back to first principles, but by recognising and promoting its ethical, political, rhetorical and aesthetic dimensions. The demand that archaeology should create a disinterested and objective understanding of the past has left it impoverished and etiolated.

Recapitulation: archaeology and modernity

This last chapter will take the form of a series of suggestions for ways in which a 'counter-modern' archaeology might be achieved. The term 'counter-modern' is preferred to 'post-modern' because the approach is one that draws on ideas and ways of thinking that are in many cases as old as modern thought itself. For as long as there has been a modern condition there have been a series of critiques of modernity, and these have been based in traditions of thought that run parallel with modern thinking (Bauman 1992: 115; Kolakowski 1990: 11). These have included phenomenology, hermeneutics, critical theory, post-structuralism, feminism, queer theory and aspects of romanticism. However, before we progress to a critical evaluation of modern ideas with a view to overcoming them, we should briefly reiterate the principal themes that have been central to the creation of archaeology as a discursive formation. While many of these have been discussed in relative isolation in the different chapters of this book, the intention here is to underscore their strong degree of interconnectedness. Although these elements coalesced in such a way as to enable an archaeological conception of the past to be thought, and in this sense they all served their purpose, it is possible that some remain essential while others can by now be dispensed with.

The modern world has been preoccupied with temporality, and with the notion that changes in society, culture and living things are spread out across time. Time has provided a logical structure within which difference can be ordered, and because it can be arbitrarily segmented linear time can provide a 'container' for processes and phenomena of different kinds. This concern with the temporal distribution of diversity only began to be of importance with the decline of the Middle Ages, which had been more concerned with the arc that leads from the creation to the Last Judgement. With the Renaissance, human diversity became a topic of scholarly interest. It began to be recognised that the past was unlike the present, and that in some respects the people of the past could be distinguished from those of the present. Later, a quite different way of thinking about variability emerged, which focused on norms and deviance. The idea of a norm implies a central point from which other phenomena depart, and reflects the development of a modern cosmology in which humanity is at the centre of things. This brought about a gradual shift in attitudes towards the non-Western 'Others' who were increasingly being encountered during the early modern period. Rather than being located within a continuous web of human difference, Africans and Native Americans began to be evaluated in relation to the implicit norm of the Western European. Similarly, ideas of social and technological development through time enabled correspondences to be drawn between 'savages' and 'barbarians' in the non-Western world and in the European past.

These notions of human development implied that history was directional and irreversible. This contrasted with the natural world, which was imagined by early modern science to be a changeless mechanism. Only at the end of the eighteenth century did the idea of a dynamic nature develop, and with it the need to distinguish between historical and natural change. This problem became all the more intense once conceptions of biological evolution began to be seriously entertained. However, modern thought generally identified historical change with human actions, and there was consequentially a linkage between the emerging metanarratives of modernity and the prioritisation of epistemology. If history was a process in which human beings transcended their conditions and limitations, this was understood as having been achieved through the deployment of reason, which was a question of method. Humanity and reasoned human action therefore represent the subject of history, replacing the innate tendencies of medieval teleology. The overwhelming narrative that began to emerge was that of progress and increasing complexity, in which the benefits of the application of reason demonstrated the desirability of rational conduct. As a result, planning, efficiency and order became closely identified with the good in the European nations, a tendency that survives in archaeology with optimal foraging theory and various aspects of evolutionism. With humanity at the centre of the historical process, rather than as one kind of creature amongst others before God, the modern predisposition for philosophical humanism began to take form. Humanism holds that certain aspects of human existence are fixed, essential and transcendental, and can therefore serve as a baseline for the analysis of the past.

The recognition that societies and technology change across time gave rise to stadial schemes of human development: the journey from savagery to civilisation, for instance. Perhaps the most significant consequence of this way of thinking was that modernity itself came to be recognised as a stage or a period. Modernity was often understood as the culmination of various processes in the past, but it was also sometimes identified as a transitory phase on the way to some kind of resolution of history. Yet at the same time the emphasis on human action gave rise to a concern with contingency, so that a tension emerged between the indeterminacy of particular acts and the supposed inevitability of the end of history. In any case, the understanding that it amounts to a distinct stage, which can be distinguished from other historical periods, is one of the principal features that sets modernity apart from any other condition of human existence, and gives rise to a very particular preoccupation with what has been and what will be. Certainly, this is quite different from a belief in the resolution of the *telos*, in which the prevailing social or economic conditions appear to have very little consequence for the principal dynamic processes within the world.

If historical change was now understood as being driven by the human use of reason, the belief that there were specific ways in which reason could be most effectively applied was to have fateful consequences. We have seen that during the seventeenth century a close connection began to develop between philosophy and statecraft. The crisis of political legitimacy that arose from conflicts between mercantile and landed wealth, and between Catholicism and Protestantism, stimulated forms of political thinking in which the principles of resolution and composition were applied to human societies. The result was that communities were more and more understood as systems composed of parts, the fundamental atom of which was the individual. In these political theories society was identified as a contract made between individuals, and the implication was that those individuals could exist prior to and independent from society.

The perceived universality of the method of resolution and composition promoted the belief that not just society but the whole universe was composed of fundamentally independent entities, legitimising an atomistic conception of knowledge. This meant that both history and nature could be investigated in an analytical and classificatory fashion. Worldly objects were to be apprehended by knowing subjects, and thinking minds were logically separate from physical bodies. This re-sorting of the world into separate categories of phenomena gave rise to the desire to purify knowledge, and to separate it entirely from interests, values and prejudices. Rather than knowing everything that might be known about a thing, from the seventeenth century onwards it became preferable to know only what was certain and secure. Established facts were to be disentangled from ethical, political, rhetorical and aesthetic dimensions of thought. All of this had further implications for the study of the past, for it was now recognised as both different from the present and a legitimate object of dispassionate investigation. The past was thus rendered as an externality, which must be known through scholarly inquiry rather than from what was handed down by tradition. The rationally researched historical past was explicitly distanced from myth.

Archaeology springs from the combination of this construction of the past as an object of knowledge and Bacon's conviction that one can create new knowledge by attending to the material world. Yet for modern thought that world is composed of matter which is inert, and cannot put itself into motion. Matter is passive, and subject to the action of a variety of forces. Most importantly, the twin dichotomies of mind/body and form/matter have created a view of materiality as something which is worked and sculpted by humanity, and this leads to an emphasis on design as an imposition of mind on the world. For modern thought, matter is in itself meaningless as well as passive, for meaning is an attribute of the inner world of the mind. So like designed form, meaning is bestowed on the world by human cognition. It follows from this that the material things that past people have left behind are potential sources of knowledge, and that what we can learn from them concerns the forms and meanings that they impressed upon their world. Ancient artefacts are therefore evidence for the doings of human others, now disappeared. In time, material evidence would also be recognised as an index of the intellectual, economic and social progress of past communities, facilitating a convergence between archaeological analysis and the speculative histories of the Enlightenment.

However, as well as demonstrating the gradual development of human reason and the overcoming of nature, material culture was also called upon to represent an expression of the essential character of specific ancient peoples. While archaeology is widely acknowledged to have served nationalistic agendas, this was only made possible by the more fundamental modern assumption that ethnic, cultural, linguistic and political boundaries should naturally coincide. This circumstance is by no means universal, and is actually diagnostic of the contemporary nation-state. In the modern world the nation has become a collective historical subject, but archaeology has tended to retrospectively impose this situation on the past. Thus we have either 'peoples' or 'folk' migrating across the ancient world, or 'populations' which represent sutured entities engaged in adaptive relations with a broader ecosystem. The rise of the nation-state as a form of organisation had the effect of transforming the sovereign from the inheritor of the royal line into the embodiment of the nation and the chief executive of the state. And this shift from sovereignty to bureaucratic government reinforced the emphasis on social norms, which might now be representative of a bounded polity.

Seventeenth-century philosophy sought to legitimise the ordered structure of the state, while attempting to identify the deep order that had been vested in nature by the creator. Yet the growth of classification and taxonomy in the later part of the century reflected an increasing conviction that order was always an achievement of human mental faculties. This ambiguity between the pattern inherent in observed phenomena and that imposed by the scholar has remained an underlying tension in archaeological typology and seriation.

By the eighteenth century the desire to achieve a rational society had resulted in an imperative to define human nature. Yet at the same time there was much preoccupation with the potential for a human perfection that had not yet been achieved. It was this aspiration that lent the Enlightenment metanarratives much of their force: if progress in the past could be demonstrated, the eventual achievement of the ideal condition was more assured. The theme of human progress and achievement was also manifested in the changing significance of the term 'culture', which was now drawn in to the conceptual space that had been created by the relations between mind, matter and form, in order to signify the products and habits of thought and action. Nonetheless, the eighteenth century also saw a partial reaction against modernity in the form of Romanticism, and with it a new kind of affirmation of the distant past. The ambivalent relationship between narratives of technical progress and a nostalgic attachment to the ruins of antiquity has provided another of the critical elements in the formation of archaeology.

However, the transformation of the ensemble of practices known as 'antiquarianism' into what we would now identify as archaeology was part of a more general shift in modern thinking which took place at the end of the eighteenth century and the beginning of the nineteenth. It was at this point that the nation-states of Western Europe began to throw up various forms of popular nationalism, and with them the notion of a national community. Only when such a community could be imagined could the idea of a national past take hold, leading to popular support for its material substantiation through archaeological investigation. At the same time an epochal change overtook the general conception of knowledge. An epistemological formation based on the tabulation of worldly phenomena into classificatory order was replaced by a search for deep structures underlying manifest entities. The relationship between depth and surface is the hallmark of high modernity, and characterised important changes in the study of geology, medicine, language and political economy (Foucault 1970). I have conjectured that this realignment of knowledge can ultimately be attributed to more long-term changes in conceptions of the person, and the growth of the idea of human interiority.

The modern preoccupation with depth was the final element that contributed to the forging of archaeology. It also most precisely demonstrates the reciprocal relationship between the emergence of archaeology and that of modernity in general. Modern thought creates equivalences between spatial and temporal depth, and associates hiddenness with profundity. Within the modern imagination archaeology serves to signify the search for that which is authentic and immemorial. However, I have suggested that this leads to a degree of conflation of various kinds of 'depth', and that this has significant consequences for the way that archaeology understands its own enterprise.

Critiques of modernity

If the ideas and practices of archaeology are so thoroughly knitted in to the fabric of modernity, the various critical evaluations of the modern condition that have been generated over the centuries will be of material significance to the future development of the discipline. Critiques of modernity may effectively amount to critiques of archaeology, and may point to ways in which the subject might be reformed. To begin with, one of the most evident pathologies of modern existence has been the way in which, since the Enlightenment, reason and science have been identified as the means of achieving a perfect society. The consequence of this has often been that human beings have been subjected to traumatic conditions which were the product of abstract planning: five-year plans, economic stimulus packages, regional development programmes (Falzon 1998: 66). In this way, the human sciences themselves have often been complicit in a calculative reason that seeks to overcome problems by reducing humans to numbers (Horkheimer and Adorno 1973: 7). Similarly, by applying the same logic to 'natural resources' one may achieve efficiency and economic success, but at the cost of alienating oneself from the phenomenal world. Related to this broadly Marxist argument is Nietzsche's view that human beings have come to dominate nature through a rapacious will to truth, which lays everything bare and yet provides no spiritual enrichment. Modern rationality has denied people the consolation of religious belief, but has not been able to replace it with any other kind of ideal which might invest their lives with meaning (Love 1986: 4). Precisely because the Cartesian universe is one from which meaning has been evicted the modern experience is one of a listless nihilism in which we can produce colossal quantities of information but nothing of any real worth. Undoubtedly, there must be times when we will feel that this is true of archaeology: that we are able to extract great amounts of data from excavations without being convinced that we have got any closer to the lives of those who inhabited the place in the past.

For Martin Heidegger, all of these phenomena could be attributed to modern metaphysics, which as we saw in the previous chapter has the effect of absolutising a particular horizon of disclosure. That is to say, modern thought presents everything in the universe as being comprehensible within the terms of a single rationality, while effectively denying the possibility of any other perspective which might reveal things in a different way (Young 2002: 34). If everything can be grasped within the framework of the modern technological imagination, people and things will be reduced to the raw material for an insatiable productive process. Worse still, it will be impossible for them to show up in any other way. Under these circumstances, the world loses its 'enchantment' and human beings suffer a general condition of dislocation, unable to be at home in their surroundings or experience any commitment to shared ethical values.

For many commentators, the nihilism of the contemporary West is to be blamed on the universalising tendencies of modern thought and its consequent denial of human finitude. As we have seen, Newton sought to define a set of natural laws that would hold good at all times and in all places, while the Enlightenment presented human beings as capable of transcending their material conditions through the power of thought (Falzon 1998: 9). There is thus only one array of legitimate knowledge to be had from the universe, and only one framework of understanding through which we can address it. This is precisely what Heidegger means by the making of the modern horizon into something absolute. The alternative view is that human beings are fundamentally mortal, and as such their existence is radically temporal. Mortals have a particular finite past, they exist in an embodied state, alongside others, in a concrete and contingent situation, and they have only a certain range of possibilities open to them for their future from which they must choose (Polt 2001: 59). The world and the phenomena of which it is made up are only accessible in a meaningful way to human beings, but it is the finite range of experiences, conditions and possibilities attending any particular person which enables them to show up in an intelligible fashion. In other words, it is human finitude that makes a comprehensible world possible. While thinkers like Kant argued that we must overcome the body, the passions, and our historical and cultural circumstances in order to approach the eternal and transcendental truths, it is actually only by being immersed in the sensual, social and transitory world that we can have any understanding of things at all (Falzon 1998: 28).

Modern politics and the evaluation of modernity

It will be immediately obvious that the critical views of the modern experience that we have now begun to discuss have strong political implications. If we are to argue that one of the flaws of modern thought has been its attempt to separate abstract knowledge from political and ethical values, it follows that we should acknowledge and even embrace these implications. And if we wish to enhance our archaeology by confronting its attachment to modernist shibboleths, we will need to be quite clear of the ramifications of adopting a particular position, and rejecting or retaining specific ideas or aspirations. The problem that this immediately raises is that contemporary political debate takes place within terms which are themselves a product of modernity. So while we can identify 'left-wing' and 'right-wing' perspectives on the modern condition, the distinction between left and right is one that emerged from a uniquely modern set of circumstances. In the French National Assembly in the period running up to the revolution of 1789, the First and Second Estates sat on the right, and the Third Estate on the left. This division reflected the principal socio-economic conflict of the early modern period: between the landed aristocracy and the principle of dynastic inheritance on the one hand, and the new wealth of mercantile capital on the other. While it is far too crude an argument to suggest that conservatism, liberalism and radicalism directly reflect the class interests of the aristocracy, the bourgeois and the working classes, there is doubtless a degree of correlation.

The principal point that I want to develop from this is that while liberalism broadly represents the political manifestation of the core ideas of modernity, the precise terms under which the conservative right and the radical left have both expressed concern over modern conditions have shifted considerably over the past two centuries. It is arguable that at the end of the eighteenth century the political left was animated by the ideas of the Enlightenment: that knowledge and reason can bring about perfection, provided that tradition and prejudice are swept away. Gradually, the division between socialism and liberalism became more distinct, on the basis of whether the objective of a rational and just state could best be achieved through revolution or reform, and through a centralised economy or enlightened self-interest. For liberalism, the ideal of freedom for the autonomous individual was absolute (Carroll 1993: 124). Yet both adhered to the notion of progress towards an ideal society, in which perfect harmony had been achieved through a reason that was singular and universal.

By contrast, the conservatism of the late eighteenth century gained its coherence from its opposition to the French Revolution. Edmund Burke's *Reflections on the Revolution in France* (1790), for instance, presented the view that the attempt to transform society at a stroke had placed power in the hands of a 'swinish multitude' who were unfit to govern, resulting in chaos and instability (Butler 1984). Traditional conservatism was a curious doctrine, for it held that the value of custom and tradition was not to be underestimated in that they had nurtured and sustained forms of human life that were stable, coherent and viable. It was consequentially opposed to the idea of social engineering, which might tinker with or uproot traditional forms, and in the process bring about dysfunction and collapse. The corollary of this view was that tyrannies, despotisms and moribund aristocracies could not be improved upon by deliberate human design, and must be left in place for fear of instituting something far worse. This was the lesson that had seemingly been learned from the Reign of Terror in Paris. On the other hand, by stressing the positive qualities of tradition conservatism effectively approved a pluralistic position like that of Herder, rejecting the kind of homogenised utopia of reason that had been promoted by the Enlightenment. There was no ideal social form to be achieved, and therefore all existing societies had their value.

Thomas Paine's riposte to Burke, *The Rights of Man* (1791), was phrased in terms of the universal and inalienable rights of the individual. It therefore drew directly on the legacy of the Enlightenment. I would argue that in the centuries since the exchange between Burke and Paine the left has relinquished some of its belief in human perfectibility and the ideal universal society, while the right has let go of pluralist conservatism and embraced a form of liberalism. These developments have had critical consequences for the way in which they now address the issues of modernity and post-modernity. In the period since the Second World War, the ideas of the left have been influenced by the implications of the Holocaust, liberation struggles in the former European colonies in the Third World, the women's movement and the gradual acknowledgement of the totalitarian character of 'actually existing socialism' in the Soviet Union and its satellites. We could argue that each of these factors has played a part in the demolition of Enlightenment metanarratives, and a recognition that ideal rational communities were neither the inevitable outcome of history, nor immune to the domination of sectional interests. It may be for this reason that radical politics since the 1960s has come to celebrate heterogeneity and difference, including multiculturalism, cultural hybridity and sexual diversity. At the same time a non-utopian leftist agenda could be identified in Michel Foucault's argument that liberation was not a condition but a practice. That is, the welfare of ordinary people is unlikely to be secured by a single revolutionary event which removes the government and ushers in a workers' state. There will be no 'end of history' where power has been removed from the earth, and hence the struggle to achieve social justice is an unending one, characterised by innumerable small victories and setbacks.

At the same time as the left has been adopting pluralism, the right has ceased to be truly conservative, and has instead combined economic neo-liberalism with state authoritarianism. This is the cocktail that Andrew Gamble (1988) characterised in the case of Thatcherite Britain as 'the free economy and the strong state'. Paradoxically, right-wing neo-liberalism has advocated the complete freedom of the individual to make and spend money as they please, with little taxation from a 'small state', at the same time as the state remains powerful in the international arena. This involved Britain and the United States in bellicose militarism during the 1980s Reagan–Thatcher era, and more recently has escalated to involve a willingness to indulge in social engineering or 'nation building' – where other people's countries are concerned. In theory, these activities would be anathema to a traditional conservative, although in practice the reorganisation of subject populations was fundamental to nineteenth-century colonialism. At the start of the twenty-first century the project of neo-liberalism appears to be further compromised by the role of increasingly powerful multinational corporations, which now blur the distinction between politics and economics.

The argument that I wish to draw from these points is that neither the left nor the right has maintained an unchanging attitude towards modernity over the past two centuries. On the contrary, positions have repeatedly shifted and issues that were raised from one perspective at one time have been incorporated into quite different arguments at another. For this reason,

I find no problem in drawing on aspects of the critical literature which derive from both the reactionary right and the radical left. In practice, the diagnosis of the ills of modernity arrived at from both points of view can be strikingly similar. Both ends of the political spectrum (as it is presently conceived) consider the modern condition to be in some sense pathological, while the liberal centre has been more consistently willing to adopt a Whiggish view, and to imagine that there has been continuous social and technological progress over the past four centuries. Where left and right part company is not in identifying the problem with modernity but in suggesting a solution. The former may wish to transcend and move beyond the present condition, while the latter often advocates some kind of return to more innocent, pre-modern circumstances.

These politically related attitudes towards modernity are especially evident in relation to the issue of nostalgia. We have seen that the modern world is absorbed with time and its irreversibility, and this often leads to the conclusion that past conditions are irretrievable. Modern societies at once distance themselves from a past that is understood as 'primitive' and 'unsophisticated', while revealing a longing for what has been lost (Wagner 2001: 81). The problem here is that modern thought relies so heavily on foundations and origins, and yet in an ultimate sense the origins of contemporary peoples and organisations appear to be inaccessible. This is one of the reasons why archaeology has been so important to modernity, and yet always fails to achieve what is hoped of it: to bring the past into full presence. For conservatives, archaeology operates as a means of documenting a prelapsarian condition to which modern societies might return, drawing on their cultural heritage in order to re-establish a homeostatic relationship with their surroundings. A quite different kind of nostalgia exists on the left, which might seek to identify a primitive communism in the distant past, in which the products of labour were not alienated from the artisan. Yet rather than representing a state to which contemporary people should revert, such a past serves as evidence that modern capitalism is a passing phase, and that other social and economic arrangements are conceivable. Primitive communism in the past serves as a harbinger of a communism to come. Nonetheless, the attempt to escape the confines of modern thinking should involve moving beyond nostalgia altogether. It is in its difference that the past reveals truly radical possibilities, rather than as precedent.

The world stripped bare

Modernity has created a world from which meaning has been excised. For some, an archaeology which reflects this condition is to be applauded. Hassan, for instance, argues that 'an ethical, aesthetic, historical, poetic or novelistic domain of interpretation is clearly distinct from a scientific domain' (1997: 1023). Archaeology addresses itself to a world of bare material things, which are quite separate from the realm of meaning and value, which lies inside the mind. This situation has arisen from the eclipse of a world-view in which the character of things was given by their place in a cosmic order. That which has not been subject to human design is now without meaning, and as a result the archaeological record is understood as an array of dead substance that has been subject to physical impacts or events of encoding. Ethical, aesthetic or political values are consequentially considered to be extrinsic to this material, and at most a subsidiary element of archaeological investigation. This hierarchy of legitimate archaeological concerns is a legacy of the seventeenth-century 're-sorting' of worldly phenomena, in which the phenomenal world was identified as a space of objects in which perception takes place and information is gathered. The mind was then a separate sphere in which representations were generated, and language enabled these representations to be transferred from one mind to another. In the process, meaning has come to be exclusively identified with representation, and perception has been afforded logical priority over it. Within the sphere of perception modernity has privileged vision, which allows unmediated access to physical things, and yet in a way that allows disengagement and objectivity rather than passionate and sensual engagement.

In the modern world, material things are thus primarily understood as autonomous entities from which information can be acquired, principally through the distanced gaze. This means that things are always objects in relation to a subject: they are always 'present-at-hand'. Under these circumstances, all intellectual inquiry is dominated by the problem of extracting information from the world, and epistemology gains an absolute priority over other kinds of thought. Building human knowledge is simply a matter of finding and employing the correct method (Shanks and Tilley 1987: 48). However, once we recognise that the majority of human involvement in the material world is not characterised by the object/subject relation, these arguments are overturned (see Chapter 9). As we have seen, most of the time human beings operate in such a way that they are absorbed and immersed in their surroundings, and abstract looking is actually a derived and secondary way of relating to the world. The problem is that if our archaeology takes a form that is principally analytical, objective and scientific we may learn very little about the habitual, experiential and involved character of everyday life in the past. People in antiquity did not live their entire lives as disengaged subjects gathering information from abstract objects. They dwelt in sensuous worlds of meaning, desire, suffering and labour. It is impossible to construct an understanding of the past on the basis of artefacts and structures viewed as analytical objects and to hope to somehow unfold a world of meaning out of it. Meaning never arrives on the scene after the structures of material existence have been put together.

It is for this reason that recent experiments with alternative means of expression in archaeology may have a greater importance than they are sometimes credited with. In recent years, archaeologists have become interested in unconventional photographic imagery (Shanks 1992), physical performance (Pearson and Shanks 2001), art, installations and aesthetics (Campbell and Hansson 2000; Schülke 2000), poetry (Giles 2001) and alternative forms of writing (Edmonds 1999) as ways of addressing aspects of past experience which cannot be conveyed by standard academic discourse. The significance of these approaches is not that they should replace analytical forms of archaeology but that they should complement them, broadening our appreciation of the richness and unfamiliarity of lives that were lived in the distant past. Contrary to modernist dogma, investigations that have been shorn of aesthetics, rhetoric and poetics are impoverished rather than more secure in their conclusions, for they arrive at patterns of understanding which exclude significant dimensions of human existence.

Ethics and difference

If the modern insistence on rationality and objectivity has resulted in a limitation of the forms of expression employed in archaeology, a rather more worrying phenomenon is the neglect of ethical issues within the discipline. On the whole, ethical debates in archaeology have been restricted to questions of the control of cultural property, whether to excavate or preserve sites, and the professional responsibilities of archaeologists in the field (Vitelli 1996). These are important issues, but they have largely been approached through universalising frameworks based around rights and codes of conduct. Furthermore, the question of how we conceptualise people in the past is also an ethical one. We may choose to focus on the universality of social roles and innate drives, or alternatively we may concentrate on the surprise we experience in the face of unfamiliar humanities. This is not a morally neutral choice, for our attitude to other persons in the present will be deeply affected by whether we emphasise the unity or the diversity of human existence. My argument will be that an ethics that relies upon the sameness of all human beings is vulnerable in the face of atavism and racism.

We saw in Chapter 2 that the Enlightenment faced the problem of attempting to find a rational foundation for ethical conduct. This issue arose out of the decline of tradition and religious conviction. Traditional values or a conception of cosmological order can provide the basis for a shared moral vision. But where customary practice and the centrality of the deity had been replaced by reason and Man, a need arose for an independently grounded moral order. As we have seen, it was human nature and reason which were called upon as the foundation of this new order, which sought to establish the kinds of rules that an autonomous, self-enclosed, rational being could be expected to observe. In Kant's version of this argument the free agent must choose whether or not to obey the dictates of the moral law, and only the acts of a free individual can be moral (Laidlaw 2002: 314). As rational beings, humans are universally aware of the moral law, which is a priori rather than learned. Moreover, our moral behaviour in relation to other human beings is a function of their also being autonomous individuals, whose own rational will must not be made subject to ours. Yet we noted that this scheme was flawed, for the proper application of reason in social life would have required human beings to have already achieved a degree of perfection that had not yet been arrived at through social progress (see Chapter 6). As a result, universalising moral schemes came to be based on rights instead of reason, and on the role of protest and the uncovering of wrong-doing as means of maintaining those rights (MacIntyre 1981: 69). Rights therefore become place-holders for the moral absolutes of earlier, traditional ethical systems.

The concept of inalienable human rights is a metaphysical one, and is linked to essentialist views of human nature and individuality, and to contract theories of society. The dignity and worth of a person are derived from their uniqueness and unrepeatability, rather than from their place in a cosmic order that modernity has liquidated. From an archaeological point of view such an ethics is unsatisfactory not simply because it is opposed to the values of community and solidarity but because it assumes that there is only one way to be human, and it is fragile in the face of the idea that some people are not properly human at all. Rather than starting from the proposition that human beings are all unique in the same way, a way that can be fully accounted for by science, it may be more profitable to consider the otherness of the other human being. The other person always exceeds our comprehension because we cannot be them, or see the world from their point of view. They can never be reduced to our conception of them. While the rights of the modern individual are conceived in monadic terms, the difference of the other person can only be understood relationally. An ethics that takes this relationship as its point of departure is better placed to acknowledge that we could not be human at all if it were not for other people (Levinas 1983: 100). We are born into a community with cultural and linguistic traditions, and embedded coping skills, which constitute us as human actors. Our lives emerge out of our dealings with others, and this demands an ethics which is based not on autonomy but on heteronomy (Critchley 2002: 12). Once we relinquish the idea that we are autonomous individuals we can begin to understand ourselves as ethical subjects (Critchley 1999: 75).

This is very much the argument that Emmanuel Levinas (1998) proposes when he suggests that ethics, rather than epistemology or ontology, should have the status of first philosophy. For Levinas, it is the face-to-face relationship with the other person that is fundamental to our existence as ethical beings. In this relationship we confront an alterity that is irreducible, and which cannot be described objectively as if from the outside. This is not to fall back into some notion of the primordial individuality of the other person so much as to say that the lived practice of being human is too rich, complex and strange to be fully encompassed conceptually. By challenging our ability to typify neatly everything in our world, the relationship with the other troubles our whole horizon of intelligibility. A Kantian ethics would emphasise the relationships between conscious, rational subjects, transcending and overcoming their embodiment and their physical passions. Yet for Levinas the ethical relationship is one not between abstract intelligences but between embodied, sensible, sensuous beings (Critchley 1999: 63; Waldenfels 2002: 65). This means that ethics cannot be addressed through an analytical epistemology, since it exceeds and overflows the possibilities of explicit knowledge. One does not contemplate the other person like an object of scientific investigation; one engages in a dialogue with them. This is a practice of being in relation to the other.

Kant's ethics was concentrated around respect for the moral law; more recent modern moral codes have demanded the observance of the rights of individuals. A relational ethics, however, is concerned not with rights but with our *responsibility* to the other person (Davies 2002: 162). Since we cannot exist except in relation to others, this responsibility is overwhelming. It is infinite, beyond our capacity to meet, and yet it cannot be avoided (Critchley 2002: 22). The ethical relationship is one of openness to the radical alterity of the other, in which we confront them in their concrete, contingent reality as a being who enjoys pleasure and feels pain. While Kant stresses the individual's freely willed choice to follow the moral law, Levinas is more concerned with the obligation to offer unconditional hospitality to the other person in their suffering. Where modern reason struggles to find a ground for believing that other human beings are conscious and capable of feeling at all, Levinas's insistence that we can only be in relation to the other renders such doubts meaningless (Davies 2002: 164). The senselessness of the suffering of the other person is literally unbearable, and yet we cannot encompass it intellectually: it simply demands an unlimited response.

Advocating an ethics which replaces personal rights with responsibility to the other is not a position that should be adopted lightly. In the period since the Second World War the discourse on human rights has contributed immensely to struggles against oppression and intolerance. The Civil Rights movement in the United States is only one example of what has been achieved by insisting that a certain entitlement is universal and non-negotiable. However, rights are finite, while our responsibility to the other is infinite. There are ways of denying that another person is the same as us, rendering them 'subhuman', and thus declaring them ineligible for human rights. But there is no way of avoiding the otherness of the other person. We cannot fail to recognise another as an embodied being who speaks to us, and issues a call to which we must respond. Our responsibility to the other person in their alterity and in their suffering cannot be neglected. In recent years, the language of responsibility has been appropriated by conservative politicians in order to argue that citizens should not automatically expect to be supported by the state. Instead, it is suggested that they should conform to the demands that the state or the market places upon them. This is very far removed from what Levinas means by our responsibility to the other. Indeed, it is worth considering how a recognition of responsibility towards the suffering of other human beings might affect the conduct of those who presently hold power in the Western nations.

Archaeology is concerned with the difference of the past. That is, it investigates the alterity of other human beings who now no longer exist. In what sense could we be said to have an ethical relationship with people who have been dead for centuries? If those people can no longer act or feel, and if they exist as no more that a handful of bones, can we really have any responsibility towards them? I want to argue that we do, in that our attitude towards the distant people whom we study is indicative of our attitude towards other human beings in general. We cannot harm these people, or offend them through what we write about them, but there is an extent to which the relationship that we establish with past humanities is formative of ourselves as persons in the present. Where we treat other human beings as scientific specimens we transform them into fully comprehensible objects. They become a kind of raw material for the production of knowledge. It makes little difference that the people that we study through archaeology cannot look or speak back to us. If we reduce them to the atoms of a past social system, or to rational foraging organisms, we subject them to a totalising logic. By failing to recognise that human lives exceed our conceptual schemes, we do not learn from the past so much as organise it (Wyschogrod 2002: 191). Most critically, where we seek to nullify the difference of the past by identifying people who are 'just like us' (having the same ways of thinking, bodily experiences, emotional responses, values and beliefs) we transform that difference to a universal sameness. This is a totalisation that is closely related to totalitarianism: it contains the same urge to impose order on the world and annihilate whatever does not fit. By acknowledging this difference we recognise that it exceeds our ordering capabilities. The ethical task of archaeology is thus *to bear witness to the past other*. This is by no means straightforward, for there is the abiding danger of wilfully constructing a bizarre and exotic past for the sake of spectacle (Hodder 1999: 154; Shanks and Tilley 1989: 7). The problem is one of letting the difference of the past reveal itself *as* itself, rather than allowing it to dissipate into a set of mere images which can be absorbed by the more general economy of signs that dominates contemporary existence.

Analogy and difference

If archaeology is to adopt a counter-modern position, and challenge the expectations that modern thought inflicts on the past, it will require a variety of strategies for opening up the difference of past horizons. One such strategy might lie in a reconsideration of the way in which ethnographic analogy can be employed. At the most basic of levels, a general awareness of ethnography is essential for any archaeologist, simply because it demonstrates that the social practices and values of the modern West are not shared by the whole of humanity. However, there are immediate problems that we face as soon as we seek to establish comparisons between past societies and those of the non-Western world. First, although throughout this book I have been making a case that modernity is a unique condition, which in some ways stands apart from other forms of human existence, it would be quite wrong to imagine that all pre-modern and non-modern communities are broadly comparable with each other. This kind of homogenisation of the spatial and temporal other sets up a simplistic polarity between 'the West' and 'the rest' (Stahl 1993: 236). While it is sometimes tempting to imagine that we can directly compare the material traces of past communities with contemporary accounts of non-industrial groups in Africa, New Guinea or Amazonia and hope to 'read off' social practices, this is reductive in the extreme. Similarly, analogy has long formed an element of the comparative method in archaeology and anthropology, but this has often revolved around the stadial schemes which operate by pigeonholing particular communities within an evolutionary sequence of social 'types'.

Ethnographic analogy conventionally involves the selective transfer of information from one context to another. Generally this transfer takes place from a relatively well-known source community in the present to a less well-understood subject community in the past (Wylie 1985). Wylie points out that only a partial similarity between past and present context is ever implied, as a means of fleshing out the past and enabling further questions to be posed and further salient information to be sought. However, there are inherent drawbacks in the use of analogy, for it implies that social or cultural systems are naturally composed of 'traits', or atomic elements of behaviour which can be extracted from one context and introduced to another (Lucas 2001: 182). Moreover, as Barrett and Fewster (1998) remind us, the transposition of aspects of social form from contemporary to past communities may promote idealised and static conceptions of social formations. Despite this, it is notable that the use of ethnographic examples has been enthusiastically adopted in recent years within forms of archaeology which are actually opposed to an unreflective uniformitarianism (e.g. Bradley 1990; Edmonds 1999; Richards 1991; Tilley 1996; Whittle 1997: 143–51). I take this to be an encouraging trend, and suggest that the way in which archaeologists have been using analogies has subtly shifted over the past twenty years or so. It may be helpful to draw out the implications of this change.

Much of the classic literature on the use of analogy is actually directed towards quite different problems to those posed by the employment of ethnographic material in recent 'post-processual' archaeology. As Wylie (1985) presents it, the dilemma of American archaeology in the 1950s was to choose between a use of analogy that relied quite explicitly on uniformitarianism in order to place artefacts in a social context, and accepting a sterile 'artefact physics'. In the face of these difficulties, Ascher (1961: 319) attempted to define a 'new analogy' in which the appropriateness of particular analogues could be distinguished according to specified boundary conditions. However, as Stahl (1993) demonstrates, attempts to define such boundary conditions invariably cause further problems. The choice of source cases generally rests on their attribution to a particular stage of social evolution, or on their combination of ecological circumstances and technological development. The latter was the case in Grahame Clark's study of the mesolithic site of Star Carr in Yorkshire, in which he argued that women would have been responsible for hide-working on an analogy with recent Native American groups (Clark 1972; Hodder 1982b: 16). This implies that the sexual division of labour is determined by environment and technology.

But with the rise of the New Archaeology in the 1960s analogy was forcibly rejected. Analogy was seen as inductive, while the hypothetico-deductive method was now understood as a means by which reliable knowledge of the past could be generated from the archaeological evidence alone. So analogy was redundant and, as Binford (1983a) put it, there was no reason to suspect that any amount of information about present societies could increase our knowledge of the past at all. However, as a number of authorities have pointed out (and as we saw in Chapter 3), the attempts that were made to replace inductive logic with a thoroughgoing science of the archaeological record or of physical and ecological relationships were themselves, ultimately, analogical (Wylie 1985). In all of these arguments, the analogical relationship is generally considered to be one between 'past' and 'present' contexts. In other words, the ethnographic context is already understood under the rubric of the same, because it is directly observable, and only the past is different because it is unknown. Ultimately, the past too can be reduced to the same, once it has become fully known and demonstrated to abide by the universal laws of human culture. From this point of view, the virtue of analogy is that it gives access to the behaviour of people following particular subsistence strategies, or using particular kinds of technology, or inhabiting particular ecosystems, or living at a particular stage of socio-cultural evolution. It is not their cultural *difference* that is at issue.

It is in this respect that I will argue that the attraction of interpretive or post-processual archaeology to ethnography has been different in kind from that of traditional and processual archaeologies. Admittedly, structural Marxism has sometimes encouraged us to see past societies as representative of a particular mode of production. But more often the reason for our fascination with African or Melanesian communities has been because they live lives that are so unfamiliar to us in the modern West. What I take this to mean is that interpretive analogies (if we can call them that) involve relations between not two, but three contexts. That is, there is the context within which we archaeologists work; and the temporal other of the past; and the ethnographic or spatial other. With its emphasis on dispassionate observation, processual archaeology tended to occlude the first of these contexts, rendering the archaeologist's perspective a 'view from nowhere'. From an interpretive point of view, the triangulation between these contexts becomes quite complex, because much of the point of the analysis lies not in demonstrating that the source and subject contexts are commensurate but that aspects of both are distinct from our own everyday modern experience.

This book has dwelt on the paradox that archaeology has been made possible by modernity, yet that it is our position in the modern world that makes it difficult for us to comprehend the distant past. Nonetheless, ethnography may provide us with a kind of leverage which enables us to recognise that our personal experiences of the manufacture and circulation of goods, or of gender roles, or of domestic relations are by no means universal. In light of the arguments concerning disclosure, background and pre-understanding developed in Chapters 8 and 9, it should be evident that the most important role of ethnographic analogy lies not in filling in the gaps in our knowledge of prehistoric societies but in troubling and disrupting what we think we already know. This kind of analogical argument is not aimed at establishing a testable hypothesis about what the past was like. Instead, it takes a measure of presumed similarity between two contexts as a starting point and asks: *what if* it was like this? In other words, it sets up a kind of analysis in which we work through the implications of an initial act of defamiliarisation.

In a broad sense, this is what successful analogies have always done. When antiquarians like Dugdale and Plot used observations on non-Western peoples to suggest that what had hitherto been identified as 'thunderstones' or 'elf shot' were actually prehistoric stone tools, this attribution was not an end in itself. Rather, it raised the question of what the ancient inhabitants of Europe had been like, and challenged the images that had been developed from biblical and classical sources. In the same way, when we take ethnographic observations of gift exchange, or different conceptions of personhood, or the meanings of places in the landscape, and suggest that something similar might have applied in the past, the point is not to say that neolithic Wessex or Bronze Age Denmark was just like the New Guinea Highlands or southern Madagascar. Rather, we establish implications that can be taken back to the material evidence, and which reveal it to us in a new light. Barrett and Fewster (1998) have argued that we should not be seeking to impose fixed structures of meaning on the past, but to understand how symbols were reworked and recontextualised by human agency. But analogy *can* serve to tell us that that agency takes forms that are very different from those with which we are familiar, and that those symbols can be used in ways that we may not have personally encountered.

The ethical relation and dialogue

Our discussion of analogical reasoning in archaeology has emphasised difference, and the relationships between past and present, and different cultural horizons. This brings us back abruptly to the issue of ethics. Following Levinas's argument that the encounter with the other is essentially one of conversation between embodied beings, it will be through opening ourselves to the difference of the past that our practice as archaeologists becomes ethical, and the interpretive use of analogy may be one way in which this can be achieved. Inevitably, in choosing one or more analogies with non-Western societies as our point of departure we organise the past and subject it to our own analytical logic. But where we follow up the implications of our 'what if?' questions we enable the past context to surprise us, we avoid closure, and the relationship becomes dialogical. I want to suggest that this emphasis on dialogue will have a more general significance in developing a counter-modern archaeology. While modern thought has emphasised non-contradiction and resolution, a pluralist dialogical ethics would recognise that different points of view need not be reduced to one another for the encounter between them to be productive. Equally, the modern emphasis on the bounded individual has involved an expectation that each person will have a coherent and internally consistent point of view. In practice, we may each adopt a variety of different positions on different issues, and dialogue with others may be a means by which we develop these positions and work out the implications of their incommensurability. Dialogue with the past and amongst the living involves openness, and yet it can be agonistic, with different forces coming into play against each other (Falzon 1998: 57). Rather than arriving at a synthetic or unified perspective, the benefit of engaging in dialogue is that the encounter with others that cannot be encompassed by our own views actually enriches our understanding. This argument is complementary to Hodder's suggestion that we should not expect the tensions between different archaeological theories to be resolved, and that these enduring tensions should be seen as productive rather than problematic (Hodder 1999: 58).

These ideas of dialogue are of particular importance to the relations between the respective archaeological traditions of different regions and states. As a discipline, archaeology emerged in those nations most closely associated with the development of modern thought: France, Britain, Germany, Denmark, Italy, Sweden, and the United States. As Olsen (1991: 211) points out, the pattern in recent decades has been for the archaeologies of particular countries (notably the US and Britain) to be able to claim a universal and international status, while others are judged marginal, parochial and provincial. In some cases, a knowledge of the past of African, Asian or Australasian peoples produced by Euro-American academics is judged more significant than that created by indigenous archaeologists. This is a form of scientific colonialism (ibid.: 214). Such a situation is undesirable enough in itself, but there are good reasons why archaeologists who occupy the metropolitan centres of academic power should attend to other traditions (Holtorf and Karlsson 2000: 8). For one thing, a critical distance from the 'core' areas of the Enlightenment project can facilitate a more clear-sighted evaluation of the implicit values of archaeological methodologies. Indian archaeologists, for instance, have been particularly alert to the connections between culture-history and colonialism (Paddaya 1995: 134). But perhaps more interesting is the possibility that archaeological ideas and approaches can be recontextualised and transformed by being translated into different traditions from those in which they were generated.

A suggestive example of this recontextualisation can be found in the work of the Nigerian archaeologist Bassey Andah. Andah drew on the ecological processual archaeology of David Clarke, Lewis Binford and others, but deployed these influences in a distinctively African fashion. Andah's view was that a characteristically imperialist archaeology made use of European norms as an implicit yardstick by which to measure the divergence of African customs and artefacts. Once these had been stigmatised as bizarre and exotic they could form the basis for classifications and typologies, and these in turn established 'monstrous' cultural entities that were far removed from indigenous experience (Andah 1995a: 98). This was an external view, which constructed African identities as essentially removed from a European sameness, and organised the African past into ethnic groupings in much the same way as colonial administrators reordered living populations. In opposition to such totalising frameworks, Andah sought to understand the particular ways in which specific communities made use of material culture in order to cope with contingent environmental conditions (ibid.: 104). Thus he was able to recruit ideas from what is generally considered to be a generalising approach to archaeology, and yet use them to challenge the blandly homogenising practice of culture-history (Andah 1995b). It is this way in which new dimensions of ideas may be 'found in translation' which may represent another means of overcoming the modernist conventions of the discipline. Without demanding that different regional and national traditions give up their distinctive character, an increased dialogue between archaeological communities would maximise the potential for putting ideas into unfamiliar contexts, revealing unexpected strengths and weaknesses.

Fieldwork and dialogue

In Chapter 3 we discussed the implications of the modern separation of method from interpretation for archaeological practice in the field. The belief that an explicit epistemology can be formulated before any engagement with the material world, and that this can be fully implemented before any interpretation begins, lies behind the present separation between professional field archaeology and the academy. I want to suggest that the recognition that observation and interpretation cannot be distinguished from each other in archaeological excavation and survey should encourage us to reconsider the social relationships that constitute fieldwork. In this connection the idea of an ethics of conversation is once again germane, for we can argue that an archaeological field project is a site in which a dialogue takes place between numerous persons and things, leading to the creation of knowledge about the past.

This conception of field archaeology as a series of interlocking conversations is far removed from approaches which present excavation as a form of objective data-gathering. Binford (2001: 676) has recently argued that our theory-building activities should be kept quite distinct from the observations that we make on archaeological sites. Fieldwork should be designed in order to substantiate hypotheses that have been generated from large-scale pattern-recognition exercises, which correlate existing archaeological evidence with a variety of other data-sets, including climatic, biogeographical and ethnographic information. The effect of this procedure is that the focus of archaeological investigation becomes displaced from the archaeological site and the immediacy of our experience of the evidence. When we *do* then excavate it is in order to address 'referral arguments' that have been generated off-site: arguments which, presumably, most of the field crew have not had a role in formulating. Binford's somewhat Mandarin outlook suggests that the important elements of 'research' take place at a distance from any archaeological site. It may be that a variety of research problems formulated by different people are pertinent to a single excavation, but it is nonetheless tempting to characterise this argument as *anti-democratic*. That is to say, it places the excavator in the position of implementing 'cognitive conventions' generated elsewhere, or of gathering data that will assist in the construction of further arguments. So for the archaeologist on site the implications of this procedure are much the same as those of rescue archaeology, in which excavation can take place without any particular questions about the past having been framed. In either case, the digger might as well be a data-collecting robot.

Once we dissolve the separation between observation, description and interpretation, this characterisation of the fieldworker as a gatherer of atoms of information is no longer tenable. It is not simply, as Hodder (1999: 81) suggests, that the description of evidence involves a subjective element. Rather, the way that this evidence reveals itself to us depends upon a particular background of pre-understanding which is already interpretive. As we saw in Chapter 3, our experience of material things always requires that we experience them *as* something or other, rather than as objective sense data. Each excavator brings a particular pre-understanding to bear on their experience of the archaeological site, and this is not composed of a set of analytical ideas lodged in their mind but of habituated skills and coping practices. These form the basis for their ability to proceed with their on-site tasks at any given point. In the excavation context, skills such as finding the edge of a feature or distinguishing a layer in a section embody an understanding which is already interpretive, even if it is not verbalised. These skills are often intensely physical, involving ways of inhabiting fragmentary spaces and structures which reiterate or invert acts of digging and construction that took place in the far past (Lucas 2001: 203).

This means that our explicit interpretations, relating to the past events that took place in a specific location, are grounded in innumerable acts of understanding carried out by the excavators (see Andrews *et al.* 2000: 526). Therefore, the final account of the site that finds its way into the excavation report is not the outcome of a linear process in which 'bits' of information collected by the diggers are gathered together and cognitively 'processed' by the site director. Conventionally, a single person has the prerogative to collate the results of archaeological investigation and render them comprehensible through a definitive and singular interpretation. But in reality interpretation emerges in the field of relationships constituted by the excavation team as a whole, through a process of negotiation and contestation. In other words, the interpretation of the site gradually crystallises through the innumerable *conversations* that we have on site.

My own experience is that workers on archaeological sites are continually engaged in conversations about the features that they are digging. They say 'do you think I've got the edge here?', or 'can you see another layer in there?', or 'do you think this post was withdrawn, or did it rot away?' In asking these questions of each other they verbalise understandings of the materiality that they are confronted with, which have been developed through their inchoate interpretive skills. This means that the excavation team as a whole is an interpretive community, which engages with a material location collectively, using embodied skills and sometimes trying to rationalise what they have discovered. On site, we find ourselves 'thrown' into a material situation, and we struggle to make sense of it, just as the people who occupied the site in the past found *them*selves inhabiting a materiality and struggling to make sense of it. Tim Ingold (1993) has suggested that we should think of excavation as the most recent episode of dwelling or inhabitation on a site, and all such dwelling involves the gradual development of an inconspicuous familiarity with the place. Sometimes we come to our interpretations of a site less because of any explicit observation that we have made and more because we have spent a period of weeks or months in the place and have 'got the measure of it'.

Excavators on site occupy different subject positions, and have different experiences of the work. They see the site from their own particular ditch or post-hole, and they bring their own biographical resources to the site. They may have worked on a variety of different projects before, and be familiar with different subsoils, different chronological periods, different methods of recording. If as a result they take a stand on the site which is agonistic in relation to others this may actually be productive. As Chantal Mouffe has observed, it is the ability to sustain differences, even incommensurate differences, that defines democracy (Mouffe 1993). Beyond this, the continuous conversation that takes place on any archaeological site is not a disembodied dialogue between abstract minds: it is spatially and materially situated. We are constantly asking questions of the site and its component parts: testing it, picking at it, encouraging it to disclose new relationships. So although obviously archaeological sites are not animate beings, it makes sense to think of our conversation as one in which the site itself is a participant. This point is clearest in the case of a multi-season project, in which the team returns to the site each year with new questions that have been suggested by the analysis of the previous season's findings.

For the most part, the social organisation of archaeology in the field still reflects a linear and hierarchical model of procedure, in which many people collect facts and objects and pass them on to a rarefied stratum of specialists, and then ultimately to the director who will synthesise the whole. It is increasingly recognised that just as we want to recognise a wider range of voices in the past, we should acknowledge more of the diverse experiences of the excavators on site, and allow these to find their way into the textual representation of the project. However, much of the recent debate has come to focus on the roles of information technology and recording systems (for instance, see Hodder 1999: ch. 10). While these developing technologies are extremely helpful, they are essentially tools, and they are not inherently liberating in and of themselves. So while computer networks *can* allow the circulation and sharing of information and site diaries, they can also channel information and constrain observation in ways that actually enhance hierarchy (a point explicitly recognised by Hodder 1998: 214). Equally, while single-context recording places the primary record in the hands of the excavator her- or himself, it can also disaggregate and segment the record in such a way that it becomes difficult to relate the feature one is excavating to the site as a whole. In this connection, Chadwick (1997) notes that while the Harris matrix was originally devised as a means of interpretation, it has latterly been reduced to a means of objectifying the different elements of an archaeological site.

What really matters is how these technologies are put to work, and this is a function of the pattern of social relations on site. Or to put this another way, the interpretive discourse of an archaeological site is an effect of power, and will be qualitatively different depending upon whether the power relations concerned are more or less democratic. Social relations are not merely the context within which we make our interpretations, they actually generate our understanding. The relations between people and people, and between people and things on site, constitute a field of productivity in which meaning is developed. The significance of a site is not created in a single mind but through the *working* of a series of relationships which are more than just inter-subjective. Therefore, the difference between a hierarchical and a democratic excavation is more than a matter of management style: it actually constitutes the web of relations in which the site reveals itself to us through the dialogical process.

The implication of this is that we need to attend far more closely to the micro-politics of excavation. What kinds of freedom of action people have, what kinds of access they are given to the site and to the information generated from it, how they move across the site, and what kinds of opportunity they have to speak and to be heard will directly affect the degree of diversity of the interpretations being generated. It may be that the traditional quasi-military social structure of archaeological field projects is not best suited to the production of a plurality of interpretive discourses (Lucas 2001). And it may be that we can imagine other arrangements that are more productive. Perhaps in some circumstances the position of site director is actually superfluous, and even limits the richness of what can be said about the site. It may not be entirely unrealistic to imagine a field project run as a collective, or in which different people take turns at directing different phases of the investigation. Nonetheless, just as we cannot imagine a society without power, so any field project will involve power relations of one kind or another. Power does not automatically amount to domination, and the important point is the establishment of relations that enable the participants to contribute to the project. While this will generally be achieved by making the conversation as democratic as possible, much field archaeology is conducted on a training basis, and here it will be relationships of productive tutelage and apprenticeship that need to be considered.

Epilogue

Archaeology was a constituent part of the process by which the modern world came into being. In the form in which it is presently practised, archaeology could not have developed in any other set of conditions. In this form it produces a past which serves particular ends and interests: it aspires to the creation of factual knowledge which can be drawn on as the grounding for contemporary projects and identities. However, the object that archaeology studies – the past – is absent, and the discipline continually strives for a degree of certainty that it finds hard to deliver. As part of the structure of modern thought, archaeology seeks clarity, objectivity, and a reduction to law-like or mathematical terms. It demands precision, unambiguous resolution, universality and the transcendence of local conditions. All of this is achieved by declaring the world to be object-like and free of meaning. Meaning is a function of human ordering abilities, and consequentially it is possible to regard the world in a way that brackets out ethics, rhetoric and social relations. None of these applies to mere objects.

The counter-modern archaeology that has been proposed in this chapter is one that begins from the premise that meaning and materiality cannot be separated. Archaeological practice is always conducted by finite mortal beings whose experience of the traces of the past is always contingent. Their interpretations of those traces will arise from different sets of pre-understandings and may thus be irresolvable. Despite this, their accounts of the past will gain in richness from a process of dialogue that is not intended to reach a definitive, non-contradictory point of closure. It is acknowledged that these different accounts of the past will be politically situated. Moreover, our relationship with the past people whom we study is an ethical one, in which we recognise that we cannot fully apprehend and appreciate their lives through analytical frameworks alone. It is for this reason that the 'rhetorical' aspects of archaeology (performance, poetry, art) are important complements to the strictly academic component of the discipline, for they seek to evoke and delineate the absence of aspects of the past that cannot be addressed scientifically.

All of this follows from the recognition that archaeology has been complicit in a process of 'disenchantment' which has engendered modern nihilism. However, once we accept that our world is inherently meaningful, it is no longer possible to see archaeology as anything other than embodied, socially situated, finite and freighted with ethical and political significance. Yet this is not to suggest that we should return to a pre-modern teleology, which presents meaning as a consequence of cosmic order. We need not accept the anthropocentrism of the Enlightenment to recognise the value of modernity's stress on historicity: the recognition that history happens through human social action. Rather than the unfolding of reason towards a static utopia, history involves the unending play of social forces within which humans emerge as subjects and are empowered to act. Furthermore, it is history itself that produces the conditions of finitude under which we practise our archaeology.

BIBLIOGRAPHY

Note: amongst the older works referenced, the original date of publication appears within square brackets, while the later date is that of the edition consulted.

Althusser, L. 1971 Ideology and ideological state apparatuses. In: L. Althusser, *Lenin and Philosophy and Other Essays*, 121–73. London: New Left Books.

Andah, B.W. 1995a European encumbrances to the development of relevant theory in African archaeology. In: P.J. Ucko (ed.) *Theory in Archaeology: A World Perspective*, 96–109. London: Routledge.

Andah, B.W. 1995b The theory and practice of African archaeology: a critical reflection. In: B.W. Andah (ed.) *Rethinking the African Cultural Script: Overview of African Historiography*, 69–111. Ibadan: University of Ibadan.

Anderson, B. 1983 *Imagined Communities: Reflections on the Origin and Spread of Nationalism*. London: Verso.

Andler, D. 2000 Context and background: Dreyfus and cognitive science. In: M. Wrathmall and J. Malpas (eds) *Heidegger, Coping, and Cognitive Science*, 137–60. Cambridge, Mass.: MIT Press.

Andrews, G., Barrett, J.C. and Lewis, J.S.C. 2000 Interpretation not record: the practice of archaeology. *Antiquity* 74, 525–30.

Anthony, D. 1995 Nazi and eco-feminist prehistories: ideology and empiricism in Indo-European archaeology. In: P. Kohl and C. Fawcett (eds) *Nationalism, Politics and the Practice of Archaeology*, 82–96. Cambridge: Cambridge University Press.

Appleby, J., Covington, E., Hoyt, D., Latham, M. and Sneider, A. 1996a Introduction: knowledge and postmodernism in historical perspective. In: J. Appleby, E. Covington, D. Hoyt, M. Latham and A. Sneider (eds) *Knowledge and Postmodernism in Historical Perspective*, 1–20. London: Routledge.

Appleby, J., Covington, E., Hoyt, D., Latham, M. and Sneider, A. 1996b The scientific revolution and Enlightenment thought: introduction. In: J. Appleby, E. Covington, D. Hoyt, M. Latham and A. Sneider (eds) *Knowledge and Postmodernism in Historical Perspective*, 23–8. London: Routledge.

Ardrey, R. 1970 *The Social Contract*. London: Collins.

Armstrong, R.H. 1999 The archaeology of Freud's archaeology: recent work in the history of psychoanalysis. *International Review of Modernism* 3, 16–20.

Arnold, B. 1990 The past as propaganda: totalitarian archaeology in Nazi Germany. *Antiquity* 64, 464–78.

Arnold, B. and Hassman, H. 1995 Archaeology in Nazi Germany: the legacy of the Faustian pact. In: P. Kohl and C. Fawcett (eds) *Nationalism, Politics and the Practice of Archaeology*, 70–81. Cambridge: Cambridge University Press.

Ascher, R. 1961 Analogy in archaeological interpretation. *Southwestern Journal of Anthropology* 17, 317–25.

Atherton, M. 1998 Locke and the issue over innateness. In: V. Chappell (ed.) *Locke*, 48–59. Oxford: Oxford University Press.

Ayer, A.J. 1986 *Voltaire*. London: Faber and Faber.

Ayers, M. 1997 *Locke: Ideas and Things*. London: Phoenix.

Bacon, F. [1605] 1920 *The Advancement of Learning*. Oxford: Clarendon.

Bacon, F. [1620] 1878 *Novum Organum*. Oxford: Clarendon.

Bailey, G. 1981 Concepts, time-scales and explanations in economic prehistory. In: A. Sheridan and G. Bailey (eds) *Economic Archaeology*, 97–118. Oxford: British Archaeological Reports S96.

Barakat, S., Wilson, C., Simcic, V.S. and Kojakovic, M. 2001 Challenges and dilemmas facing the reconstruction of war-damaged cultural heritage: the case study of Pocitelj, Bosnia-Herzegovina. In: R. Layton, P.G. Stone and J.S. Thomas (eds) *Destruction and Conservation of Cultural Property*, 168–81. London: Routledge.

Barceló, J.A. 2000 Visualising what might be: an introduction to virtual reality techniques in archaeology. In: J.A. Barceló, M. Forte and D.H. Saunders (eds) *Virtual Reality in Archaeology*, 9–35. Oxford: British Archaeological Reports S843.

Barker, P.W. 1977 *Techniques of Archaeological Excavation*. London: Batsford.

Barrett, J.C. 1994 *Fragments from Antiquity*. Oxford: Blackwell.

Barrett, J.C. 1999 Chronologies of landscape. In: P.J. Ucko and R. Layton (eds) *The Archaeology and Anthropology of Landscape*, 21–30. London: Routledge.

Barrett, J.C. and Fewster, K.J. 1998 Stonehenge: is the medium the message? *Antiquity* 72, 847–52.

Bassin, M. 1987 Imperialism and the nation state in Friedrich Ratzel's political geography. *Progress in Human Geography* 11, 473–95.

Bateman, J. 2000 Immediate realities: an anthropology of computer visualisation in archaeology. *Internet Archaeology* 8. http://intarch.ac.uk/journal/issue8/bateman/index.html

Baudrillard, J. 1988 *Selected Writings*. Cambridge: Polity Press.

Bauman, Z. 1989 *Modernity and the Holocaust*. Cambridge: Polity Press.

Bauman, Z. 1991 *Modernity and Ambivalence*. Cambridge: Polity Press.

Bauman, Z. 1992 *Intimations of Postmodernity*. London: Routledge.

Bauman, Z. 1993 *Postmodern Ethics*. Oxford: Blackwell.

Bender, B. 1975 *Farming in Prehistory*. London: John Baker.

Bender, B. 1989 The roots of inequality. In: D. Miller, M. Rowlands and C. Tilley (eds) *Domination and Resistance*, 83–95. London: Unwin Hyman.

Bender, B. 1999 Subverting the western gaze: mapping alternative worlds. In: P.J. Ucko and R. Layton (eds) *The Archaeology and Anthropology of Landscape*, 31–45. London: Routledge.

Berger, J. 1972 *Ways of Seeing*. Harmondsworth: Pelican.

Berlin, I. 2000 *Three Critics of the Enlightenment: Vico, Hamann, Herder*. London: Pimlico.

Berman, M. 1982 *All That is Solid Melts Into Air: The Experience of Modernity*. London: Routledge.

Bernauer, J. 1988 Michel Foucault's ecstatic thinking. In: J. Bernauer and D. Rasmussen (eds) *The Final Foucault*, 45–82. Cambridge, Mass.: MIT Press.

Bernfeld, S.C. 1951 Freud and archaeology. *American Imago* 8, 107–28.

Berry, C. 1989 Adam Smith: commerce, liberty and modernity. In: P. Gilmour (ed.) *Philosophers of the Enlightenment*, 113–32. Edinburgh: Edinburgh University Press.

Best, S. 1995 Sexualizing space. In: E. Grosz and E. Probyn (eds) *Sexy Bodies: The Strange Carnalities of Feminism*, 181–94. London: Routledge.

Binford, L.R. 1965 Archaeological systematics and the study of culture process. *American Antiquity* 31, 203–10.

Binford, L.R. 1968 Some comments on historical versus processual archaeology. *Southwestern Journal of Archaeology* 24, 267–75.

Binford, L.R. 1972a Archaeological perspectives. In: L.R. Binford, *An Archaeological Perspective*, 78–104. New York: Seminar Press.

Binford, L.R. 1972b Comments on evolution. In: L.R. Binford, *An Archaeological Perspective*, 105–13. New York: Seminar Press.

Binford, L.R. 1977 General introduction. In: L.R. Binford (ed.) *For Theory Building in Archaeology*, 1–10. New York: Academic.

Binford, L.R. 1981 Behavioural archaeology and the 'Pompeii premise'. *Journal of Anthropological Research* 37, 195–208.

Binford, L.R. 1982 Objectivity – explanation – archaeology 1981. In: C. Renfrew, M.J. Rowlands and B. Seagraves (eds) *Theory and Explanation in Archaeology*, 125–38. New York: Academic Press.

Binford, L.R. 1983a Middle-range research and the role of actualistic studies. In: L.R. Binford, *Working at Archaeology*, 411–22. New York: Academic.

Binford, L.R. 1983b *In Pursuit of the Past: Decoding the Archaeological Record*. London: Thames and Hudson.

Binford, L.R. 1985 Human ancestors: changing views of their behaviour. *Journal of Anthropological Archaeology* 4, 292–327.

Binford, L.R. 1987 Data, relativism and archaeological science. *Man* 22, 391–404.

Binford, L.R. 1989 The 'New Archaeology', then and now. In: C.C. Lamberg-Karlovsky (ed.) *Archaeological Thought in America*, 50–62. Cambridge: Cambridge University Press.

Binford, L.R. 2001 Where do research problems come from? *American Antiquity* 66, 669–78.

Binford, L.R. and Sabloff, J.A. 1982 Paradigms, systematics and archaeology. *Journal of Anthropological Research* 38, 137–53.

Boast, R. 1997 A small company of actors: a critique of style. *Journal of Material Culture* 2, 173–98.

Bourdieu, P. 1990 *The Logic of Practice*. Cambridge: Polity Press.

Bowden, M. 1991 *Pitt Rivers*. Cambridge: Cambridge University Press.

Bowdler, S. 1996 Freud and archaeology. *Anthropological Forum* 7, 419–38.

Bradley, R.J. 1983 Archaeology, evolution and the public good: the intellectual development of General Pitt Rivers. *Archaeological Journal* 140, 1–9.

Bradley, R.J. 1990 *The Passage of Arms: An Archaeological Analysis of Prehistoric Hoards and Votive Deposits*. Cambridge: Cambridge University Press.

Braidwood, R.J. 1952 *The Near East and the Foundations for Civilization*. Eugene: Oregon State System of Higher Education.

Brück, J. 1998 In the footsteps of the ancestors: a review of Christopher Tilley's 'A Phenomenology of Landscape: Places, Paths and Monuments'. *Archaeological Review from Cambridge* 15, 23–36.

Brück, J. 2001a Body metaphors and technologies of transformation in the English Middle and Late Bronze Age. In: J. Brück (ed.) *Bronze Age Landscapes: Tradition and Transformation*, 149–60. Oxford: Oxbow.

Brück, J. 2001b Monuments, power and personhood in the British neolithic. *Journal of the Royal Anthropological Institute* 7, 649–68.

Brumfiel, E.M. 1992 Breaking and entering the ecosystem – gender, class and faction steal the show. *American Antiquity* 61, 453–62.

Bryant, C.G.A. 1985 *Positivism in Social Theory and Research*. London: Macmillan.

Burckhardt, J. [1860] 1995 *The Civilization of the Renaissance in Italy*. New York: Modern Library.

Burke, E. 1790 *Reflections on the Revolution in France*. London: J. Dodsley.

Burnham, D. 2000 *An Introduction to Kant's Critique of Judgement*. Edinburgh: Edinburgh University Press.

Busby, C. 1997 Permeable and partible persons: a comparative analysis of gender and body in south India and Melanesia. *Journal of the Royal Anthropological Institute* 3, 261–78.

Butler, J. 1990 *Gender Trouble: Feminism and the Subversion of Identity*. London: Routledge.

Butler, J. 1993 *Bodies That Matter: On the Discursive Limits of 'Sex'*. London: Routledge.

Butler, M. 1984 Introductory essay. In: M. Butler (ed.) *Burke, Paine, Godwin and the Revolution Controversy*, 1–17. Cambridge: Cambridge University Press.

Campbell, F. and Hansson, J. (eds) 2000 *Archaeological Sensibilities*. Gothenburg: Department of Archaeology, Gothenburg University.

Carroll, J. 1993 *Humanism: The Wreck of Western Culture*. London: Fontana.

Carruthers, P. and Chamberlain, A. 2000 Introduction. In: P. Carruthers and A. Chamberlain (eds) *Evolution and the Human Mind: Modularity, Language and Meta-Cognition*, 1–12. Cambridge: Cambridge University Press.

Cassirer, E. 1951 *The Philosophy of the Enlightenment*. Princeton, N.J.: Princeton University Press.

Caverero, A. 1996 Towards a theory of sexual difference. In: S. Kemp and P. Bono (eds) *The Lonely Mirror: Italian Perspectives on Feminist Theory*, 189–221. London: Routledge.

Chadwick, A. 1997 Archaeology at the edge of chaos: further towards reflexive excavation methodologies. *Assemblage* 3, http://www.shef.ac.uk/assem/3/3chad.htm

Cheah, P. 1996 Mattering. *Diacritics* 26, 108–39.

Chernykh, E.N. 1995 Postscript: Russian archaeology after the collapse of the USSR. In: P. Kohl and C. Fawcett (eds) *Nationalism, Politics, and the Practice of Archaeology*, 139–48. Cambridge: Cambridge University Press.

Childe, V.G. 1940 *Prehistoric Communities of the British Isles*. London: Chambers.

Childe, V.G. 1942 *What Happened in History*. Harmondsworth: Penguin.

Childe, V.G. 1950 *Prehistoric Migrations in Europe*. Oslo: Aschehaug.

Childe, V.G. 1956 *Piecing Together the Past: The Interpretation of Archaeological Data*. London: Routledge and Kegan Paul.

Childe, V.G. 1957 *New Light on the Most Ancient East*. New York: Grove Press.

Clark, J.G.D. 1972 *Star Carr: A Case Study in Bioarchaeology*. Addison-Wesley Modules in Anthropology. New York: Addison-Wesley.

Clarke, D.L. 1968 *Analytical Archaeology*. London: Methuen.

Clarke, D.V. and Sharples, N. 1985 Settlements and subsistence in the third millennium B.C. In: C. Renfrew (ed.) *The Prehistory of Orkney*, 54–82. Edinburgh: Edinburgh University Press.

Cohen, I.B. 2002 Newton's concepts of force and mass, with notes on the laws of motion. In: I.B. Cohen and G.E. Smith (eds) *The Cambridge Companion to Newton*, 57–84. Cambridge: Cambridge University Press.

Cohen, I.B. and Smith, G.E. 2002 Introduction. In: I.B. Cohen and G.E. Smith (eds) *The Cambridge Companion to Newton*, 1–32. Cambridge: Cambridge University Press.

Coley, N. 1991a French science in the seventeenth century. In: D. Goodman and C.A. Russell (eds) *The Rise of Scientific Europe, 1500–1800*, 171–96. London: Hodder and Stoughton.

Coley, N. 1991b Science in seventeenth-century England. In: D. Goodman and C.A. Russell (eds) *The Rise of Scientific Europe*, 197–226. London: Hodder and Stoughton.

Collingwood, R.G. 1945 *The Idea of Nature*. Oxford: Clarendon.

Collingwood, R.G. 1961 *The Idea of History*. Oxford: Clarendon.

Condorcet, M. [1795] 1822 *Esquisse d'un Tableau Historique des Progrès de l'Esprit Humain*. Paris: Masson.

Conkey, M. 1990 Experimenting with style in archaeology: some historical and theoretical issues. In: M. Conkey and C. Hastorf (eds) *The Uses of Style in Archaeology*, 5–17. Cambridge: Cambridge University Press.

Connerton, P. 1989 *How Societies Remember*. Cambridge: Cambridge University Press.

Cooney, G. 2002 So many shades of rock: colour symbolism and Irish stone axeheads. In: A. Jones and G. MacGregor (eds) *Colouring the Past*, 93–107. London: Berg.

Cosgrove, D. 1984 *Social Formation and Symbolic Landscape*. London: Croom Helm.

Cosmides, L. and Tooby, J. 1994 Origins of domain specificity: the evolution of functional organisation. In: L. Hirschfield and S. Gelman (eds) *Mapping the Mind: Domain-Specificity in Cognition and Culture*, 85–116. Cambridge: Cambridge University Press.

Cottingham, J. 1988 *The Rationalists*. Oxford: Oxford University Press.

Cottingham, J. 1992 Cartesian dualism: theory, metaphysics and science. In: J. Cottingham (ed.) *The Cambridge Companion to Descartes*, 236–56. Cambridge: Cambridge University Press.

Crawford, O.G.S. 1932 The dialectical process in the history of science. *Sociological Review* 24, 165–73.

Critchley, S. 1999 *Ethics, Politics, Subjectivity*. London: Verso.

Critchley, S. 2000 Heidegger for beginners. In: J.E. Faulconer and M.A. Wrathmall (eds) *Appropriating Heidegger*, 101–18. Cambridge: Cambridge University Press.

Critchley, S. 2002 Introduction. In: S. Critchley and R. Bernasconi (eds) *The Cambridge Companion to Levinas*, 1–32. Cambridge: Cambridge University Press.

Cummings, V. 2002 All cultural things: actual and conceptual monuments in the neolithic of western Britain. In: C. Scarre (ed.) *Monuments and Landscape in Atlantic Europe*, 107–21. London: Routledge.

D'Agata, A.L. 1994 Sigmund Freud and Aegean archaeology. Mycenaean and Cypriote material from his collection of antiquities. *Studi micenei ed egeo-anatolici* 34, 7–41.

Daniel, G. 1950 *A Hundred Years of Archaeology*. London: Duckworth.
Daniel, G. 1980 *A Short History of Archaeology*. London: Thames and Hudson.
Dant, T. 1999 *Material Culture in the Social World*. Buckingham: Open University Press.
Darwin, C. 1859 *Origin of Species by Means of Natural Selection*. London: J. Murray.
Davidson, J.L. and Henshall, A.S. 1989 *The Chambered Cairns of Orkney*. Edinburgh: Edinburgh University Press.
Davies, P. 2002 Sincerity and the end of theodicy: three remarks on Levinas and Kant. In: S. Critchley and R. Bernasconi (eds) *The Cambridge Companion to Levinas*, 161–87. Cambridge: Cambridge University Press.
Day, A. 1996 *Romanticism*. London: Routledge.
De Bolla, P. 1996 The visibility of visuality. In: T. Brennan and M. Jay (eds) *Vision in Context*, 63–82. London: Routledge.
Deetz, J. 1968 The inference of residence and descent rules from archaeological data. In: L. Binford and S. Binford (eds) *New Perspectives in Archaeology*, 41–8. Aldine: New Mexico University.
Deigh, J. 1991 Freud's later theory of civilisation: changes and implications. In: J. Neu (ed.) *The Cambridge Companion to Freud*, 287–308. Cambridge: Cambridge University Press.
Derrida, J. 1978 Structure, sign and play in the discourse of the human sciences. In: J. Derrida, *Writing and Difference*, 278–93. London: Routledge and Kegan Paul.
Descartes, R. [1637] 1912 *Discourse on Method*. New York: E.P. Dutton.
Díaz-Andreu, M. and Champion, T.C. 1996 Nationalism and archaeology in Europe: an introduction. In: M. Díaz-Andreu and T.C. Champion (eds) *Nationalism and Archaeology*, 1–23. London: UCL Press.
Diderot, D. [1754] 1999 *Thoughts on the Interpretation of Nature*. Manchester: Clinamen.
Disalle, R. 2002 Newton's philosophical analysis of time and space. In: I.B. Cohen and G.E. Smith (eds) *The Cambridge Companion to Newton*, 33–56. Cambridge: Cambridge University Press.
Donald, M. 1991 *Origins of the Modern Mind: Three Stages in the Evolution of Culture and Cognition*. Cambridge, Mass.: Harvard University Press.
Donald, M. 1993 Précis of Origins of the Modern Mind: three stages in the evolution of culture and cognition. *Behavioural and Brain Sciences* 16, 737–91.
Donald, M. 1998 Hominid enculturation and cognitive evolution. In: C. Renfrew and C. Scarre (eds) *Cognition and Material Culture: The Archaeology of Symbolic Storage*, 7–18. Cambridge, UK: McDonald Institute.
Dowson. T.A. 2001 Queer theory and feminist archaeology: towards a sociology of sexual politics in rock art research. In: K. Helskog (ed.) *Theoretical Perspectives in Rock Art Research*, 312–29. Oslo: Novus Forlag.
Dreyfus, H.L. 1992 *What Computers Still Can't Do: A Critique of Artificial Reason*. Cambridge, Mass.: MIT Press.
Dreyfus, H.L. 2000 Could anything be more intelligible than everyday intelligibility? Reinterpreting Division I of *Being and Time* in the light of Division II. In: J.E. Faulconer and M.A. Wrathmall (eds) *Appropriating Heidegger*, 155–74. Cambridge: Cambridge University Press.
Dreyfus, H.L. and Rabinow, P. 1982 *Michel Foucault: Beyond Structuralism and Hermeneutics*. Brighton: Harvester.

Dunbar, R. 2000 On the origins of the human mind. In: P. Carruthers and A. Chamberlain (eds) *Evolution and the Human Mind: Modularity, Language and Meta-Cognition*, 238–53. Cambridge: Cambridge University Press.

Eaglestone, R. 2001 *Postmodernism and Holocaust Denial*. Cambridge: Icon Books.

Earle, T.K. 1991 The evolution of chiefdoms. In: T.K. Earle (ed.) *Chiefdoms: Power, Economy and Ideology*, 1–15. Cambridge: Cambridge University Press.

Edmonds, M.R. 1999 *Ancestral Geographies of the Neolithic*. London: Routledge.

Evans, J. 1860 On the occurrence of flint implements in undisturbed beds of gravel, sand, and clay. *Archaeologia* 38, 280–307.

Fagan, B. 1977 *Elusive Treasure: The Story of Early Archaeologists in the Americas*. New York: Macdonald and Jane's.

Falzon, 1998 *Foucault and Social Dialogue: Beyond Fragmentation*. London: Routledge.

Ferguson, A. [1767] 1819 *An Essay on the History of Civil Society*. Philadelphia, Pa.: A. Finley.

Feyerabend, P. 1976 *Against Method: Outline of an Anarchistic Theory of Knowledge*. London: Verso.

Fisher, P.F. 1999 Geographical information systems: today or tomorrow? In: M. Gillings, D. Mattingley and J. Van Dalen (eds) *Geographical Information Systems and Landscape Archaeology*, 5–11. Oxford: Oxbow.

Flannery, K.V. 1972 Culture history vs. culture process: a debate in American archaeology. In: M.P. Leone (ed.) *Contemporary Archaeology*, 102–7. Carbondale: South Illinois University.

Fodor, J. 1983 *The Modularity of Mind: An Essay on Faculty Psychology*. Cambridge, Mass.: MIT Press.

Foucault, M. 1967 *Madness and Civilization: A History of Insanity in the Age of Reason*. London: Routledge.

Foucault, M. 1970 *The Order of Things: An Archaeology of the Human Sciences*. London: Tavistock.

Foucault, M. 1972 *The Archaeology of Knowledge*. London: Tavistock.

Foucault, M. 1973 *The Birth of the Clinic: An Archaeology of Medical Perception*. London: Tavistock.

Foucault, M. 1977 *Discipline and Punish: The Birth of the Prison*. New York: Vintage Books.

Foucault, M. 1978 *The History of Sexuality. Volume 1: An Introduction*. Harmondsworth: Penguin.

Foucault, M. 1979a Cuvier's position in the history of biology. *Critique of Anthropology* 13/14, 125–30.

Foucault, M. 1979b Governmentality. *Ideology and Consciousness* 6, 5–21.

Foucault, M. 1980 Two lectures. In: C. Gordon (ed.) *Michel Foucault: Power/Knowledge*, 78–108. Brighton: Harvester.

Foucault, M. 1984 On the genealogy of ethics: an overview of work in progress. In: P. Rabinow (ed.) *The Foucault Reader*, 340–72. Harmondsworth: Penguin.

Foucault, M. 1987 *The Use of Pleasure: The History of Sexuality, Volume 2*. Harmondsworth: Penguin.

Foucault, M. 1988a *The Care of the Self: The History of Sexuality, Volume 3*. Harmondsworth: Penguin.

Foucault, M. 1988b Technologies of the self. In: L. Martin, H. Gutman and P. Hutton (eds) *Technologies of the Self*, 16–49. London: Tavistock.

Foucault, M. 1997 The hermeneutic of the subject. In: P. Rabinow (ed.) *Michel Foucault: The Essential Works. Volume 1: Ethics*, 93–106. London: Allen Lane.

Foucault, M. 2001 The political technology of individuals. In: J.D. Faubion (ed.) *Michel Foucault: The Essential Works, Vol. 3: Power*, 403–17. London: Allen Lane.

Fowler, C. 2000 The individual, the subject, and archaeological interpretation: reading Luce Irigaray and Judith Butler. In: C. Holtorf and H. Karlsson (eds) *Philosophy and Archaeological Practice: Perspectives for the 21st Century*, 107–33. Gothenburg: Bricoleur Press.

Fowler, C. 2001 Personhood and social relations in the British neolithic with a study from the Isle of Man. *Journal of Material Culture* 6, 137–63.

Fowler, C. 2002 Body parts: personhood and materiality in the earlier Manx neolithic. In: Y. Hamilakis, M. Pluciennik and S. Tarlow (eds) *Thinking Through the Body: Archaeologies of Corporeality*, 47–69. Dordrecht: Kluwer.

Frede, D. 1993 The question of Being: Heidegger's project. In: C. Guignon (ed.) *The Cambridge Companion to Heidegger*, 42–69. Cambridge: Cambridge University Press.

Freud, S. [1919] 1938 *Totem and Taboo: Resemblances Between the Psychic Lives of Savages and Neurotics*. Harmondsworth: Penguin.

Freud, S. 1927 *The Ego and the Id*. London: Hogarth Press.

Freud, S. 1930 *Civilisation and its Discontents*. London: Hogarth Press.

Freud, S. 1946 *Collected Papers, Vol. 3: Case Studies*. London: Hogarth Press.

Gadamer, H.J. 1975 *Truth and Method*. London: Sheed and Ward.

Gamble, A. 1988 *The Free Economy and the Strong State: The Politics of Thatcherism*. Basingstoke: Macmillan Education.

Gamble, C. 1986 *The Palaeolithic Settlement of Europe*. Cambridge: Cambridge University Press.

Gamwell, L. 1989 The origins of Freud's antiquities collection. In: L. Gamwell and R. Wells (eds) *Sigmund Freud and Art: His Personal Collection of Antiquities*, 21–32. London: Freud Museum.

Gamwell, L. 1996 A collector analyses collecting: Sigmund Freud on the passion to possess. In: S. Barker (ed.) *Excavations and Their Objects: Freud's Collection of Antiquity*, 1–12. Albany: State University of New York Press.

Gardiner, S. 1991 The unconscious. In: J. Neu (ed.) *The Cambridge Companion to Freud*, 136–60. Cambridge: Cambridge University Press.

Gatens, M. 1992 Power, bodies and difference. In: M. Barrett and A. Phillips (eds) *Destabilizing Theory: Contemporary Feminist Debates*, 120–37. Cambridge: Polity Press.

Gatens, M. 1996 *Imaginary Bodies: Ethics, Power and Corporeality*. London: Routledge.

Geertz, C. 2000 *Available Light: Anthropological Reflections on Philosophical Topics*. Princeton, N.J.: Princeton University Press.

Gellner, E. 1983 *Nations and Nationalism*. Oxford: Blackwell.

Gibson, K. 1996 The biocultural human brain, seasonal migrations, and the emergence of the upper palaeolithic. In: P. Mellars and K. Gibson (eds) *Modelling the Early Human Mind*, 33–46. Cambridge, UK: McDonald Institute.

Giddens, A. 1974 Introduction. In: A. Giddens (ed.) *Positivism and Sociology*, 1–22. London: Heinemann.

Giddens, A. 1991 *Modernity and Self-Identity: Self and Society in the Late Modern Age*. Cambridge: Polity Press.

BIBLIOGRAPHY

Giles, M. 2001. Taking hands: archaeology, poetry and photography. *Staple* 51, 28–31.

Glendinning, S. 1998 *On Being with Others: Heidegger, Derrida, Wittgenstein*. London: Routledge.

Goodman, D. 1991 Europe's awakening. In: D. Goodman and C.A. Russell (eds) *The Rise of Scientific Europe, 1500–1800*, 1–31. London: Hodder and Stoughton.

Gouldner, A. 1970 *The Coming Crisis of Western Sociology*. London: Heinemann.

Gray, J. 1995 *Enlightenment's Wake: Politics and Culture at the Close of the Modern Age*. London: Routledge.

Guignon, C. 1983 *Heidegger and the Problem of Knowledge*. Indianapolis, Ind.: Hackett.

Guignon, C. 2001 Being as appearing: retrieving the Greek experience of *Phusis*. In: R. Polt and G. Fried (eds) *A Companion to Heidegger's Introduction to Metaphysics*, 34–56. New Haven, Conn.: Yale University Press.

Guilbaud, G.T. 1959 *What is Cybernetics?* London: Heinemann.

Hall, H. 1993 Intentionality and world: Division I of *Being and Time*. In: C. Guignon (ed.) *The Cambridge Companion to Heidegger*, 122–40. Cambridge: Cambridge University Press.

Hall, M. 2002 Blackbirds and black butterflies. In: C. Hamilton, J. Taylor, M. Pickover, G. Reid and R. Saleh (eds) *Refiguring the Archive*. Cape Town: David Philip.

Härke, H. 1995 'The Hun is a methodical chap': reflections on the German tradition of pre- and proto-history. In: P.J. Ucko (ed.) *Archaeological Theory: A World Perspective*, 46–60. London: Routledge.

Harris, E. 1989 *Principles of Archaeological Stratigraphy*. San Diego, Calif.: Academic Press.

Harris, M. 1968 *The Rise of Anthropological Theory*. New York: HarperCollins.

Hassan, F.A. 1997 Beyond the surface: comments on Hodder's 'reflexive excavation methodology'. *Antiquity* 71, 1020–25.

Hedges, J.W. 1984 *Tomb of the Eagles: A Window on Stone Age Tribal Britain*. London: John Murray.

Heidegger, M. 1962 *Being and Time*, translated by J. Macquarrie and E. Robinson. Oxford: Blackwell.

Heidegger, M. 1971a The origin of the work of art. In: M. Heidegger, *Poetry, Language, Thought*, 15–88. New York: Harper and Row.

Heidegger, M. 1971b The thing. In: M. Heidegger, *Poetry, Language, Thought*, 163–86. New York: Harper and Row.

Heidegger, M. 1977 *The Question Concerning Technology and Other Essays*. New York: Harper and Row.

Heidegger, M. 1993a Modern science, metaphysics, and mathematics. In: D.F. Krell (ed.) *Martin Heidegger: Basic Writings* (2nd edn), 267–305. London: Routledge.

Heidegger, M. 1993b Letter on humanism. In: D.F. Krell (ed.) *Martin Heidegger: Basic Writings* (2nd edn), 213–65. London: Routledge.

Heidegger, M. 1993c What is metaphysics? In: D.F. Krell (ed.) *Martin Heidegger: Basic Writings* (2nd edn), 89–109. London: Routledge.

Heidegger, M. 2001 *Introduction to Metaphysics*. New Haven, Conn.: Yale University Press.

Hekman, S. 1990 *Gender and Knowledge: Elements of a Postmodern Feminism*. Cambridge: Polity.

Hempel, C. 1966 *Philosophy of Natural Science*. Englewood Cliffs, N.J.: Prentice-Hall.
Herb, H. 1989 Persuasive cartography in *Geopolitik* and National Socialism. *Political Geography Quarterly* 8, 289–303.
Higgs, E.S. and Jarman, M.R. 1969 The origins of agriculture: a reconsideration. *Antiquity* 43, 31–41.
Higgs, E.S. and Jarman, M.R. 1972 The origins of animal and plant husbandry. In: E.S. Higgs (ed.) *Papers in Economic Prehistory*, 3–14. Cambridge: Cambridge University Press.
Higgs, E.S. and Jarman, M.R. 1975 Palaeoeconomy. In: E.S. Higgs (ed.) *Palaeoeconomy*, 1–8. Cambridge: Cambridge University Press.
Hill, C. 1967 *Reformation to Industrial Revolution*. Harmondsworth: Penguin.
Hill, J.N. 1970 Prehistoric social organisation in the American southwest: theory and method. In: W.A. Longacre (ed.) *Reconstructing Prehistoric Pueblo Societies*, 11–58. Albuquerque: New Mexico University.
Hill, J.N. 1972 A prehistoric community in Eastern Arizona. In: M.P. Leone (ed.) *Contemporary Archaeology: A Guide to Theory and Contributions*, 320–32. Carbondale and Edwardsville: Southern Illinois University Press.
Hill, J.N. 1994 Prehistoric cognition and the science of archaeology. In: C. Renfrew and E. Zubrow (eds) *The Ancient Mind: Elements of Cognitive Archaeology*, 83–92. Cambridge: Cambridge University Press.
Hill, J.N. and Gunn, J. 1977 Introducing the individual in prehistory. In: J.N. Hill and J. Gunn (eds) *The Individual in Prehistory: Studies of Variability in Style in Prehistoric Technologies*, 1–12. New York: Academic.
Hoare, R.C. [1812] 1975 *The Ancient History of Wiltshire*. Wakefield: EP Publishing.
Hobbes, T. [1651] 1996 *Leviathan*. Cambridge: Cambridge University Press.
Hodder, I.R. 1982a Theoretical archaeology: a reactionary view. In: I.R. Hodder (ed.) *Symbolic and Structural Archaeology*, 1–16. Cambridge: Cambridge University Press.
Hodder, I.R. 1982b *The Present Past: An Introduction to Anthropology for Archaeologists*. London: Batsford.
Hodder, I.R. 1986 *Reading the Past*. Cambridge: Cambridge University Press.
Hodder, I.R. 1992 Symbolism, meaning and context. In: I. Hodder *Theory and Practice in Archaeology*, 11–23. London: Routledge.
Hodder, I.R. 1997 'Always momentary, fluid and flexible': towards a reflexive excavation methodology. *Antiquity* 71, 691–700.
Hodder, I.R. 1998 Whose rationality? A response to Fekri Hassan. *Antiquity* 72, 213–17.
Hodder, I.R. 1999 *The Archaeological Process: An Introduction*. Oxford: Blackwell.
Hodder, I.R. 2000 Agency and individuals in long-term process. In: M.A. Dobres and J. Robb (eds) *Agency in Archaeology*, 21–33. London: Routledge.
Hodder, I.R. and Preucel, R. (eds) 1996 *Contemporary Archaeology in Theory: A Reader*. Oxford: Blackwell.
Hodgen, M.T. 1964 *Early Anthropology in the Sixteenth and Seventeenth Centuries*. Philadelphia, Pa.: University of Pennsylvania Press.
Holtorf, C. and Karlsson, H. 2000 Changing configurations of archaeological theory: an introduction. In: C. Holtorf and H. Karlsson (eds) *Philosophy and Archaeological Practice*, 1–12. Gothenburg: Bricoleur Press.
Hooper-Greenhill, E. 1992 *Museums and the Shaping of Knowledge*. London: Routledge.

Horkheimer, M. and Adorno, T.W. 1973 *Dialectic of Enlightenment*. London: Allen Lane.
Horowitz, A. 1987 *Rousseau: Nature and History*. Toronto: University of Toronto.
Hroch, M. 1988 Real and constructed: the nature of the nation. In: J.A. Hall (ed.) *The State of the Nation: Ernest Gellner and the Theory of Nationalism*, 91–106. Cambridge: Cambridge University Press.
Hunter, J. and MacSween, A. 1991 A sequence for the Orcadian neolithic? *Antiquity* 65, 911–14.
Hutton, J. [1788] 1795 *Theory of the Earth*. Edinburgh: Cadell and Davies.
Hutton, P.H. 1988 Foucault, Freud, and the technologies of the self. In: L.H. Martin, H. Gutman and P.H. Hutton (eds) *Technologies of the Self: A Seminar with Michel Foucault*, 121–44. London: Tavistock.
Ingold, T. 1993 The temporality of the landscape. *World Archaeology* 25, 152–74.
Jameson, F. 1984 Post-modernism or the cultural logic of late-capitalism. *New Left Review* 146, 53–93.
Jardine, L. 1999 *Ingenious Pursuits: Building the Scientific Revolution*. London: Abacus.
Jay, M. 1973 *The Dialectical Imagination: A History of the Frankfurt School and the Institute of Social Research, 1923–50*. London: Heinemann.
Jay, M. 1986 In the empire of the gaze: Foucault and the denigration of vision in twentieth-century French thought. In: D.C. Hoy (ed.) *Foucault: A Critical Reader*, 175–204. Oxford: Blackwell.
Jay, M. 1993 *Force Fields: Between Intellectual History and Cultural Critique*. London: Routledge.
Johnsen, H. and Olsen, B. 1992 Hermeneutics and archaeology: on the philosophy of contextual archaeology. *American Antiquity* 57, 419–36.
Johnson, G.A. 1978 Information sources and the development of decision-making organisations. In: C.L. Redman, M.J. Berman, E.V. Curtin, W.T. Langhorne, N.M. Versaggi and J.C. Wanser (eds) *Social Archaeology: Beyond Subsistence and Dating*, 87–112. New York: Academic Press.
Johnson, M.H. 1989 Conceptions of agency in archaeological interpretation. *Journal of Anthropological Archaeology* 8, 189–211.
Jones, A. 2000 Life after death: monuments, material culture and social change in neolithic Orkney. In: A. Ritchie (ed.) *Neolithic Orkney in its European Context*, 127–38. Cambridge, UK: McDonald Institute.
Jones, A. 2001 Drawn from memory: the archaeology of aesthetics and the aesthetics of archaeology in earlier Bronze Age Britain and the present. *World Archaeology* 33, 334–56.
Jones, G.D.B. 1984 *Past Imperfect: The Story of Rescue Archaeology*. London: Heinemann.
Jones, R.F. 1961 *Ancients and Moderns: A Study of the Rise of the Scientific Movement in Seventeenth-Century England*. New York: Dover.
Jones, S. 1997 *The Archaeology of Ethnicity: Constructing Identities in the Past and Present*. London: Routledge.
Jones, S. and Richards, C.C. 2000 Neolithic cultures in Orkney: classification and interpretation. In: A. Ritchie (ed.) *Neolithic Orkney in its European Context*, 101–6. Cambridge, UK: McDonald Institute.
Jordanova, L. 1989 *Sexual Visions: Images of Gender in Science and Medicine Between the Eighteenth and Twentieth Centuries*. London: Harvester Wheatsheaf.
Kant, I. [1790] 1988 *Critique of Judgement*. Oxford: Clarendon.

BIBLIOGRAPHY

Kant, I. [1797] 1998 *Groundwork of the Metaphysics of Morals*. Cambridge: Cambridge University Press.
Klindt-Jensen, O. 1975 *A History of Scandinavian Archaeology*. London: Thames and Hudson.
Knapp, A.B. and Meskell, L. 1997 Bodies of evidence in prehistoric Cyprus. *Cambridge Archaeological Journal* 7 (2), 183–204.
Kohl, P. and Fawcett, C. 1995 Archaeology in the service of the state: theoretical considerations. In: P. Kohl and C. Fawcett (eds) *Nationalism, Politics, and the Practice of Archaeology*, 3–20. Cambridge: Cambridge University Press.
Kolakowski, L. 1990 *Modernity on Endless Trial*. Chicago: University of Chicago Press.
Kristeva, J. 1984 *Revolution in Poetic Language*. New York: Columbia University.
Kristiansen, K. 1985 *Archaeological Formation Processes*. Copenhagen: Nationalmuseet.
Kuspit, D. 1989 A mighty metaphor: the analogy of archaeology and psychoanalysis. In: L. Gamwell and R. Wells (eds) *Sigmund Freud and Art: His Personal Collection of Antiquities*, 133–51. London: Freud Museum.
Laidlaw, J. 2002 For an anthropology of ethics and freedom. *Journal of the Royal Anthropological Institute* 8, 311–32.
Latour, B. 1987 *Science in Action*. Milton Keynes: Open University Press.
Latour, B. 1993 *We Have Never Been Modern*. London: Harvester Wheatsheaf.
Lawson, H. 1985 *Reflexivity: The Post-Modern Predicament*. London: Hutchinson.
Leroi-Gourhan, A. 1982 *The Dawn of European Art: An Introduction to Palaeolithic Cave Painting*. Cambridge: Cambridge University Press.
Levinas, E. 1983 Beyond intentionality. In: A. Montefiore (ed.) *Philosophy in France Today*, 100–15. Cambridge: Cambridge University Press.
Levinas, E. 1998 *Entre Nous: Thinking-of-the-Other*. New York: Columbia University Press.
Lévi-Strauss, C. 1977 The scope of anthropology. In: C. Lévi-Strauss, *Structural Anthropology, Volume II*, 3–32. London: Allen Lane.
LiPuma, E. 1998 Modernity and forms of personhood in Melanesia. In: M. Lambek and A. Strathern (eds) *Bodies and Persons: Comparative Perspectives from Africa and Melanesia*, 53–79. Cambridge: Cambridge University Press.
Lloyd, C. 1986 *Explanation in Social History*. Oxford: Blackwell.
Lock, G. and Harris, T. 1992 Visualising spatial data: the importance of Geographic Information Systems. In: P. Reilly and S. Rahtz (eds) *Archaeology in the Information Age*, 81–96. London: Routledge.
Locke, J. [1690] 1998 *Essay Concerning Human Understanding*. Ware, Herts.: Wordsworth.
Longacre, W.A. 1964 Archaeology as anthropology: a case study. *Science* 144, 1454–5.
Lorenz, K. 1963 *On Aggression*. London: Methuen.
Love, N.S. 1986 *Marx, Nietzsche and Modernity*. New York: Columbia University Press.
Lowe, E.J. 1995 *Locke on Human Understanding*. London: Routledge.
Lucas, G. 2001 *Critical Approaches to Fieldwork: Contemporary and Historical Archaeological Practice*. London: Routledge.
Lukes, S. 1973 *Individualism*. Oxford: Blackwell.
Lyell, C. 1830 *Principles of Geology*. London: John Murray.

Lyman, R.L. and O'Brien, M. 2001 Introduction. In: G.R. Willey and P. Phillips, *Method and Theory in American Archaeology*, 1–78. Tuscaloosa: University of Alabama Press.
Lyotard, J.-F. 1984 *The Postmodern Condition: A Report on Knowledge*. Manchester: Manchester University Press.
Macbeath, M. 1989 Kant. In: P. Gilmour (ed.) *Philosophers of the Enlightenment*. Edinburgh: Edinburgh University Press.
McCann, B. 1987 The national socialist perversion of archaeology. *World Archaeological Bulletin* 2, 51–4.
McCann, E. 1994 Locke's philosophy of body. In: V. Chappell (ed.) *The Cambridge Companion to Locke*, 56–88. Cambridge: Cambridge University Press.
McCannell, J.F. 1996 Signs of the fathers: Freud's collection of antiquities. In: S. Barker (ed.) *Excavations and Their Objects: Freud's Collection of Antiquity*, 33–56. Albany: State University of New York Press.
MacIntyre, A. 1981 *After Virtue: A Study in Moral Theory*. London: Duckworth.
McNay, L. 1994 *Foucault: A Critical Introduction*. New York: Continuum.
McVicar, J.B. 1984 Social change and the growth of antiquarian studies in Tudor and Stuart England. *Archaeological Review from Cambridge* 3, 48–67.
Marion, J.L. 1992 Cartesian metaphysics: the simple natures. In: J. Cottingham (ed.) *The Cambridge Companion to Descartes*, 115–39. Cambridge: Cambridge University Press.
Marion, J.L. 1996 Heidegger and Descartes. In: C. Macann (ed.) *Critical Heidegger*, 67–96. London: Routledge.
Marx, K. 1970 *Capital, Volume One*. London: Lawrence and Wishart.
Mattrie, J.O. [1748] 1994 *Man a Machine*. Indianapolis, Ind.: Hackett.
Mellars, P. and Gibson, K. 1996 *Modelling the Early Human Mind*. Cambridge, UK: McDonald Institute.
Merleau-Ponty, M. 1962 *Phenomenology of Perception*. London: Routledge.
Meskell, L. 1996 The somatisation of archaeology: institutions, discourses, corporeality. *Norwegian Archaeological Review* 29, 1–16.
Meskell, L. 1998 Intimate archaeologies: the case of Kha and Merit. *World Archaeology* 29, 363–79.
Meskell, L. 1999 *Archaeologies of Social Life*. Oxford: Blackwell.
Meskell, L. 2000 Writing the body in archaeology. In: A.E. Rautman (ed.) *Reading the Body: Representations and Remains in the Archaeological Record*, 13–24. Philadelphia, Pa.: University of Pennsylvania Press.
Miller, D. 1987 *Material Culture and Mass Consumption*. Oxford: Blackwell.
Miller, D. 1994 *Modernity: An Ethnographic Approach: Dualism and Mass Consumption in Trinidad*. London: Berg.
Mithen, S. 1996 *The Prehistory of the Mind: A Search for the Origins of Art, Religion and Science*. London: Thames and Hudson.
Montesquieu, C. de S. [1748] 1750 *The Spirit of the Laws*. London: J. Nourse and P. Vaillant.
Moran, D. 2000 *Introduction to Phenomenology*. London: Routledge.
Morgan, L.H. 1877 *Ancient Society, or Researches in the Lines of Human Progress from Savagery through Barbarism to Civilization*. Chicago, Ill.: Charles H. Kerr.
Morris, B. 1991 *Western Conceptions of the Individual*. Oxford: Berg.
Mouffe, C. 1993 *The Return of the Political*. London: Verso.

Mouffe, C. 1995 Democratic politics and the question of identity. In: J. Rajchman (ed.) *The Identity in Question*, 33–45. London: Routledge.
Mouffe, C. 1996 Deconstruction, pragmatism, and the politics of democracy. In: C. Mouffe (ed.) *Deconstruction and Pragmatism*, 1–12. London: Routledge.
Munn, N. 1986 *The Fame of Gawa: A Symbolic Study of Value Transformation in a Massim (Papua New Guinea) Society*. Durham, N.C.: Duke University Press.
Newton, I. [1687] 1995 *Principia Mathematica*. Santa Fe, N. Mex.: Green Lion Press.
Nozick, R. 1974 *Anarchy, State and Utopia*. Oxford: Basil Blackwell.
Olafson, F.A. 1995 *What is a Human Being? A Heideggerian View*. Cambridge: Cambridge University Press.
Olsen, B.J. 1991 Metropolises and satellites in archaeology: on power and asymmetry in global archaeological discourse. In: R.W. Preucel (ed.) *Processual and Postprocessual Archaeologies: Multiple Ways of Knowing the Past*, 211–24. Carbondale, Ill.: Centre for Archaeological Investigations.
Olsen, B.J. 2001 The end of history? Archaeology and the politics of identity in a globalised world. In: R. Layton, P. Stone and J. Thomas (eds) *The Destruction and Conservation of Cultural Property*, 42–54. London: Routledge.
Outhwaite, W. 1985 Hans-Georg Gadamer. In: Q. Skinner (ed.) *The Return of Grand Theory in the Human Sciences*, 21–40. Cambridge: Cambridge University Press.
Paddaya, K. 1995 Theoretical perspectives in Indian archaeology: an historical review. In: P.J. Ucko (ed.) *Theory in Archaeology: A World Perspective*, 110–49. London: Routledge.
Paine, T. 1791 *The Rights of Man: Being an Answer to Mr. Burke's Attack on the French Revolution*. London: J.S. Jordan.
Patrik, L. 1985 Is there an archaeological record? In: M.B. Schiffer (ed.) *Advances in Archaeological Method and Theory, Volume 3*, 27–62. London: Academic Press.
Patterson, E.C. 1970 *John Dalton and the Atomic Theory*. New York: Doubleday.
Patterson, T.C. 1995 *Toward a Social History of Archaeology in the United States*. Fort Worth, Tex.: Harcourt Brace.
Paul, R.A. 1991 Freud's anthropology: a reading of the 'cultural books'. In: J. Neu (ed.) *The Cambridge Companion to Freud*, 267–86. Cambridge: Cambridge University Press.
Pearson, M. and Shanks, M. 2001 *Theatre/Archaeology*. London: Routledge.
Peters, R. 1956 *Hobbes*. Harmondsworth: Peregrine.
Pickstone, J.V. 2000 *Ways of Knowing: A New History of Science, Technology and Medicine*. Manchester: Manchester University Press.
Piggott, S. 1976 *Ruins in a Landscape: Essays in Antiquarianism*. Edinburgh: Edinburgh University Press.
Piggott, S. 1985 *William Stukeley: An Eighteenth-Century Antiquary*. London: Thames and Hudson.
Plog, S. 1977 Archaeology and the individual. In: J.N. Hill and J. Gunn (eds) *The Individual in Prehistory: Studies of Variability in Style in Prehistoric Technologies*, 13–21. New York: Academic.
Plog, S. 1978 Social interaction and stylistic similarity: a reanalysis. In: M.B. Schiffer (ed.) *Advances in Archaeological Method and Theory, Vol. 1*, 143–82. London: Academic.
Plot, R. 1686 *A History of Staffordshire*. Oxford.

Pluciennik, M. 2001 Archaeology, anthropology and subsistence. *Journal of the Royal Anthropological Institute* 7, 741–58.
Pollock, G. 1988 *Vision and Difference: Femininity, Feminism and the Histories of Art*. London: Routledge.
Polt, R. 2001 The question of nothing. In: R. Polt and G. Fried (eds) *A Companion to Heidegger's Introduction to Metaphysics*, 57–82. New Haven, Conn.: Yale University Press.
Poster, M. 1986 Foucault and the tyranny of Greece. In: D.C. Hoy (ed.) *Foucault: A Critical Reader*, 205–20. Oxford: Blackwell.
Prior, N. 2002 *Museums and Modernity*. Oxford: Berg.
Rahtz, P.A. 1974 Rescue digging past and present. In: P.A. Rahtz (ed.) *Rescue Archaeology*, 53–72. Harmondsworth: Penguin.
Rand, A. 1983 *Capitalism: The Unknown Ideal*. New York: Signet.
Reinhard, K. 1996 The Freudian things: construction and the archaeological metaphor. In: S. Barker (ed.) *Excavations and Their Objects: Freud's Collection of Antiquity*, 57–80. Albany: State University of New York Press.
Renfrew, C. 1973a Monuments, mobilisation and social organisation in neolithic Wessex. In: C. Renfrew (ed.) *The Explanation of Culture Change*, 539–58. London: Duckworth.
Renfrew, C. 1973b *Social Archaeology*. Southampton: Southampton University.
Renfrew, C. 1977 Space, time and polity. In: J. Friedman and M.J. Rowlands (eds) *The Evolution of Social Systems*, 89–112. London: Duckworth.
Renfrew, C. 1979 *Investigations in Orkney*. London: Society of Antiquaries.
Renfrew, C. 1985 *Towards an Archaeology of Mind*. Cambridge: Cambridge University Press.
Renfrew, C. and Bahn, P. 1991 *Archaeology: Theories, Methods and Practice*. London: Thames and Hudson.
Richards, C.C. 1991 Skara Brae: revisiting a neolithic village in Orkney. In: W.A. Hanson and E.A. Slater (eds) *Scottish Archaeology: New Perceptions*, 24–43. Aberdeen: Aberdeen University Press.
Richards, C.C. 1993 Monumental choreography: architecture and spatial representation in late neolithic Orkney. In: C.Y. Tilley (ed.) *Interpretative Archaeology*, 143–78. London: Berg.
Ricoeur, P. 1974 *The Conflict of Interpretations: Essays in Hermeneutics*. Evanston, Ill.: Northwestern University Press.
Robertson, W. 1777 *History of America*. London: Cadell and Davies.
Rorty, R. 1979 *Philosophy and the Mirror of Nature*. Princeton, N.J.: Princeton University Press.
Rose, G. 1993 *Feminism and Geography: The Limits of Geographical Knowledge*. Cambridge: Polity Press.
Rosenberg, D. 2001 An eighteenth-century time machine: the Encyclopaedia of Denis Diderot. In: D. Gordon (ed.) *Postmodernism and the Enlightenment*, 45–66. London: Routledge.
Roskams, S. 2001 *Excavation*. Cambridge: Cambridge University Press.
Rowlands, M. 1989 A matter of complexity. In: D. Miller, M. Rowlands and C. Tilley (eds) *Domination and Resistance*, 29–40. London: Unwin Hyman.
Sackett, J. 1986 Isochrestism and style: a clarification. *Journal of Anthropological Archaeology* 5, 266–77.

Samuels, R. 2000 Massively modular minds: evolutionary psychology and cognitive architecture. In: P. Carruthers and A. Chamberlain (eds) *Evolution and the Human Mind: Modularity, Language and Meta-Cognition*, 13–46. Cambridge: Cambridge University Press.

Saunders, N.J. 2001 Matter and memory in the landscapes of conflict: the Western Front 1914–1999. In: B. Bender and M. Winer (eds) *Contested Landscapes: Movement, Exile and Place*, 37–54. London: Berg.

Schnapp, A. 1996 *The Discovery of the Past*. London: British Museum.

Schnapp, A. and Kristiansen, K. 1999 Discovering the past. In: G. Barker (ed.) *Companion Encyclopaedia of Archaeology*, 3–48. London: Routledge.

Schorske, C.E. 1991 Freud: the psychoarchaeology of civilisations. In: J. Neu (ed.) *The Cambridge Companion to Freud*, 8–24. Cambridge: Cambridge University Press.

Schouls, P.A. 1989 *Descartes and the Enlightenment*. Edinburgh: Edinburgh University Press.

Schrift, A.D. 1995 Reconfiguring the subject as a process of the self: following Foucault's Nietzschean trajectory to Butler, Laclau/Mouffe, and beyond. *New Formations* 25, 28–39.

Schülke, A. 2000 Archaeology and art. In: C. Holtorf and H. Karlsson (eds) *Philosophy and Archaeological Practice*, 261–76. Gothenburg: Bricoleur Press.

Segal, E.M. 1994 Archaeology and cognitive science. In: C. Renfrew and E. Zubrow (eds) *The Ancient Mind*, 22–8. Cambridge: Cambridge University Press.

Shanks, M. 1992 *Experiencing the Past*. London: Routledge.

Shanks, M. and Tilley, C.Y. 1987 *Re-Constructing Archaeology: Theory and Practice*. Cambridge: Cambridge University Press.

Shanks, M. and Tilley, C.Y. 1989 Archaeology into the 1990s. *Norwegian Archaeological Review* 22, 1–54.

Shapin, S. 1996 *The Scientific Revolution*. Chicago: University of Chicago Press.

Sheridan, A. 1980 *Michel Foucault: The Will to Truth*. London: Tavistock.

Shildrick, M. 1997 *Leaky Bodies and Boundaries*. London: Routledge.

Simon, B. and Blass, R.B. 1991 The development and vicissitudes of Freud's ideas on the Oedipus complex. In: J. Neu (ed.) *The Cambridge Companion to Freud*, 161–74. Cambridge: Cambridge University Press.

Simons, J. 1995 *Foucault and the Political*. London: Routledge.

Smart, B. 1992 *Modern Conditions, Postmodern Controversies*. London: Routledge.

Smith, A.D. 1995 National identities: modern or medieval? In: S. Forde, L. Johnson and A.V. Murray (eds) *Concepts of National Identity in the Middle Ages*, 21–46. Leeds: Leeds Texts and Monographs.

Smith, A.D. 1998 *Nationalism and Modernism*. London: Routledge.

Smith, A.M. 1998 *Laclau and Mouffe: The Radical Democratic Imaginary*. London: Routledge.

Smith, G.E. 1937 *In the Beginning: The Origin of Civilization*. London: Watts.

Smith, N.H. 2002 *Charles Taylor: Meaning, Morals and Modernity*. Cambridge: Polity Press.

Smith, W. 1816 *Strata Identified by Organised Fossils*. London: W. Arding.

Sollas, W.J. 1911 *Ancient Hunters and their Modern Representatives*. London: Macmillan.

Sontag, S. 1967 *Against Interpretation*. London: Eyre and Spottiswode.

Sorell, T. 1987 *Descartes*. Oxford: Oxford University Press.

Spaulding, A. 1968 Explanation in archaeology. In: S.R. Binford and L.R. Binford (eds) *New Perspectives in Archaeology*, 33–40. New York: Aldine.
Sperber, D. 1992 Culture and matter. In: J.C. Gardin and C.S. Peebles (eds) *Representations in Archaeology*, 56–65. Bloomington: Indiana University Press.
Stahl, A. 1993 Concepts of time and approaches to analogical reasoning in historical perspective. *American Antiquity* 58, 235–60.
Stanislawski, M.B. 1973 Review of 'Archaeology as anthropology: a case study' by W.A. Longacre. *American Antiquity* 38, 117–22.
Startin, W. and Bradley, R.J. 1981 Some notes on work organisation and society in prehistoric Wessex. In: C.L.N. Ruggles and A.W.R. Whittle (eds) *Astronomy and Society in Britain During the Period 4000–1500 BC*, 289–96. Oxford: British Archaeological Reports 88.
Strathern, M. 1988 *The Gender of the Gift*. Berkeley: University of California Press.
Strathern, M. 1990 Presentation for the motion (1). In: T. Ingold (ed.) *The Concept of Society is Theoretically Obsolete*, 4–11. Manchester: Group for Debates in Anthropological Theory.
Strathern, M. 1996 Cutting the network. *Journal of the Royal Anthropological Institute* 2, 517–35.
Strauss, L. 1952 *The Political Philosophy of Hobbes: Its Basis and its Genesis*. Chicago, Ill.: Phoenix.
Sturrock, J. 1993 *Structuralism*. London: Fontana.
Sumner, W.G. [1906] 1960 *Folkways: A Study of the Sociological Importance of Usages, Manners, Customs, Mores, and Morals*. New York: Mentor Books.
Symmons, J. and Simpson, D.D.A. 1975 Introduction. In: R. Colt Hoare, *The Ancient History of Wiltshire*, 1–16. Wakefield: EP Publishing.
Tarlow, S. 2002 Bodies, selves and individuals. In: Y. Hamilakis, M. Pluciennik and S. Tarlow (eds) *Thinking Through the Body: Archaeologies of Corporeality*, 23–7. Dordrecht: Kluwer.
Taylor, C. 1985 *Human Agency and Language: Philosophical Papers I*. Cambridge: Cambridge University Press.
Taylor, C. 1988 Nationalism and modernity. In: J.A. Hall (ed.) *The State of the Nation: Ernest Gellner and the Theory of Nationalism*, 191–218. Cambridge: Cambridge University Press.
Taylor, C. 1989 *Sources of the Self: The Making of the Modern Identity*. Cambridge: Cambridge University Press.
Taylor, C. 1993 Engaged agency and background in Heidegger. In: C. Guignon (ed.) *The Cambridge Companion to Heidegger*, 317–36. Cambridge: Cambridge University Press.
Taylor, C. 2000 What's wrong with foundationalism? Knowledge, agency and world. In: M. Wrathmall and J. Malpas (eds) *Heidegger, Coping, and Cognitive Science*, 115–34. Cambridge, Mass.: MIT Press.
Taylor, W.W. 1948 *A Study of Archaeology*. Carbondale: Southern Illinois University Press.
Thomas, C. 1974 Archaeology in Britain 1973. In: P.A. Rahtz (ed.) *Rescue Archaeology*, 3–15. Harmondsworth: Penguin.
Thomas, J.S. 1993 The politics of vision and the archaeologies of landscape. In: B. Bender (ed.) *Landscape: Politics and Perspectives*, 19–48. London: Berg.

Thomas, J.S. 1996 *Time, Culture and Identity: An Interpretive Archaeology*. London: Routledge.
Thompson, E.P. 1963 *The Making of the English Working Class*. Harmondsworth: Pelican.
Tilley, C.Y. 1989a Excavation as theatre. *Antiquity* 63, 275–80.
Tilley, C.Y. 1989b Claude Lévi-Strauss: Structuralism and beyond. In: C.Y. Tilley (ed.) *Reading Material Culture*, 3–81. Oxford: Blackwell.
Tilley, C.Y. 1994 *A Phenomenology of Landscape: Places, Paths and Monuments*. London: Berg.
Tilley, C.Y. 1996 *An Ethnography of the Neolithic: Early Prehistoric Societies of Southern Scandinavia*. Cambridge: Cambridge University Press.
Tooby, J. and Cosmides, L. 1992 The psychological foundations of culture. In: J. Barkow, L. Cosmides and J. Tooby (eds) *The Adapted Mind: Evolutionary Psychology and the Generation of Culture*, 19–136. Oxford: Oxford University Press.
Toulmin, S. 1990 *Cosmopolis: The Hidden Agenda of Modernity*. Chicago: University of Chicago Press.
Treherne, P. 1995 The warrior's beauty: the masculine body and self-identity in Bronze Age Europe. *Journal of European Archaeology* 3, 105–44.
Trigger, B.G. 1989 *A History of Archaeological Thought*. Cambridge: Cambridge University Press.
Trigger, B.G. 1995 Romanticism, nationalism and archaeology. In: P. Kohl and C. Fawcett (eds) *Nationalism, Politics, and the Practice of Archaeology*, 263–79. Cambridge: Cambridge University Press.
Tringham, R.E. 1991 Households with faces: the challenge of gender in prehistoric architectural remains. In: J.M. Gero and M.W. Conkey (eds) *Engendering Archaeology*, 93–131. Oxford: Blackwell.
Tuck, R. 1989 *Hobbes*. Oxford: Oxford University Press.
Ucko, P.J. 2001 Unprovenanced material culture and Freud's collection of antiquities. *Journal of Material Culture* 6, 269–322.
Ucko, P.J., Hunter, M., Clark, A.J. and David, A. 1991 *Avebury Reconsidered: From the 1660s to the 1990s*. London: Unwin Hyman.
Van der Leeuw, S.E. 1981 Information flows, flow structures and the explanation of change in human institutions. In: S.E. van der Leeuw (ed.) *Archaeological Approaches to the Study of Complexity*, 229–329. Amsterdam: Amsterdam University.
Vattimo, G. 1988 *The End of Modernity: Nihilism and Hermeneutics in Post-Modern Culture*. Cambridge: Polity Press.
Veit, U. 1989 Ethnic concepts in prehistory: a case study on the relationship between cultural identity and archaeological objectivity. In: S.J. Shennan (ed.) *Archaeological Approaches to Cultural Identity*, 33–56. London: Unwin Hyman.
Vico, G. [1725] 1948 *The New Science*. Ithaca, N.Y.: Cornell University Press.
Vitelli, K. (ed.) 1996 *Archaeological Ethics*. Walnut Creek, Calif.: Altamire.
Voltaire [1745] 1829 *Essai sur L'Histoire Générale et sur les Moers et l'esprit des Nations*. Paris: Chez Werdet et Lequieu Fils.
Wagner, P. 2001 *Theorizing Modernity: Inescapability and Attainability in Social Theory*. London: Sage.
Waldenfels, B. 2002 Levinas and the face of the other. In: S. Critchley and R. Bernasconi (eds) *The Cambridge Companion to Levinas*, 63–81. Cambridge: Cambridge University Press.

BIBLIOGRAPHY

Walker, R. 1998 *Kant and the Moral Law*. London: Phoenix.
Wanklyn, H. 1961 *Friedrich Ratzel: A Biographical Memoir and Bibliography*. Cambridge: Cambridge University Press.
Warnke, G. 1987 *Gadamer: Hermeneutics, Truth and Reason*. Cambridge: Polity.
Wheeler, R.E.M. 1954 *Archaeology from the Earth*. Oxford: Clarendon.
White, L. 1949 *The Science of Culture: A Study of Man and Civilisation*. New York: Grove Press.
Whittle, A.W.R. 1997 *Sacred Mound, Holy Rings: Silbury Hill and the West Kennet Palisade Enclosures*. Oxford: Oxbow.
Wiessner, P. 1984 Reconsidering the behavioural basis for style: a case study among the Kalahari San. *Journal of Anthropological Archaeology* 3, 190–234.
Wilkie, L.A. and Bartoy, K.M. 2000 A critical archaeology revisited. *Current Anthropology* 41, 747–77.
Willey, G. and Phillips, P. [1958] 2001 *Method and Theory in American Archaeology*. Tuscaloosa: University of Alabama Press.
Willey, G. and Sabloff, J. 1980 *A History of American Archaeology*. New York: Academic Press.
Witcher, R.E. 1999 GIS and landscapes of perception. In: M. Gillings, D. Mattingley and J. van Dalen (eds) *Geographical Information Systems and Landscape Archaeology*, 13–22. Oxford: Oxbow.
Wiwjorra, I. 1996 German archaeology and its relation to nationalism and racism. In: M. Díaz-Andreu and T.C. Champion (eds) *Nationalism and Archaeology*, 164–88. London: UCL Press.
Wobst, H.M. 1977 Stylistic behaviour and information exchange. In: C.E. Cleland (ed.) *For the Director: Research Essays in Honour of James B. Griffin*, 317–42. Ann Arbor: Research Papers of the University of Michigan 61.
Wrathmall, M. 2000 Background practices, capacities, and Heideggerian disclosure In: M. Wrathmall and J. Malpas (eds) *Heidegger, Coping, and Cognitive Science*, 93–114. Cambridge, Mass.: MIT Press.
Wylie, A. 1985 The reaction against analogy. In: M.B. Schiffer (ed.) *Advances in Archaeological Method and Theory, Vol. 8*, 63–111. London: Academic Press.
Wylie, A. 1991 Gender theory and the archaeological record: why is there no archaeology of gender? In: J.M. Gero and M.W. Conkey (eds) *Engendering Archaeology*, 31–56. Oxford: Blackwell.
Wylie, A. 2002 *Thinking from Things: Essays in the Philosophy of Archaeology*. Berkeley: University of California Press.
Wynn, T. 2000 Symmetry and the evolution of the modular linguistic mind. In: P. Carruthers and A. Chamberlain (eds) *Evolution and the Human Mind: Modularity, Language and Meta-Cognition*, 113–39. Cambridge: Cambridge University Press.
Wyschogrod, E. 2002 Language and alterity in the thought of Levinas. In: S. Critchley and R. Bernasconi (eds) *The Cambridge Companion to Levinas*, 188–205. Cambridge: Cambridge University Press.
Young, J. 2002 *Heidegger's Later Philosophy*. Cambridge: Cambridge University Press.
Ziarek, K. 2002 Art, power and politics: Heidegger on *Machenschaft* and *Poiêsis*. *Contretemps* 3, 175–86.
Zimmerman, M. 1990 *Heidegger's Confrontation with Modernity: Technology, Politics, Art*. Bloomington: Indiana University Press.

INDEX

action at a distance 10, 206
action, human 23, 185, 225
Adorno, Theodor 50
African archaeology 243
agency 121–2, 147, 192, 209
agriculture 91–5
Alberti, Leon Battista 5, 179
Aldrovandi, Ulisse 24–6
alienation 124, 156, 208
Altamira 220
alterity 147, 235–41
altheia 219
Althusser, Louis 138
analogy 238–41
Andah, Bassey 243
Anderson, Benedict 104
anima 204
animals 153, 172, 196
anthropocentrism 87, 248
antiquarianism 7, 149, 157–8, 228
Antiquaries, Society of 20
anti-Semitism 108, 164
anxiety 188
a priori concepts 35–6, 177
archaeological record 73, 210–12
Ardrey, Robert 75
Aristotle 5, 8, 31, 129, 182, 202–3, 206
Aristotelianism 9, 21, 31, 62, 80, 175, 203–4
artificial intelligence 136, 183, 185–6
Ascher, Robert 240
Ashmolean museum 15
assertive style 213
as-structure, the 66, 73, 75, 143, 217, 244

atomism 29, 62, 100, 116, 135, 160, 183, 194, 204, 226
atoms 214–15
Aubrey, John 20, 24, 107
Augustine, Saint 128, 130, 150, 156
Australopithecenes 74–5
Avebury 33, 107
axes, stone 219

Bahn, Paul 181
background 184–7, 190, 241
Bacon, Francis 7, 11–13, 16–21, 30, 48, 57, 59–61, 80, 171, 204, 227
Barrett, John 239, 241
Bartoy, Kevin 121
Baudrillard, Jean 209
Bauman, Zygmunt 3, 49, 105
Bender, Barbara 220
Bentham, Jeremy 180
Bernfeld, Susan Cassirer 164–5
Bernifal 220
Binford, Lewis 69–75, 90, 111, 180, 211–12, 240, 243–4
Boast, Robin 213
Bourdieu, Pierre 121
Bowdler, Sandra 166
Boyle, Robert 20–1
Braidwood, Robert 93–4
brain 182–5
Brain, Charles 74–5
Brixham Cave 44
Brück, Joanna 147
Brunelleschi, Filippo 179
Bruno, Giordano 21, 79
Buckland, William 44

INDEX

Buffon, Georges Louis Leclerc 87, 150
Burckhardt, Jacob 127
Bure, Johan 107
Burke, Edmund 231
Busby, Cecilia 125
Butler, Judith 143, 215–17

cabinets of curiosity 13–15, 24–6
capitalism 2, 136
Carnap, Rudolf 90
Carter Ranch Site 70
catastrophism 44
cathode ray tube 214
cave painting 220
Chadwick, Adrian 246
Charles II 20, 107
Cheah, Pheng 216
chemistry 214
Childe, Vere Gordon 93–5, 112–13, 211
Chomsky, Noam 189
Christian IV (Denmark) 107
Christianity 4–5, 7, 17–18, 30, 44, 79, 97, 127–8, 133, 174
citizenship 98
Civil Rights movement 237
Clark, Grahame 240
Clarke, David Leonard 243
classification 23–6, 61–3, 66–9, 157, 161, 211, 227
cognition 173, 180, 196, 227
cognitive archaeology 180–2
cognitive psychology 173, 182, 185, 190
collecting 13, 26
Collingwood, Robin George 154
computers 136, 183–6, 190, 194, 198–201
Condorcet, Marie Jean Antoine Nicolas de Caritat 32, 86, 94
confession 127, 151, 163
Conkey, Margaret 212
consciousness 17, 53, 133, 162, 172
conservatism 231–2
Constantinople, fall of 5
Cooney, Gabriel 219
Copenhagen, Battle of 109

Copernicus 5, 8, 21, 79
corpuscular theory 17, 22, 204–7
Cosmides, Leda 189, 192, 196
cosmology 15, 21, 89, 91, 126, 132, 153, 203–4, 225
Counter-Reformation 151
Crawford, O.G.S. 2
cremation 147
Crowley, Aleister 135
culture 82–4, 228
culture-history 64, 66–7, 69, 111–16, 212
Cummings, Vicki 221
Cunnington, William 43
Cuvier, Georges 39, 44, 88, 89

Dalton, John 214
Daniel, Glyn 158
Dart, Raymond 74–5
Darwin, Charles 45, 89, 168
  Origin of Species 45
Deetz, James 70
depth and surface 23, 149–70, 228
deism 30, 83
Derrida, Jacques 161
Descartes, René 3, 7, 11–12, 16–22, 30, 39, 55–65, 69, 72, 79, 126, 130–5, 152, 162, 171–8, 182, 195, 200, 204, 207
  Discourse on Method 16–17, 55
design 3, 202, 227
dialogue 242–3
Diana, Princess 144
Diderot, Denis 28, 87
  Encylcopaedia 28
diffusionism 91
Dilthey, Wilhelm 140, 156
diluvialism 44
disclosure 187–8, 216–18, 241
disease 153
disenchantment 42, 229, 248
dividuals 124
Donald, Merlin 190, 193–5
domestication 94–5
Dowson, Thomas 170
Dreyfus, Hubert 185
Duns Scotus 203
Durkheim, Emile 103

269

efficient causes 9, 11, 80
Ego 166–7
Ego-Ideal (Superego) 167–8
Emblemic style 213
empathy 134, 144, 179
empiricism 11–13, 20, 57, 171–3, 175–6, 207
enframing (*Gestell*) 42, 218–19
English Civil War 7
Enlightenment 12, 27–34, 37, 40, 43, 45–6, 53, 56, 65, 84–8, 91, 106, 135, 138, 140, 174, 176, 227–32, 243, 248
Epicurus 31
epistemology 7, 18, 53–61, 69, 76–7, 225, 234
Erasmus 6, 128
Eros 162
essentialism 109, 141, 170
ethics 35–7, 65, 83, 133–7, 176, 230, 234–8, 242–3, 247
ethnicity 104, 108, 111–16, 120
ethnography 241
Evans, Arthur 161
Evans, John 45
events 122
evolutionary psychology 189–92
excavation, archaeological 76–7, 229, 244–7
exchange 123
experiment 57–61
explanation 61
external symbolic storage 194–5

Ferguson, Adam 86
feminism 141–2, 215–16, 224
fetishism of commodities 208
feudalism 96–7, 99
Fewster, Katherine 239, 241
Ficino, Marsilio 5
fieldwork, archaeological 243–7
finitude 28, 37–9, 230
First World War 47–8, 110
Fodor, Jerry 190
Font-de-Gaume 220
form 202, 212–14
fossils 24, 158

Foucault, Michel 8, 10, 38–9, 44, 97, 107, 126–7, 150–4, 217, 232
The Archaeology of Knowledge 150
The Birth of the Clinic 153
Discipline and Punish 151
foundations 29, 60, 69, 73, 108, 130, 135, 223, 233
Fowler, Christopher 147
frame problem 190
Frankfurt School (critical theory) 47–8, 163
Frazer, James George 163
Frederik III (Denmark) 15, 109
free will 57, 121, 130, 134–5
French Revolution 29, 34, 43, 139–40, 230–1
Freud, Sigmund 154, 161–9, 216
Civilisation and its Discontents 165
functionalism 120–1

Gadamer, Hans-Georg 1, 29, 156
Galileo (Galilei) 5, 8, 11, 21, 64, 79, 87, 171
Gallehus horns 109
Gamble, Andrew 232
Gamwell, Lynn 165
Gassendi, Pierre 87
Gellner, Ernest 97, 108
Gemeinschaft and *Gesellschaft* 113
gender 83, 120, 124, 132–3, 138, 199
genocide 49
Geographical Information Systems (GIS) 198–201
geology 64, 159–60, 169, 228
Gestell, see 'enframing'
Giddens, Anthony 121
Glendinning, Simon 132
government 98, 105, 107, 227
graphical representation 27
gravity 206–7
great chain of being 43, 47
Greece, ancient 218–19
Gunn, Joel 120
Gustavus Adolphus 107

Halley 33
hand-axes 181
Harris, Edward 160–1

INDEX

Harris matrix 160
Hassan, Fekri 65, 233
Hedges, John 113
Hegel, Georg Wilhelm Friedrich 154, 219
Heidegger, Martin 39–42, 130, 143, 156, 188, 209, 215–19, 229–30
  Being and Time 156
Hempel, Carl 90
Herder, Johann Gottfried von 106–7, 109, 111, 231
hermeneutics 65–6, 156, 224
Hesiod 5, 78
Higgs, Eric 94
Hill, James 70, 120
historical change 46, 78–95, 225–6
Hoare, Sir Richard Colt 43
Hobbes, Thomas 18, 22–3, 30, 37, 61, 80–2, 84–5, 99–100, 101–3, 111, 116, 130, 137, 173
  Leviathan 23, 101, 102, 137
Hodder, Ian 55, 76, 113, 121, 144–7, 213–14, 223, 242, 244, 246
Holocaust 48–50, 232
Holy Roman Empire 98
Hooke, Robert 17, 20–1
Hooper Greenhill, Eilean 4, 15
Hoover, Herbert 140
humanism, philosophical 30, 119–48, 225
humanism, Renaissance 4–6, 46, 128
human nature 23, 84, 130, 134, 228
Husserl, Edmund 48, 175
Hutton, James 38, 43, 158
  Theory of the Earth 158
Hypothetico-deductive method 69

Ice Man 144–7
Id 167
ideology 138, 154
Ikhnaton 119
Incest taboo 168–9
individual, human 23, 98, 103, 105, 108, 117, 119–48, 178, 226, 231, 236
individualism 2, 46, 106, 132, 139–40
Industrial Revolution 2
information processing 181–4

Ingold, Tim 245
Innate ideas 176–7
interiority 127–8, 132–3, 150–4, 163, 228
interpretation 72, 142, 156, 212
intuitive physics 197

Jameson, Frederic 3, 151, 154, 156
Jarman, Michael 94
Johnson, Matthew 121
Jones, Andrew 27
Jones, Siân 113–14
Jonston, John 24
Jordanova, Ludmilla 153
Joyce, James 129

Kant, Immanuel 3, 35–7, 49, 83, 134–5, 137, 150, 155, 175, 180, 182, 230, 235, 237
  Critique of Judgement 150
Kenyon, Kathleen 160
Kepler, Johannes 5, 8, 11, 16–17, 79
kinship 124
Knap of Howar 113
Knapp, Bernard 121, 140–1
Knossos 161
Kossinna, Gustaf 110–11
  Herkunft der Germanen 111

labour theory of value 207–8
Lamarck, Jean-Baptiste 43, 89
landscape 179
landscape archaeology 199
language 16, 141, 143, 147, 174, 196
Lascaux 220
Latour, Bruno 22, 46, 51, 64–5
laws 63–4, 83–4, 91, 106, 133–4, 151
Leakey, Louis and Mary 74
Leibniz, Gottfried Wilhelm von 205
Leroi-Gourhan, André 220
Levinas, Emmanuel 236–8
Lévi-Strauss, Claude 37, 155–6
Lhwyd, Edward 20, 24
liberalism 231–2
life 88
Linnaeus 87
LiPuma, Edward 124–5

INDEX

Locke, John 3, 18, 22–3, 28, 30, 37, 48, 61–2, 66, 81–2, 99–100, 111, 116, 129–35, 139, 163, 172–3, 176–7, 205–6
  Essay Concerning Human Understanding 28, 176
Longacre, William 70
Lorenz, Konrad 75
Löwy, Emmanuel 165
Lucas, Gavin 66, 159
Lucretius 31, 78
Luther, Martin 6, 128
Lyell, Charles 44, 158
  Principals of Geology 158
Lyotard, Jean-François 40, 50, 79

Machiavelli, Nicolo 97
MacIntyre, Alasdair 135, 136
madness 152–3
magic 15
Mahudel, Nicholas 32–3
Makapansgat 74
Malthus, Thomas 94
Man [sic] 37–9, 45–6, 51, 53, 150–4, 235
Man, Isle of 147
Marx, Karl 208
Marxism 93, 154, 229, 240
mass 207
massive modularity hypothesis 190
material culture 66, 78, 83, 111–12, 116, 202, 208, 227
materiality 143, 144, 202–22, 227, 248
matter 204–5, 208, 210, 217, 227
Mattrie, Julian Offray de la 87
McCann, Edwin 204
meaning 41–2, 60, 72, 133, 156, 175, 212–14, 224, 227, 233–5, 246–8
medicine 143, 153–4
megaliths 221–2
Melanesia 123–5
memory 177, 195
mental architecture 182, 194, 196–8
Merleau-Ponty, Maurice 199
Meskell, Lynn 121–3, 126, 136, 140–1, 144

metanarratives 31, 47, 50, 89, 135, 225, 228, 232
metaphor 149–50, 191, 196
metaphysics 61, 90, 129, 157, 180, 207–9, 216, 229
microcosm and macrocosm 8–9
microstructural organisation 62, 206
Middle Range Theory 72–6
mind 16, 63, 82, 129, 132–3, 136, 156, 161–9, 170, 171–201, 228
mind-body dichotomy 12, 77, 83, 131–2, 172, 174, 176, 180, 227
Mirandola, Giovanni Pico della 5
Mithen, Steven 192, 195–8
modernity, definition of 2–4
  specificity of 51
  critiques of 229–30
modules, mental 189–92, 196
Mohenjo-Daro 181
Montaigne, Michel de 133
Montelius, Oscar 111
Montesquieu, Charles de Secondat 85–6, 99
mood 188
moral order 35–7
motor habits 120–1
Mouffe, Chantal 139, 246
Munch, Edvard 151
Munn, Nancy 124
museums 15, 26–7

Nabonidus 4
nationalism 50, 96, 98, 106–11, 116, 118, 227–8
nation-states 7, 50, 96–118, 227–8
natural history 23, 59, 62, 66, 88
naturalism 90, 96
natural selection 189, 191–2
nature 11–12, 17–18, 20–7, 29–30, 32–3, 36–9, 41–2, 44, 46–7, 53, 56–7, 61–4, 78–95, 103, 150, 179, 197, 225, 227
Nazi regime 110, 137
Neanderthals 196
Neurath, Otto 90
New Archaeology 69–72, 90, 240
New Right 119, 136–7

272

INDEX

Newton, Isaac 20–3, 26, 28, 30, 33, 38, 44, 61, 63, 79, 83, 172–3, 206–7, 211, 214, 230
  Principia Mathematica 21
Nietzsche, Friedrich 229
nostalgia 233
novels 128
Nozick, Robert 136–7
Nyrup, Rasmus 109

Oasis theory 93
objectivity 63–6, 70, 73, 121–2, 157
Oedipus 161, 164, 167
Olduvai 74
Olsen, Bjørnar 223, 242
optics 178
order, problem of 3, 23, 61–3, 225
origins 87, 161, 165
Orkney, Neolithic 113–16
other minds, problem of 132, 174, 191
Oxenstierna, Count Axel 107

Paine, Thomas 231
Palaeoeconomy 94–5
palaeopsychology 180
Panopticon 180
Paracelsus 204
Patrik, Linda 210
perception 12, 18, 48, 78, 143, 171–201, 198–201, 234
perfectibility, human 53, 81
personhood 140–1
perspective art 179
Perthes, Jacques Boucher de 44
Petrie, Flinders 159
phenomenology 48, 156, 225
Phillips, Phillip 67
philosophical histories 84–7
physis 218–19
Pickstone, John 12
Piggott, Stuart 2
Pitt Rivers, Augustus 66, 159, 163
planetary motion 205, 207
Plato 5, 16, 23, 31, 60, 96, 126, 176
Pleistocene foragers 189
Plog, Stephen 120
Plot, Robert 20, 51, 241
  History of Staffordshire 51

Pluciennik, Mark 32
poisis 42, 218–19
politics 230–3
Pompeii 165
positivism 47, 69–72, 90, 157
post-modernity 42, 223, 232
post-processual archaeology 55, 122, 140
power 215–16, 232
Preconscious 167
prejudice 1, 29, 63, 73–4, 136, 224, 226
Prestwich, Joseph 45
Preucel, Robert 113
Primal crime 168–9
primary and secondary qualities 206
processual archaeology 116–7, 120–1
Protestantism 128
psychoanalysis 128, 156, 161–9
Ptolemy 8
public-private dichotomy 133

racism 108, 235
Rand, Ayn 140
rationalism 11, 17, 20, 57, 150, 152, 171–6
Rat Man 165
Ratzel, Friedrich 109
realism 178
reason 16–18, 22, 28–9, 35–7, 46, 57, 63, 81, 84, 103, 126, 177, 225, 227, 229, 231, 235–6
recapitulation 166
Reformation 6, 55, 97, 104, 128
Renaissance 6, 8, 12–16, 20, 31–2, 51, 79, 127–8, 149, 225
Renfrew, Colin 116–17, 181
repression 163
resolution and composition, method of 59, 99, 226
responsibility 237
Ricardo, David 23, 39, 99
Richards, Colin 113–14
rights 101, 136–7, 236
Robertson, William 86
rock art 170
Romanticism 42–3, 107, 140, 224, 228

273

INDEX

Rome 165
Rorty, Richard 3
Roskams, Stephen 160
Rousseau, Jean-Jacques 30–1, 43, 81–2, 86, 91–2, 103, 130, 163
Royal Society 20

Sabloff, Jeremy 111
Sackett, James 213
Sade, Marquis de 135
Samuels, Richard 189
Saussure, Ferdinand de 155
Schiemann, Heinrich 161, 164
Schliermacher, Friedrich 140, 156
Schnapp, Alain 2
scholasticism, medieval 5, 202, 204
scientific revolution 8–16, 21, 28, 83, 99, 157, 183
sensory experience 57–61
Shanks, Michael 90, 223
Shannon, Claude 182
Simmel, Georg 208–9
simple natures 205
single-context recording 160
Skara Brae 113
Smith, Adam 23, 99, 130–1, 179
Smith, Grafton Elliot 91–3
Smith, William 38, 43, 158
  Strata Identified by Organised Fossils 158
social archaeology 116–17
social contract 81, 100–103, 105, 116, 136–7, 226
Social Darwinism 140
social engineering 23, 49, 231
socialism 231
social physics 98–100, 116, 118
Sollas, William Johnson 51–2
Sontag, Susan 156
Soviet Union 118, 232
Spaulding, Albert 64, 69
Spinoza, Baruch 130
stadial schemes of development 32, 66, 85, 225, 239
Stahl, Ann 240
Star Carr 240
state of nature 31, 37, 81, 101
Stonehenge 33, 107

Strathern, Marilyn 123–4, 133
stratigraphy 158–61, 166–9
structuralism 155–6, 166, 169, 214
Stukeley, William 20, 33
style 212–14
subjectivity 63, 121–2
subject-object relation 18, 56, 77, 131, 157, 176, 234
substance 204, 210, 214–16
Sumner, William Graham 140
systems theory 121–2

Taylor, Charles 126, 133, 186
Taylor, Walter 67–9
taxonomy 23, 26, 88, 227
techne 42
teleology 9, 22, 31–2, 80, 85, 126, 133, 135, 152, 175, 203, 225–6
temporality 224
Thirty Years War 7, 98
Thomsen, Christian 33–4, 37, 109, 158–9
Thomson, J.J. 214
three-age system 32–3, 37
thrownness 143, 186
Tilley, Christopher 90, 223
Tonnies, Ferdinand 103
Tooby, John 189, 192, 196
Toulmin, Stephen 7, 19
totalisation 238
totemism 168–9
Tradescant collection 15
traditional societies 29–30, 40–1
Treherne, Paul 141–3
Trent, Council of 7, 151
Troy 161, 164
Trigger, Bruce 2, 6, 45
Turgot, Robert Jacques 32
Typology, artefact 24, 62, 66

unconscious 163
uniformitarianism 73
United States 138, 140
universals, human 64, 106, 123, 134, 137, 145, 235
un-worlding 42, 187, 189
Upper Palaeolithic 192–4, 196, 220–1
Utopias 3, 22, 53, 91, 99

Varro 31
Vattimo, Gianni 50
Versailles peace conference 110
Vico, Giambattista 87
Vinci, Leonardo da 79
Virtual Reality Modelling (VRM) 198–201
vision 178–80, 183, 199–200, 212, 234
Voltaire (Francois Marie Arouet) 30, 85, 94

warrior graves 141
weights, Indus Valley 181
Westphalia, Treaty of 117
Wheeler, Mortimer 160
Whig view of history 233
White, Leslie 119

Wiessner, Polly 213
Wilkie, Laurie 121
Willey, Gordon 67
Wilser, Ludwig 110
Winckelmann, Johann Jochim 24
Wobst, Martin 213
Woolf, Virginia 129
world 185, 216
world-picture 39, 130
Worm, Ole 107
Worsaae, Jen Jacob 34, 110, 159
Wylie, Alison 239
Wynn, Thomas 181

Yugoslavia (former) 118

Ziarek, Krysztof 217–18

eBooks – at www.eBookstore.tandf.co.uk

A library at your fingertips!

eBooks are electronic versions of printed books. You can store them on your PC/laptop or browse them online.

They have advantages for anyone needing rapid access to a wide variety of published, copyright information.

eBooks can help your research by enabling you to bookmark chapters, annotate text and use instant searches to find specific words or phrases. Several eBook files would fit on even a small laptop or PDA.

NEW: Save money by eSubscribing: cheap, online access to any eBook for as long as you need it.

Annual subscription packages

We now offer special low-cost bulk subscriptions to packages of eBooks in certain subject areas. These are available to libraries or to individuals.

For more information please contact webmaster.ebooks@tandf.co.uk

We're continually developing the eBook concept, so keep up to date by visiting the website.

www.eBookstore.tandf.co.uk